SOCIALISM AND DEMOCRACY IN CZECHOSLOVAKIA
1945–1948

SOVIET AND EAST EUROPEAN STUDIES

SOVIET AND EAST EUROPEAN STUDIES

Books in the series

SOCIALISM AND DEMOCRACY IN CZECHOSLOVAKIA 1945-1948

M. R. MYANT

CAMBRIDGE UNIVERSITY PRESS

CAMBRIDGE

LONDON   NEW YORK   NEW ROCHELLE

MELBOURNE   SYDNEY

Published by the Press Syndicate of the University of Cambridge
The Pitt Building, Trumpington Street, Cambridge CB2 1RP
32 East 57th Street, New York, NY 10022, USA
296 Beaconsfield Parade, Middle Park, Melbourne 3206, Australia

First published 1981

Printed in Great Britain by
Western Printing Services Ltd, Bristol

British Library Cataloguing in Publication Data
Myant, M. R.
Socialism and democracy in Czechoslovakia,
1945–1948.—(Soviet and East European studies)
1. Czechoslovakia—Politics and government—1945—
I. Title II. Series
943.7′042 DB2218.7 80–41951
ISBN 0 521 23668 1

Contents

Contents

Acknowledgements

It would be impossible to name individually all those who have contributed in one way or another towards this work. Numerous people have provided advice, ideas and encouragement at various stages and conversations with many of those who lived through the events covered in the book were extremely helpful. Without their comments it would have been very difficult to make much sense of what was happening.

Special mention must be made of Vladimír Kusín who supervised my PhD at Glasgow University and made innumerable useful suggestions. I would also like to thank those who made it possible for me to spend a year in Prague on a British Council studentship. My supervisors there were Čestmír Amort and Václav Král and they gave some helpful general advice. They also made access to some sources easier as did Mrs Blühova of Bratislava on an earlier occasion. More recently the editors of the NASEES monograph series gave helpful advice on how to reduce the work to publishable length.

I am also indebted to C. Crampton, Myra Black, Ella Kininmonth, and Janette Johnstone who typed various parts of the work, and to those who provided financial assistance. For two years at Glasgow University I was supported by a Francis T. Hunter Scholarship and for a period after that I was dependent on my wife who also spent a great deal of time improving the successive versions of the work.

Abbreviations

ČKD	Českomoravská Kolben Daněk (Prague engineering combine).
ČNR	Česká národní rada; Czech National Council.
DS	Demokratická strana; Democratic Party.
HSL'S	Hlinkova slovenská l'udová strana; Hlinka Slovak People's Party.
JSČZ	Jednotný svaz českých zemědělců; United Union of Czech Farmers.
JZSR	Jednotný zväz slovenských rol'níkov; United Union of Slovak Farmers.
Kčs	Koruna československá.
KSČ	Komunistická strana Československa; Communist Party of Czechoslovakia.
KSS	Komunistická strana Slovenska; Communist Party of Slovakia.
LD	*Lidová demokracie*; People's Democracy (see bibliography).
LS	Lidová strana; People's Party.
NATO	North Atlantic Treaty Organisation.
NKVD	Narodny komisariat vnutrennikh del; People's Commissariat of Internal Affairs.
NS	National Socialist, abbreviated from ČsSNS Československá strana národně socialistická; Czechoslovak National Socialist Party.
PL	*Právo lidu*; Right of the People (see bibliography).
ROH	Revoluční odborové hnutí; Revolutionary Trade Union Movement.
RP	*Rudé právo*; Red Right (see bibliography).
R–3	Rada tří; Council of Three.
SČM	Svaz československé mládeže; Union of Czechoslovak Youth.
SD	Social Democrat.
SNR	Slovenská národná rada; Slovak National Council.
SS	*Svobodné slovo*; Free Word (see bibliography).
UNRRA	United Nations Relief and Rehabilitation Administration.
ÚPK	Ústřední plánovací komise; Central Planning Commission.
ÚRO	Ústřední rada odborů; Central Council of Trade Unions.
ZVOJPOV	Zväz vojákov povstania; Union of Soldiers of the Uprising.

Introduction

A considerable amount has been written, both in Czechoslovakia and in the West, on the events in Czechoslovakia in the 1945–8 period. This is not surprising, as in three different respects it is of great importance for modern European history. The events of February 1948 had considerable international significance at the time in the division of Europe into opposing blocs. The governments of the United States, Britain and France even issued a joint declaration suggesting that the February events were a threat to their own political institutions. They were subsequently quoted as a major argument for setting up NATO. Today the period has a second international significance as certain Western European Socialist and Communist Parties have hoped to unite in implementing socialist changes within a multi-party system. Although Czechoslovakia's experience after 1945 can neither prove nor disprove the feasibility of a similar social transformation in another place and at another time, it remains a unique example of a democratically elected multi-party government implementing socialist changes in what, even then, was one of the most advanced countries in Europe. This experience is therefore invaluable for the sharpening and clarification of a number of theoretical concepts that have recently become more topical.

The third reason for attaching importance to Czechoslovakia's immediate post-war experience is that events in the late 1960s and in more recent years too have served to highlight the inadequacies of the model of socialism developed since 1948. Study of the 1945–8 period may therefore provide useful ideas for the evolution of a model of socialism more suited to conditions in Czechoslovakia and possibly other Eastern European countries too.

This work is therefore directed at two related questions. The first is to explain how socialism, understood in a broadly Marxist sense, was established in Czechoslovakia. The second is to see why it took a form basically similar to the Soviet model which, as later experience showed, was ultimately unsuitable for so advanced a society. To provide the basis for serious answers to these questions an approach is needed which shows not only what did happen but also what else could have happened. That, it must be emphasised, does not mean writing extensively on what did not happen. Nevertheless, there clearly were alternatives available and the events that took place were not all inevitable. Otherwise, of course, Czechoslovak experience would refute the ideas of those in the East and in the West who hope for a more democratic model of socialism. That, however, is not the conclusion of this work.

The starting point is the creation of the Czechoslovak state in 1918. This longer historical view can be justified on the grounds that the records of the various parties throughout the inter-war period were extremely important in the political struggles immediately after World War II. Moreover, there were some analogies between the situations after the two world wars: references to events in the 1918–20 period were very common in the 1945–8 period and undoubtedly influenced the various parties' strategies.

The centre of attention, however, is the development of the Communists' thinking to see how far they were able to prepare themselves for the role they took on in later years. It becomes clear that, although in this period as in the post-war years their ideas cannot be seen as a simple imposition from outside, the Comintern was of decisive importance in preventing the development of a strategy for socialism relevant to Czechoslovakia. Nevertheless, the party was able to build up and retain a significant body of support before the destruction of the republic in 1938 and 1939.

The occupation is discussed in more breadth, including consideration of the Nazis' aims and of the strategy of Beneš who led the administration in exile in London. This provides the necessary background for an understanding of how the Communists were able to evolve a strategy that won them a prominent place in post-war politics. To some extent this showed that there was flexibility in their ideas and that the heritage of the Comintern did not rule out all development. The Communists' post-war prestige can also be attributed in part to the apparent failure of the pre-Munich republic and hence of all the parties that had shared in its government. The

Communist Party then appeared to many, on the basis of its past record, as the most credible vehicle for a more just and a more secure republic. This historical background therefore goes a long way towards explaining the general strength of the Communist Party after May 1945 and the general direction of post-war events. To understand the precise model of socialism that emerged the analysis of the crucial post-war events has to be far more detailed.

It is important to adopt a broad methodological approach in interpreting the nature of the changes that took place. It is quite inadequate to follow the typical approach of émigré writers, especially in the early 1950s, who portrayed events as a perfidious plot by Communists to subvert Czechoslovak democracy. It is just as unconvincing to follow the approach that was used inside Czechoslovakia during the same period when the only permissible analytical framework was one derived from Lenin's writings on the 1905 and 1917 revolutions. Both of these approaches are far too simplistic and overlook much of what was taking place. Above all, they implicitly deny what becomes obvious from a detailed study of the period i.e. that a novel revolutionary process was taking place leading towards a new model of socialism.

Moreover, despite conflicts and various sources of discontent, this new model of socialism was extremely popular. It was widely felt to be a real advance that all legal parties were united in a 'National Front' government and were committed to maintaining national unity while implementing deep changes in society. It seemed as if constructive unity had replaced the divisions and bickering between politicians that were believed to have weakened the pre-Munich republic. It also seemed to many in Czechoslovakia that they *were* treading a new path heading towards a synthesis of parliamentary democracy and socialism. Although not the first to recognise this, the Communist Party began cautiously suggesting that they were following their own, specifically Czechoslovak, road to socialism which would not require the establishment of the 'dictatorship of the proletariat'.

The framework adopted in this work aims to reveal both the potential of these steps towards a new model of socialism and the reasons for its ultimate demise. It owes a great deal to the writings of Czechoslovak historians in the 1960s. Special mention must be made of one of Karel Kaplan's works.[1] His starting point was a detailed analysis of what he felt to be the most important revolutionary measure, the nationalisation of industries in 1945. He showed the interaction of forces that brought it about culminating in widespread acceptance of a multi-sector economic structure. This destruction of the power of big business confronted political leaders with completely new problems as it gave them the power to shape and direct the economy. Kaplan discussed the programmatic principles of the political parties against this background thereby showing how well or badly equipped they were to confront the problems and possibilities raised by the nationalisations.

This work differs from Kaplan's approach as it does not seem valid to single out one aspect of the revolutionary changes of 1945 as being more important than the others. The revolution was a broad and wide ranging process and recognition of that is itself important for an understanding of the model of socialism that was emerging.

Discussion of the revolutionary process naturally involves consideration of the Communist Party's role within it. It certainly does seem valid to refer to the party exercising a leading role, although this is very different from the absolute and rigid notion of leadership embodied in the concept 'the dictatorship of the proletariat'. Under the conditions of a coalition government, broadly speaking, they were able to win support for, and implement, proposals that were well thought out and generally corresponded to the needs of the time. This was the basis for the gradual evolution of a model of socialism including nationalised industries, the beginnings of economic planning and a considerable equalisation of living standards. This goes a long way to refute arguments from many quarters that socialism and democracy are incompatible.

This of course leads to the crucial question of why the Communist Party felt it necessary to take an effective monopoly of power in February 1948. Although there certainly were sources of conflict in the social structure these are hardly adequate to explain the intensity and nature of the struggle that developed in the last months of 1947. Czech historians argued about this during the 1960s and two opposing positions emerged. In Opat's view the 'blame' should be placed primarily on the beginnings of the cold war which, he argued, led to a political offensive from the Czech right wing.[2] The alternative, put by Belda, placed the principal emphasis on the long-standing aim of the Communist Party inherited from the Comintern.[3]

Neither of these views is accepted in total in the present work. Although the principal political offensive did come from the Communists, Belda seems to have underestimated the flexibility and uncertainty in their thinking. It seems more accurate to place the roots of the fight for power in the impact of the beginnings of the cold war on Soviet foreign policy and hence on Communist Party strategy, which underwent an unmistakable change in the latter part of 1947.

This work also differs from many previous ones on the same subject as it does not stop at the February events. A look at the first few months after February serves to illustrate quite dramatically the unsuitability of the new political power structure for Czechoslovak society at the time. This does not mean that the pre-February system was in any sense an ideal. The intense competition between a small number of parties could itself restrict serious discussion and this made it possible for some, both inside and outside the Communist Party, to believe that February might lead to a more genuine form of democracy. Even if such views were to prove sadly mistaken, it certainly does seem that a simple reversal of the February events is neither a precondition for, nor necessarily the best way to achieve, a democratisation of Czechoslovak political life.

I

The development of the Communist Party
of Czechoslovakia

I THE ROAD TO A COMMUNIST PARTY

The Czechoslovak state came into being at the end of October 1918 out of the ruins of the Austro-Hungarian empire. Leadership in the new republic was soon in the hands of the progressive Czech politician Masaryk and his assistant Beneš. They had spent the war in emigration where they succeeded in creating an army of legionnaires from prisoners of war and deserters: it apparently numbered 128,000 men at the end of the war. This enabled them to win some measure of international recognition for a Czechoslovak state in the autumn of 1918 and Masaryk then returned home to be elected Czechoslovakia's first President. Beneš stayed in Paris to negotiate the Czechoslovak case at the peace conference. His strategy was to incorporate Czechoslovakia's cause into the emerging French strategy for Central Europe. This meant becoming part of a potential counter to German influence and a defence against the spread of 'Bolshevism'.[1]

He therefore advocated firm measures against opposition to the new state from the large German minority as this strengthened his standing at the peace conference where there was strong anti-German feeling.[2] He also argued for the maximum show of domestic stability and this helped persuade the more right-wing members of the first Czechoslovak government to welcome the Social Democrats into the government and to allow the speedy enactment of social reforms including the eight-hour day, social insurance measures and emergency unemployment benefits.[3] There was also a conscious effort to strengthen the standing of the cautious right wing within Social Democracy by encouraging confidence that 'socialisations' – i.e. establishing social ownership of the means of production – were

6

imminent.[4] Even the National Democrats, the most explicitly bourgeois of all Czech parties, complied with this.[5]

This helped to ensure working class support for the regime. In fact, despite talk of the threat of 'Bolshevism', there had been no real inclination towards revolution. Workers, like Czechs generally, were gripped by nationalistic euphoria and they expected the new state to lead naturally to socialism.[6]

Thus the strategy evolved by Masaryk and Beneš set the most general direction for the consolidation of the Czechoslovak state. It was pro-Western, anti-German, and capitalist but some important social reforms were implemented and a fairly broad coalition government was established. Marxist historians were for a long time unable to understand the meaning of this for the creation of a political-power structure as they tended to imply that Czechoslovakia was simply capitalist and therefore ruled by the bourgeoisie. A more thorough analysis revealed a less rigid structure including the President, the coalition parties and big business.[7] The relationship between these three centres had already assumed a fairly permanent form by the end of 1919 at the latest. The relationships within the coalition were an important part of this, particularly after local elections on 16 June 1919 which gave the Social Democrats 30% of the Czech vote. A secret agreement was then reached between Masaryk and Švehla, the astute leader of the moderately conservative Agrarian Party, giving the right-wing Social Democrat Tusar the post of Prime Minister. Far from being a step towards 'socialisation' this was intended only to give the government a socialist appearance to help withstand the dangers of 'Bolshevism'.[8] Švehla himself took the key post of the Interior so as to dominate the police force which he regarded as the 'backbone of the state'.[9]

In purely electoral terms the Social Democrats were the strongest of the Czech parties and yet they seemed unable to take any independent, let alone united, initiative. Their leaders have been condemned for 'betraying' the movement in this period and there certainly were issues on which they joined in the deliberate deception of their own members. Nevertheless, this can hardly be an explanation for the absence of a socialist revolution during the 1918–20 period or for the policies actually pursued by the Social Democrats. The real point was that, although there certainly was scope for a more vigorous policy, the only alternatives presented at the time were singularly unattractive. This can be seen from a discussion of the party's three main possibilities; Šmeral's strategy during World War I, allegiance to the Russian October revolution and the policy of participation in the post-war coalition.

Šmeral, who led the Czech Social Democrats up to 1917, had advocated support for the Austrian war effort. His argument for this was partly simple opportunism, partly fear of the consequences should Austria be defeated by Tsarist Russia and partly a belief that Austria-Hungary, containing as it did several nationalities, could become the nucleus of a future United Socialist States of Europe.[10] He strongly opposed the idea of an independent Czech, or Czechoslovak, state on the grounds that it would be very dangerous to try to satisfy Czech national aspirations at the expense of the rights of the German nationality.[11] The point was that to be economically viable and militarily defendable, a Czechoslovak state had to incorporate significant German and Hungarian minorities who were opposed to its creation.

Nevertheless, Šmeral's thinking was overwhelmingly rejected by the Czech population after the Tsarist regime had been overthrown and, above all, after the entry of the United States into the war had sealed the fate of the Central Powers. After October 1918 he became an object of public derision as other Czech politicians tried to imply that he alone had been responsible for the pro-Austrian policy that they had all accepted in the early years of the war.[12] When the campaign of vilification led to an assassination attempt in a Prague tram, Šmeral quietly left the country.[13]

The second major alternative for Czech socialists was to ally themselves with the Russian October revolution. This was not publically advocated by anyone in 1917 or 1918 partly because the news which penetrated through Austrian censorship was so distorted that even the most sympathetic view was that the Bolsheviks might not be responsible for everything bad in Russia.[14] Not surprisingly, it was unanimously agreed that their 'methods' were quite unsuitable for Czechoslovak conditions. Moreover, the Czech national cause had been damaged by the Bolshevik revolution which, particularly after Brest-Litovsk, removed one of Austria's potential enemies from the war scene. Even if some Social Democrats felt a class sympathy with the Bolsheviks their national aspirations seemed to be better served by Masaryk.[15]

As Soviet Russia was clearly too weak to protect the new Czechoslovak state, orientation towards the Bolsheviks could only be based on allegiance to the idea of a world revolution which was too abstract to appeal to the Czech working class. This was quickly realised by the small number of Czech Communists, mostly former legionnaires, who returned home with eye-witness accounts of the revolution. They therefore postponed their original intention of forming a Communist Party and took the opportunity to work within Social Democracy.[16]

In practice the Social Democrats participated in the Czechoslovak government and could thereby claim some of the credit for the establishment and consolidation of the new state. Although, as has been shown, there was no serious and attractive alternative to this strategy, it still caused doubts within the party, stemming at first from a traditional suspicion of participation in bourgeois governments. This general issue therefore had to be debated at the party's Twelfth Congress in November 1918 where it was accepted that the party should remain in the government on the assumption that 'socialisations' were imminent. Should that not be the case, then another congress was to be held.[17] There was no debate around the real problem of *how* the Social Democrats should use their positions in the government. The leadership was therefore left to drift without needing to take any initiative on socialisations, which they even began to argue would be positively damaging.[18] They were also indecisive on land reform policy and allowed the Agrarians to dominate village politics and to consolidate a rural base by very slowly implementing a land reform that benefited the wealthier peasants at the expense of the nobility but gave nothing to landless labourers.[19]

It is hardly surprising that grave doubts about the general direction of the party's policy continued during 1919, especially as the promises of socialisations were not backed up with action. It was only after strikes and demonstrations in the mining industry that the Social Democrat Ministers proposed a start, but even that ultimately led only to a law confirming the existing powers of workers' organs in mining.[20]

Shortly after this those with serious doubts about the leadership's policies formed the 'Marxist Left'. It was to be a temporary body aiming to bring forward issues for discussion at the party's next congress. They produced a strongly worded programmatic statement calling for the development of worker's councils and ultimately the establishment of the 'dictatorship of the proletariat'.[21] Most of this remained empty rhetoric as, in deference to the party leadership and presumably from fear of being condemned as 'Bolshevik', the Left still made no attempt to get involved in workers' struggles. The weakness of their political perspective was revealed at a conference chaired by Zápotocký, on 7 March 1920, shortly before the first parliamentary elections. While forcefully opposing the leadership's coalition policy, the only alternative presented was an 'oppositionist' policy in parliament allowing M.Ps to take up a 'pure and principled proletarian stand.'[22] This did persuade the leadership to adopt a strongly worded election programme setting out the need to direct all activity 'to the socialisation of the republic',[23] but it did not ensure that they would try to implement any part of the programme even after the elections confirmed that there was a strong desire for change. The party emerged with 25.7% of the total vote. Thanks particularly to big gains by the German Social Democrats, the socialist parties together, including the explicitly non-Marxist Czech National Socialists, won 47.5% of the vote.[24]

The Left responded to these results by opposing the formation of another coalition, preferring to leave responsibility for 'the collapsing capitalist regime' to the bourgeoisie.[25] This naivety made it easy for Tusar to win the party's representatives for a new coalition with the Agrarians without any conditions on its programme. The point was that there seemed to be no other possible government. Nevertheless, the new government itself appeared to be only a provisional arrangement pending some future act of clarification.[26] The fundamental weakness was within Social Democracy as the leadership could not avoid betraying its own policies and incurring the uncontrollable wrath of its left wing.

In a bid to avoid defeat at his party's forthcoming congress, Tusar withdrew from the government in September 1920 and successfully advocated the creation of a 'government of officials' excluding all political parties. He could then claim that there was no longer any urgency in holding the congress as the central issue of dispute, participation in the coalition, had been resolved. The Left, however, were determined to proceed with the congress as quickly as possible and achieved something of a tactical success by attracting the great majority of the previously elected delegates.

The real task for the congress, however, was to formulate definite policies as the Left could no longer survive on little more than opposition to the right. This onerous task was taken up by Šmeral whose political ideas had been re-thought after a visit to Russia in early 1920.[27] He saw the need to bring together individual policies towards social change, the Czechoslovak state and the Russian revolution into one coherent whole. He had to answer the central point in the right's argument which was that the 'methods' of the Russian revolution were unsuitable for Czechoslovak conditions so that there was no alternative to the coalition policy. He also had to answer arguments from those who advocated immediate affiliation to the Comintern by total acceptance of Lenin's stringent 21 conditions.[28]

He rejected claims that the Left's aim was the destruction of the Czechoslovak state: instead, he accepted it as 'the given base and assumption of the class, social, revolutionary struggle' which would only be disrupted and delayed if nationalist feelings were once more inflamed by border disputes. He went on to deny the security of the existing state, maintaining that militarism and conservatism could not protect it: ultimately the only security for a small nation in Central Europe was a 'brotherhood of nations' which, Šmeral argued, was synonymous with a 'United Socialist States of Europe'. The applause this received indicates how strongly the Left understood the need to combine nationalism with an international perspective. At the same time, the rest of the party and of the population were seemingly more convinced by Beneš's approach of placing faith in the strength of the victorious Western powers. From Šmeral's position followed opposition to the suppression of minorities within Czechoslovakia and the advocacy of a different idea on which to base the state: 'the idea of socialism must triumph over the idea of nationalism'.

Šmeral laughed at the suggestion that the Left was following 'orders from Moscow' pointing out that the Russian example was not a general blueprint. The Bolsheviks were to be followed in their dedication, creativity and loyalty to the revolutionary cause but not in the details of particular tactics: 'in precisely this question we are the only one among European states to differentiate our tactics from the start from the model tested by the Russian comrades'.

The principal divergences from Russian conditions were seen as the impossibility of staging an isolated revolution in Czechoslovakia – owing to its size and geographical position – and the higher level of economic and social development so that, unlike the Russian revolution, the winning of political power would be associated with positive support for socialism from the majority of the population. From this followed a different approach to the creation of a Communist Party which by then seemed to be accepted as the inevitable consequence of the division of Social Democracy. As revolution was dependent on events in neighbouring countries, particularly Germany, and on winning the support of the mass of the workers, Šmeral believed that it was not on the immediate agenda. There therefore seemed to be every justification for proceeding cautiously. An attempt could be made to win over the whole of the two Social Democrat Parties rather than rushing to create a Communist Party as a small sect as had been done in Russia. He therefore played down the issue of affiliation to the Comintern on the grounds that it was not urgent.

As an alternative to acquiescence within the coalition Šmeral proposed an action programme to direct the party towards class struggle. The central point was the expropriation of large landholdings, banks and industrial enterprises while smaller ones were to be left in private ownership. This, it was hoped, would inspire the working class and unite the different nationalities. He believed that active campaigning around a positive programme could lead to a parliamentary majority for the three socialist parties (i.e. Czech and German Social Democracy and the Czech National Socialists) and thence to a workers' government. He thought, however, that 'the present holders of power in the state' would react like the leadership of Social Democracy and try to impose a 'dictatorship of the minority' once the basic interests of the bourgeoisie were threatened. He then argued that the workers would have to 'organise a firm government, a dictatorship of the proletariat in the interests of the majority for the enforcement of socialist aims'. It should be added that he never elaborated on his conception of the 'dictatorship of the proletariat' although he did vaguely differentiate it from the parliamentary system.

Despite Šmeral's references to active class struggle, and the subsequent success of the Left in organising the majority of the old party within their ranks, they still did not take an initiative in trying to coordinate or lead extra-parliamentary struggles. They were therefore woefully unprepared for a major political confrontation when the party's right wing took legal action and used the police to regain control of the party headquarters, thereby overruling the will of the majority of the old party's members. The Marxist Left had no choice but to call a general strike. Not surprisingly, it remained confused and uncoordinated and it is difficult to estimate the number of participants: claims range between 160,000 and one million.[29] It was called off after only a few days.

This fiasco confirmed beyond any doubt the general character of the Czechoslovak state and also the irreconcilability of the split within the Social Democrats. It also showed the Left their own weaknesses and encouraged the search for new ideas. This meant that it was a blow to Šmeral's ideas too, as his hope for a socialist coalition government seemed quite unrealistic. Instead, criticism of Šmeral mounted and the feeling grew for the speediest possible affiliation to the Comintern.

This was only the start to damaging strife that was to persist within the Communist Party throughout the 1920s. To some extent it could be blamed on the Comintern's leadership: Zinoviev especially totally distrusted Šmeral.[30] Nevertheless, it would be wrong to present the fundamental cause of conflicts as the attempts of the Comintern leadership to impose their will on the Czech Left and later on the KSČ. As Šmeral pointed out later on, criticisms of his policy were often far stronger at home than in the Comintern.[31]

The conflict seemed rather to grow naturally out of the Czech situation. Šmeral continued to believe that Czech Marxists had to work out their own strategy: he therefore feared becoming 'a component of a great whole' if that meant that 'decisions about us will no longer depend on us'.[32] The alternative view was that, after the failure in the general strike, it was impertinent to criticise or question the 21 conditions:[33] implicit in this approach was the notion that revolution was such a simple process that it needed no more than loyalty to the cause. The application of 'orders from Moscow' would then be adequate.

Such a view fitted with the primitive militancy of much of the Left. It also reflected their general ignorance of what the Russian revolution had involved: they knew nothing of the problems and preparations that preceded and surrounded it and seemed rather to believe that its essence had been revolutionary spontaneity.[34] They therefore viewed with the utmost suspicion Šmeral's insistence that capitalism was not on the point of collapse and that revolution was not imminent: it seemed to many that he was following the same road as the reformist leaders. There was therefore always a good audience for critics of Šmeral even when they presented no serious alternative policies and based much of their case on distortions, exaggerations and some outright lies.[35]

In the spring of 1921 even the imprisoned strike leaders from the militant mining town of Kladno, later to be close allies of Šmeral, shared the belief that joining the Comintern would give them the line whereby 'communism must win'.[36] There was also strong pressure along similar lines from the left within German Social Democracy.[37]

Despite all this pressure, Šmeral was able to delay the Founding Congress of the KSČ until May 1921 when he succeeded in winning almost the whole of the Marxist Left for the new party. Polish and German groups were still excluded as Šmeral consistently argued against an overhasty merger of nationality groups, fearing lest it should lead to a later bitter separation. Following sharp criticism at the Comintern's Third Congress he accepted that there was no case for further delay and the KSČ was founded as an international party at the beginning of November 1921.

So the Communist Party was finally formed with a membership of around 170,000. It was at this time one of the largest sections of the Comintern, but its membership subsequently declined fairly steadily to a low point of barely over 20,000 during the depression. After that it gradually increased again.[38] Behind these figures lies a more complex history than one of a party simply and directly preparing itself for power.

2 THE COMMUNIST PARTY IN OPPOSITION

During the first months of the Communist Party's existence Šmeral's supporters were in the minority on the Executive Committee, but their position was gradually strengthened throughout 1922. Moreover, changes in the Comintern, and especially Radek's rise and advocacy of the idea of a united front leading to a workers' government, encouraged Šmeral to develop further his ideas on the possible means of transition to socialism in Czechoslovakia.

An enormous stimulus to this was a major strike in May 1922 by engineering workers in Prague which greatly strengthened the left wing within the National Socialist Party. Even the party's leadership declared its support for the strike and then entered discussions with the KSČ on the possibility of leaving the existing coalition if a

feasible alternative could be proposed.[39] Although shortly afterwards the National Socialists expelled their left wing, Šmeral was
encouraged enough to propose the idea of a workers' government
to the Comintern's Executive in June 1922.

He was always cautious about what this government could hope
to achieve, but he did emphasise very clearly that it was not a
synonym for the 'dictatorship of the proletariat'. A number of
articles in party journals tried to elaborate on this. There were
even references to a process of 'revolutionary evolution' during
which the government would announce measures from above while
factory councils would implement them and control production. It
was left open when the decisive struggle for power would arise.[40]

It was only in this period in the early 1920s, before the rigid
centralisation of the Comintern around condemnations of 'right
deviations', that there was any theoretical sophistication in ideas
on the means of transition to socialism. There were still unanswered
questions. Although the means of transition evidently involved
respect for the institutional framework that had grown up since
1918 – especially the parliamentary system – nothing definite was
said about the ultimate forms of political power in a socialist
society. Neither did the KSČ clarify the role of political parties
within its conception of democracy. Although Šmeral understood
the 'dictatorship of the proletariat' in a fairly flexible way, he did
not develop beyond those of Lenin's polemical pamphlets that
pointed only to the class nature of political power. Nevertheless a
theoretical base was being created during the period of Šmeral's
leadership from which ideas could have been developed making
the KSČ far better prepared to lead Czechoslovak society after
1945.

The idea of a workers' government might have been raising the
prestige of the KSČ but the party still could not overcome its
inability to formulate a clear policy on Czechoslovak statehood
and that very probably reduced its attractiveness. The point was
strikingly demonstrated when, in response to an attempted Habsburg
restoration in Budapest in October 1921, Beneš, who was Prime
Minister at the time, ordered a mobilisation of the army to meet the
implicit threat to the Czechoslovak state. Šmeral decided to support
the mobilisation because, as he did not see socialist revolution as
an immediate possibility, to do otherwise would have amounted to
tacit support for the Habsburg restoration.[41]

By contrast, the 'left' advocated 'utilising the chaos and war tension to free the road to socialist revolution which alone can really solve the organisation of European relations'.[42] The extent of the difference between these two approaches could for a time be masked as the danger to the Czechoslovak state passed so quickly and the party could then be reunited essentially around the left's position.[43] A similar position was maintained at the party's First Congress in February 1923 which simply condemned the Versailles system and called for a revolution over the whole of Europe.[44]

This probably reveals the greatest obstacle the Communists faced to extending their influence. They were unable to embrace unequivocally any particular single nationalism. Their very concept of a workers' government and of the alliances they wanted to create was not to be based on the existing Czech national development. Instead, it was to be explicitly socialist and unreservedly internationalist: it required a fundamental change in the direction of thinking of most Czechs.

The Social Democrats, by contrast, were firmly committed to the existing Czechoslovak state and re-entered a government in 1922 without ever attempting to challenge the right-wing dominance within the coalition.[45] This does not mean that they, or the National Socialists who pursued a similar policy, made no difference to the government's policies. Rather they defended the status quo against *both* alternatives – both a shift to the right and a shift to the left[46]

Despite the extent of these domestic obstacles, the development of Šmeral's ideas was ultimately brought to an end by Zinoviev's rise within the Comintern and the propagation of the new slogan of the 'Bolshevisation' of the Communist Parties. It was made quite clear that the slogan arose in the struggle against the danger of 'right opportunist' interpretations of the united front tactic. Radek's views were over-ruled, the idea of a workers' government was equated with the dictatorship of the proletariat and an armed uprising was presented as the only means to reach that dictatorship.[47] This meant an abrupt end to the ideas Šmeral had been developing.

Zinoviev's hostility was probably aggravated by Šmeral's unwillingness to be drawn into condemning Trotsky. This did not reflect agreement with all of Trotsky's policies, although Šmeral must have regretted the demise of Radek, Trotsky's ally. Probably as important was Šmeral's belief that it was wrong to intervene in the internal affairs of other parties as he believed that the KSČ should be able to develop their own policies without direct interference.[48] Instead, the Comintern leadership intervened more decisively than ever before. They changed the KSČ leadership and even instructed Šmeral to leave Czechoslovakia to work in the Comintern. This kept him away until the mid 1930s.

The new leadership was thereby given ample opportunity to develop their policies. Unfortunately their simplistic over-optimism, which dovetailed with the ideas propagated by the Comintern, prevented them from presenting realistic ideas. They were therefore unable to improve the party's standing. The optimism they encouraged led only to disillusionment thereby creating scope for a new 'left' opposition within the party.[49]

This provided the internal conditions for another change in party leadership following the further lurch to the 'left' in the Comintern associated with Stalin's defeat of Bukharin. The belief then was that a revolutionary upsurge was imminent provided the danger from the 'right' was eliminated. This was associated with a number of further axioms. There was, it was said, to be no intermediate stage within the advanced capitalist countries before the 'dicatorship of the proletariat', and the revolution itself was to be an armed uprising. Any united front 'from above' was completely rejected and Social Democratic parties condemned: the term 'social fascist' was gradually used to characterise them. All this was presented as a policy of 'class against class'. It had, of course, always been the belief of Communist Parties that their policies were based on the principles of class struggle. Šmeral, however, had accepted that other parties could also represent the working class. His conception of the 'dictatorship of the proletariat' was therefore ambiguous: it was not necessarily to be a one-party state. By 1928, however, it was dogmatically insisted that only the Communist Party represented the working class: the 'dictatorship of the proletariat' therefore acquired a clearer meaning as a one-party state, in line with Soviet practice. Such notions were to become deeply entrenched and hampered the development by the KSČ of a more complete strategy even after the dissolution of the Comintern.

Despite the inaccuracy of the party's position, it could command internal support thanks to its strident partisanship and blanket condemnation of all other movements. Nevertheless, intervention from the Comintern was again essential to ensure Gottwald's election as General Secretary at the party's Fifth Congress in February 1929. His new Central Committee was largely working class, dominated by young and little known individuals who were generally founding members of the party but lacked experience in the old Social Democracy. This made it easier for them to condemn the old leadership and Šmeral in particular, but they were unable to retain the loyalty of most former leading members. The party soon faced a major internal crisis and a catastrophic drop in membership: its vote also declined from 13.2% in 1925 to 10.2% in the general election of October 1929.

Under these circumstances it is not surprising that the party still could not adequately solve the problem of Czechoslovak statehood. It must have lost them some Czech support when, whilst not proposing any alternative to the existing state, Kopecký emphasised 'the right for all parts of the German nation to join into one whole'. He added the proviso that this could not be done by 'the imperialist expansion of German capitalism . . . but only by proletarian revolution',[50] thereby indicating renewed illusions of a coming German revolution.

Nevertheless, despite rhetoric about an armed uprising, they clearly rejected revolutionary adventurism in their domestic policies and proved moderately successful in their stated aim of organising struggles for the defence of the daily interests and demands of the working people.[51]

Particularly impressive was the movement of unemployed workers which was led effectively exclusively by the KSČ around a minimum demand of proper unemployment benefit to be paid by the state.[52] As even the Social Democrats were generally quite cynical in their rejection of this movement, the Communists' indiscriminate and total condemnation of all other parties presented no immediate problems. Among employed workers, however, no serious action could be taken without involving the members of other parties and trade unions. This was demonstrated during the important strike by miners in the Most area in March 1932 in response to attempted sackings in one of the mines.[53] The Social Democrat trade unions opposed strike action and leadership went to elected committees dominated by Communists but including members of other parties. At first it seemed to the Communists that their aim of a united front 'from below', spanning nationality and political allegiance, had been achieved and that the 'treachery' of 'the social fascist leaders' had once again been revealed,[54] but the real lesson of the Most strike was to highlight the inadequacies of their own sectarianism. For the point was that united action had been possible only when they *played down* references to 'social fascists'.[55] This led the KSČ leadership to begin to rethink their attitude towards the Social Democrats: they even made a cautious and hesitant proposal for a united front 'from above' after von Papen's putsch in Prussia. Gottwald then referred, at the Comintern Executive's Twelfth Plenum, to the possibility of unity against the threat of fascism. Shortly afterwards, however, the Comintern intervened to reassert a more sectarian line.[56]

There was perhaps some justification for a return to the 'social fascist' position as repressive laws, aimed and used to a certain extent against German fascists, were combined with increasing repression of the KSČ. Legal work became extremely difficult. Moreover, the Social Democrats hardly presented an attractive alternative for committed socialists as they made no effort to implement their socialist programme and consistently opposed any working class actions against the consequences of the depression.

Nevertheless, the discussions within the KSČ leadership at the time of the Most strike are of great importance for an assessment of the party's history throughout the inter-war period. Some historians have tried to present the 'class against class' period as if it revealed the real essence of the KSČ,[57] while Skilling has argued that it amounted to a destruction of the party Šmeral had created.[58] Both these views are exaggerations as there had been very sectarian attitudes within the party before and some of Šmeral's ideas seemed to reappear continually.

There was a certain continuity in KSČ history, but it would be naive to search for a simple 'essence'. The point was that the party had set itself very ambitious aims but then had to reconcile them to the complex realities of Czechoslovak society. There was always a tendency to subordinate analysis to a simple proclamation of Communist identity, of exclusive loyalty to the Communist Party and hence of opposition to all other parties. There was also always a tendency to grapple with the changing complex reality and to seek a political strategy within the existing society. During the 'class against class' period, development along these lines was effectively blocked by the Comintern, but the tendency was still there. It was soon to lead part of the new leadership back to the idea of a government of socialist parties which had been firmly condemned by the Comintern shortly before.

The immediate stimulus for this change was the impact inside Czechoslovakia of the rapid consolidation of the Nazi regime in Germany. Henlein's Sudeten German Party grew to win the largest number of votes in the Czech lands in the elections of May 1935 and many on the right of Czech politics, especially within the Agrarian Party, looked admiringly towards Germany. Masaryk and Beneš did not share this view and sought better relations with the USSR against possible German expansion while the Social Democrats responded to the new dangers by sticking ever more firmly to their coalition policy: given the President's opposition to a fascist dictatorship, they maintained that it was safest to stay within the government so as to dissuade the right from attempting to establish fascism.

Changes within the KSČ followed Dimitrov's rise to prominence in the Comintern and his exposition of the Popular Front strategy. Gottwald was in Moscow at the time and he quickly became an enthusiastic supporter of Dimitrov's ideas. This left Šverma, Slánský and, from early 1935, Šmeral as the main architects of KSČ policy. Their first attempt to apply the more flexible approach developing in the Comintern involved a reversion to the idea of a government of socialist parties and they even definitely proposed this in November 1934.

The Social Democrats were unmoved by the proposal but, paradoxically, it was the Comintern leadership that prevented its further development by insisting that there had been no retreat from 'class against class' policies: they also reaffirmed that a workers' and peasants' government was synonymous with the dictatorship of the proletariat.[59]

The Comintern's line was further clarified by Dimitrov's speech at the Seventh World Congress. This itself contained ambiguities. It seems that the new line was emerging as a compromise in which advocates of the 'old' position still held influence and were willing to concede only so long as they were not roundly condemned.[60] So, despite Dimitrov's celebrated idea of a workers' united front, broadened by other social strata into an anti-fascist Popular Front and leading hopefully to a government that Communists could support, there was still no question of allowing a return to Šmeral's ideas of the early 1920s. Dimitrov still insisted that there could be no 'special intermediate stage lying between the dictatorship of the bourgeoisie and the dictatorship of the proletariat',[61] and claimed that the aim was 'the organisation of a mass political strike'.[62]

These ambiguities and contradictions in the Comintern line discouraged the KSČ leaders from committing themselves on controversial issues like the possibilities for a government of socialist parties. Nevertheless, they did initiate a cautious inner-party discussion on how the Comintern's new line should be applied and they did definitely follow Dimitrov's general advice on becoming more involved in the immediate problems of Czechoslovak politics. Particularly important was their active support for Beneš's Presidential candidature in 1935 when he faced possible defeat at the hands of a right-wing coalition.

It is impossible to say how the KSČ line could have developed from there. In February 1936, when ideas were still in a flexible and formative state, Gottwald returned from Moscow with a firm condemnation of the party's effective leadership and immediately closed the discussion.

He seems to have been responding to criticisms of the KSČ line from sectarian elements within the Comintern and from Trotskyists who had been using the KSČ as an example with which to condemn the whole Comintern line.[63] To answer these criticisms, which Stalin's purges suggest were taken with the utmost seriousness by the Soviet leadership, Gottwald seems to have wanted a clearer differentiation of the party's position from Social Democracy so as to leave no scope for the view that there had been a change to full support for 'bourgeois democracy'. He therefore insisted that any new policy would still require a fight against the reformist leaderships as the Social Democrats, he claimed, could not be won as a whole for united action.[64]

The KSČ congress was finally held in April 1936 and, not surprisingly, was dominated by Gottwald's exposition of the party's policy. He made it clear beyond any doubt that the KSČ had adopted the defence of the Czechoslovak state as their central aim. This no longer needed to conflict with friendship with the USSR or with support for revolutionary struggles in Europe because, under the actual conditions prevailing in Europe at the time, defence of the republic meant opposition to Nazi expansionism. Moreover, the Soviet Union was militarily more powerful than ever before and Gottwald's faith in the Red Army was such that he could even advocate a foreign policy of almost exclusive friendship with the USSR.[65]

The central theme for domestic policy was the strengthening of the republic's defensive capabilities, but Gottwald maintained that this could not be achieved by an alliance or compromise with bourgeois parties: he insisted instead on class struggle against the bourgeoisie around four sets of demands. These were: first, the social and economic demands of the working people of town and country; secondly, greater democratic rights and freedoms; thirdly, equal rights for the different nationalities; and, fourthly, democratisation and purging of the army.[66] It was hoped that, with enough 'pressure from below' around these demands, the government socialist parties could be persuaded to abandon the existing coalition and form a government of the left, following the examples of France and Spain.

There were ambiguities throughout Gottwald's ideas and particularly around his conception of democracy. He argued that all those opposed to fascism should be given the maximum of freedom, but that there should be no compromise with those who supported fascism. This, of course, does not exhaust the problem. He had indicated his willingness to defend the bourgeois democratic Czechoslovak republic and he advocated the creation of a new coalition government of socialist parties still within a parliamentary framework. At the same time leading Communists assiduously avoided suggesting that such a government could implement truly socialist measures and indicated considerable distrust towards the other socialist parties and especially towards Beneš and the so-called 'left wing of the bourgeoisie'.[67]

Although Gottwald was most emphatic that only a Popular Front could protect the republic against fascism, there were clear indications that, in so far as the party had clarified its ideas at all, the Popular Front was still seen as no more than a tactic, or as a brief introductory period before a socialist revolution which was understood just the same as before – as the exclusive affair of the KSČ. Any references to an armed uprising or the creation of soviets were enthusiastically received by the Congress, particularly if it was suggested that they were on the agenda for the very near future. Šverma was thunderously applauded for criticising his own failure to understand 'that we are building a party that has to lead an armed uprising and revolution in Czechoslovakia!',[68] and Gottwald insisted that the republic could only survive via the liquidation of the regular army and a strategy of 'Jacobin' defence.[69]

Nevertheless, the Communists were making enough of a political impact to force comments from socialists and from those close to the President who had previously been content to dismiss them as irrelevant. There was a sudden spate of articles and pamphlets trying to discredit the KSČ by arguing either that it had completely capitulated to Social Democracy and hence had no further justification for an independent existence,[70] or that it really had not changed its policies at all.[71] There was even an extraordinarily bitter attack from the normally liberal journalist Peroutka in an article that he must have later regretted. He firmly rejected any thought of cooperation with the Communists who he condemned in emphatic terms as 'the root of all contemporary evil'.[72]

Generally, then, none of the other parties showed any interest in abandoning the existing coalition. The Social Democrats, although willing to drop their earlier bitter attacks on the Soviet Union and to seek any help that could be available against Nazi Germany, still stuck to their policy of coalition with the Agrarians. The alternative of 'fierce class struggle' would, they believed, force the right wing 'to threaten the very existence of the state by an experiment of the fascist type'.[73]

Meanwhile, censorship and repressive measures continued against the KSČ. There was a ban on references in any of the press to the danger of a German attack: this even affected warnings against it by Communist MPs.[74] As the final local elections in 1938 revealed, the KSČ policy was winning them more support than ever before in solidly Czech areas, where the Social Democrats were losing ground. In Slovakia, however, despite all their efforts the Communists were losing support.

Overall, despite the twists and turns in policy, the KSČ had maintained a sizeable body of support throughout the whole inter-war period. This obviously cannot be explained by looking only at the party's internal strife. Its faults have to be compared with those of other parties and, in particular, the other socialist parties. It often seemed to be the only party defending and fighting for the interests of many industrial and rural workers and maintaining the promise of a better, socialist future. It probably maintained a reputation and a degree of respect as a workers' party among more than just its own voters. Moreover, there was no equivocation over defence of the Czechoslovak state when it really mattered. Despite weaknesses in the Communists' policies in the late 1930s, their firm stand against compromising with Nazi Germany was to serve them well in the future.

Their prestige, however, was that of an opposition party and they could not point to any concrete positive achievements. This was reflected in the simplicity of the ideas they developed which left them unprepared to answer many questions that were to confront them on entering the post-war government. Much of the blame for this lies with the Comintern which gave theoretical coherence to the crude sectarianism that seemed to emerge spontaneously within the party and which, on several occasions, prevented the elaboration of the idea of a government of socialist parties. Without that starting point it was impossible to consider seriously what form a socialist transition, let alone socialism itself, would take in Czechoslovakia. Nevertheless, over the next six years the KSČ was able to expand its support enormously and to win a place for itself at the forefront of Czechoslovak politics.

2

War and occupation

I NAZI STRATEGY

The notorious Munich agreement of September 1938 confronted the Czechoslovak government with the demand to abandon immediately all areas where more than half the population was of German nationality. Beneš acquiesced to this pressure and also ceded territory in the south of Slovakia to Hungary even though resisting would have received massive support from the Czech people, the left-wing parties and the armed forces. He also ignored the possibility of Soviet help partly because he thought it might not be adequate, but primarily because of its internal and international political implications.[1]

This led to the Second Republic in which the Agrarians firmly dominated the Prague government. They succeeded in banning the KSČ and merging the right-wing parties, including the National Socialists, into one party leaving the Social Democrats to play the role of a docile legal opposition. Slovakia was granted greater autonomy and the right-wing Catholic nationalist party led by the priest Tiso, the HSL'S, succeeded in merging other right-wing forces into a single party bloc at a meeting of its Executive Committee in Žilina in October. The new Slovak government, headed by Tiso, soon banned all opposition.

After barely five months the Nazis, ignoring the Munich agreement's guarantee of Czechoslovakia's existence, used strong threats to persuade the Slovak leaders to proclaim an independent state. Using the pretext that Czechoslovakia had ceased to exist, the Czech lands were occupied on 15 March 1939 and the 'Protectorate' established.

At first there was no clear Nazi plan for the Czech lands: the immediate rationale for the sudden occupation had been the desire to pre-empt any anti-German action from Czechoslovakia at some point in the future. Gradually, through successive changes and modifications, they evolved a definite strategy.[2] Their first consideration was to ensure control and this was achieved both by exploiting the unwillingness of many Czech leaders to actively oppose the occupation and by progressively strengthening the position of specifically German institutions. They were even willing to allow a Protectorate government powers that at first appeared to be greater than those enjoyed by any Czech institution within the Austrian empire.

In fact, although it would be wrong to accuse all participants in the Protectorate government of actively helping the Nazis, and hence of collaborating, they were very soon involved in helping the repression of real political opposition and they could do nothing against 'Germanisation' policies. These involved giving marked privileges to the German minority while denigrating the Czech language and culture. The most dramatic anti-Czech measure was the closing of Czech universities on 17 November 1939 and the execution of student leaders following street demonstrations on 28 October 1939. Although presented as a response to political opposition, this was also part of a plan to eliminate Czech education and was followed by instructions for the gradual limitation even of Czech school education.[3]

The eventual aim was to 'Germanise' the Czech lands by persuading most Czechs to accept German nationality: the more stubborn ones were to be executed or forcibly removed from Central Europe.[4] Solid refusal from Czechs to renounce their nationality forced the occupiers to postpone their plan. Nevertheless, the necessary research for such a project was started whenever the Nazis thought victory was at hand, particularly after the fall of France and to some extent also when Moscow's fall seemed imminent.

In the autumn of 1941 the war situation, the activisation of Czech opposition to the occupiers and the refusal of the Czech nation to accept voluntary 'Germanisation' all contributed to a shift in Nazi strategy. This was personified in the appointment of the ruthless Heydrich as Protector in 1941. He did not anticipate rapid 'Germanisation' but took a far tougher line with active opposition so as to maintain political stability and steady military production. He dissolved the Protectorate government and ordered the execution of its Prime Minister, Eliáš. Even though terror was never far below the surface, he did not unleash the barbarity used in Poland, Yugoslavia or parts of the Soviet Union. There was always space left for compliance so that active resistance never appeared as the best means of survival. Moreover, there was always scope for believing that things could be worse and this feeling was fully and subtly exploited. So, when on 27 May 1942 Heydrich was assassinated by parachutists sent from London as part of Beneš's plan to win international recognition,[5] the response was one of carefully controlled ruthlessness. Active resistance organisations were demolished: with a few exceptions, they disappeared or had to be rebuilt from scratch again afterwards. The mass of the people, however, were terrorised into passivity by these widespread executions and above all by the massacre of the villages of Lidice and Ležáky. These were not the usual Nazi atrocities, ordered by a local commander to avenge a local partisan attack, but were centrally decided and widely publicised acts deliberately accompanied by rumours of the impending liquidation of the Czech nation.[6] Although this may have discouraged active resistance it simultaneously encouraged a feeling of helplessness leading to a grim hatred for Germans in general who, in the Czech lands at least, actively applauded the act.[7]

Heydrich's aim was, quite simply, to minimise the scope for active resistance and thereby help raise military production. The Czech people could help the Nazis in two ways: the first was by providing labour for German industry, thereby replacing German workers who were needed in the armed forces. The second was by raising the military output of the industries within the Czech lands.[8] The first aim became so imperative after the German defeat at Stalingrad that all young Czechs born within a particular year were drafted to work in Germany: this probably affected in all 600,000 Czechs and 200,000 Slovaks who returned home with a deep hatred for Germany.[9] The second aim, which increased in importance from late 1943 as bombing affected industry in Germany itself, involved, as soon as August 1942, the compulsory lengthening of the working week to 60 hours and then the expansion of the labour force by drafting in peasants, the urban petty bourgeoisie, the intelligentsia, office workers, housewives, former students, the old and even invalids. As these sources were exhausted, so labour was transferred from useful consumers' goods industries. In August 1944 all production not directly related to the war effort was prohibited.

This process, with the progressive proletarianisation of the Czech nation and concentration of workers into bigger factories, could appear like the economic prelude to a socialist revolution leading to a planned economy. This, however, cannot be concluded from the situation in the Czech lands. Concentration was associated entirely with military production and hence declining living standards: one of the first post-war tasks would have to be a reversal of this trend. Moreover, to judge from the nature of Nazi repression and how it was most widely felt, the objective conditions were being created for a national rather than a socialist revolution. Although social or socio-economic aspects of repression became important, particularly towards the end of the war, they could never take precedence over, or stand independently from, national repression. Czech historians have therefore argued that 'the basic contradiction of society . . . was . . . between the majority of the nation and the occupiers plus those who linked their social and individual destinies with them'.[10]

Against this background it is not surprising that there was a deep craving for national unity and a widespread longing for a restoration of the Czechoslovak state. There was, however, no escaping the fact that the pre-Munich republic had ended in disaster. Calls for its restoration were therefore frequently combined with strong criticisms of the ideas on which it had been based and above all of its inclusion of large national minorities, its dependence on France and its capitalist system. This last point was potentially especially divisive. The point was that those who had suffered from a socially subordinate position before had been willing to reconcile themselves to the realities of the situation partly because of the threat to the state. This had been the basis of the Social Democrats' thinking. It seemed, though, that the sacrifices made by workers and by their representatives in the government had led only to disaster. It is therefore not surprising that ideas about the restoration of the Czechoslovak state were often associated with calls for fundamental changes in its social system. In fact there was a strong tendency for active resisters to move to the left and to seek the causes of Czechoslovakia's collapse in its internal social and political system as well as in its nationalities policies and international orientation.

So the Nazi occupation created the objective conditions for a very broad opposition, covering almost the whole Czech nation, but one which could not be completely united in its aim. Nazi strategy, however, was also such that opposition tended not to take active forms. Even in big factories resistance rarely went beyond individual sabotage acts: it is unclear to what extent they contributed to the 13% decline in productivity between 1939 and 1944.[11]

The general picture, then, was of a Czech nation which deeply hated the occupiers but showed this primarily only in small individual acts of defiance. It was against this background that more detailed ideas took shape for a resistance strategy and for the future form of the Czechoslovak state.

2 BENEŠ

The most important anti-Nazi tendency was led by Beneš, who was pressurised by Germany into resigning the Presidency shortly after Munich and then went into emigration. Only after the establishment of the Protectorate did he begin political activities in London and he soon established himself as the leading Czechoslovak émigré politician.[12] His strength was based on his standing as the former President, on his opposition to Munich and on his ability to formulate a definite plan for the re-establishment of the Czechoslovak state. This was an adaptation from his World War I experience centring on the claim that the Czechoslovak state, as it had been destroyed by external force, still legally existed and that he was still legally its President. He resolved to create, and win international recognition for, the trappings of a constitutional state including a government, a parliament and an army. His hope was that these would be able to return home as the recognised supreme bodies at the end of the war.

Supremacy among émigrés was established once his government in exile had won a degree of international acceptance. He insisted that it should include no political parties, although much later he seemed to be willing to include KSČ representatives. Meanwhile, he carefully manipulated its composition to incorporate and thereby eliminate most opposition. Only the far right, some Social Democrats and the KSČ refused his terms for participation.

Winning full international recognition was more difficult as Britain and France tried to keep their options open on the future for Central Europe. Beneš, however, kept trying to persuade them that Czechoslovakia was a potentially viable barrier to German expansion and that its collapse stemmed not from inherent weaknesses but from the failure of its Western allies to give it the necessary support in 1938. He was therefore extremely sensitive to suggestions that Czechoslovakia should have fought in 1938 as that would imply that its collapse was not entirely the fault of the West. He hoped the outbreak of war would convince Britain and France of their mistake and lead to a clear renunciation of Munich. Ultimately it was only after the Soviet Union had been brought into the war and taken the initiative in recognising his government in exile that Britain finally gave him recognition. Then, a year later, Britain was behind the Soviet Union again in categorically renouncing the Munich agreement.

Within his strategy, the activities of the domestic resistance were clearly subordinated to his activities in emigration. They could help him by providing valuable intelligence information or, hopefully, by staging a coup to proclaim him President again in the event of a collapse of German power. For a time he even hoped that this would be achieved by elements within the Protectorate government and he maintained good contacts with Eliáš who was regarded even by the KSČ as a genuine resister.[13] After June 1941, fearing lest contacts with the Protectorate should alienate Soviet sympathy,[14] Beneš ordered the Protectorate government to resign. With the exception of Eliáš, members of the government preferred to subordinate themselves to Nazi authority. Even then, Beneš made excuses for them until after Lidice when his London government had won full recognition in the West.

Despite such equivocations, Beneš's activities in emigration won him enormous popularity at home. An image was even created of him as the legendary future liberator of the Czech lands and this was shared by many who stood politically well to his left.[15]

He was well informed of the leftward shift in popular feeling. Apparently even right-wing Czechs were calling for him to advocate more radical policies as early as the autumn of 1940. They feared that otherwise it would be impossible to withstand the danger of 'Bolshevism'.[16] Beneš was prepared to go along with this feeling and accepted that there could be no exact restoration of the pre-Munich republic. Instead he worked out policies for major internal changes which were partly intended to ensure that the republic could never again be threatened by nationality problems. He also believed that reforms would be the best way to weather the expected danger of revolution in the immediate aftermath of war. He therefore advocated nationalisation of large-scale industry and land reform which he hoped would lead to a society in which Marxism would no longer have any relevance.[17] He even hoped to incorporate and thereby silence the KSČ within a broader party of the left.[18]

Nationalities policies, primarily aimed at preventing another Munich, could make social reforms easier as a great deal was to be achieved through measures against Germans. Beneš even formulated the notion of a combined national and social revolution. The most ambitious proposal in this was the expulsion of most of the German minority. The demand proved extremely popular with the non-Communist domestic resistance, but could only be seriously advocated after the approval of the great powers. Britain showed some reluctance, but gave general approval in June 1942. The USSR prevaricated until the middle of 1943.

The Slovak national question was for Beneš less fortunate and led eventually to conflict with the domestic resistance. He firmly adhered to the 'Czechoslovakist' position whereby only a single 'Czechoslovak' nation was recognised. This, he argued, was the only way to convince the great powers that a Czechoslovak state could be viable: admission of a separate Slovak nation would either justify a separate Slovak state or a Czechoslovak state with no national majority and consequently no justification for denying equal rights to all the minorities.[19]

Of even greater importance was Beneš's attitude towards the USSR. Broadly speaking he understood Soviet foreign policy as either a desire to export revolution, which he naturally feared, or as the pragmatic actions of a great power, which he could understand and sometimes even welcome. The Nazi–Soviet pact and then the desire for cooperation with the West seemed to indicate the supremacy of the latter element but Beneš, particularly during and after Soviet military successes in mid 1943, feared the possibility of the USSR defeating Germany alone and deciding the fate of Central Europe.[20] To avert this danger he firmly advocated East–West cooperation, hoping that it could continue even after the war, giving the West a say in Central Europe. He believed, and he had supporting evidence, that the USSR would see a strong, democratic, anti-Nazi Czechoslovakia as being in their own best interests.[21] He hoped that the Soviet leaders would recognise the alleged inapplicability of Communist ideas to Czechoslovakia and that, still needing the cooperation of the West to rebuild their economy,[22] they would not try to force revolution onto Czechoslovakia.[23]

During 1943, as his hopes of liberation and also his fears of its consequences mounted, Beneš began discussions on a treaty of friendship with the USSR. His aim was to ensure that the Soviet leaders firmly recognised the restoration of a Czechoslovak state with him as President as one of their war aims: this he described as 'non-interference' in Czechoslovakia's internal affairs.

He was eventually able to win British approval for his plan and went to Moscow in December. After discussions with Stalin and Molotov he was apparently in a state of elation: they seemed to regard him as a basic part of their plans for Central Europe.[24] Beneš also held discussions with the KSČ leaders during which he generally gave non-committal or subtly flattering replies to suggestions for resistance strategy and measures in post-war Czechoslovakia.[25] His main conclusion in fact was that the Communists, albeit with some reservations, acknowledged his right to be President. This meant that the London government could make detailed preparations for returning home,[26] thereby effectively ignoring the different ideas of the KSČ.

Beneš's confidence was raised still higher in May 1944 by a further treaty giving power to a 'government delegate' rather than the Soviet authorities on Czechoslovak territory as it was liberated. The delegate appointed was the right-wing Social Democrat F. Němec and he left for Moscow in August 1944.

3 COMMUNIST STRATEGY

While Beneš was evolving his ideas on the future shape of Czechoslovakia and preparing to put them into practice, Communist policy was following a tortuous path of development. At first, like the whole Czech nation, they were disoriented by Munich. They had centred their activity on the willingness of the government socialist parties to resist and, when they and Beneš capitulated, there seemed to be no sense in attempting 'Jacobin' defence.[27] During the Second Republic the KSČ tried to develop unity to defend what was left of pre-Munich democracy, but this proved to be an illusory hope as political developments led instead to the banning of the KSČ. Communists were again surprised by the sudden Nazi occupation and many were quickly arrested.

Nevertheless, the KSČ alone among parties held out against the right-ward, pro-German trend in Czech politics while its leaders sought safety in emigration. Only a few went to Moscow, probably because of the Soviet leadership's fear of foreigners,[28] and most went to France. By mid 1939 the KSČ in Paris, led by Šverma and obviously maintaining good contacts with Moscow, had formulated their assessment of Munich. They argued that Czechoslovakia should and could be restored within the international context of a world-wide anti-fascist front with the USSR wielding a powerful influence in Europe. Communists were to work for this both in emigration and at home by trying to create broad national unity; the term 'National Front' even appeared.[29] Leadership within this, it was argued, could be taken only by the KSČ.

Although they wrongly believed that Beneš had completely discredited himself, and were also unduly optimistic in expecting the Protectorate government to be completely isolated at home from the very start, their solid rejection of any form of collaboration could well have won them a position of genuine leadership in the nation as the Protectorate government gradually did become isolated. Instead, the start of World War II, for which the KSČ in Paris had been implicitly working, brought a sudden switch in Comintern strategy amounting to a subordination to the tactical needs of Soviet foreign policy.

At first the KSČ domestically and in Paris seem to have accepted the Nazi–Soviet pact purely as a tactic and even seen its revolution-ary potential as the war would, they presumed, follow a similar course to World War I. This would enable the USSR to intervene in a revolutionary way when the warring powers had exhausted themselves.[30] Perhaps the dominant aspect of KSČ activity – fully in line with such a perspective – was waiting, trying to learn the methods of underground activity and conserving an organisation 'in deep illegality not only from the German police but also from the nation'.[31] This was encouraged by the savage repression of demonstrations in October and November 1939 after which im-mediate mass action was regarded as being too dangerous both by Beneš in London and by the KSČ in Moscow. Nevertheless, the change in Comintern line threw the Communists into confusion. There were long delays between messages from Moscow to the disoriented domestic organisation and important aspects of the new line were clarified only very slowly.[32] Soon, however, there was a definite acceptance of increasingly sectarian attitudes within the KSČ. They never held a neutral attitude towards the occupation, let alone collaborated, but the KSČ leadership in Moscow did shun anything that could give preference to one side or the other in the war: they therefore isolated themselves from Beneš and the West which remained the nation's main hope of liberation.

It must be said that the Communists could find some justification for the Comintern's line not from its own strength or consistency but from the weaknesses of possible alternatives. It was impossible to choose an anti-fascist war instead as the West was involved in 'phoney war' associated with the most forceful anti-Communist propaganda since the Russian revolution. Beneš, although cautious towards the USSR, was very cutting about the KSČ. Moreover, Soviet territorial expansion seemed to suggest greater progress for Communism than the strategy of anti-fascist unity had yielded.[33]

Only after the fall of France, which upset the Comintern's basic predictions on the course of the war and awakened fears of an attack on the USSR, did the KSČ leadership in Moscow begin to rethink their ideas. According to Kopecký, wide-ranging discussions were held amounting to a reassessment of the 1918–20 period on the basis of Lenin's works on the 1905 and 1917 revolutions. It was argued that the left's strategy had been for an immediate socialist revolution while the concrete tasks confronting them made possible only a national democratic revolution, analogous to the bourgeois democratic revolution discussed by Lenin. By ignoring broader issues, the revolutionary working class movement, so it was claimed, allowed itself to be isolated from the peasants and was therefore defeated in the 1920 general strike.[34]

Although this is hardly an adequate interpretation of that period, such ideas undoubtedly did develop before the end of the war and the view outlined by Kopecký became the orthodox KSČ position. A similar notion of a two stage revolution was, in fact, being proposed by Šmeral in mid 1939 and again in late 1940.[35] Nevertheless, in published documents in late 1940 and early 1941 at least, the re-emphasis on national liberation was still linked very directly with socialist revolution and there was no mention of a separation of the revolutionary process into two distinct stages

Whatever changes may have been taking place within the Comintern in early 1941, the decisive change came not from any rethinking of revolutionary strategy but, just as had been the case in 1939, as a sudden reaction to a major world event. The Nazi invasion of the USSR meant that all else was subordinated to the aim of preventing the defeat of the Soviet Union. This had two immediate consequences for KSČ policy.

The first was insistence on the urgency of active resistance against the Nazis involving individual acts of sabotage and, after the massacres at Lidice and Ležáky, the formation of partisan units. In practice, very little headway could be made with this second aim until much later in the war. The principal obstacles were the geography of the Czech lands, the lack of arms and the Nazi occupiers' strategy, which left considerable scope for passive acquiescence. In fact, even Gottwald had been sceptical of the idea, which was firmly rejected in London, and had for a time resisted pressure from the Comintern.[36]

The second consequence was the avoidance of an outright clash with Beneš who was seen as a likely proponent of East–West cooperation. The re-establishment of the Czechoslovak state was therefore recognised as a war aim. The KSČ, however, refused to join Beneš's government in exile ostensibly because of his rejection of their insistence that its principal immediate task was the encouragement and mobilisation of the domestic resistance. They may also have been keeping their options open as the war could have ended by revolution inside Germany or by complete Soviet domination of Central Europe in which case Beneš could have become an irrelevant embarrassment to them.

In practice, however, unity with Beneš became increasingly important to the KSČ. It would be totally wrong to present this as a simple compliance with the needs of Soviet diplomacy. A comparison with Yugoslavia and Poland reveals the point, as in both those cases unity with London émigré governments proved impossible and Communists, against the wishes of Moscow, adopted radical programmes for social change. In the Czech lands the situation was very different: Beneš commanded immense prestige and was much more friendly to the Soviet Union and Communists generally than others in the West. The domestic KSČ therefore willingly followed the line of establishing the broadest possible national unity.[37]

A more complete policy for Czechoslovakia's future only evolved with time particularly as, in 1943, the Soviet Union's position improved and it became possible to predict the likely course of the war. Major landmarks for the KSČ were the Comintern resolution on Czechoslovakia[38] of 5 January 1943 and then the dissolution of the Comintern. After that, direct advice from Stalin and Dimitrov covered only the very most basic policy issues. Then, roughly coinciding with Beneš's visit to Moscow, the journal *Československé listy* started publication in Moscow thereby providing a platform for semi-programmatic articles.

The policy that the party leaders developed owed a great deal to ideas evolved during the Popular Front period. There were inevitably important differences: above all the new line was worked out in greater detail and with a greater sense of realism. The starting point was the view that the pre-Munich republic had failed. To create a strong and viable Czechoslovakia there therefore had to be major changes rather than a simple restoration of the old state. Some aspects of this were spelt out fairly clearly but others, especially the social and economic content of the proposed revolution, were left remarkably vague.

The starting point was the conception of political leadership in the resistance which was to be carried through into the new state. Gottwald, unlike Beneš, always believed that collaboration and resistance were primarily political questions. An active resistance therefore required leadership which could be provided only by those who had never betrayed the nation's interests and who had the social base and political past to differentiate themselves from collaborators. He argued that this pointed to a bloc of socialist parties which should be seen not as the representative of the left, but as the representative of the whole nation.[39] The KSČ even argued that right-wing parties such as the Agrarians, who were judged to have betrayed the republic in the fateful Munich period, should be banned.[40]

They also advocated replacing the existing state apparatus with National Committees which were to assume much wider powers than in 1918, when they had emerged in localities to proclaim the new state but then quickly ended their activities. This time they were to start as uniting and coordinating organs for the resistance and then were to take over from the existing state machine at the time of liberation.[41] Although presented as an expedient for a brief period only – coinciding with the 'transition period' of a few months which Beneš foresaw separating liberation from the re-establishment of a parliament – the KSČ evidently hoped that National Committees would become permanent.

On nationalities questions the KSČ gradually recognised the crucial importance of a clear and unambiguous policy if there was to be an active resistance movement. They were, however, reluctant to accept Beneš's idea for mass expulsions of Germans and stuck for as long as possible to hopes that an anti-Nazi movement would develop among Sudeten Germans so that a future Czechoslovak republic could solve nationality questions on the basis of equality.[42] Gradually, however, hopes of this faded and the KSČ moved remarkably close to Beneš's notion of a combined national and social revolution.

By contrast they clashed with Beneš over the Slovak question when they tried to convince him of the need to recognise the existence of a separate Slovak nation: they believed this to be the precondition for an active resistance in Slovakia. Slovak historians have criticised the timid way in which Kopecký in Moscow approached this question,[43] but the KSČ were left with little scope to develop their ideas without incurring the extreme wrath of Beneš. He expressly requested that there be no questioning of his positions on Slovakia and on Munich[44] as, for reasons already explained, this was essential to his plan for regaining the Presidency. The Communists seem largely to have complied with his wishes.

The KSČ also viewed favourably the Polish and Ukrainian minorities and opposed the suggestion that any of them should be expelled. Instead, undoubtedly largely as an application of the Slavonic idea that Stalin was reviving in the Soviet Union, the new Czechoslovakia was to be based on several Slavonic nationalities rather than just a single nation. Meanwhile, Germans and Hungarians were to be 'weakened and ousted'.[45]

Gottwald even went beyond this to give the anti-German policy a status within Marxist theory when he claimed that Lenin had presented the main problem of every revolution as 'which class, which nation has power in its hands and into which nation's or class's hands that power is passing'.[46] It would probably have been better to regard the expulsion of large numbers of Germans as at the very best a regrettable necessity limiting the degree to which the revolution can be described as democratic.[47]

Clarity on these questions contrasts strikingly with the KSČ's cautious approach to social and economic measures and their obvious unwillingness even to mention state ownership of industries. They evidently foresaw a two stage revolution with the first, national

democratic revolution, so clearly differentiated from a later, socialist
stage that it need have no explicit socio-economic content at all.
This may have stemmed from the fear that references to socialist
changes would disrupt national unity[48] but Beneš himself spoke of
nationalisations. This makes it seem likely, and other circumstantial
evidence suggests this too, that Stalin, who need not have known or
understood Beneš's thinking, specifically advised the Communists not
to mention nationalisations.[49] Although he was willing to encourage
a momentous reversal on nationalities policy, he still implicitly insisted
that genuine socialist change was to be exclusively the affair of the
Communist Party. There could therefore still be no thought of a
process of 'revolutionary evolution' as had been suggested in the
period of Šmeral's leadership.

Instead, all the emphasis was placed on the need to prevent
immediate economic collapse – the influence of Lenin's *Threatening
Catastrophe* is obvious. This meant that Factory Councils and
National Committees were to take over the property of Germans
and collaborators as quickly as possible, while the ultimate fate of
this property was left completely open until an elected parliament
could decide. The outcome was a conception of revolution placing
primacy on immediate political power questions,[50] and leaving the
same ambiguities as in the earlier Popular Front policy. Above all,
although it was clear that the KSČ wanted unity to defeat fascism,
it was not explained how this related to socialist revolution and to
the earlier conception of the 'dictatorship of the proletariat'.

The issue was clarified a little when Gottwald was finally confronted in liberated Eastern Slovakia in early 1945 by Communists
who saw cooperation with other political forces as a very transient
phenomenon. Although Gottwald's argument was expressed in
terms of the situation in April 1945, it was probably worked out in
general terms considerably before. He pointed out that, *from the
point of view of its political power,* the bourgeoisie's position was
greatly weakened by the war and its outcome. It was, for example,
unable to use a state apparatus from the pre-Munich republic, from
the period of occupation or one constructed in emigration.[51]

He thereby did not rule out a future fight for power between anti-
fascist forces. He even gave credence to the view that cooperation
could not be permanent when he justified it as follows: 'We cannot
govern alone and they cannot govern alone either . . . There
remains the necessity for cooperation with the other political group

which is forced to cooperate with us'.[52] Nevertheless, he rejected ideas of an early fight for power. There was apparently even a hope that the socialist parties would gradually come closer together and eventually merge to leave a single party effectively dominating political life.[53] The 'dictatorship of the proletariat' could then have been achieved without a further violent revolution.

This problem was approached in a slightly different way by KSČ organisations at home. In general, the extent of Nazi repression – in all there were five Illegal Central Committees, each one created after its predecessor had been decimated – greatly restricted their ability to formulate any coherent ideas. By 1944, however, when their fortunes were at their lowest ebb, Czech Communists began relating their setbacks to ambiguities about theoretical questions and about the future form of the republic.

The most sophisticated example was the work of the group *Předvoj* (Vanguard) which was led primarily by former students with no pre-war political experience. They tried to provide an answer to 'dogmatic sectarians' by means of a justification for the line of national liberation struggle as received from Moscow Radio.[54] Unlike Gottwald, they emphasised from the very start and unequivocally that the coming revolution would be 'social in content and national in form'.[55] They even elaborated a programme of social changes including the democratisation of industrial management, steps towards pay equalisation and land reform.[56] Post-liberation events leave little doubt that many of these demands accurately reflected the workers' feelings, but it would be wrong to suggest that the domestic KSČ had a more sophisticated approach than that of Gottwald. Plenty of points remained unanswered. There was no mention of the world context, of the German minority, of Beneš or of other political parties.

It seemed as if the KSČ inside the Czech lands, operating in such deep illegality as to be unable to estimate the political diversity to be expected in the new republic, was able simply to assume Beneš out of existence. The party's leadership in Moscow, however, had deliberately formulated its ideas in the hope that an agreement with Beneš could be reached. It was therefore important that he was strikingly unimpressed by what they were proposing.

There is an analogy to his over-simplified interpretation of Soviet policy as, broadly speaking, Beneš could understand the KSČ policy either as subordination to his authority or as an attempt to

stage a revolution against him: most of KSČ policy he and his
associates interpreted as the latter. Their Slovak policy he believed
was intended to weaken the republic making it a more willing
instrument of Communist policies.[57] Proposals on National Committees were seen as the prelude to a 'Soviet revolution'[58] and he
particularly feared the suggestion that his London government
should not return home: he preferred to alter its composition after
a period 'in which a certain stabilisation of conditions at home could
occur'.[59]

He was, however, optimistic that his understanding with the
Soviet leadership would enable him and his government to return
home without making any major concessions to the KSČ. He was
forced into a major reappraisal of the situation only during the
gradual liberation of Czechoslovakia.

4 THE SLOVAK NATIONAL UPRISING

The initial episode in the lengthy process of Czechoslovakia's
liberation was the uprising in Slovakia. It was to have important
consequences for Slovakia's future internal political life and also
had implications for the Communist Party's strategy. Most immediately, however, it began the process whereby Beneš's dominance
over Czechoslovak politics was undermined.

Its roots lay in Slovakia's war-time development which was very
different from that of the Czech lands.[60] Rather than resorting to
an open occupation, the Nazis had been able to rely on the subservience of a formally independent Slovak state led by a right-wing
Catholic movement. Although many Slovaks at first doubted its
viability, and it was never able to command much really enthusiastic and active support, the new state did create a significant mass
base during 1940 and 1941. It could genuinely claim to be the
'lesser evil' as Slovakia was kept out of the war.

Nazi Germany had a strong and increasing influence over policies
as was clearly demonstrated in the privileges given to the German
minority, the subordination of the economy to German war needs,
anti-Jewish measures culminating in their sale to Germany,[61] and
military subordination leading to involvement in the war in the
East. Nevertheless, leading economists could argue that close relations with Germany were a sound basis for advance and the
economy did seem to be functioning better than before.[62] Moreover,

Jewish property was given not to Germans but to Christian Slovaks and this met with considerable approval.[63] Even peasants were generally able to prosper from the war even though a land reform which was promised was not fully implemented.[64]

The Slovak government could therefore claim to be advancing the Slovak national interest and succeeded in incorporating the pre-war bourgeois parties within one ruling party without ever using repressive measures as strong as those that became common in the Protectorate. This obviously limited the possibilities for a broad opposition movement and, in addition to the sectarian past traditions of the party in Slovakia, probably helped to give the Comintern's line of the 1939-41 period a greater appeal among Slovak Communists. They formed a separate party – the KSS – which was still subordinated to the KSČ within the Comintern. They even responded to Soviet actions in the Baltic states by formulating the aim of a 'Soviet Slovakia' meaning incorporation into the USSR.[65] This slogan was firmly refected in Moscow, but the KSS was very half-hearted in attempts to establish anti-fascist unity even after July 1941. Their approach was changed somewhat in 1943 by a new leadership made up of Šmidke, a pre-war MP who returned to Slovakia with the Comintern's resolution of 5 January 1943, Husák and Novomeský

Their hope of a united anti-fascist movement culminating in a national uprising appeared more realisable as the regime's credibility began to crumble. Its weaknesses were shown up as the course of the war made reliance on Nazi Germany appear as a recipe for disaster rather than a guarantee of security. Even state officials began expressing preference for a new Czechoslovakia. Particularly in Central Slovakia, with its large working class and Protestant population, the security forces lost the power to dominate the courts and sometimes even turned a blind eye to resistance organisations.[66] Even some of the highest figures in the state prepared to change sides and, in one way or another, helped the preparations for the uprising.

In this atmosphere resistance groups multiplied, established contacts with each other and made preparations for an uprising. There were broadly three plans for how this could be done. The first centred on army chief of staff Golian who based himself in Banská Bystrica in Central Slovakia. He always owed his first allegiance to Beneš with whom he worked out plans for an army putsch prepared entirely by conspiratorial means. The Soviet commanders regarded this with great scepticism as the Slovak army would very probably have to confront German troops from a position of encirclement.[67] Instead, they and the KSČ leadership favoured the maximum encouragement of partisans in Slovakia aiming for 'a mass transition of Slovak soldiers and of Slovaks generally to the partisan units'.[68] To encourage this, and much to the annoyance of Beneš's military representatives in Moscow, who saw it as the prelude to the incorporation of Czechoslovakia into the USSR,[69] they sent trained partisan units into Slovakia.

The third plan, worked out by the Communists inside Slovakia, was roughly for a synthesis of those two military tactics – an army putsch backed up by partisans.[70] In addition, they wanted to establish a new supreme Slovak political organ which would not accept total subordination to Beneš and would provide the basis for greater Slovak national rights within a future Czechoslovak state. Towards this end they approached the Protestant former Agrarians Ursíny and Lettrich who led one of the most serious of many small resistance groups. They, in turn, welcomed the prospect of unity with the Communists who they felt would wield immense power in the likely event of Slovakia being liberated from the East.[71]

Although there were plenty of strong differences of opinion, these two groups were able to agree on a joint platform in December 1943 and established the Slovak National Council (SNR) as the potential supreme representative of the Slovak nation. During 1944 they made contact with Golian and agreed roughly on military plans for an uprising. Šmidke and Lt. Col. Ferjenčik then went to the USSR to try to coordinate their plans with the Soviet army. There were, however, unexplained delays and then a dramatic political change in Rumania which made Slovakia irrelevant to Soviet military plans. The uprising therefore started without the approval of any great power.

A general offensive by partisan units, culminating in the occupation of several towns where National Committees emerged to take power, provoked an invasion by Nazi troops on 29 August 1944. Although the partisans were unsuccessful over most of the country, a consolidated area was established in Central Slovakia where the Slovak army, along with the partisans, was able to mobilise perhaps 80,000 men and to hold out for two months after which a fairly successful partisan war was continued until liberation.

Real military success for the uprising would only have been possible after much greater external help and there have been accusations that the Soviet Union deliberately allowed it to suffer defeat. In fact they were persuaded by Gottwald that the uprising's leaders were friendly to the Soviet Union[72] and thereupon launched the Carpathian operation. Despite enormous losses, they failed to open a route into Central Slovakia until after the uprising had been defeated.

The West was even more reluctant to help and the British government was easily deterred by signs of Soviet reticence although no formal veto to the air-lifting of military supplies was ever sent. This could encourage doubts about the sincerity of Britain's support for the uprising, a point which must have been an embarrassment to Beneš. Perhaps for this reason he later claimed that there had been a Soviet veto on British involvement.[73]

Nevertheless, the uprising certainly was a blow to Beneš's supremacy. From the start the London government tried to present it as their own operation so as to exploit it 'on the international forum in London'.[74] They therefore hoped for statements of unqualified recognition from the uprising's leaders.

In practice, however, the Communists took the initiative from the start thanks both to their strength in National Committees and to firm and determined support from partisan units. Despite some confusion at the very beginning, they were able to exploit the disunity of the rest of the anti-fascist movement to establish the SNR as the supreme political organ and to ensure that half its members were either Communists or their close allies.[75] They held a similarly strong position in the Board of Commissioners, effectively a Council of Ministers.

The SNR had already clearly stated its views on the relationship between the domestic resistance and the emigration. In a statement in July 1944 they accepted continuity with the pre-Munich republic 'only with respect to foreign countries and in international relations'. Beyond that they demanded changes arguing that only a clear statement that Czech–Slovak relations were to be on the basis of equality could win the ordinary working people to fight for Czechoslovakia.[76] Beneš could not accept their arguments, particularly when they adopted the KSČ position of recognising his right to be President but not the right of the London government to return home.

A further disappointment for Beneš was the creation of a Slovak party-political structure based on two parties. At first the KSS seemed to be almost completely dominant as the only organised political force within the uprising. Its strength within the working class was clearly demonstrated at its congress on 7 September 1944 when, to the surprise of both Moscow and London, a merger was accomplished with the Social Democrats.

It would, however, be wrong to exaggerate the Communists' strength by implying that they alone could claim all the credit for the uprising. As one of Beneš's informants commented, they certainly were the most impressive with their serious hard work, but they alone could not win the peasants, the intellectuals and the whole army for revolutionary action.[77] The uprising's strength was in fact derived from its ability to bring together such diverse social and political forces into a genuinely broad movement which no single grouping has any right to claim for itself alone.

Nevertheless, their clear ability to take the initiative frightened the diverse non-socialist groups into forgetting their differences and merging to form the Democratic Party.[78] This new body could not start with a clear programme: in practice its strength was derived from flexibility rather than clarity of principles. It could claim joint credit for the uprising and thereby appear as a genuinely anti-fascist and also non-Communist force able to hold together very diverse tendencies. In 1946 this latter characteristic became still more prominent.

This two party system was a disappointment to Beneš who had advocated the revival of the National Socialists as a Czechoslovakist force. Uhlíř, representing his position in Slovakia, tried to convince Lettrich of the need for a third party. He argued that the Communists might win outright in an election against only one opponent as they had a head's start with their clear programme, organisational unity and their energetic young leadership. Moreover, unlike the Democrats, they were definitely refusing to entertain people associated with the previous regime. Lettrich, however, believed that an electoral majority could be won by exploiting widespread fears of Communism which had been accentuated by the indiscipline of some partisans.[79]

Nevertheless, the Communists certainly were assured of considerable support and the course of the uprising seemed to confirm the general applicability of their conception of national democratic revolution. Their success would clearly have been impossible without the policy of a broad anti-fascist struggle rejecting both immediate socialist revolution and simple subordination to Beneš. Despite accusations in the early 1950s that the Slovak Communist leaders had succumbed to 'bourgeois nationalism' their line was very close to that of the Moscow KSČ. This was confirmed when Šverma arrived with some other Communist leaders on 28 September 1944.

Nevertheless, there were some differences of approach and the uprising could have led to some rethinking of the social content of the national democratic revolution. At the start, however, political-power changes were seen as the most pressing with precedence given to the establishment of National Committees and the dissolution of fascist organisations. Questions like land reform and the nationalisation of industries were delayed on the grounds that they would threaten the unity of the anti-fascist front and thereby hamper mobilisation of the armed struggle.[80] Soon, however, Husák was suggesting that explicitly social demands would actually *strengthen* the anti-fascist struggle.[81]

In practice, simple opposition to fascism was proving an inadequate basis for the mobilisation of an anti-fascist movement. The Slovaks' experience of independent statehood also meant that restoration of a Czechoslovak state alone was not immediately attractive either. At a conference of Factory Committees at Podbrezová on 15 October 1944 there were even renewed, powerful calls for a 'Soviet Slovakia'. It seemed that workers' representatives would only support the uprising enthusiastically when given assurances that a new Czechoslovakia would be closely allied to the USSR and would advance their social status.[82]

The extent of economic problems ruled out immediate wage rises, although that was the most widespread working class demand.[83] Instead, the resolutions from Podbrezová called rather for workers' involvement in the running of their factories through a continuation of the enormous powers already assumed by some Factory Committees and by the immediate statisation of the property of enemies and traitors.[84]

Over the issue of land reform events were less dramatic, as preoccupation with military affairs prevented any positive steps, but the KSS leaders again differed from the Moscow KSČ. Their ideas were not fully worked out but they broadly advocated a

'general' land reform on 'class' lines[85] rather than one on national
and anti-fascist lines, i.e. by the expropriation of Germans,
Hungarians and traitors.[86] This followed from the view held in
Moscow, based purely on an understanding of the Czech situation,
that land reform could be closely linked to national liberation.
Slovakia had already been described as effectively German occupied[87] and the German minority as an instrument of foreign
imperialist domination.[88]

Although these differences did not lead to sharp conflicts at the
time, they did make themselves felt again after liberation. The
differences between Beneš and the SNR were to prove even more
important as they affected the political complexion of the first post-
war government.

5 THE KOŠICE GOVERNMENT

After the defeat of the uprising, Beneš could renew his hope that
organs of power would emerge to express unquestioning loyalty to
his London government. He was, however, quickly disappointed
when the Soviet army reached the Sub-Carpathian Ukraine, an
area occupied by Hungary in 1939.

Far from giving power to Němec, the Soviet troops were greeted
by a powerful movement demanding incorporation into the Soviet
Ukraine. As the territory did become part of the USSR, no detailed
or objective account exists of how far this was instigated or encouraged by the Red Army or the NKVD. The different accounts do,
however, roughly agree on the ultimate breadth and strength of
the movement which led to Němec's isolation.[89]

Beneš was confronted with an extremely embarrassing situation.
Despite the treaty of May 1944, the Soviet authorities seemed to
be if anything encouraging local organs which rejected his authority.
If he complied with the evident Soviet wish that he should give his
blessing to the de facto situation, then there would be nothing to
prevent a repeat of the same course of events among the Ukrainians
of Eastern Slovakia and then in Slovakia generally. The London
government might gradually find itself as irrelevant to events at
home as its Polish counterpart. Moreover, Beneš's fears were compounded as the Soviet leaders evidently understood the treaty
agreements not just as an insurance against 'non-intervention' but
rather as the basis for a united approach on international questions:
they therefore expected him to recognise the Polish Lublin govern-

ment, which he was unwilling to do. Despite growing signs of Soviet distrust towards him, he stuck to the constitutionally correct position over the Sub-Carpathian Ukraine and only formally ceded the territory in June 1945.

The liberation of Slovakia must have increased Beneš's worries as the Soviet and Czechoslovak armies established direct contacts with local National Committees, often completely dominated by the KSS. They ignored Němec and recognised the SNR as the supreme authority, quite simply because it was the only anti-fascist body with any authority.[90] So, far from being defeated and forgotten, the uprising proved to be of all-Slovak significance. The prospect of the SNR playing a role like the Polish Lublin government was reaffirmed when hopes of even the Czech lands being liberated from the West faded during the renewed and vigorous Soviet offensive of January 1945.

Beneš finally started making real concessions. He recognised the Lublin government, accepted at last that the Agrarian Party could not be renewed in any form and signed a law on punishing collaborators meaning that a Minister in any Protectorate government could go before a special court.[91] The hardest concession of all was acceptance that the London government could not return home and that a new government would be formed on the basis of discussions in Moscow. Although sometimes presented as a mistake, Beneš's decision appeared as the only way to retain influence at home as the country was being gradually liberated from the East. He hoped that it would be only a temporary concession with free elections roughly reaffirming the pre-war political situation.[92]

The discussions were held in Moscow between 22 March 1945 and 29 March 1945. Beneš took no direct part and behaved instead as a non-party President leaving the formulation of policies to a meeting of the three socialist parties. The Catholic People's Party was also represented but in practice that made no difference to the course of the discussions. The conclusions from the meeting were presented to representatives of the SNR who argued only on the question of Czech–Slovak relations. The National Socialists and Social Democrats had no firm organisation in emigration or at home so that their representatives in the Moscow discussions and subsequent government became the new party leaderships.

Dominance in the Social Democratic Party went to its left wing which had been taking shape from the beginning of the war.[93]

Particularly prominent figures were Laušman and Fierlinger, who Beneš had appointed ambassador to Moscow. Central points in the programme they developed were close friendship with the USSR and an assessment of the main error in 1918–20 as hesitancy which let slip a golden opportunity for socialism:[94] they thought conditions in 1945 would be even more favourable and were therefore surprised by the Communists' moderation.[95] They must, however, have welcomed the chance to take part in forming a new government in Moscow.

The National Socialists seemed during the war to be seeking a new political base. They started incorporating former members of right-wing parties and their programmatic documents suggested fear of the KSČ establishing a monopoly of power rather than concern with the concrete problems of liberating and rebuilding the country.[96] Not surprisingly, they were very nervous of discussions in Moscow[97] and still hoped that the Western powers would reach Prague first. To be prepared for this eventuality Ripka, Beneš's closest aide, remained in London.

During the actual discussions the KSČ took the initiative and directed attention first and foremost onto the programme of the new government. They presented a 32-page draft based on the ideas they had been developing in Moscow: this was accepted as the only basis for discussion. Although there was considerable disagreement on some points, the draft was generally accepted with only stylistic corrections.[98] To achieve this the Communists were prepared to compromise on several issues by making it clear that the programme only referred to immediate tasks within the transition period before a parliament could be established. This gave the National Socialists real grounds for hoping that the programme could be altered fairly quickly, particularly as it was made explicit that the government was to be broadened to include representatives of the domestic resistance very soon after liberation.

The only really sharp disagreements arose over Czech–Slovak relations. The KSČ approach was dominated by discussions involving Dimitrov, who had advocated a symmetrical arrangement of Czech–Slovak relations each having their own governments alongside a common federal Czechoslovak government.[99] Gottwald never committed himself to any definite state form largely because this advice conflicted with the tactical need, as reiterated by Stalin, to be accommodating towards Beneš.[100]

By evading a statement of definite aims on the Slovak issue, and instead subordinating it to the needs of a compromise with Beneš, the KSČ gained enormously in the Moscow discussions. The Slovak presence took the form of a united SNR delegation basing itself on a programme presented by the KSS: this prevented the formation of a united front of Czech and Slovak right-wingers. Nevertheless, Gottwald felt obliged to persuade the KSS to weaken their position on Czech–Slovak relations so as to avoid a major conflict with Beneš's followers.[101] Agreement was then finally reached on a formulation leaving a final decision on the powers of the SNR to elected representatives of the Czech and Slovak people.

Perhaps equally fierce were disagreements over the actual composition of the government, although the record of the discussions shows only unanimous agreement. The National Socialists wanted some of the 'key' Ministries and were not averse to Gottwald becoming Prime Minister.[102] Perhaps this would have made it easier to change the government later on the grounds that it was Communist dominated. In practice Fierlinger, who was intensely disliked by many of those close to Beneš because they saw him as being 'more Soviet than the Soviets',[103] was accepted as Prime Minister with a 'Government Presidium' containing one representative of each party. These were Ursíny (DS), Široký (KSS), J. David (NS), Šrámek (LS) and Gottwald (KSČ). The whole government was then agreed to and individual Ministers were required to express agreement with its composition and programme. This became known as the Košice Programme because the government formally assumed office there.

The rest of the government was as follows;

Interior	V. Nosek	(KSČ)
Information	V. Kopecký	(KSČ)
Agriculture	J. Ďuriš	(KSS)
Foreign Affairs	J. Masaryk	(non-party)
Defence	L. Svoboda	(non-party)
Finance	V. Šrobár	(DS)
Industry	B. Laušman	(SD)
Food Supply	V. Majer	(SD)
Foreign Trade	H. Ripka	(NS)
Justice	Jaroslav Stránský	(NS)
Posts	F. Hála	(LS)
Health	A. Procházka	(LS)

Internal Trade	I. Pietor	(DS)
Transport	A. Hasal	(non-party)
Education	Z. Nejedlý	(non-party)
Social Security	J. Šoltész	(KSS)

There were also 'State Secretaries' to give Slovaks representation in Ministries which had no equivalent in the Board of Commissioners:

Foreign Affairs	V. Clementis (KSS)
Defence	M. Ferjenčík (non-party)
Foreign Trade	J. Lichner (DS)

So the Communists had a strong but not completely dominant position. Moreover, several non-party Ministers would be unlikely to oppose them in a crisis. Particularly important was Svoboda who had been appointed commander of the Czechoslovak forces in the Soviet Union; Nejedlý was actually a KSČ member.

Not surprisingly, émigré writers have often characterised the outcome of the Moscow discussions as a disaster for their side. Nevertheless, despite KSČ ideas of a bloc of three parties or of a much wider National Front to include mass organisations, the programme had been agreed in emigration by four Czech parties and the government gave equal representation to all of them. This enabled the National Socialists to return home with more prestige as a political party than their role in the domestic resistance warranted. They could help build a political system based on competing political parties, and look forward with optimism to free elections.

Moreover, the creation of the government and agreement on its programme was still not enough to ensure its survival in a liberated Czechoslovakia. Beneš, in fact, felt that the KSČ was over-represented following their 'trick' over the Slovak ministers. Perhaps this was the thinking behind the National Socialists' reluctance to give clear recognition to the SNR. He still expected the alleged conservatism of the Czech lands to show itself after liberation and to force changes in the government.[104] He kept his own options open by refraining from approving the Košice Programme. A great deal was still undecided and could depend on how Prague was liberated and on what political character the Czech resistance would assume in the last days of the war.

This was uncertain right up to the last minute as the Czech resistance remained fragmented and organisationally weak. There were about 7500 partisans in the Czech lands in the spring of 1945, but they remained geographically isolated and could not create a centralised leadership.[105] There were also many attempts to form local National Committees: their composition, origins and political character were very diverse but, once the fighting was over, the majority could be seen to be dominated by Communists or by those who quickly joined the KSČ.

Amid this picture of fragmentation, as if the same uprising were being prepared by a multitude of different groups, the KSČ, ÚRO (an underground trade union organisation which developed from within the Protectorate unions and was close to the Communists' position) and R-3 joined to create the ČNR (Czech National Council). All three claimed credit for the initiative, but only R-3 had contacts with the outside world. It recognised Beneš as President but stood politically to his left: its leaders actively encouraged partisan groups and this brought them closer to the KSČ.[106]

The ČNR was formally founded at the end of April and remained firmly under the dominance of trade unionists and Communists.[107] An attempt was made to broaden representation by including, among others, members of underground army groups and of the political parties represented in the Košice government. This gave it a somewhat artificial appearance and, unlike the SNR, it accepted from the start that its existence was only temporary and that it was completely subordinated to the Košice government.[108]

Although there could be no authoritative organ without the three founders of the ČNR, they did not initiate the Prague uprising which began spontaneously on 5 May 1945 and showed an energy surprising even to its leaders. Only as the element of surprise wore off did the immensely superior Nazi forces recover and regroup. They even seemed to be within sight of victory when, on 9 May 1945, the uprising was saved by the arrival of Soviet forces.

This, however, marked the end for the ČNR which, in recognition of its own weakness, had sought gains through negotiations with the Nazi authorities. Soviet distrust, leading to categorical demands for the ČNR's dissolution, was engendered by the right-wing's approaches to Vlasov's forces and a strange compromise of 8 May 1945 whereby German forces were to be allowed to keep their arms and pass through Prague to escape from the Red Army and surrender in the West.[109]

The greatest difficulty facing the ČNR, apart from their own shortage of arms, was their ignorance of the rapidly approaching

Soviet forces and of the complex intrigues involving foreign help and intervention. Beneš had already disappointed R-3 by not sending arms and even argued in Košice that it was too late.[110] Infuriatingly, this was combined with continuing calls from London for armed action. This was an obvious cause of bitterness to Grňa of R-3 who attributed the comparative weakness of the Czech partisan movement entirely to the absence of such outside help.[111] There is no clear evidence that it can all be attributed to a refusal from Stalin to allow the delivery of arms that had already been loaded into British aircraft.[112] The alternative suggestion, that Britain was refusing to help any such uprising as would directly aid the Soviet advance,[113] also lacks substantiation. Beneš and his associates in London were always conspicuously silent on what the explanation could be.

Meanwhile Ripka, still in London, negotiated over a possible US advance to Prague. Despite pressure from within the State Department and from Churchill,[114] Eisenhower opposed this attempt to secure a strong bargaining position against the Soviet Union partly because he lacked the resources for a direct clash with the USSR and partly because their help was still wanted against Japan.[115]

The Soviet leadership was undoubtedly opposed to any such US operation as they too were fully aware of the political significance of liberating Prague. Fierlinger expressed opposition to allowing US troops into Prague as it would help 'conservative elements'[116] and Marshall Koniev himself emphasised the political significance of a speedy action to prevent any direct Western share in Prague's liberation.[117] The Soviet military operation to reach Prague, which had already been prepared before the uprising,[118] was therefore quickly set in motion. On 9 May 1945 Soviet tanks reached the capital.

So the Košice government, which arrived in Prague on 10 May 1945, could quickly establish its authority without any opposition from the domestic Czech resistance.

3

The national revolution

As the new government was welcomed back to Prague so organs
of the new Czechoslovakia were establishing their authority over
the territory of the state. Officially the government was to be
subject to alteration and a Provisional National Assembly was to be
created as quickly as possible. In practice the 'transition period'
lasted almost six months and in the meantime many revolutionary
measures were implemented. Generally this was referred to as the
'national revolution' and the term is adopted here. Its guiding
document was the Košice Programme, which received exceptionally wide publicity, although many comments even by leading
politicians suggest that its actual contents were rarely remembered
exactly. It could anyway not be a precise blueprint for the revolution: it quickly became clear that in some fields it was not being
applied rigorously while in others the revolutionary changes went
further than had been laid down.

This complex revolutionary process cannot be reduced to terms
of one class taking power from another, as Czechoslovak historians
especially in the early 1950s felt obliged to do, and neither can it
be reduced to the perfidious acts of Communists in subverting
Czechoslovak society as was implied by a number of émigré writers
in the same period. Both of those approaches grossly oversimplify
what took place and neither provides a sound basis for understanding the subsequent evolution of Czechoslovak society. That
does not mean that there was no social content to the revolution or
that the Communist Party did not have an extremely important
role, but it does mean that the revolution cannot be reduced entirely
to such simplistic terms.

It is extremely important to emphasise the complexity of the
revolutionary process: the social formation that emerged was the

53

outcome of a complex interaction of ideas and intentions with sometimes unexpected consequences. Discussion of the national revolution therefore has to be wide ranging, covering the changes in organs of power, in the media, in the nationalities structure of Czechoslovak society, in industry and in economic mechanisms generally.

I BACKGROUND TO REVOLUTIONARY CHANGES

In the first six months rule was by the seemingly highly undemocratic means of Presidential decree, but this did not mean that Beneš behaved as a dictator. He tried to stick to his principle of standing above parties and, although on occasion he did disagree with government decisions, he made no attempt to use his prestige publicly against the Communists. In his many public speeches he seemed to be searching for the middle ground towards which all parties could compromise: he accepted the need for rapid social change, even characterising the regime as a 'socialising democracy', and he generally provided a constitutional rubber stamp to decisions of the government.

Although four Czech parties were created, the KSČ undeniably held the initiative. Organisations emerged from illegality or were formed quickly after liberation and the party was the first to hold a big rally in Prague. Gottwald, however, insisted that they had to exploit their initiative within the multi-party structure that had been created in Moscow. He rejected the very popular suggestion that there should be an immediate merger of the three socialist parties on the grounds that it would be premature. He feared that it would leave the right wing of Social Democracy with the freedom and potential strength to create a significant anti-Communist organisation. He therefore advocated encouraging the continued independent existence of Social Democracy, which could in practice be dominated by the left.[1] A similar argument applied for the National Socialists, so that Gottwald implicitly encouraged their domestic leaders to revive their organisation although they had at first even suggested a merger with the KSČ.[2]

Nevertheless, the National Socialist Party was still too weak to take advantage of the stipulation in the Košice Programme that the government was to be altered to include representatives of the domestic resistance. They therefore had to accept a compromise whereby the three socialist parties formed a bloc committed to supporting the Košice Programme as the basis for the new republic. The agreement also covered approval for the idea of united mass organisations, such as trade unions, and committed the parties to reaching agreement on policies prior to government meetings. In return the National Socialists were assured that there would be parity between parties in National Committees wherever possible and in the Provisional National Assembly. The National Socialists' Chairman Zenkl would also be re-elected to his pre-war position of mayor of Prague.[3] Although the National Socialists did not keep to the agreement for long it was extremely important for a time in preventing the creation of a bloc of the two right-wing parties.

Alongside the Socialist Bloc was the National Front which was to prove far more permanent and became effectively the supreme political body. The KSČ wanted it to include mass organisations alongside the parties, but they eventually had to accept the supremacy of the four-party structure that had been created in Moscow. Resolutions of this body were binding both on the government and, when it was formed, on parliament. This helped to smooth over all sorts of disagreements so that, in the whole period up to 1948, there were hardly any cases in which a vote in parliament was contested.[4] It also meant that the four parties could decide over an enormous range of political and social questions.

They agreed that none would try to organise as an all-state party i.e. covering both Slovakia and the Czech lands. They also arrogated for themselves the right to decide whether any new party could be formed and they insisted that all legal parties should be in the government. They thereby agreed on the banning of the pre-war right-wing parties.

Thus the basic outline of the new political structure took shape. It gave the KSČ scope to exercise considerable authority but they were constrained both by the need to reach compromise agreements and by the immensity of the economic problems confronting the new republic.

It is extemely difficult to estimate the extent of losses due to the war as there were no statistics at the time of liberation. The occupation had led to gross distortions in the economy which were compounded by damage from bombing and fighting and also by the removal of industrial and transport equipment by the occupiers at the close of the war. One, possibly conservative, estimate puts the total losses as equal to the total national income produced in the six year period 1932–7.[5] Moreover, damage was particularly severe in the key sectors of transport and energy. It was therefore necessary to continue, as in war-time, with strict controls over scarce products and inputs.[6]

There were also very acute food supply shortages. Significant help came from the Red Army, and this was well publicised in all the press, and also from UNRRA, the United Nations aid body, whose help was extremely important in the following months for both food and essential industrial raw materials.[7] It proved possible to increase rations at the end of 1945 so that an adult would receive 1800–1900 calories instead of 1300: this was still way below the desirable level.[8] Majer summed the situation up with the assurance that the population would not actually starve over the winter, but that difficulties would continue for several years.[9]

Difficulties in restoring the economy were compounded by labour problems as the war economy had relied heavily on compulsion, and for many industrial workers liberation meant an opportunity to take a holiday. Others saw in it a chance to shift their employment, particularly from heavy manual labour such as mining, into more desirable jobs in offices.[10] Moreover, there was also a striking drop in hours worked and a sharp rise in absenteeism. Although it is impossible to know how much of this was caused by industrial disorganisation, it became usual to refer to a collapse in labour morale as one of the worst consequences of the occupation.

In this extremely serious situation revolutionary measures had to be judged to a great extent by how far they would help in overcoming immediate problems. This makes nonsense of the suggestion that the KSČ could have seized power and ruled alone from the time of liberation.[11] That view could only stem from a realistic assessment of the numerical weakness of all other parties but not from an appraisal of the Communists' actual ability to overcome alone the difficulties they would have faced.

2 NEW POLITICAL POWER STRUCTURES

As the power of the occupiers collapsed, National Committees emerged to proclaim the authority of the new state. At first, with all else in a state of disarray, they could be the only organs of the new state in localities and the KSČ, fearing that they might soon be dissolved, as had happened in 1918, consistently called on them to take the maxumum power they could. A full structure was quickly created with Local (místní), District (okresní) and two Regional (Zemský) National Committees – for Bohemia and Moravia. The parties could usually agree to constitute them on the basis of parity, but at the lowest levels the KSČ did not accept this. Arguing that all four parties did not have organisations everywhere and that popular control was to be very direct for Local National Committees, they often insisted on elections at public meetings. In consequence the Communists had 36% of places and 46% of chairmen of National Committees in Bohemia and Moravia in early 1946.[12]

Parity was, however, pretty strictly maintained in the more important higher units in the structure. The selection of their members still involved public participation as open meetings were held by Local National Committees to vet delegates, presented by parties and mass organisations, who then formed the District National Committees and so on up the structure to the Provisional National Assembly. This procedure was not presented as an ideal, but the KSČ leadership persuaded their own members to accept it and argued strongly against an immediate competitive ballot on the grounds that the maximum unity was needed to confront economic tasks.[13]

Despite Communist hopes, the National Committees rapidly receded from the centre of political attention. Part of the reason for this was that attention generally shifted onto economic questions which could only be solved by the central government. The principal reason, however, was that the new state established its own central-ised organs, such as the police and army, because the National Committees alone could not guarantee the security of the new state. Their highly fragmented armed groups, which had grown out of the uprising and probably numbered around 160,000, lacked the discipline and experience for the tasks they had to face, especially in the frontier regions. It was therefore decided, on 4 June 1945, that they should either be disarmed or incorporated into the polic the army or the factory militia groups.

The most important of these in military terms was the army, which was soon expanding rapidly on the basis of two years com-pulsory national service. At first it seemed that it would fulfil the Communists' hope of an army based on those units created in the USSR plus other active anti-fascists, but the shortage of officers and demobilisation of the armies created during the war – many of their officers wanted different employment anyway – meant that 70% of the new officers were from the pre-Munich army. Among these were many who had done nothing during the occupation.[14] All this suggests a considerable success for the National Socialists' idea of restoring basically the same pre-war army.

In practice, however, the parties had far less influence within the army than in other institutions. It was neither a major subject of political controversy nor a significant political force. There is no real evidence on the political thinking of army officers or ordinary soldiers because they did not involve themselves in politics as a united force. Soldiers were allowed to join political parties, but only outside their barracks. Joining the KSČ was not a help in promotion prospects because the ultimate authority in deciding on appointments was Beneš. There were a few Communist organisations within the army which, strictly speaking, were illegal, but there is no evidence that they were influential.[15] Communist strength was primarily among Political Education Officers and this was the basis for an unwieldy and rudimentary organisation of party activity.[16]

So, for reasons that would require further study, the establishment of the army did not alter the balance of strength between the political parties.

In practice the principal immediate consequence of its establishment was to aid the consolidation of the Czechoslovak state thereby allowing the two liberating armies to withdraw. At first they had been welcomed as liberators but in time, owing to misunderstandings and some indisciplined behaviour, there were unpleasant incidents that could have developed into serious inter-state conflicts.[17]

In practice the Red Army did not intervene directly in Czech politics although their presence undoubtedly had a strong moral impact and Gottwald often referred to it. Further East, Soviet involvement had been more direct. The exact situation in the Sub-Carpathian Ukraine remains unknown, while the NKVD was certainly active in Eastern Slovakia. Apparently in an effort to secure the army's rear, Slovaks, mostly from leading positions in fascist organisations, were taken to Soviet prison camps and only gradually returned: cases of unjustified arrest that were taken up with the Soviet authorities by Clementis remained unheeded until after 1956.[18] Lettrich put the number of prisoners at 7000 and claimed that many were still in the USSR in the early 1950s.[19] The

Slovak Democrat MP Linczenyi raised the issue in parliament and gave the figure of 3000.[20]

By the autumn of 1945 it seemed that a withdrawal of Soviet troops would be a useful reassurance that they had no lasting ulterior designs towards Czechoslovakia. In negotiating for this, Beneš privately requested that the US army should stay – although at that time the US had no interest in Czechoslovakia, which they regarded as being under complete Soviet domination[21] – so as to ensure that the Red Army was not left as the only occupation force.[22] The outcome of negotiations was that the two armies departed simultaneously in November 1945.

Contrasting with this largely non-political role for the army, the police force was of enormous importance in the rivalry between parties. As with the army, the KSČ, in line with their general conception of the national democratic revolution, argued that the old force had failed the republic in 1938 and a new one had to be built up firmly committed to anti-fascist politics.[23] In this case, however, they achieved their aim after a purge of the old police force plus the incorporation of the best elements from revolutionary armed groups. Legal proceedings for war-time activities were started against 1619 policemen in the Czech lands,[24] but the new, purged police force contained 25,000 from the old force plus 12,000 new policemen: most of the new ones, who had to provide proof of resistance activity, went to the frontier.[25] In the interior the tendency was to change just the leading posts.[26] Overall the police force was bigger than in 1938 and its frontier units were particularly well armed.

This gave the KSČ the opportunity to go beyond their stated policy and to secure a very strong position within the police. Nosek never left any doubt that, as Minister of the Interior, he held the ultimate authority on personnel questions. In the atmosphere of a purge, which he insisted for some time was unfinished, there was a very strong incentive for police officers seeking security or promotion to join the party of the Minister in charge of these questions. The KSČ was also quite happy to recruit policemen with real experience of their work. Nosek, albeit speaking at a later period, indicated what was happening when pointing out to a meeting of KSČ policemen on 19 January 1948: 'party membership does not entitle him [i.e. the KSČ member] *merely* to personal advancement and promotion'.[27]

The Communists' position was still further strengthened by their insistence on dominating posts concerned with police affairs at National Committee level. In this too Nosek's position of power was extremely important: he had no hesitation in resolving a deadlock over the allocation of posts in the Regional National Committee in Prague decisively in favour of the KSČ after even the government and the National Front had failed to reach agreement.[28]

All this indicated an extraordinary determination to gain the maximum of control over the organs of public order, even at the risk of exacerbating conflicts between parties. Nevertheless, there was very little sign in this early period of the whole police being used systematically in intra-party rivalries. Rather than preparations for a 'police coup', the Communists' activities appear as a consequence of their general belief that some sort of decisive struggle for power would come and the political complexion of the police force could then make the decisive difference.

Moreover, the Communists did not aim *at any cost* for complete domination of the police. The realities of the multi-party system meant that Nosek had to be able to answer criticisms from other parties and, while half the leading positions were given to Communists,[29] he also succeeded in working in harmony with the senior officials in his ministry who held differing views. To this end he consistently insisted that appointments were made on merit alone without reference to political affiliations. Although this was not strictly true, his actions had to give it some degree of credibility.

The National Socialists were Nosek's most consistent critics. The start was made by O. Hora as soon as the Provisional National Assembly had been formed,[30] but his criticisms amounted to the denial of any need for changes from the pre-Munich force. Not surprisingly, even though the National Socialists intensified their verbal attacks, the other parties did not join in and the Social Democrats were even led effectively to express full confidence in Nosek's activities.[31] The police could certainly claim to be doing a competent job in keeping order, which was probably what most people would have noticed at the time.

Finding themselves politically isolated, the National Socialists joined with the other parties in unanimously approving Nosek's report to parliament on the activities of his ministry.[32] This followed a fierce argument behind the scenes, which certainly indicated that there was cause for real concern. There had apparently been an attempt by the Communist head of the intelligence service in Prague to fabricate evidence of war-time collaboration against the National Socialist leader Krajina. There is no reason to believe that the KSČ leadership had any prior knowledge of what was being attempted and Nosek, following strong representations from the National Socialists, was prepared to remove the man from his post, but not from intelligence work altogether.[33]

There were also bitter disagreements over the legal system, which was the ultimate responsibility of the National Socialist Minister of Justice. The Communists never defined precisely their conception of the role of the legal system but the basic outlines were already clear in 1945. They did not regard legality as totally irrelevant, but they expected it to confirm rather than contradict the revolutionary changes. Most immediately, they wanted legal proceedings to confirm the public rejection of traitors and collaborators. This, they argued, was not a question of revenge, but a question of justice and of the security of the state as firm punishments would be a strong lesson to all who might consider betraying the republic in future.[34]

The first Presidential decrees, although not exactly as the KSČ wanted, did confirm that the punishment of traitors was a special measure in which normal legal practices could not be used.[35] There were to be special National Courts in Prague and Bratislava and also Peoples' Courts in the Districts. The Communists had some direct say in their verdicts as, although the chairman was to be a professional judge, four more judges were to be selected from the people. The decrees made every provision for rapid trials with no right of appeal and death sentences to be implemented with minimal delay. The maximum sentence was to be public execution for those guilty of particularly numerous and horrendous crimes.

Despite speed with the original decree, Gottwald soon complained that the legal processes were going more slowly than in other European countries. This began to threaten the revolutionary changes even in the economic field as individuals who had not been tried, or who had not been found guilty, were soon demanding back their property and positions. The KSČ therefore advocated a broadening of the law so that even those whose crimes were not serious enough for the Peoples' Courts could still not claim complete innocence. In particular they wanted District National Committees, rather than the legal apparatus to have the decisive power.[36] This led to the decree on offences against 'national honour' which could apply even to those who were not outright traitors. National Committees were thereby given powers to imprison for up to one year and had up until 26 May 1946 before the decree would expire.[37] Apparently 8000 were found guilty and these were predominantly from the ranks of the bourgeoisie.[38]

At the same time the Communists stepped up their criticisms of the slow operation of the People's Courts and the light sentences they were giving. Zápotocký even argued in a parliamentary debate that some judges should be removed and that the legal apparatus should be purged.[39] Just as the National Socialists had stepped back before challenging Nosek's authority, so the KSČ refrained from publicly attacking Drtina or voting against his report in parliament. He had replaced Jaroslav Stránský as the National Socialists' Minister of Justice and was therefore the member of government ultimately responsible.

This left the legal apparatus with considerable independence and strength with which to control organs of power. The same was also to a great extent true of the media although they too very quickly became a source of controversy. Kopecký, as the Minister of Information, had powers over key personnel appointments, but he was restricted by his determination to deny that he was pursuing a one-sided policy.

In the radio, headed by the Communist Laštovička, it was revealed in 1947 that 44% of leading positions were held by Communists,[40] but early complaints about the alleged political bias of broadcasts did not stand up to close scrutiny. The situation in the press was more complex. The individual legal political parties had their own daily papers which expressed their own, partisan viewpoints on events. The mass organisations also published daily papers which, although not neutral in political disputes, generally tried to give a more balanced account of events. There were also weeklies and other periodicals, some produced by parties, some by mass organisations and some by specialist bodies.

Exaggerated claims by National Socialist politicians that the freedom of the press was greatly restricted when compared with the pre-Munich republic[41] were generally rejected as, for the first time ever, there was no pre-publication censorship. The only serious grounds for criticising the Ministry's practices were that one paper (i.e. *Rudé právo*) was allowed a larger print, while others could never satisfy demand.[42] In fact, with time, all papers expanded and all the parties produced more periodicals so that the force even of that complaint declined.

Nevertheless, there was one important new restriction, as it was no longer possible for private individuals to publish. This could be circumvented by creating an organisation that could then claim to be the publisher: it was thereby possible for Peroutka to publish a daily, *Svobodné noviny*, and a weekly, *Dnešek*, although his pre-war journal, *Přítomnost*, could not explicitly be revived.

This restriction in the number of papers was justified by Kopecký in his own inimitably bombastic manner. He argued that the mass of private owners before the war had generally helped the enemy while Czechoslovakia, he claimed, had to be strong and not allow full freedom for fascists. He also pointed out that the critics of the new system, who seemed to want the 'weakest possible democracy', had previously favoured strong measures against the KSČ.[43] The opposing view, as presented by Jan Stránský, was that the post-war organisation of the press was tolerable only because of an acute shortage of paper.[44]

3 EXPULSION OF GERMANS

One of the measures with the most far-reaching economic and social consequences was the Czech occupation of the frontiers and the expulsion of Germans. This went considerably further than the cautious statements in the Košice Programme and indicated the depth of hatred towards Germans, particularly in the Czech interior. The notion that Germans were *collectively* guilty unless proved innocent was confirmed by law. All privileges were taken away from them and all except proven anti-fascists were given the same level of rations as had been given to Jews.[45] Germans were then given compulsory duty to repair war damage under the supervision of the District National Committees,[46] while Nazi criminals were sent to labour camps to perform unpaid work:[47] according to Fierlinger this applied only to active Nazi party members.[48]

These tough measures were evidently partly an attempt to alleviate the sectoral labour shortages but essentially they were a prelude to wholesale expulsion for which international agreement was needed. Discussions were slow as, although the principle was generally accepted at Potsdam and the occupation authorities in the

Soviet zone were willing to help, the US zone did not accept any Germans until early 1946.[49] Expulsion then proceeded rapidly through 1946 until the US zone imposed a 'temporary' halt. By the spring of 1947 the international climate had changed so that the expulsions were effectively stopped. Overall, there had been an enormous movement of people with 660,000 leaving voluntarily or by unorganised expulsions, 2,256,000 leaving by organised transports, and then a further 80,000 left in 1947.[50] In the end Czechoslovakia was left with only 100,000 Germans that the US zone would not take, and those judged to be unreliable were moved away from the frontier and scattered in the interior. There were another 100,000 from mixed marriages who were allowed to stay.[51] This inevitably meant that the population of the Czech lands declined and in some frontier areas the density did not even reach half the pre-war level. Overall, there was a 20% drop in Bohemia's population between 1930 and 1947 and a 13% drop in the population of Czechoslovakia as a whole.[52]

There were at first suggestions that the expulsions might be delayed because of the labour shortage, particularly in factories in the frontier zones.[53] It certainly seemed that German forced labour was a lifeline for coal mining during the winter of 1945–6. The industry was again confronted with enormous problems as Germans left through the summer of 1946.[54] Nevertheless, thoughts of using Germans in this way for a longer period were rejected for two reasons; first, it was assumed that the Germans expelled would be balanced by returning Czechs of whom there were said to be two and a half million scattered around the world. This included probable over-estimates of 500,000 and 600,000 in Germany as political prisoners and drafted labour respectively:[55] it seems that only 748,000 Czechs returned home in 1945.[56] Secondly, there was a hardening of attitudes against Germans on all sides leading to a united insistence, irrespective of economic considerations, that they should go. Beneš claimed that they were all responsible for Lidice[57] and leading Communists maintained that more than 90% had followed Henlein[58] and were therefore implicated in his attempts to incorporate the Sudetenland into Nazi Germany. This was probably an accurate estimate of how they had voted in local elections in 1938.

The National Socialists went the furthest in condemning absolutely all Germans and proclaiming that they would never say of

any German that he was an anti-fascist.[59] The Communists generally took a strong nationalist line too. Expulsions were justified in
nationalistic historical terms as finally reversing the White
Mountain,[60] although there had in fact been a German population
within the area occupied by Czechoslovakia even before that. When
confronted with their internationalist past, however, the Communists
often argued that Germans as such were not necessarily bad, and
that expulsions were necessary only because, and in so far as, the
Germans had supported the Nazis. Nevertheless, the fact remains
that the KSČ stopped looking for German anti-fascists and dropped
attempts to develop an anti-Nazi movement among Germans.
Instead, they welcomed the fact that the first Germans to leave
voluntarily were Communists going to take leading positions in the
Soviet zone of Germany.[61]

Undoubtedly this hardening of Czech political attitudes was
encouraged by the situation in the frontier regions after liberation.
Throughout the summer of 1945, stores of arms and elements of the
underground Nazi organisation 'Werwolf' were uncovered: in practice these did not present a serious threat to the regime although
they could well have become very dangerous in a changed international situation.[62] More immediately worrying were reports of
sabotage acts and frequent acts of violence which were automatically being blamed on Germans. There were cases of Czech acts of
violence and revenge against Germans, but much of the endemic
violence very probably was caused by Germans. It must, however,
be added that, although the fact was not publicised at the time,
help from Germans in uncovering various plots and organisations
was a crucial factor enabling the Czech organs to establish control.[63]

That obviously raises the question of whether Czech attitudes and
policies were not far harsher than necessary. In effect Germans
were deprived of all rights and the atmosphere among Czechs was
such that nobody would speak up in their defence. The revolution
can therefore hardly be described as democratic in its treatment of
Germans and this, it has been argued, was a possible contributory
factor to later extra-legal practices by security organs: they were
already getting into the habit of behaving outside the law and
treating part of the population with contempt and at times even
brutality.[64] This, however, made at most only a minor contribution
to later practices. Their extension to part of the Czech population
ultimately depended on the relaxation of controls on the power of

the police and on the conscious decision to give them power to act independently of the legal system.[65]

Nevertheless the policy towards Germans was a remarkable reversal of thinking, especially for the KSČ. Faced with a similar dilemma to that confronted by Šmeral during World War I they implicitly accepted his argument that a Czechoslovak state on the pre-Munich model could not be viable. Instead, they accepted a nationalities policy that would have been unthinkable before. It is, however, difficult to see a credible alternative. Repeating Šmeral's proposals would hardly have been realistic and even the ideas of the Popular Front period would have been dangerous if that meant allowing Germans to elect their own representatives. Apart from giving power in predominantly German areas to German Communists or Social Democrats, an option obviously unacceptable to the Czech right wing, some significant reduction in the German population inside Czechoslovakia was probably the only possible approach. The KSČ were probably encouraged to insist on the expulsion of almost all Germans, partly because of the enormous popularity of the measure among Czechs and partly because of the scope it created for the social advancement of the Czech rural poor.

As Germans were losing their property and privileges and as preparations were made for their expulsion, so Czechs moved in to settle in the frontier areas. At first, however, they did not bring order and stability: many were just out for rapid financial advancement while the new Czech organs were often corrupt and unable to quell indiscipline even among Czechs.

The Communists, arguing that quickly settling the frontiers was essential for the security of the state, soon saw the need for a more systematic approach. The key to attracting suitable and reliable settlers was not industry, which could only be properly organised later, but agriculture. Communist officials in the Ministry of Agriculture worked out and then administered the first post-World War II land reform which aimed to create 'a mass of Czech peasants, firmly settled on their own land' who would solidly support the new republic.[66] Knowledge that they would become owners of land was a necessary incentive for them to move. The plan was therefore for units with a maximum size of 13 ha which, although not reckoned to be ultimately the most economically productive form of organisation, was the best way to encourage settlement and thereby maximise immediate production with the smallest possible loss of labour from the interior.[67]

There were doubts about this as some within the KSČ wanted to organise collective farms and Social Democrats also criticised the subdivision of existing holdings.[68] More important was outright opposition from Beneš who only signed the relevant decree after it had been unanimously backed by a second vote in the government. He had wanted Czech settlers to pay more than the minimal amount, only twice the annual harvest, that the KSČ was advocating.[69]

So settlement of agricultural land could proceed quickly through the autumn of 1945. Previously there had been 160,000 German enterprises supporting 800,000 to 900,000 people[70] and by the winter there were 110,000 Czech families amounting to 500,000 people.[71] In social terms this gave much greater weight to the 'middle' peasant while previously there had been considerable differentiation among both Czech and German landowners.[72] The beneficiaries from the Czech interior tended to be the poorest peasants, or landless labourers. A side effect was therefore to reduce pressure for land reform in the interior which at that time was to be based on the expropriation of traitors and collaborators.

4 CHANGES IN INDUSTRY

From the very start in the liberated republic events in industry suggested that changes would be deeper, more varied and more sweeping than anything suggested in the Košice Programme. They went way beyond the changes in 1918, making any attempt to find an analogy quite meaningless. Formally speaking, 'National Administrators' were to be installed where it was felt necessary in the interests of reviving or continuing production.[73] Even this seemed only just to be keeping up with events.

As National Committees took power in localities so Factory Councils took even more all-embracing powers in industry and other places of work. Soon they confirmed their allegiance to ÚRO, which became the supreme trade union body after liberation, and followed its guidelines for holding elections. In basic industries the Communists seem to have been completely dominant, but elsewhere councils could be formed before any party had established an organisation. In all cases, though, they seem to have been the first reliable support in places of work for the new regime. For a time they therefore enjoyed enormous power.

Their rise was closely linked with the purging of management structures and the restarting of production. The purge itself was officially aimed against open collaborators and was generally administered by the Factory Councils.[74] The numbers removed varied enormously between factories depending on specific local conditions and feelings. Sometimes, against the protests of the work force, key specialists were kept on despite their wartime record.[75] More generally, the purge reflected a widespread distrust towards all managers who were accused by workers of indecisiveness in their attitude towards the occupation.[76] Sometimes Factory Councils even insisted that every single managerial post was elected – apparently this could be a precondition for persuading workers to repair war damage and restart production[77] – and they took clear initiatives in selecting the new managements in the biggest factories. Laušman was then presented with a fait accompli which he could only confirm, thereby giving legal status to the changes.[78]

The exercise of such immense power inevitably made the Factory Councils highly controversial bodies, and the most controversial of their activities was their control of the lightly armed Factory Militia groups. Membership was not exclusive to any one party: there was, in fact, no sign of a KSČ attempt to create significant armed workers' groups,[79] but the Factory Militia was persistently attacked as an illegal body intending to use its arms in internal political conflicts.[80] They certainly were defended in political terms, as one of the working class's 'gains from the national revolution',[81] but their actual tasks appeared to be far less exciting than their opponents' more colourful criticisms suggested. Available evidence indicates that they were concerned with protecting their enterprises against Germans and guarding Germans in internment camps.[82] In the autumn of 1946, probably partly in response to persistent criticisms, the trade union leadership agreed to a reduction in their strength so that all available able-bodied workers could be engaged in production.[83] The militia was still not completely dissolved because, apart from anything else, the shortage of police meant that nobody else could guard factories.[84]

The immense power taken by the Factory Councils during and after May 1945 also led to disagreements among trade unionists about the role of new workers' organs. There was no disagreement that they greatly enhanced the power of the working class in the state generally. The point at issue was their precise role within a model of management of the economy and of society. This came into the open during a 'lively discussion' at a Prague trade union congress in July 1945 where one view, which gained significant support, was put by Veltruský. He appears to have argued that workers could take the full task of industrial management and that would give ÚRO at least the status of a parallel government.

This was opposed by Zápotocký who had been unanimously elected chairman of ÚRO on 7 June 1945, immediately after his return from a concentration camp. He argued that it was neither necessary nor possible to have absolute power in industry. It was adequate to 'control' production so that it could never be dominated by private capitalist interests, but at the same time workers could still not run industry without 'capitalist engineers and technicians': he did, however, suggest that some workers would eventually take management positions after they had gained the necessary experience.[85]

Meanwhile, trade union bodies within a factory were left with a seemingly more limited function. They had to organise, educate and develop the work force both in defence of its own interests and to overcome its broken morale. They had to convince the workers that production, and even potentially unpopular reorganisations of production, were the precondition for higher wages and social benefits. They therefore made it clear that they would not support wage demands and saw themselves as 'a great school of education and persuasion'.[86] In practical terms this meant the need for a deeper organisational form than just the small, elected Factory Councils. Zápotocký's return was therefore followed by a call to create separate single united trade union branches in each workplace and to start voluntary recruitment to them.[87] In practice this was a slow process and Factory Councils remained the more important bodies for some time. By the end of 1945 the unions had 1,442,816 members and soon after that could claim to organise 61% of workers and 53.6% of all employees.[88]

This, it should be added, was not the position worked out in emigration where all the emphasis was placed on the trade unions as a *political* force. From this, and from the experience of the uprising in Slovakia, it seemed that they could be based on Factory Councils.[89]

By contrast, the activities of trade unions at the all-state level were very close to earlier KSČ ideas. Zápotocký insisted that there could be no serious 'non-political' trade union movement, but that did not mean following the line or programme of any one party. Instead, they restricted themselves to immediate social and economic questions which directly affected employees, irrespective of their political affiliations, and combined this with firm commitment in general terms to the national revolution and government programme. They were thereby able to command enormous loyalty from employees, especially manual workers, and became unique among mass organisations in their extraordinary strength and unity of purpose.

There is no doubt that Communists held an extremely strong position within them. This stemmed partly from the KSČ's organisational strength and partly from the clarity of their conception of the role of trade unions. Figures need not reveal the extent of this dominance. Out of 2753 posts in the whole apparatus on 15 May 1947 the KSČ held 31.2%, the Social Democrats 31.9%, the other parties 10.3% and 26.6% were non-party.[90] The real point, however, was that the members of other parties generally did not challenge the KSČ. There were two principal reasons for this, one of which was that the KSČ was well organised enough to establish a firm grip on personnel policy within much of the trade union movement and thereby to ensure the election only of those fully prepared to cooperate with them.[91] The second was that there were prominent and capable trade unionists, particularly among Social Democrats, who did not significantly disagree with KSČ policy on those questions which concerned trade unions, at least until the autumn of 1947. Among these were J. Kubát and E. Erban who rose through the Protectorate unions and played very important roles in the Prague uprising.

The leading National Socialist trade unionist was O. Wünsch who also broadly accepted the KSČ line on the nature and role of trade unions. Some other National Socialists shared his approach and they were implicitly disowned by their party, which could still feel itself to be represented on the Presidium by A. Vandrovec and V. Šplíchalová.[92] They evidently were too few in number and unclear in their ideas to make any impact until the autumn of 1947.

The strength in national politics of these workers' representative organs was demonstrated very quickly after liberation when they sent delegations to Laušman demanding the nationalisation of at least some industries. The government was forced to take their demands seriously when miners in the Ostrava area staged a demonstration strike.[93] Shortly afterwards their colleagues in Most sent a very strongly worded resolution to Laušman.[94] Before the KSČ gave this prominent publicity, Gottwald sought and received a definite assurance from Beneš that he would be prepared to sign a decree for the nationalisation of some key sectors of the economy *before* the opening of the Provisional National Assembly.[95] Then, following approval of the government, Laušman could begin work on proposals for the immediate nationalisation of heavy and key industries. He foresaw further discussions and a gradual process of nationalisation of other important industries when a parliament had been formed.[96] This corresponded closely to the thinking of all the parties of the Socialist Bloc.

Nevertheless, the KSČ leadership were nervous that there might be serious opposition leading to a split in the National Front and that Beneš and his allies would try to procrastinate until the formation of a parliament. They therefore encouraged pressure 'from below': resolutions were sent in from National Committees, and from meetings in places of work which expressed enthusiastic approval for the proposals. The crucial point was that they also demanded speedy nationalisation of their own enterprises. This effectively took the discussion on the detailed pace and extent of nationalisations outside the government and led to the adoption of a measure more radical than anything anybody had advocated beforehand.

Political differentiation then took place not around the question of nationalisations as such, but principally around the desirability of this pressure 'from below'. The Social Democrats, trade unions and Communists gave full publicity to resolutions that were sent in, thereby willingly allowing themselves to be carried along on the wave of increasing demands. The National Socialist and People's Parties were placed in an embarrassing position: they could hardly oppose such powerful expressions of popular feeling and therefore took their stand from Beneš's position which, as Gottwald had predicted, was to delay rather than to oppose outright.[97] The National Socialist press was therefore full of warnings against ill-considered and hasty decisions taken in response to public pressure.

These arguments, coinciding with delays while discussions were held in the government, resurrected memories of the promises of 'socialisations' in 1918 and 1919.[98] Perhaps partly through fear of a partial repetition of that experience, and perhaps partly seeing their chance in view of the uncertainty of their potential opponents, the KSČ leadership again gave encouragement to the resolutions 'from below'. This gave them the strength to argue in the government for the nationalisation of an enormous amount of Czechoslovak industry by Presidential decree *before* the creation of the Provisional National Assembly. That deadline finally set the limit to the extent of nationalisations as demands for continued extension of the scope of the decree were used by the National Socialists as a pretext for delays in the government.[99] Zápotocký therefore ultimately called for an end to the flow of resolutions.[100]

On 24 October 1945 the President signed decrees on the nationalisation of certain industries and on the powers of Factory Councils. These were practically the last measures before the opening of the Provisional National Assembly and meant that nationalisations could be celebrated on 28 October 1945, thereby firmly linking the decrees with the creation of the Czechoslovak state in 1918. The decrees laid down complicated guide-lines for individual industries, so that only those enterprises above a particular size – expressed in terms of the number of employees – were nationalised. In a few sectors nothing was to be publicly owned: an important example was internal trade. The overall picture is shown in Table 1.

Although these nationalisation decrees were never publicly challenged inside Czechoslovakia, this was by no means the end of all disagreements over industrial policy. There were still ambiguities in the decrees, the most troublesome of which concerned the fate of 'confiscates', i.e. the former property of Germans or traitors that did not automatically qualify for nationalisation. Moreover, the very fact of the nationalisation of industries raised questions of the relationship between the public and private sectors and of the exact organisational structure and powers of different organs within the public sector.

It very soon became clear that the post-nationalisation reorganisation of industry gave the opportunity for a great expansion of the operations of parties into the economic field. They inevitably clashed with each other as they manoeuvred behind the scenes to win representation for their own members in leading positions in industry. The Communists and Social Democrats were in a

Table 1 *Percentage of Czechoslovak industry nationalised by sector*[101]

Industry	Percentage of employees in nationalised enterprises	Percentage of technical units nationalised
All	61.2	16.4
Mining	100.0	100.0
Metallurgy	99.4	97.8
Power	99.1	88.5
Chemicals	76.4	25.7
Engineering	72.6	22.2
Sugar-mills	69.8	63.3
Glass	67.4	10.8
Building materials and ceramics	63.4	24.3
Paper	60.7	19.3
Leather	58.5	6.5
Textiles	54.3	22.1
Woodworking	26.3	5.7
Distilleries	26.0	5.9
Breweries and malt	24.5	7.3
Flour-mills	20.1	7.3
Saw-mills	15.8	5.7
Foodstuffs	14.4	5.2
Building	13.4	2.8
Clothing	13.1	2.7
Printing	2.7	3.8
Water works	0.7	2.5

particularly strong position as their members could be presented as firm supporters of the idea of nationalisations. This is to some extent reflected in figures for early 1948 when, out of 18 central directors, three were Communists, four Social Democrats, four National Socialists, one Slovak Democrat and six were non-party.[102] Figures for individual enterprise directors indicate a more definite predominance of the left.[103]

Reorganisation following the elimination of private ownership was more explicitly intended to give scope for direct workers' representation in management and provision was made for this in the nationalisation decrees. They laid down a management structure for individual enterprises which was a peculiar compromise between collective and one-man management.

A single manager was to be appointed but his actions could be examined by a board that had the power to complain about him directly to the Ministry of Industry. This board was to be one third nominated by the employees while the remaining two thirds were nominated from the centre with the employees having an ill-defined right to comment on their acceptability.[104] In practice, the board never became an important instrument of control. Elections of its worker members were inexplicably delayed and surrounded by minimal publicity.

Very probably they were regarded as irrelevant in comparison with Factory Councils, which continued to be the most important workers' representative organs at the work-place level. Their powers were even confirmed in a decree published simultaneously with the nationalisation decrees.[105] It evidently owed a great deal to ideas developed by Zápotocký as Factory Councils were encouraged to take as much power and responsibility as possible without actually supplanting the specialist abilities of management.

Alongside their task of attending to the basic interests of employees, they were expected to play an important role within the developing model of management of the economy which, as the general reorganisation of industry indicated, involved centralisation in preparation for central planning. Factory Councils therefore clearly could not be in any sense genuine organs of self management. Instead, they were to be the social conscience for the whole factory, ensuring that its narrow, sectional interest was subordinated to the interests of the economy as a whole.

This was in line with the Communists' ideas, but was not fully accepted by the other parties, who successfully argued for Factory Councils to receive a 10% share in profits. Later, when Factory Councils were expected to be pressing for price reductions, it was noticed that many were dividing this share up among the workers.[106] ÚRO advocated centralising these into one fund so that loss making industries, such as mining, could share in it. They had great difficulty in winning support for this even in big factories.

In practice Factory Councils seemed to be even more powerful than the decree suggested. Managers were at first scared to assert their authority for fear of becoming unpopular and being sacked. Their survival and their success depended on good relations with workers' organs while their own prestige among the work-force remained low.[107] Factory Councils often seemed to be the executive organ of and at least an equal partner with management[108] especially on personnel questions.

5 POLITICS AND THE MARKET IN ECONOMIC MANAGEMENT

While nationalisations and the reorganisation of industry could lay the basis for new economic policies, they could not instantaneously solve the immediate economic problems. Production and productivity remained very low, the authority of management was badly shaken and economic organisation was in a state of collapse: the situation was particularly bad in the basic industries. By the late summer of 1945 improvement in the economic situation was seen by the KSČ leadership as the party's principal task. Communists took a clear initiative in organising voluntary efforts to clear away war damage and set about establishing an economic apparatus – including top managers, trade union officials and members of Factory Councils – which gave them enormous power and influence within the nationalised industries. Other parties were never so systematic in their economic organisations although the Social Democrats went some way towards copying the KSČ.[109]

This, it must be emphasised, does not mean that KSČ organisations tried to decide over everything. Detailed managerial tasks or directly technical matters were to be left alone. The KSČ conception of economic activity indicated that the party organisations should make their contribution to economic recovery by concerning themselves with broader questions like labour morale, the competence of Factory Councils and trade unions and relations between the working class and intelligentsia.[110] Even then they did not believe that trade union bodies alone, or even political parties, could solve the problem of low productivity. By January 1946, when industrial production was still running at only 50% of the 1938 level, they therefore encouraged and gave unceasing publicity to new organs known as Production Committees which had spread by September 1946 to over 1000 factories, i.e. about one third of all factories with over 50 employees.[111]

They were not based on any foreign example, but had definite similarities to the production committees of the British war economy.[112] There were no clear directives on their composition or size and they included representatives of all grades of employees, of the Factory Council, of political parties and of trade unions.

Their function was distinct from all these as they were to be a channel for constructive communication uniquely concerned with raising production. In no sense could they be seen as organs of potential political power and they were explicitly defined as advisory and not executive organs.[113]

Their actual impact is impossible to quantify although it was claimed that there were masses of simple ways in which workers' suggestions could be collated and used to help raise productivity.[114] They were also given the task of quickly working out a plan for their individual factories which could be presented to a full meeting of the whole factory, thereby winning commitment for it from all types of employees.[115]

It is evident from the Communists' ideas for Production Committees that one of the keys to raising production was the co-operation of different types of employees. The main obstacle to this, as was continually reiterated in trade union and factory journals, was an atmosphere of distrust between manual workers and the technical intelligentsia. A crucial precondition for overcoming this was an acceptable pattern of income distribution and Communist leaders were not scared to present their views on what this should be, even insisting that there should be no embarrassment about paying specialists even more than they had received from capitalists, if their work and abilities warranted it.[116] It was then hoped that mutual envy could be eliminated once all were reasonably well paid and adequately covered by social insurance.[117]

This led them to criticise publicly some Factory Councils for alleged 'excessive' egalitarianism.[118] Many manual workers, while otherwise solidly supporting the KSČ, were bitterly opposed to such arguments and called for those in positions of authority to be paid no more than workers.[119] It is therefore not surprising that tension and mistrust between the social groups essential to industrial production remained and influenced political events both before and, perhaps to an even greater extent, after February 1948.[120]

It also proved difficult for the KSČ to win working class conviction in their most direct attempts to encourage greater productivity. These were most systematically tried in the mining industry, which was faced with enormous problems after liberation.[121] Economic realities ruled out the use of material incentives alone to counter the post-liberation collapse in labour discipline. Instead, insisting that German forced labour could only be a very temporary solution, the KSČ placed great emphasis on combining material with moral incentives. One aspect of this was that factories were encouraged to send Czech workers for brief spells in the mines. The labour was formally voluntary but significant material rewards were given and institutions refusing to contribute were given to understand that they would receive no coal.[122]

There were also attempts to imitate Soviet experience in 'socialist competition' and in the Stakhanovite movement. These were not regarded as special expedients for a problem industry: there were soon references to mining being the most advanced sector of the economy in its production planning and in the careful following and publication of results.[123] There apparently was some success later in encouraging widespread interest in economic performance by competition between factories and workshops.[124] The Stakhanovite movement, however, made no impact outside mining. A survey of 1200 workers in an engineering factory outside Prague showed that 20% were against it in principle while 50% had definite reservations. They generally equated Stakhanovism with increasing the intensity of labour and instead of welcoming attempts to increase productivity their attitude was more reserved. 'On the whole the workers favour honest and average work from all employees. The workers reject shirking of work and also high performances of individuals and excessive talk about work.'[125]

Even in the mines near Ostrava only 18% participated in socialist competition in the autumn of 1945, although significant material rewards were given to groups attaining high productivity.[126] There was also enormous publicity for individual Stakhanovites who were invited to Prague to see the President, and the best of them all, Viktor Gach, was elected to the KSČ Central Committee. These individuals recorded quite amazing results. Gach even claimed a world record for a single shift when, with twelve helpers, he reached one hundred times the average productivity.[127] In 1946 publicity around these Stakhanovites disappeared which suggests, despite earlier claims to the contrary, that the movement was little more than a publicity stunt with limited effectiveness in raising productivity in the coalfield as a whole.

It is clear from all these attempts that the KSČ saw their increased involvement in economic life as much more than a temporary measure to overcome special difficulties. Nevertheless they also fully recognised that political involvement alone would not produce an ideal model of economic management. Along with the other parties, they worked out measures for monetary stabilisation and for an adjustment of the price and wage level which were intended to make possible greater reliance on market relations rather than central administrative controls.

The need for far-reaching measures stemmed from the methods used during the occupation. Wages were high enough to create surplus purchasing power but finances were divorced from the actual functioning of the economy, which was based on direct controls and rationing. This meant both that relative wages were not always in harmony with the desired or rational allocation of labour between sectors and that immense personal savings had been accumulated.

This latter problem could be seen in the growth of bank notes and small currency, which increased almost nine-fold over the Protectorate's territory, and in a huge increase in current and deposit accounts.[128] The imbalance had to be corrected before greater reliance could be placed on the market mechanism without leading to inflationary chaos. The most drastic measure was a freezing of savings. The economic importance of this can be seen from figures for 31 December 1945 showing circulating currency as 30,384 million Kčs, assets in financial institutions as 57,399 million Kčs and frozen assets as 257,815 million Kčs.[129] Sometimes these savings were derived from wartime profiteering by sharp businessmen, but there were many more people who were affected because they had at least *some* savings: there were therefore continual calls for the freeing of savings at least for those suffering particular hardships.

Government administered wage and price adjustments also had very broad effects. Their aim was to reach an approximate balance and overcome the most extreme inter-sectoral anomalies so that administrative controls could be relaxed. The hope was that it all could be done in one go with approximately a 300% rise in the wage and price levels. At the same time there were larger rises for the poorest and the elimination of a whole number of inequalities created during the occupation.[130] Nevertheless, many new anomalies were created by the changes and it was estimated that 48% of workers actually suffered a decline in their real wages.[131] This left plenty of scope for discontent at the new wage and price system over the following years.

There was also a realisation of the need to reintroduce market relations in agriculture and the Košice Programme therefore promised a gradual ending of the Protectorate's system of fixed quotas for compulsory deliveries. The hope was that free market sales above the quotas could gradually be expanded until the market mechanism alone could suffice to ensure adequate food supplies. Gottwald returned to this point several times, emphasising its importance as a counter to propaganda from former Agrarians who he believed were trying to prevent fulfilment of quota obligations.[132]

Unfortunately, the supply situation was far too serious to allow for any relaxation, but it was at least decided to increase the price paid for compulsory purchases. Moreover, the new prices were differentiated with rises of 77% for peasants holding under 20 ha, 65% for those with 20–50 ha and 44% for those with over 50 ha. This triple price system was the Communists' idea and they defended it against increasingly open criticisms from all the other parties on the grounds that it was no more than a temporary measure to be superseded later by a whole complex of new agricultural policies including a progressive tax system, social insurance and help for mechanisation. In the meantime it amounted to helping the poorest in the only way administratively practicable when conditions were very hard for all.[133]

Other changes in the economy, particularly the nationalisations and consequent state control over industry, could also affect peasants. The first problem was, again, related to prices as the price scissors moved ever more sharply against agriculture with general price adjustments in late 1945.[134] This could only create greater scope for a renewal of the ideas of a common peasant interest from which the Agrarian Party had drawn its strength. The KSČ, having previously argued that nationalisations could help reverse the steady trend against agriculture in price changes in the inter-war period,[135] felt obliged later to advocate and press for actual price changes to give this promise some credibility.[136] The second way in which nationalisations could help was by directing production towards the mechanisation of agriculture,[137] but that was still a few years away.

It is clear from this discussion of agriculture both that the KSČ had a greater share than any other party in deciding on policies and that there was no definite policy of restricting private enterprise. Even the new price system could not directly harm larger farms as they too benefited from price rises and therefore had a greater incentive to sell to the state. Nevertheless, the KSČ could not create a powerful peasants' union and instead found themselves bogged down in lengthy arguments over the nature and purpose of the proposed JSČZ (United Union of Czech Farmers). The balance between the left (i.e. the Communists and Social Democrats) and the right was roughly even at local congresses of the union[138] and over the following months it proved impossible for representatives of the Czech parties to agree on what a common peasant interest was. Unlike the trade unions, the peasants' union therefore could not become a significant political or social force and suggestions on agricultural policy invariably originated from the parties.

6 A CZECHOSLOVAK MODEL OF SOCIALISM?

The national revolution brought deep changes in the structure of Czech society and this raises the question of how to assess its significance. The KSČ, as will be argued, were unable to understand fully what had happened, as they tried to deny the socialist content of the revolution. In the late 1960s some Czechoslovak historians, most notably Kaplan, cautiously argued that it should be seen as the start to the Czechoslovak model of socialism.[139] There seems to be no reason for not going along with this. A major change certainly had taken place within Czech society as the power of big business had been demolished and the whole apparatus of political power had been transformed. Moreover, although society differed markedly from the Communists' earlier conception of socialism, it was comparatively free from sharp internal conflicts: it was in no sense inevitable that it would be just a transitional stage on the way to a totally different model of socialism.

That does not mean that social conflicts, let alone further development of the social order, had ended. Although there was a strong feeling of, and desire for, national unity, there was plenty of scope for discontent, especially over living standards. For, although income inequalities were undoubtedly much smaller than in the Protectorate or the pre-Munich republic, any inequalities were a possible source of bitterness as the period was characterised by the utmost hardship. One quarter of the population could not even afford to buy the goods allocated to them through the ration system.[140] There also seemed to have been an equalisation within society by means of its 'petty-bourgeoisification', particularly as a consequence of the expropriation of Germans. This however, did not lead to a homogenisation of political thinking. There was instead a definite differentiation between the 'old' and the 'new' petty bourgeoisies and similarly between those who had held high positions over many years and those who were newly promoted. As the discussion below of individual social groups indicates, the revolutionary changes meant great social advancement for some, but aroused nervousness and fears in other sections of society.

There was, in fact, a gradual political differentiation between those who fully supported the revolution, represented by the Communists and Social Democrats, and those who to various degrees retained reservations. The necessary background for understanding this is a summary of how the social and economic changes affected the various social groups in Czech society. Table 2 shows the approximate breakdown of the economically active population into workers, peasants, small businessmen and the intelligentsia, these being the categories generally used at the time.

Table 2 *Approximate social composition of the active Czech population in the 1945–48 period in percentages*[141]

Workers	53	
in nationalised industries		15
in private industries		10
others not included elsewhere		4
Peasants (with no other source of income)	12	
all those employed in agriculture		20
Small businessmen	9	
all those employed in small businesses		25
Intelligentsia	17 ⎫	26
Foremen, non-manual employees in industry	9 ⎭	
Total	100	100

Of the individual social groups, the largest was the working class. In general they could see immediate benefits or promises of gain from measures that covered all working people such as the institution of equal pay for women, of allowances for children and in the promise of an adequate social insurance scheme. The lowest paid also benefited from wage increases. There was some evidence of dissatisfaction from the more skilled workers as their differentials were decreased but this division was less important than that between workers in nationalised enterprises and those in private firms which generally employed under 250 workers. As Table 2 shows, the former were only a minority of the working class, but they had been affected the most by the revolutionary changes. They were likely to be well organised in trade unions or even political parties, and could identify most completely with the revolution as a whole, which seemed in no way to threaten them. At the other pole were workers dispersed in very small enterprises, typically in agriculture, distribution or services, and even workers who worked in their own homes: many of these were women and few of them played an active role in politics. Between these two extremes were the large numbers employed in private industrial enterprises. Although even those in the smallest enterprises had common interests with workers in larger, nationalised enterprises, their perception of how they had gained or could gain in comparison with the pre-Munich republic was different. This led to a different attitude towards active involvement in politics.

Miners, working in a well-organised, nationalised industry where wages were centrally decided and controlled, expected their social advancement to be supported by the government. Acutely aware of the shortage of miners, it was prepared to give them some relative privileges, such as the highest hourly pay of any manual workers and a special insurance scheme, but they still hoped for more. They looked forward to future changes after which they would be 'valued at their worth'.[142] Nevertheless, building workers, whose industry was largely privately owned and fragmented into small units, could almost catch up with the miners' hourly rate of pay. Owing to the labour shortage, and despite official disapproval, employers were paying them 'black' wages which rose steadily irrespective of government policies.[143]

Leading Communists favoured the apparent social responsibility of the miners' situation and Zápotocký even referred to workers in private industry sometimes being 'bought off' by their employers. By this he meant not that they were siding politically with capitalists, but that their Factory Councils were not using the full powers that they were given by law. They were happy to settle for wage increases and leave questions of production to the employers.[144] In this way they were implicitly happy to set their own sectional interests against those of the nation as a whole.

It was in mining and other large nationalised enterprises that workers were most likely to see political decisions of the government as the key to their social advancement. They indentified with the revolution and the KSČ most actively. Even they, however, could find grounds for distrust towards the party. Many workers were unimpressed by pressures for increased productivity and also by the continued existence of large inequalities even within their own enterprises. Many KSČ members rejected the leadership's position and argued that managers who had joined the party should not have higher pay than workers.[145] In practice, heads of nationalised enterprises had secretly negotiated salaries comfortably above those of government ministers.[146]

Among peasants there was far more scope for doubts about government policies. Important social changes had been brought about by the new price policy and above all by the land reform whereby those in the 5–20 ha range increased their share of agricultural land from 42% to 51%.[147] This small but significant change was almost entirely a result of settling the frontier areas, which benefited poor or landless peasants. Their commitment to the new regime and to the KSČ was very strong.

The middle peasants in the Czech interior were unlikely to have so clear-cut a political position. In one sense land reform was a blow to them as it accentuated the labour shortage in agriculture. Generally, they were less directly affected by the revolutionary changes than were other social groups and were therefore less likely to feel themselves directly involved in politics: their attitudes remained unclear up to, and even after, the 1946 elections.

One factor bringing them towards the KSČ was their close links with industrial workers, many of whom lived in villages and even owned a little land. There was, however, plenty of scope for mutual distrust because of the serious food shortages in the towns and because the price scissors – the relationship between agricultural and industrial prices – moved steadily against agriculture during 1945 and 1946.[148] This was an issue on which all peasants had a common interest. It could therefore bring the middle peasants close to the richer peasants who had stronger grounds for objecting to the discriminatory triple price system and for fearing a further, more egalitarian, land reform.

There was even more diversity within the urban petty bourgeoisie. Small businessmen, often employing no labour outside their own family, were economically important, especially in handicraft production, internal trade, distribution and services. They could respond to the revolutionary changes in a contradictory way – favouring some measures while opposing others – but their existence did not seem to be immediately threatened. In fact, their numbers increased dramatically after liberation as German businesses were given to Czechs and as other Czechs sought more agreeable occupations than employment in industry. Even the KSČ welcomed this for a time as 'part of our national revolution',[149] but even the firmest supporters of private enterprise began to advocate restrictions when there were 90,000 small businesses in Prague alone with an average of 600 requests per day to establish new ones.[150]

Even if small businessmen need not have feared imminent expropriation, many resented the banning of their party and felt they had valid grounds for dissatisfaction over the shortages of labour and raw materials.[151] They feared that nationalised industries were receiving preferential treatment and this reinforced fears that the nationalisations could be the prelude to an elimination of private enterprise. Moreover, they were aware of some hostility from workers relating especially to the black market which apparently provided a source of income for roughly half of all small businesses.[152] Workers, however, could barely afford the high prices demanded.

There were even clearer grounds for discontent from sections of the intelligentsia. This term was used to describe a very diverse social group. Particularly the 'creative' intelligentsia – writers, poets etc. – tended to commit themselves firmly to the idea of revolution. To some extent this was a natural consequence of their wartime experiences as it could never be forgotten that the Nazis had aimed to destroy the Czech intelligentsia. Even before that, many had identified with the KSČ, which, with its greater willingness to accept some degree of diversity, seemed able to give them a more definite place of honour.

There was, however, a basis for really widespread discontent from office workers. Their numbers were growing rapidly and they constituted 17% of the economically active population in 1947.[153] In May 1946 almost 80% claimed to be dissatisfied with the government.[154] There can be no doubt that this stemmed from real hardship as almost all had suffered from pay adjustments during and after the occupation: they were, in absolute terms, worse off than before the war. This was particularly true for that large section of office workers with civil service status. As there had been a narrowing of differentials within their ranks, it was particularly the older civil servants who had remained in office during the occupation who were likely to be negative towards the regime.[155] Among the newer recruits there could be more support for the government. By way of contrast, in those fields most deeply affected by the revolutionary changes, such as industry and the police, there was likely to be firm support for the government from those individuals who had experienced rapid advancement into top positions precisely because of their membership of the KSČ.

Capitalists were a likely source of firmer opposition to the regime, but in numerical terms they were very weak. One generous estimate put the numbers of owners of nationalised and private factories and other enterprises at 80,000.[156] In their social position and attitude towards the revolution there is no need to draw any distinction between actual owners of capital who had been expropriated and those managers who had been purged. All had lost immensely. Those who had been spared during the nationalisations were likely to be highly nervous about the course of developments. On their own, though, they had minimal political influence.

Although this suggests that outright opposition to the revolution was likely to be weak, there clearly was considerable scope for differentiation of political attitudes within Czech society. The firmest commitment could be expected among workers in nationalised industries and peasants in frontier zones, but they both still had grounds for discontent. Outright hostility was likely only from a small minority while there was a large area in between in which many could feel reservations about certain revolutionary changes. There were also many who were in no way threatened by the revolution but were not actively involved in it either: this applied even to much of the working class.

Surveys of public opinion, although still at an experimental stage and therefore not to be taken too exactly, revealed this gradual differentiation. It was quite unmistakable that approval ran in a descending scale from readers of the Communist press through readers of Social Democrat, National Socialist and the People's Party papers. For the general question of satisfaction with the government the figures, from a survey in May 1946, were 95%, 89%, 73% and 67% respectively giving an overall figure of 81.6%.[157] When questioned in March 1946 on National Committees, 72% of Communist supporters thought they were better than previous local councils compared with figures of 40% and 45% for People's Party and National Socialist supporters.[158]

Support for political parties can be related to social class by the approximate breakdown for the membership of the individual parties in Table 3. Unfortunately the People's Party did not keep accurate enough records so that the comparison is restricted to the other three Czech parties.

Table 3 *Membership of Czech political parties by social group* (000s)[159]

	Date for which figures apply	Workers	Office worker intelligentsia	Peasants	Small businessmen
All parties		780	275	296	230
Communists	March 1946	577	92	129	41
National Socialist	April 1946	100	123	89.5	143
Soc. Democrat	mid 1946	120	60	77.6	46

Evidently, no party was restricted to one particular social group, but there were marked differences in social composition. Small businessmen seem to have been particularly willing to join parties and generally opted for the National Socialists where they constituted the largest group. The intelligentsia showed something of the same tendency, but they were spread more evenly among the parties. Also striking was the tendency for workers to join the KSČ. They constituted, in March 1946, almost 70% of the party's membership or, to put it the other way round, almost 75% of workers who joined any party joined the KSČ.

This brings out the social content of the revolution, but it must still be emphasised that the revolutionary changes cannot be reduced to the simplistic terms of one class taking power from another. Such a formulation would not describe or summarise the actual changes within organs of power for, although the working class did benefit greatly from the revolution, they still generally received the lowest incomes and individual workers were not greatly involved beyond their own workplaces. In National Committees, for example, at the Regional and District levels, only 10% were workers while 57.5% were from the intelligentsia. At the District level only 16.6% of KSČ representatives were workers and the figure was much lower for other parties.[160] Even in such a revolutionary centre as Kladno the first National Committee with 39 members was dominated by professional people and contained only six workers.[161] Irrespective of its very real power within its own factories, the working class did not directly dominate in the state as a whole.

Evidently, society was complex and diversified enough for it to be possible for workers' organs to wield great power without making any direct difference to much of the Czech population. This could be confirmed by a survey on attitudes towards Factory Councils. 48% thought they were a step forward while 13% did not. When broken down further 77% of those well informed felt they were a step forward while 16% did not. So, more striking than outright opposition was ignorance and indifference.[162] The attitudes towards voluntary brigades revealed a similar sort of differentation.[163]

Moreover, Czech experience indicates another important aspect in which revolution in an advanced and complex society would differ from the Communists' interpretation of the Russian revolution. Irrespective of its social content, the revolution cannot be understood purely in terms of political power. Little is gained even from attemps to adapt Gramsci's view that, in an advanced society, there would be a more gradual and drawn out 'war of position' rather than a short, sharp 'frontal attack' or 'war of manoeuvre'.[164] The real point, as was widely recognised by Czechoslovak historians in the 1960s, was that politics had become far less a question of 'war' and increasingly a question of conscious and constructive involvement in the shaping of new institutions and relationships.

Politics therefore acquired far greater importance for people's everyday lives than ever before. In the first place, practically everyone was affected by at least some aspects of the revolution. In addition to this, as much of this chapter indicates, political parties, the government or other elected bodies were taking decisions that would previously have been left to private businessmen, managers, impersonal market forces or non-political specialists. It was already true that, to quote Brus, 'the political aspect' had become 'an integral element of the analysis of the economic system'.[165]

It must be re-emphasised that there was a discernible differentiation in the extent to which individuals were affected by politics and this corresponded roughly to the propensity among different social groups to join political parties. As an example, peasants in the Czech interior, and this was even more true in less advanced Slovak villages, were less closely integrated and less likely to be actively concerned about politics; by contrast, many office workers, policemen and employees of the media could find their jobs and livelihoods directly dependent on political allegiances. This, stemming from the generally higher level of development and hence greater degree of integration of society, gave the political, social and economic changes in Czechoslovakia in and after 1945 a somewhat different character from those associated with the Russian revolution of 1917.

This is the background for an understanding of the steady growth in the membership of parties until about 40% of the adult population had joined one or other of them. Their domination of both elected and non-elected posts was often referred to as a very regrettable feature of post-war life, but alternatives such as a political structure based on Factory Councils or National Committees were not practical possibilities. Such bodies could certainly have enjoyed greater autonomy from parties – meaning in practical terms that the latter would have been less monolithic – but the nature of the national revolution meant that primacy had to go to the parties. The crucial point was that parties were not just representative bodies or even organs of power. They presented themselves with definite conceptions of society and of social development. Either explicitly or implicitly they had *programmes* for how, in broad outline, society should be organised and developed. Thus a Factory Council could have a place within a party's conception of democracy, but the converse was not the case. Moreover, it was inherent in the revolutionary changes that problems like the role of Factory Councils had to be confronted and solved.

Parties were also, of necessity, the only bodies able to present solutions on international questions and foreign policy and on the general outlines of all-state economic policy. The whole of Czechoslovakia's preceding history left no doubt that conscious political involvement in these sort of questions could have a major impact on people's everyday lives. Simple involvement in controlling the immediate aspects of life, by means of the new local institutions of democracy was, in all probability, at most a secondary interest, or a means to ensure the most basic aim of preventing a repetition of the stark tragedies of the past.

This provides the terms of reference for analysing the individual Czech parties. They cannot be seen just as the representatives of classes or as passive articulators of interests. Their role within society was much broader than that and they must therefore be analysed and judged against their ability to provide solutions to the concrete problems confronting Czechoslovak society after the national revolution.

In this context the internal regimes of the various parties were of great importance. Very little tangible information is available. The issue is not how far they complied with any model of formal democracy: the point rather is the concrete influences and mechanisms whereby they shaped their policies. Superficially all the leaderships seemed to be fully in control exercising, as Michels argued 'unlimited power'.[166] This might seem to support his view that a multi-party system is in no way beneficial, as it amounts to the dictatorship of a group of oligarchs in place of an individual dictatorship.[167]

The particular sort of multi-party system that developed in Czechoslovakia, however, differed in important respects from the effectively one-party structure that emerged after February 1948. The National Front system had two clear and obvious advantages over an absolute monopoly of power for one party. The first was that the existence of several parties within a coalition, irrespective of their precise policies, made it impossible to silence all alternative views. Proposals had to be discussed between parties before implementation. This took place to a certain extent in front of the public and therefore left scope for the consideration of a wide range of opinions. Moreover, although formally speaking the only views considered were those adopted by parties, there was scope for expression and elaboration of opinions by genuine specialists and it was also impossible to keep quiet the existence and nature of pressure 'from below', such as strikes in factories. Under such circumstances mass organisations could never become transmission belts for any single party. Trade union bodies had to make a definite effort to win loyalty from members for the policies they advocated.

Even within parties no leadership could eliminate all diversity because the need to compete with other parties forced them to encourage the maximum recruitment. As will become clear in Chapter 10, the situation was very different after February 1948.

The second advantage was that it enabled a number of parties, none of which had all of the best policies, to make a contribution to the development of a Czechoslovak model of socialism. Although there had been important differences of opinion, the revolutionary changes had been achieved within the context of broad national unity. All the parties accepted the desirability of continuing with this. Ultimately, however, it was dependent not on good intentions, but on their behaviour towards each other.

In practice, all parties must take some blame for the gradual increase in tension between them, part of which stemmed from the need to compete against each other for votes. Although it might have been hoped that this competition would take a responsible and restrained enough form to allow for continuing cooperation, there can be no doubt that the 1946 election campaign soured relations, especially between the Communists and the National Socialists.

To the question, then, of how far the Czech national revolution laid the basis for a new model of socialism, the answer must be equivocal. The destruction of the power of the Nazi occupiers and of the ruling groups that had dominated pre-war political and economic life left open a number of options. The future development of Czech society then depended on how the political parties responded to the problems confronting society and, above all, on how they behaved towards each other. This is the background to the analysis of the individual parties in Chapter 5. It is, however, useful to look first at the course of the revolutionary changes in Slovakia which must also be seen as a component of the wider Czechoslovak revolution.

4

The national revolution in Slovakia

Slovakia was not at the centre of attention throughout the first year after liberation and its importance for the future of the whole state was only demonstrated by the Democratic Party's sweeping electoral victory. This followed a period of development in Slovakia which was in many ways different from that in the Czech lands. Moreover, Communist policy, decided by the KSČ leadership first in Moscow and then in Prague, was not based on an appreciation of the specificity of Slovakia's development and that greatly aggravated the difficulties the KSS was to face.

Differences between the two parts of the republic were revealed at the time of liberation as, although Communists often took the initiative in establishing National Committees in Slovakia too, the genuine breadth and depth of their influence remains unclear.[1] Illegal activity had often amounted only to small groups in towns which then emerged to establish the new organs of power: much of the countryside remained sympathetic to the Slovak state to the end. Aware of the presence of the Red Army and the NKVD, Slovak Communists were often content to consolidate their strength by avoiding free elections to National Committees in which they would probably have been defeated. In some places, however, they were unable to gain any representation at all, so that, over 14 Districts in liberated Eastern Slovakia on 8 April 1945, Local National Committees contained 1765 Communists, 1404 Democrats and 862 non-party members.[2]

The worst case was in Michalovce where the NKVD was accused of removing a non-Communist District National Committee.[3] The KSS felt themselves entitled to administer the area alone on the grounds that the Democratic Party had made cooperation impossible: they had allegedly recruited former fascists, called for the destruction of the KSS, and even staged an armed attack on the newly created militia.[4] The real point, however, was not the Communists' attitude towards other parties, but their arrogant attitude towards the population as a whole and the accumulation of privileges for themselves.[5] Communist leaders were horrified at this and warned of the necessity to win firm political support in the countryside rather than allowing activities to 'degenerate into terror from the militia'.[6] Gottwald was adamant that the composition of National Committees should be decided somehow by the will of the people, either through secret voting or through an assembly of the population.[7] There seem, in fact, to have been less problems in the transition to the new state power in areas liberated later in Central Slovakia where there were more partisans and where experiences of political work during the uprising were useful.[8]

There was still no easy cooperation between the two parties, but the Communists believed that they could identify two trends within the Democratic Party. One they saw as being genuinely democratic and anti-fascist and they therefore aimed to help it gain dominance. The other apparently wanted to renew the old Agrarian Party: this was felt to be unacceptable owing to that party's past record, particularly in 1938 when it had joined forces with the Hlinka movement.[9] In practice, this division did not show itself, probably because even the leading Democrats in the uprising were mostly former Agrarians. Instead, the Democratic Party consolidated its unity and posed more direct opposition to Communist leadership of the revolution than anybody in later months in the Czech lands. They argued stubbornly before accepting that National Committees should replace the old administrative apparatus[10] and reorganisation of the police force left them with a stronger influence than the KSS, although Communists did dominate the non-uniformed branch.[11]

This gulf between the two Slovak parties has to be set against the background of Slovakia's recent past which left a far stronger base for clear opposition to the revolution than existed in the Czech lands. The Slovak state had much wider support than the Protectorate and there were many important figures who did not regret the Žilina agreement of 1938 or even the establishment of the Slovak state but who had also played important parts in the uprising. Many regarded the Slovak state as, in general, a gain over the pre-Munich republic and therefore had some degree of nervousness about the new republic. There were, as has been mentioned, areas where the Slovak state enjoyed considerable support to the very end and almost everywhere there were signs of a certain amount of indifference towards the new regime.[12] Moreover, an underground network had been left behind at the end of the war: during 1946 the police discovered six clandestine groups some of which possessed arms and produced illegal publications.[13]

In isolation these underground groups could not seriously affect political developments: they had first to penetrate legal organisations. This was not so true of the Catholic church which had always been a solid support for the Slovak state. It, however, did not risk presenting a general political programme or insisting on creating a new Catholic party: that was made very difficult by the down-fall of the Slovak state and by the imprisonment or arrest of so many cadres of political Catholicism. By mid 1945, however, the church hierarchy began to feel their strength returning. A pastoral letter from Slovak bishops on 8 July 1945 proclaimed their definite opposition to the nationalisation of schools[14] which had been a basic demand during the uprising. They were prepared only to accept a return to the pre-1938 situation in which 40% of all pupils attended exclusively Catholic schools.[15] Archbishop Kmet'ko and others even presented a draft Catholic programme to Beneš in which they made clear the church's support for private property, private enterprise and church schools.[16]

Although this was a comparatively mild intervention compared with previous years, it was soon followed by an attempt to form a Catholic party. Husák's reaction, referring to 'clerical reaction' as the source of 'a new fifth column of Gardist terror and Nazism',[17] left little doubt that he saw the church hierarchy as potentially more dangerous than any discernible rightward trend in the Democratic Party. Nevertheless, he continued to hope for cooperation with 'progressive' elements in the church. In practice, the only sort of political Catholicism to emerge was approved of by the church hierarchy and took a firmly right-wing form.

The scope for a coherent right wing, actively opposing the KSS, was increased by the backwardness of Slovak society. The working class was small and scattered among small enterprises. Only $9\frac{1}{2}\%$ of the economically active population worked in industrial enterprises employing over 50 workers[18] and over much of Slovakia there were no factories at all. This meant that, although after the 1945 nationalisation decrees 66.6% of employees worked in nationalised enterprises,[19] many areas could be left completely untouched. Moreover, the importance of large scale industry at the start of the revolution was further reduced by the great extent of war damage,[20] so that there were only a few parts of the country where an organised working class could dominate political life. Later, as industry recovered and grew, the organised section of the workers became far more powerful than its simple numerical strength would suggest.

Their political influence was actively encouraged by the KSS which was predominantly a working class party, more so even than the KSČ in the Czech lands. Laluha provides figures showing 63% of KSS members being workers, and 16% peasants and small businessmen at the end of 1946 while in industrial areas the KSS was almost exclusively working class.[21] Moreover, Communists held absolute dominance within the trade unions, which the Democrats treated with disdain. They could afford to do this because the working class was small, and, most important of all, had no direct influence over much of the countryside where the majority of the population lived.

Unlike the Czech lands, the dominant economic activity in Slovakia was agriculture employing directly 40.8% of the active population compared with 18.2% in Bohemia and Moravia.[22] There was a slightly greater degree of differentation in land holdings than in the Czech lands, with almost 70% of those working in agriculture owning under 5 ha: they often had to seek employment elsewhere or enter increasingly into debt. Roughly 25% owned from 5 to 20 ha and could, in periods of economic boom such as the war, produce enough to yield a surplus over their needs. Even the richer peasants, owning over 20 ha, generally remained close to the rest of the village in their life style, but they could profit from the war boom and often supported the Slovak state.[23] In so far as there was a Slovak bourgeoisie at all, these constituted its most influential part.

This picture of differentiation within the village with extreme poverty at its lower end gave great potential scope for ideas of egalitarian land reform, but there could be little meaning to the concept of national revolution developed for the Czech lands. Most Slovak villages were culturally isolated from towns and from the working class: they were strongly under the influence of richer peasants and, above all, of the Catholic Church which was often the most effective contact with the outside world.

The Democratic Party therefore had no difficulty in building up organisations and support in rural areas. Membership figures show that small producers, mostly peasants, constituted about 80% of membership: non-agricultural capitalists were of minimal importance.[24] So, despite initial signs of willingness to cooperate with the KSS, they had no difficulty at all in asserting their independence from the Communists and quite openly resurrected the heritage of the Agrarians. Ursíny, himself a wealthy farmer and former Agrarian, was soon fully justifying the policies of the old party even in 1938.[25] There was no real sign of a genuine and distinct anti-Agrarian left-wing so that the KSS strategy of developing cooperation with part of the Democratic Party while conducting the sharpest possible struggle against 'reactionary elements' could never succeed.

In fact, the Democrats were able to follow the example of the Agrarians in 1919. They were able to delay land reform, thereby allaying the fears of richer farmers, but they could also claim credit for everything that was achieved in agriculture, as the whole apparatus of agricultural policy, including cooperatives and financial institutions, came under their control during 1945.[26] Above all, a reorganisation of the Board of Commissioners on 11 April 1945 gave Agriculture to the Democrat Kvetko in exchange for Communist control over Education and the Interior.

This meant that political divisions rapidly overshadowed cooperation between the parties and the KSS felt the initiative slipping out of their hands. It is therefore hardly surprising that many Slovak Communists feared free elections and began to advocate abandonment of the National Front in favour of a one-party state modelled on the Soviet example.[27] There were even suggestions that Slovakia should leave the Czechoslovak state and affiliate to the USSR.[28] Such ideas had a firm basis in the whole history of the Slovak Communist movement, within the sectarianism of its more immediate past and within the political structure of Slovak society itself. Many Communists must have felt that they had a great deal of power where it mattered, particularly through the organised strength of the working class, but little direct influence over the great mass of peasants.

There was, however, an alternative which was not based on indifference towards the majority of the nation. There was scope for a revolutionary movement among the peasants provided it was recognised that the Slovak revolution was far less of a national and far more of a social revolution than its Czech counterpart. This view could be developed directly out of the experience of the uprising. Moreover, the SNR manifesto of 4 February 1945, which was more or less identical to KSS policy of the time, left little doubt that there were to be 'great social reforms' giving the land to those who worked it.[29] Slovak Communists saw this as the starting point for a broad transformation of the whole of Slovak society to be followed by mechanisation, technical improvement and industrialisation to absorb the rural over-population.[30] Its immediate impact, however, would have been to broaden support for the KSS by enabling the largest possible number of poor peasants to gain from the new republic. There certainly was considerable potential support for this as there were even isolated cases in the spring of 1945 of peasants taking the law into their own hands and simply dividing up the land of loyal Czechs or Slovaks and even of the church.[31] Although it is impossible to estimate the full breadth of the movement, the issue of land reform undoubtedly attracted more interest than any other issue as areas were liberated. In some areas at least, the KSS was probably beginning to establish a base among poor peasants.

Gottwald, however, met Husák in February 1945 and persuaded him to defer talk of general land reform and instead to emphasise only the national aspect. Apparently the KSS leaders assumed that this would be a very temporary compromise and that Parliament would decide on a general land reform quickly after liberation.[32] They were already aware of the limited immediate possibilities for an anti-fascist land reform. Nevertheless, as in the Czech lands, land reform had to be based on nationalities policy.

There were no doubts about the need to expel the German population. Their representative bodies were regarded as the major proponents of a policy of moving closer to, or incorporation into, Nazi Germany.[33] In fact, most Germans were evacuated by the retreating German armies who left behind only about 20,000 out of an estimated 140,000.[34] This land was settled quickly, but it was not enough to significantly alleviate the widespread hunger for land.[35] The real hopes were placed in settling the fertile agricultural areas in Southern Slovakia that had been annexed by Hungary in 1938. This obviously meant that at least some of the indigenous Hungarian population of over one half million was to be expelled, but that was a far trickier problem than the expulsion of the German minority. There certainly was plenty of anti-Hungarian feeling in wartime Slovakia and there were calls for expelling the national minorities,[36] but leading Slovak Communists argued against condemning the Hungarian minority as a whole. Novomeský, for example, maintained that 'very many . . . always remained more faithful to the republic than many Slovaks and Czechs'[37] and Husák advocated a policy of 'general nationality tolerance' at the KSS Central Committee in February 1945.[38] This was accepted by the SNR so that, although there was no doubt about the intention of establishing firm Slovak control over Hungarian areas, the new state power was to be created in conjunction with selected advisory committees of 'democratic thinking' Hungarians. Moreover, Hungarians were to be allowed nationality rights such as their own schools.[39]

There were great difficulties in this early period for the new Czechoslovak organs of power, as even many Communists of Hungarian nationality believed that Hungary should retain at least some of its territorial gains.[40] The real change in policy, however, was prompted by acceptance of the line evolved in emigration in London and adopted by the Moscow KSČ leadership. It could not seriously be denied that the Hungarian question was less dangerous than the German question,[41] but the two were effectively lumped together. Both non-Slavonic minorities were judged to have been collectively guilty of causing the downfall of the Czechoslovak state so that, even if anti-fascists could retain political and civil rights, they could not retain nationality rights, such as their own schools. This could only mean assimilation or expulsion. Husák accepted this only when assured that it was backed by the Soviet leadership.[42] The Democrats, however, had no hesitation in fully supporting it so that, by the summer of 1945, there was, in public at least, a united Slovak insistence on the complete elimination of nationality problems.[43]

This naturally encouraged great hopes among Slovak peasants who, particularly in March and April 1945, often gave their first preference to colonising the South, but they began looking for other possible sources of land inside Slovakia when their hopes remained unfulfilled. The real obstacle was the failure to convince the great powers of the need to expel the 500,000 Hungarians who had lived in Czechoslovakia before 1938. Nevertheless, the decision was taken to continue as if the Hungarians would leave and to start settling the area with Slovaks pending an international or inter-state agreement.[44] This was linked with a very tough policy whereby Hungarians were sent to work on farms in Bohemia. Not surprisingly, there was mounting resistance when it became clear that non-fascist Hungarians with their whole families were to be permanently shifted to the Czech frontier.[45]

Meanwhile the great powers insisted on negotiations between the Czechoslovak and Hungarian governments and these progressed slowly. Finally, in February 1946, an agreement was reached whereby pre-Munich frontiers were accepted but, instead of any immediate expulsions, there were to be only voluntary exchanges of equal numbers on both sides.[46] In practice this too went slowly and together with the expulsion of post-1938 settlers affected less than 15% of the Hungarian population. Czechoslovakia pressed at the Paris peace conference for international support for the expulsion of a further 200,000 Hungarians but, despite active support from other Slavonic delegations, it was outvoted by the Western powers.[47]

Throughout these delays the land hunger of the Slovak peasants remained unsatisfied. Already in mid-1945 this gave renewed strength to the demand for a general land reform. A movement developed over the whole of Slovakia which was apparently so strong 'that no force could stop it'.[48] KSS leaders began to talk openly of radical social change. Their attention was directed above all to the question of a further stage to the land reform because 'the land to be divided up is not enough'.[49]

So, as the Democrats were building up their strength in the villages and spreading rumours of a KSS plan to force peasants into kolkhozes, the Communists answered with proposals for a further land reform along the lines of the SNR manifesto. This was to be presented as proof that the KSS aim was not the destruction but the strengthening of private ownership.[50] Unfortunately for the Communists, they were prevented from applying or even campaigning for such a policy by the leading Communists in Prague who were becoming increasingly doubtful of the KSS leadership's ability to handle the situation in Slovakia.

Their concern seemed justified by the situation within the KSS. It was far less united than the Czech party and the leadership lacked the full confidence even of older members: there were especially strong doubts on the basic issues of nationalities, land reform and the National Front itself. There were, of course, doubts within the KSČ too, but they were not so serious and could largely be overcome by inner-party discussions before the Eighth Congress and then at various later periods. The KSS did not hold a congress and neither did it take part in the discussions for the KSČ Eighth Congress. This meant that KSS members never fully and publicly clarified and united their position either on all-state or on specifically Slovak questions.

Doubts and uncertainties could only be encouraged by the real problems encountered in the summer of 1945. 'Reactionary' attitudes towards Czechs, Jews and the Soviet Union were beginning to appear. The Democratic Party was becoming a firmly right-wing party and reconstruction work was going slowly. This seems to have led to growing doubts among leading KSS representatives in Prague – those who had not been involved in the uprising – about KSS policy. They argued that Slovakia, although liberated before the Czech lands, was 'lagging behind' in development. Surprisingly, they presented economic reconstruction as the most important aspect of this, although war damage in Slovakia was very extensive and there was not even a decision on much needed help from the central government until late in July.[51]

The root of Slovakia's 'lagging' was, however, attributed to weaknesses and mistakes within the KSS.[52] It was therefore decided at a meeting in Prague, attended by Gottwald, Slánský, Nosek, Široký, Šoltész and Ďuriš, to change the leadership and policies of the KSS. This was done in the absence of Šmidke, the KSS chairman, and the venue for the change was to be a KSS conference already planned for Žilina in August. That same small group even worked out both the final resolution for the Žilina conference and the composition of the new leadership. Although there was discussion at Žilina it did not alter the outcome.[53] Široký was, in fact, sent as the representative of the KSČ Central Committee[54] to take over the leading position in the KSS and he delivered the principal speech at Žilina without prior consultation with the KSS Presidium.

So, although formally an independent party in line with the letter of the National Front agreement that no party should be organised at an all-state level, the KSS was in practice firmly subordinated to the KSČ leadership and forced to accept an analysis of the Slovak situation that had been worked out in Prague. This was presented by Gottwald and Široký who seem to have transposed their assumptions about the Czech situation onto Slovakia. They identified the roots of the problem as 'reaction's' treacherous activity aimed at ruining 'the consolidation and stabilisation of our political and economic life'.[55] Gottwald supported this with evidence that the fascist underground was still active,[56] but that was a long way from proving that they could be blamed for economic difficulties. The remedy they proposed was to fight 'reaction' and build the republic by national unity around the Košice Programme. No consideration was given to the possible need for an alternative Slovak policy and any such idea was dismissed as an expression of sectarian ideas within the KSS. Gottwald therefore argued that the best way to advance the Slovak revolution was by using the influence of the Prague government more against the Democratic Party.[57]

Although Gottwald several times asserted that the old KSS leadership was unjustifiably paranoid about Prague's central authority, he had in fact missed the point. There could be no thought of completely separate Slovak development: industrialisation, accepted by all Communists as the central aim, could obviously be helped enormously by close economic relations with the advanced Czech lands. The problem rather was whether the Košice Programme, applied in every detail, could have the same impact on Slovak and Czech society. In practice large parts of Slovakia remained practically untouched by the national democratic revolution. Moreover, the disunity and confusion within the KSS could to a considerable extent be blamed on the policies on land reform and nationalities that had been imposed from Prague.

After the Žilina conference, general land reform was again firmly ruled out on the grounds that it would frighten off peasant support in the Czech countryside.[58] The KSS was then left presenting a programme to the peasants which could only generate disillusionment. Doomed to completing the first stage of the land reform first, they encountered continual lengthy delays and disputes over the definition of a foreigner or traitor. Meanwhile, only 9% of agricultural land could be divided up under this first stage, compared with a figure of 30% in the Czech lands.[59]

Other aspects of Czech agricultural policy found even less application in Slovakia. An attempt to introduce the multiple price system was stubbornly resisted by the Democrats until the government enforced it after the 1946 elections.[60] Nor could help in technical improvement seem relevant in Slovakia to the owners of tiny holdings. There was little scope for encouraging spontaneous initiatives from the peasants to overcome their production problems: in the Czech lands this was apparently not difficult and ways were found to alleviate labour and fuel shortages.[61]

So, in the interests of KSČ policy in the Czech countryside, a policy suitable for Slovakia was ruled out. At the same time, the Czech policy could not be applied in full because so much of it depended on a higher technical level generally.

As the Žilina conference placed emphasis on continuing with a land reform on national lines, so too it encouraged anti-Hungarian measures within the KSS. This, however, was not as easy as the anti-German policy in the Czech lands as it was unpalatable to many prominent Slovak and Hungarian Communists. For a time Hungarian anti-fascists were accepted into the KSS with the same rights as Slovaks and at Žilina there were requests for producing KSS publications in the Hungarian language.[62] These seem to have been brushed aside but the differences still came into the open, particularly over the party leadership's refusal to propose the parliamentary candidature of Š. Major. He had been the most prominent pre-war Slovak Communist of Hungarian nationality, and refused to assume Slovak nationality.[63] Many Slovak Communists believed that he should have been given the place within the KSS leadership that his abilities and past record warranted.[64]

In the following months there were quite obvious doubts from within the KSS about the leadership's policy, and party organisations in the South took up the complaints of the Hungarian population against forced transportation to the Czech frontiers.[65] Nevertheless, Široký insisted on strengthening the anti-Hungarian line and demanded that Communists of non-Slavonic nationality be suspended from the party.[66] This led to the depletion of many KSS organisations and could never fully unite the party. Neither could the Communists completely dissociate themselves from their internationalist past or rival the Slovak nationalist appeal of the Democratic Party.

Moreover, an unfulfilled and unfulfillable programme for land reform based on nationality could only serve to heighten national tensions as social aspirations were automatically translated into national antagonisms. Nationalist feelings against Hungarians could grow still stronger and it proved difficult to counter a revival of anti-Jewish feeling.

Anti-semitism had definite roots in Slovak society, but it too found a new basis within the context of post-war social changes. The issue was brought dramatically into public attention by a violent demonstration – described at the time as a pogrom – against Jews in Topol'čany on 2 October 1945. Even KSS members took part and justified the action by arguing that they did not want Jewish children at the convent school alongside their own Christian children.[67] Over the following weeks it proved impossible for Peroutka to find a non-Communist Slovak who would write an article firmly condemning the incident.[68]

This reappearance of anti-semitism was more than just a survival from the propaganda of the Slovak state as it was also related to the issue of aryanised property. In the Czech lands Jewish property had been taken by Germans and was generally nationalised in 1945. In Slovakia, however, aryanisation appeared to be beneficial to the Slovak nation. Jewish owned land was sometimes even divided among poor peasants. Nobody could advocate returning this confiscated property to rich Jews but, after much equivocation, it was decided that Jews had to be treated at least as well as German or Hungarian anti-fascists. Property confiscated and divided up under the Slovak state could still not be returned, but the state promised to pay full compensation.[69]

This interweaving of national and social questions, more complex and confused than in the Czech lands, led to the immediate stimulus for the demonstration in Topol'čany. It occurred as 700 out of the 3500 pre-war Jewish population returned from concentration camps and demanded back their property. The new owners refused to comply.[70]

Evidently the Žilina conference made it even harder for the KSS to formulate policies that could make it the leading force in Slovak society. Instead, as the 1946 elections drew nearer, attention shifted to alterations to the party-political structure that might damage the Democratic Party. During the autumn of 1945, all the other parties were seeking ways to strengthen themselves by becoming all-state parties, hoping thereby to eliminate the privileged position the Communists had won during the Moscow discussions.

The Social Democrats wanted to establish an organisation in Slovakia thereby reversing the merger of the two parties in 1944. This was an important issue for them in their quest to assert an independent identity and it was the only issue at their 1945 Congress on which they obviously and openly disagreed with the KSČ. It was therefore no surprise when the Party of Labour was formed on 20 January 1946. Its programmatic statement was read in parliament on 8 March 1946 by the Democratic Party's former Vice Chairman Šabršula. He expressed firm support for the government programme and nationalisations and he maintained that the new party, although formally independent, was the sister to Czech Social Democracy. He predicted that more of the Democratic Party's MPs would join the new party. Although it was made clear that it was not to be created at the expense of the KSS,[71] the Communists were suspicious of this new party. They also resented attempts to revive the National Socialist Party in Slovakia. These made little headway and National Socialists soon accepted that their best hope was to support the efforts of Šrobár. He was a veteran Slovak politician who had generally been close to Beneš's position. He nevertheless played a very prominent role in the uprising. He never felt fully at home in the Democratic Party and formulated the idea of a new party to 're-educate' former supporters of the Slovak state.[72]

Gottwald, however, did reach the conclusion that the two-party structure was not advantageous and began to hope that the Democrats would be seriously damaged by the emergence of a third party which would work more closely with the KSS. His hopes centred on a group of Catholics not openly associated with the Slovak state who announced the formation of a 'Christian Republican Party'.[73] Apparently the Communists could not believe that it would not stand 'at least by a millimeter' to the left of the Democratic Party[74] and it did claim to be firmly in favour of the programme of the SNR and the National Front. It even insisted that it would not allow opponents of the wartime resistance into its ranks.

The National Front discussed the new party on 13 March 1946 and was willing to accept it provided it chose a less provocative title. As proposed it was obviously trying to exploit both religion and any remaining loyalties to the Agrarian (Republican) Party. This, however, highlighted the dangers for the creators of the new party. With so little time left before the elections, they would be hard pressed to win a respectable vote unless they openly exploited the heritage of the Slovak state. That meant risking facing widespread condemnation as a reactionary party. The leadership was therefore more than willing to reach a favourable compromise with the existing Democratic Party leadership.[75]

The Democrats too were extremely worried. They had no doubts about the gradual extension of their influence at the expense of the KSS. National Committee elections in late 1945 and early 1946 generally markedly improved their position, and there were often cases of KSS members crossing over to the Democratic Party feeling disillusioned by unfulfilled promises and hopes.[76] This suggested that the Democrats could be optimistic about the elections provided their party held together. The creation of another right-wing party with the backing of the church could be disastrous for them. Lettrich, however, still insisted that there would be no compromise with 'reaction'.[77] He even tried to ward off the danger by generously offering to the KSS a fifty–fifty split of seats in uncontested elections. This the KSS rejected, because Široký was convinced that the creation of a new Catholic party would ultimately strengthen the position of the KSS.[78] Its formation was even greeted with the claim that the Democratic Party had fallen apart.[79]

The Democratic Party leadership, however, then felt obliged to approach the new party. In effect Lettrich capitulated to political Catholicism in an agreement which, although signed on 31 March 1946, became known as the April Agreement. It gave Catholics a seven to three majority in party organs to be followed by a similar reorganisation in state organs where the Democratic Party had representatives. The agreement was not published at the time, but appeared in slightly modified form in an émigré paper in the USA in December 1946. The actual details included acceptance of the church's position on schools, the dissolution of People's Courts and agreement that Tiso should receive a mild sentence. Catholics were also to control the security and intelligence apparatuses and the affairs of the Interior generally.[80]

Under these circumstances there was no need for a separate Catholic party and Šrobár was left to create his 'Freedom Party' with only four instead of the expected fourteen MPs.[81] The church showed no interest in his activities and instead supported the Democratic Party's election campaign. Their activities, however, were still comparatively restrained and Slovak bishops ordered that no priest could stand as a candidate or even speak at pre-election rallies.[82]

5

Czech political parties

The KSČ had the greatest claim to be the leading force in the national revolution. This, however, should not be interpreted too rigidly as there were spheres in which changes went even further than they expected. Moreover, their leadership was applied within the context of broad national unity and was therefore tempered by the need to reach agreement with other parties. Although this obviously prevented them from establishing a monopoly of power and was a useful check on their exploitation of control over the police and security forces, it was not a major restriction on the Communist's ability to put into practice most of their immediate social and economic policies. In fact, in industry they were soon performing a role with striking similarities to that of a Communist Party in power today.

Moreover, without their contribution there is no reason to doubt that changes in industry would have been much smaller. Although some state ownership was probably inevitable in other respects the revolution could have been little more than a repeat of 1918. In 1945, however, the KSČ did not vacillate and split as the Social Democrats had after 1918. Instead, the Communists acted with unity and decisiveness. The principal reasons for this were twofold: first, the KSČ, armed with the Košice Programme, had policies that roughly corresponded to the needs of Czech society in 1945 and, secondly, the party's organisational structure was such as to allow for united, conscious action to implement those policies.

Even if this suggests that a socialist transformation is to a great extent dependent on a clear-sighted, well organised and determined political party, such as the KSČ, it is still necessary to emphasise the other side of the coin. Leadership was being exercised in a far less

105

rigid way than the Communists' earlier ideas had suggested was possible. It seemed that the 'dictatorship of the proletariat' was not a precondition for socialist change and even the use of the term was avoided as it clearly made broad unity far more difficult. A discussion of the KSČ therefore has to show both how they were able to lead the revolution and how the heritage of ideas from the Comintern would affect their ability to continue playing a leadership role within the context of broad national unity. The easiest starting point is a discussion of the party's organisational strength.

This was indeed impressive. In numerical terms the party had 28,485 pre-war members and probably about 50,000 members in all at the time of liberation.[1] It grew very rapidly over the following months and membership passed the million mark in the spring of 1946. This indicated both a widespread willingness to join the KSČ and also a desire on the party's part to maximise its own size. This was partly a natural aim as it had to compete against three other parties. At the same time, it reflected the extremely broad role the KSČ hoped to play: it was to be much more than just a vote-catching machine or the representative of a particular section of society. It intended, within its conception of national revolution, to lead in the building of a new social order. This meant that no field of social life was felt to be outside its sphere of competence.

Mass recruitment inevitably led to a party containing considerable diversity among its members in their social standing and even their political thinking or knowledge of politics. The first members to join after liberation tended to be workers in industrial centres who joined factory organisations.[2] These were the first people to join any party and were therefore probably the most definite in their commitment. At the same time, the KSČ was eager to overcome its weakness in many essential fields of specialist ability and welcomed members of the technical intelligentsia who began to join the party shortly after liberation.[3] These individuals, as well as specialists in other spheres, often enjoyed meteoric promotion in the following months and this encouraged accusations that the KSČ was full of careerists. The party's more serious critics put this into perspective by pointing to the great mass of honest new members who had previously belonged to no party and also to the immense number of brave and heroic fighters against Nazism.[4] Even figures provided by the National Socialists, which included legionnaires with political prisoners and activist in the domestic or emigration resistance, showed that 53.2% of KSČ candidates in the 1946 parliamentary elections were in one of these categories compared with 9.5% for the People's Party, 12.3% for the Social Democrats and 15.6% for the National Socialists.[5] These illustrate both sides of the picture: there were many dedicated anti-fascists, but also many whose qualifications for leading positions must have been specialist abilities. In one sense this was very different from Lenin's concept of the party as outlined in 1902 as not every member was expected to be a dedicated revolutionary. Nevertheless, the aim was still to find an organisational form to involve the whole membership actively in the party's general task of changing society and creating a new social order. From this followed the party's concrete organisational structure.

Ideas of a dual structure with a trusted inner core – indicating a fundamental distrust towards the mass of new recruits a significant number of whom had previously belonged to other parties – were firmly rejected.[6] Instead an elaborate organisational structure was built up with basic units in factories and localities. Within both of these there were sub-divisions down to groups of about ten. These were the responsibility of a steward, thereby incorporating all members into a structure that linked up to the highest levels in the party. This was much more than a simple organisational point. It was intended to be a two-way channel of communication between the leadership and the members. It was the responsibility of the steward to win conviction about the party's policy and also to convey feelings back up the hierarchy so that the leadership could assess the overall situation in the country.[7]

This was not a model of perfect democracy and there was never any doubt that important decisions were taken at the very top of the party structure. There was very little public inner-party discussion and at the congress in March 1946 all decisions were taken by unanimous vote on the leadership's recommendation. Nevertheless, the chosen structure could enable the mobilisation of the whole party within a few hours in the event of a political crisis. More immediately, it served the practical purpose of involving the whole membership continuously in the work of the party and presumably helped smooth over doubts that individual members might have had about the leadership's policies.

As has been argued, their first policies were concerned principally with the question of political power. This was reflected in the first post-liberation months when the party leaders seemed to believe that the main obstacle to the construction of a new republic would be organised opposition from traitor and collaborator elements plus the pre-war right wing – stigmatised collectively as 'reaction' – whose objective would be a repeat of the events of 1918–20. The apparent absence of 'reaction' was met with warnings that it had by no means been fully defeated[8] and the KSČ leaders therefore felt fully justified in their insistence on dominating the police force.[9]

Alongside this emphasis on political power questions was a denial of any socialist content to the national revolution. Thus even the nationalisation of industries was presented as a purely national measure aimed against foreigners and traitors.[10] Small and medium-sized firms could thereby be reassured that they would not be affected.[11] There was, of course, even encouragement of private ownership, especially in agriculture. By insisting that the revolution was only a national democratic, and not a socialist, one, the Communists could play a leading role in revolutionary changes which did not follow the ideas evolved within the Comintern. The party therefore did not need to mention, or renounce, its earlier belief that socialist change was only possible after the establishment of the 'dictatorship of the proletariat'.

In the period immediately after liberation, placing the main emphasis on creating new organs of power was probably justified. Even in later months, it would undoubtedly have been naive to suggest that the question of political power was finally and definitively settled, in the sense that the revolutionary changes of 1945 could be regarded as permanently guaranteed. It was still possible, particularly in the eventuality of a sudden worsening in East–West relations, for the danger of 'reaction' or of fascism to reappear. Nevertheless, fascism had just suffered a crushing defeat which had opened the way for sweeping revolutionary changes which in turn raised completely new problems about Czechoslovakia's further development. By the autumn of 1945, the struggle against 'reaction' could no longer in any sense be the central issue around which all others revolved.

Perhaps surprisingly, there was some scope for an adaptation from this conception of the national revolution into a basis for general ideas on social and economic policy. In the pre-Munich republic, it was argued, big capital had exercised power by the 'divide and rule' principle of setting one social group against another to hide the essential unity of interests of the working people.[12] 'Reaction' could be expected to try to do the same again so that it would be essential to maintain the unity of the working people – i.e. workers, peasants, small businessmen, the working intelligentsia and sometimes even part of the bourgeoisie – within a national front. To defeat 'reaction' the nation had to be brought together to build a new republic.

From this followed the Communists' continual calls for unity between social groups – workers and the technical intelligentsia in industry being a good example – and their opposition to any particular social group acquiring a privileged status. Thus, instead of sectional wage increases, preference was given to price reductions in basic necessities. Particular emphasis was placed on a new social insurance scheme that was to be 'the symbol of the unity of the nation, the symbol of the unity of all strata of working people.'[13]

Nevertheless by the spring of 1946 pressures were building up on the KSČ leadership to resolve the basic contradiction between their practice and their earlier ideas. This cannot be attributed simply to the broadening of the party's social base, although diversity among members certainly did encourage the leadership to clarify their position. The more fundamental cause of the change stemmed from the party's overall political role as a party of power involved in constructing a new social order in cooperation and also in competition with other parties. Pressures became noticeable during the election campaign when the KSČ, in line with its image as a constructive force, tried to outline its ideas for the future. Generally, however, the needs of the campaign prevented any serious theoretical developments as the party was more concerned with advertising itself and evading any self criticism so as to win the maximum number of votes. This was clearly demonstrated at the Eighth Congress of the KSČ in March 1946 which was to a great extent part of the party's election campaign.

Slánský, the party General Secretary, could deliver a stirring account of activities since the Seventh Congress ten years earlier. He argued that that period had been a test of the real value of world views, of parties and of individuals.[14] His report gave the general impression that the KSČ had been right even when their arguments had seemed weak. Subsequent developments suggested that they had been right to advocate a government based on socialist parties and relying on the USSR rather than the West. With the benefit of hindsight, the firm stand at the time of Munich looked correct and there was no need for a detailed justification of the party's policy in the

1939–41 period: it was sufficient for electoral purposes to refute the exaggerations from the National Socialists that the KSČ had stopped resisting altogether.[15] Slánský could continue his account by referring to the party's role in producing the Košice Programme which could not be matched by anything from the London emigration. Moreover, should anyone still doubt the Communists' sincerity, there seemed to be adequate proof of it in the thousands of party members who had lost their lives.[16] No further comment seemed necessary on the revival of pre-war propaganda that the Communists had absolutely nothing to be proud of and just a long record of doing everything to destroy the republic.[17]

So the KSČ could present itself as the party most loyal to the national struggle. In addition, they alone could produce detailed concrete proposals for the future which were based on continuity with the Košice Programme and consolidation of what had been achieved since liberation.[18] They advocated continuing with the National Front but could see dangers, not because they believed 'reaction' had gained a firm foothold in any of the parties, but because the National Socialists were beginning to express doubts in an uncertain and flexible way.[19] Gottwald therefore argued that a reversal of the revolutionary changes could be ruled out if the Communists came first in the elections and won an overall majority together with the Social Democrats. He fully expected this to be achieved and therefore saw no need to deviate from the chosen strategy of broad national unity.[20] Neither did he suggest any need for the KSČ to win an absolute majority alone.

This provided the basis for a vigorous and attractive election campaign which could serve for a time to conceal ambiguities in their policies. There were, however, also pressures, both from inside and outside the party, for a major clarification of the party's attitude towards its previous aim of an armed uprising leading to the 'dictatorship of the proletariat'.

The most likely source of political division within the party was doubt at the policy of broad national unity and at the broadening of the party itself. This could be expected particularly from among the party's most loyal members and doubts were even expressed at Central Committee level.[21] They were never articulated into an alternative policy and the only discernable differences within the leadership itself were in attitudes towards other parties. Kopecký, Ďuriš and Nejedlý seem to have been the most narrowly partisan and to have caused the most offence while Gottwald and Nosek were generally more tactful. This obviously could have implications for how permanent they expected broad national unity to be, but it does suggest that, as in the period of Šmeral's leadership, the roots of possible differences within the party have to be sought not in precisely formulated strategies but rather in general attitudes towards one's own and other parties.[22]

Nevertheless, there was no sign of opposition to the leadership even from those new or old members who might have wanted a clear proclamation of the Communist Party's individuality as a revolutionary party. This degree of unity can be attributed partly to the success in achieving the revolutionary changes discussed in Chapter 3. That created favourable conditions for the leadership to win genuine conviction from the members by means of a wide ranging internal discussion leading up to the congress.[23] The discussion, like the congress itself, carefully evaded any serious assessment of the party's policy in relation to its past: debate was restricted to immediate policies.[24] This made it possible to reabsorb even some former leading members who had previously been disgraced and expelled.

Nevertheless, although there were no open disagreements at the Eighth Congress, the discussions held beforehand in basic organisations left no doubt that there was a widespread desire for a speeding up of the revolutionary process and there were frequent demands for a sharper struggle against *all other* parties.[25] There may even have been some wildly adventurist notions as Gottwald saw fit to explicitly reject putschist tactics. At the same time, in a speech to leading party officials, he did not rule out the use of arms to 'correct' the results of 'simple mechanical voting' in the unlikely event of an electoral disaster.[26] His exact meaning remains unclear and there is no sign of serious preparation for what perhaps inevitably would have been a putschist attempt. Perhaps Gottwald was just keeping his options open for some future eventuality and thereby passifying those within the KSČ who still clung to 'old' ideas.

Particularly the party's theoreticians seemed to be unable to think quickly and only gradually began to grapple with problems that the party had had to solve in practice without their help. They tended to warn against the 'over hasty' conclusion that bloodshed and force would not be necessary.[27] A conference of theoreticians in February 1946 concluded that an actual armed uprising might not be necessary but, despite some suggestions of a more flexible approach, it was concluded that 'the dictatorship of the proletariat', meaning 'unrestricted power for the working class', was still a precondition for socialism.[28]

More promising was a very hesitant acceptance that the national revolution was closely linked to socialist change. Perhaps to some extent in response to the ideas of Social Democrat trade unionists, Zápotocký acknowledged that the nationalisation of industry was 'the first step towards socialism' adding that there was 'no longer any transitional stage between it and socialism'.[29] He later explicitly referred to an evolutionary road to socialism as a distinct possibility.[30]

This, however, was not expressed decisively and confidently enough to enable the KSČ to appreciate the real possibilities of the situation. With the important exception of the reversal on nationalities policy, the events of the national revolution had a great deal in common with ideas evolved during the period of Šmeral's leadership. He had not dogmatically insisted on the inevitability of a 'dictatorship of the proletariat' and others around him had talked freely of a process of 'revolutionary evolution'. Such notions would have created a sounder theoretical basis for policy in 1945 and 1946 but, needless to say, they had been firmly stamped on by the Comintern.

Nevertheless, it soon became even harder to accept the argument that the question of socialist aims and of the form of transition to socialism should be evaded in the interests of the election campaign. Alongside some exaggerated accusations against the KSČ, there were more serious criticisms which genuinely queried the Communists' intentions. The most important was a perceptive article by Peroutka. He started by accepting both that the Communists could win the elections and that they were the main creators and theoreticians behind the National Front, but he still insisted that the KSČ could not claim full continuity with all past policies while remaining silent on the previously central concept of the dictatorship of the proletariat. He saw this as having immediate political relevance as 'the main question beneath the surface of our politics from which arises that atmosphere of mistrust'. He went on: 'there is a great deal of uncertainty about the reply. But it is precisely that reply that decides whether it should be possible for the other parties to agree with the Communists – or vice versa – as sincerely and as lastingly as is without any doubt demanded by the policy of the National Front ... As long as they do not publish a new programme, worked out with the same theoretical rigour, it will not be securely known whether they have cast aside their former principles or merely stored them in a drawer.'[31]

Peroutka's journal then carried plenty of replies from KSČ members trying to explain what the aims of their party really were. Generally they showed themselves to be convinced of the failure of the previous system, convinced of the need for socialism and convinced that the KSČ was the only genuine and consistent force for socialism. Above all, they could see no conflict between this and democracy as only socialism had proved itself capable of defeating fascism. Some of these letters suggested that the term 'dictatorship of the proletariat' was no longer necessary as the KSČ could win people over voluntarily.[32]

Only later was there a recognition within the KSČ leadership of the need to debate seriously with Peroutka. A number of articles then appeared in which Bareš, editor of the KSČ journal *Tvorba*, and Peroutka clarified their positions relative to each other. Bareš evidently felt that he had the better of it as the KSČ published in full the contributions from both sides.[33] Much of his answer was to accuse Peroutka of double standards in doubting the Communists' democratic credentials. The pre-Munich republic, Bareš insisted, had not been a perfect democracy and Peroutka had not complained about its shortcomings then.[34] This was a powerful debating point and one which Peroutka could not answer, but it still evaded the basic question.[35]

2 NATIONAL SOCIALIST PARTY

The most effective political rival to the KSČ was the National Socialist Party. They had not maintained an organisational structure throughout the war, but grew quickly during 1945 around a leading group which had largely been created in emigration out of Beneš's closest associates. The most articulate of these was Ripka.

They were nervous from the start about the general direction of the national revolution and for a time sought ways to alter the composition of the government and vainly called for general elections as quickly as possible. By the autumn of 1945 they could see definitely that the revolution was going further than they wanted but at the same time they were building up their own strength. Above all, the formation of a provisional parliament gave them the confidence to unilaterally abandon the Socialist Bloc[36] and also provided a platform from which they could attack specific aspects of government policy.

Their complaints about the police force and the media have already been mentioned. An article by Jan Stránský made a whole range of more general criticisms, starting with the method of elections to the Provisional National Assembly and going on to mention the alleged absence of contacts with the West and the continued presence of the liberating armies.[37] He claimed that fears had been generated by delays in the expulsion of Germans, by uncertainties as to how much would be nationalised, by the large numbers imprisoned as collaborators and by the excessive powers taken by Factory Councils while, it was claimed, workers disapproved of the new managements that had been installed and wanted back the old ones.

It was a general feature of all the National Socialists' criticisms that they did not pose a definite, positive alternative. They seemed to be cautiously trying to canvass support from those who doubted aspects of the governments' policies, but they were also trying to avoid being accused of playing the role of an opposition,[38] and they frequently claimed that they still regarded themselves as a party of the left.[39]

Rather than this cautious, tactical approach, many National Socialists would undoubtedly have preferred more determined criticisms of revolutionary changes and a full-blooded defence of the pre-Munich republic. Party chairman Zenkl insisted that it was 'for us among the most beautiful periods of our national history . . . of which we have every right to be proud',[40] but already in emigration, Beneš had accepted the inevitability of changes and to deny that after they had taken place would have been absurd. This, however, left the National Socialists with the task of formulating new policies in the completely new situation created by the success of the initiatives taken by the KSČ and by the extent of the revolutionary changes. In practice the tactical need to extricate themselves from the apparent position of full support for the government, and hence subordination to the KSČ, dominated over the formulation of a new long-term strategy. Later they listed their successes not in terms of what they had achieved but rather as what they had prevented.[41]

Although holding changes in check was the central theme of the National Socialists' policy, they did gradually evolve from that specific policies on a whole range of aspects of society. Although there is no evidence of an active inner-party democracy, their approach was undoubtedly influenced by those individuals who were attracted to the party for the first time after liberation. For, as the National Socialists failed to recapture their earlier working class support, so instead they built up a broad base among those expressing doubts and fears about the revolution. They took up the case of civil servants' pay from early on, arguing significantly that particularly those with long service deserved pay increases.[42] Their reticence about changes in the economy won them support from small businessmen. Even capitalists, with more explicitly right-wing parties banned, began placing faith in the National Socialists as the most likely defender of their interests. It was widely noted that many new and influential National Socialists were former members of banned parties or influential and wealthy people who had lost their positions after May. The friendliest view put it as an open question whether these people would be won for socialism or whether the party would be moved to the right.[43]

Owing to the difficult situation in which they found themselves, plus the differences within their own ranks, the National Socialists proved incapable of producing a new programme. This was not a crippling handicap as they never tried to be a party of visionaries attempting to create a new social order and they never aspired to leadership in the national revolution: to them politics meant the technicalities of routine government within a coalition in a parliamentary system. They could therefore even present it as a virtue that their programmatic principles could be criticised for being 'a little vague' as this was apparently better than 'a programme of rigid one-sided doctrine'.[44]

Nevertheless, any party requires some clarity and unity in its ideas and the speeches by party leaders show that there was considerable common ground in their understanding of what National Socialism ɔmant. Their starting point was a notion of Czechoslovakia as a classless society made up of small men without great inequalities. Czech nationalism could therefore be supported in total and equated directly with social justice. It could also be argued that the National Socialists, rather than representing just one class, could represent the whole nation.[45]

Although they described themselves as a socialist party, National Socialists very rarely attempted to explain what they meant by socialism. It seemed to be understood not as a social or historical phenomenon but as an idea embodying specificity and morality: it was 'a burning faith, not just an invention of cold reasoning'.[46] Of more practical relevance for the formulation of concrete policies were their concepts of freedom and democracy. It was natural, given their tactics in the autumn of 1945, that they should oppose 'any sort of limiting of criticism and of variety of opinions on individual questions'.[47] The great weakness, however, was that they believed that this variety of opinions could be adequately expressed by a small number of competing parties within a parliamentary system and free from external pressures. In their view this was the essence and seemingly also the totality of democracy. This often led to a double standard. They insisted on their right to criticise, but extra-parliamentary pressures and even articles in the Communist press could be condemned as 'terror', a term to which they gave an extremely wide meaning.

There was no social content to their conception of democracy, just as their notion of nationalism assumed away any social differences or conflicts. The only source of conflict seemed to them to be the struggles between parties, while questions of inner-party democracy were never discussed. Their draft proposals for the discussions in Moscow were almost exclusively concerned with regulating strife between parties.[48] They had even justified recreating the party in Prague in May 1945 only as a means to ensure 'democratic competition, control and criticism'.[49]

They certainly did not see the need for conscious political involvement in the economy and this was reflected in the weakness of their economic organisation. They showed little interest in voluntary labour brigades, which were even condemned as being 'unprofitable',[50] or in special measures to help particular sectors. Instead, their first contribution to economic policy was a solid defence of the powers of 'proven specialists' who, it was argued, should be allowed to get on with the job free from the 'terror' which 'reigned in many enterprises'.[51] This, of course, was a criticism of the powers of Factory Councils and of their conduct of the purge. It was also a defence of the interests of those who had suffered, or who feared that they could suffer in the future, from the powers of the Factory Councils.

The acquisition and cultivation of this social base even led to a switch in National Socialist policies from advocating the primacy of specialist abilities in appointments to the need for proportional representation of parties in economic institutions – but not, for example, in the legal apparatus which was largely unaffected by the revolutionary events – and for a revision of the purge. They thereby built up an economic policy which was no more than an application of their conception of parliamentary democracy and political pluralism into other fields.[52] Even their defence of private enterprise was justified in this way. Plurality in the economy, Ripka argued, was essential to prevent 'all the people' from becoming 'slaves of the state'. He also claimed that 'the state means the government and in such conditions the government would inevitably pass into the hands of one political party'.[53] There was still no justification for public ownership and Ripka's formulation could certainly appeal to the remaining capitalists, but hardly to workers. For them, employment in private industry could hardly be any less 'slavery' than employment in nationalised industry.

They could see no independent role for mass organisations either and generally argued that they should be subordinated to political parties by the introduction of parity or proportional representation into their elected committees. This was hardly an adequate starting point for an attractive trade union policy, particularly when the unions had already assumed such a broad role within the economy. It is therefore not surprising that the National Socialists got nowhere with their request for a fifth of the places on ÚRO.[54] The trade union leaders were always adamant that trade union unity was not to be disrupted by party organisations and that trade union elections were not to be contests between parties.

Events followed a very different course in the youth organisation, which the KSČ hoped would become a powerful political voice like the trade unions. Instead the SČM (Union of Czechoslovak Youth) could only unite 30% of the 15–25 age group within its ranks,[55] and was quickly threatened with serious divisions. The feeling for national unity alone was not enough to hold it together without a far clearer definition of its role within society.

When they renounced the Socialist Bloc, the National Socialists followed the People's Party, who had never been party to the bloc agreement, in establishing independent youth organisations: their aim at first was presented as changing the SČM.[56] In the period immediately preceding the elections, however, tension between the SČM and the National Socialist leaderships mounted until the latter called on its members to withdraw from SČM which was characterised as a simple Communist front and referred to as the 'KSČM'.[57] Unfortunately, nobody felt it necessary to produce any facts or figures that could confirm or refute this claim, but the youth union from then on could never become a significant force in national politics.

This was a success for the National Socialists not because it directly extended their own influence, but because they had immobilised a mass organisation that they were convinced would generally support KSČ policies. It was a success for their general strategy of holding in check the revolutionary changes.

As the National Socialists pursued this general strategy and tried to broaden their potential electoral support by expressing the interests of those who were nervous about the revolutionary changes, so the KSČ began to accuse them of a 'two irons' policy of fishing for the votes of 'reactionaries' while also trying to claim credit for being a government party.[58] Such accusations were good propaganda for the Communists, but there was for a long time no clear evidence that 'reaction' was exerting a major influence on National Socialist policy. The presence of former members of banned parties was not regarded in itself as anything reprehensible: there were some within all the legal parties. The point was rather 'to what extent which party makes concessions to its new members and voters'.[59] The KSČ claimed to have made none but found two issues which gave scope for determined propaganda attacks against the National Socialists. The first was a flirtation by the National Socialist leadership with prominent former Agrarians, the most important of whom was Feierabend. He had been a Minister in the London government and prior to that in the Protectorate government so that, although he claimed to have been involved in resistance activities, he could still technically have been called before the National Court. Ideally, he wanted a legalisation of the Agrarian Party itself but, failing that, sought an alternative legal base within the National Socialist Party where it was believed that his alleged continuing popularity in the countryside would help win votes.[60]

When he publicly announced at the end of March 1946 that he had joined the National Socialists, the Social Democrats were prepared to give him the benefit of the doubt on his record during the occupation but were dumbfounded by the suggestion that he was a socialist.[61] It was even suggested that he had *never* opposed socialism,[62] but his published statements left no doubt that he stood on the extreme right of Czech politics. In his memoirs he refers to 'the so-called liberation' followed by 'a period of darkness which hurled Czechoslovakia back by decades'.[63]

The Communists made far more comprehensive accusations some of which were clearly exaggerated but others remained unanswered. A particularly troublesome point was the publication of documentary evidence that Feierabend had acquired Jewish property by special agreement with the Nazi official K. H. Frank and then thought the land could still be his after liberation.[64] With so vigorous a campaign against him, Feierabend no longer served a useful purpose within the National Socialist election campaign and decided not to stand as a parliamentary candidate.[65]

The second element of flirtation with the right wing was on the question of special provision for opponents of the National Front to cast a blank vote thereby indicating general disagreement with the government. This might appear to be a trivial question but it led to the first disputed vote in parliament suggesting that it concealed a really fundamental issue.

The KSČ were in favour of allowing these blank votes, claiming that the elections could thereby become a vote of confidence in the government as well as being a contest between the parties. They accused the National Socialists of fishing for support from 'anti-state reaction' and speculating on the votes of enemies of the National Front.[66] The National Socialists produced numerous counter arguments but in essence they were arguing that all those with doubts about aspects of the new regime should reject any thought of a blank vote and support the National Socialists.[67] In the vote in parliament some National Socialists absented themselves and the outcome was 155 for blank votes and 131 against.

This was only one of several disagreements in the election campaign which at times became quite bitter. Even Peroutka, one of their MPs, accepted that the National Socialists did not conduct a clean campaign,[68] although an agreement had been reached in the National Front that all parties would refrain from unprincipled polemics or personal attacks and that all would support the Košice Programme and accept responsibility for the government's actions.

Peroutka was referring particularly to his party's emphasis on a number of very serious accusations of abuses of power by Communists, some of which may have been true but many of which had to be withdrawn either before or shortly after the elections. He felt that it had been a mistake to concentrate on this 'frontal attack' against the KSČ. Despite the ambiguities in Communist strategy, continual accusations of 'totalitarianism' could only encourage firm rebuttals even from the Social Democrats, who insisted that there was no *general* danger of totalitarianism although they did have criticisms of some Communists not keeping to the parity agreement in National Committees.[69]

Moreover, these attacks on the KSČ were not accompanied by serious positive slogans. Perhaps the National Socialists hoped that they would gain a big vote from their claim to be loyal to Beneš and Masaryk, which they plugged remorselessly and with no further elaboration. Generally their slogans did not suggest that they understood and welcomed the changes since the 1935 elections. They did not present ideas for the further development of society on the basis of the revolutionary changes of 1945. Neither did they make definite commitments on policies they would pursue. Instead many of the slogans in their press and posters seemed to reflect fears and uncertainties at the direction developments could be taking. In some localities they even called openly for 'the redemption of all the crimes of the revolution', adding 'the Košice government programme is an Eastern programme and therefore unsuitable for our conditions'.[70]

Their approach to the elections neatly summarises their strengths and weaknesses. They were soon to be proved right in their insistence that power has somehow to be controlled. The weakness in their programmatic conceptions was that this point alone could not justify mass support for the party. In practice they built up their support from doubters or opponents of the new regime and lost the sympathy of those who supported the revolutionary changes. Their ideas on plurality therefore appeared to be in opposition to, rather than a necessary complement to, socialism.

3 THE SOCIAL DEMOCRATIC PARTY

The Social Democrats emerged with completely new leaders and, as the disappearance of their pre-war right-wing coalition partners inevitably meant the end of the previous policy of expediency, they all accepted the need for a more vigorous policy. They claimed to be a Marxist party and enthusiastically supported the revolutionary changes. On immediate issues there often seemed to be no real difference between themselves and the KSČ and there were suggestions that close cooperation would lead quickly to a full merger of the two parties. This was rejected by the Communists, but in some localities the party could only exist when artificially created by the KSČ.[71]

Thus a major problem for the Social Democrats, particularly as the elections drew closer, was how they could present an identity clearly separate from the KSČ. Unlike the National Socialists, they had no desire to combine this with an assertion of independence from the general direction of the revolutionary changes. They therefore did not carry negative articles in their press but instead began by trying to clarify their own policies and the justification for their own independent existence at a party congress held on 18–20 October 1945. The only visible disagreement with the KSČ then was their call for a Social Democratic Party in Slovakia to fight the dangers of 'reaction' there.[72] There were no open disputes within the party. Beneath the surface, however, there were two lines. One continued to talk of an *eventual* merger,[73] and this generally went with a more self-critical acceptance that the party had made serious mistakes in the inter-war period.[74] The alternative was to find a continuing historical justification for the party's existence[75] and this could be linked with glorification of its past.[76]

By the spring of 1946, the Social Democrats were beginning to clarify some theoretical concepts with which they could distinguish themselves from the KSČ. They boasted of going further than the Communists in trying to produce a socialist analysis of the situation, including particular attention to questions of the relationship between socialism and democracy.[77] The revolution was said to be both national and social as measures were directed even against those capitalists who had remained loyal to the nation.[78] This did not mean that socialism had been achieved but they insisted that further development was to be a 'natural evolutionary process . . . without using a dictatorship'.[79]

Socialism itself was understood as a socio-economic system based on nationalisations and planning.[80] At the same time, the Social Democrats, unlike the KSČ, made it quite clear that not all economic activity would have to be directed by the state. Agriculture, for example, was to be based not on large collective farms, but on self-sufficient peasant small holdings of 8–15 ha.[81] They also saw a lasting place for small businessmen and could justly claim to be the first party to offer them anything concrete:[82] by way of contrast, the Communists simply stated goodwill and the National Socialists made very general pronouncements about support for private enterprise.

The Social Democrats looked seriously at how to confront their economic and social problems[83] and there was even a congress of Social Democrat small businessmen.[84] It seemed there that the party was presenting a position far closer to the National Socialists: there was no mention of how nationalised industries could help but rather calls for fair treatment in the allocation of raw materials and full scope for private enterprise.[85]

This aspect of social policy was surprisingly unimportant in moving the Social Democrats away from their close relationship with the KSČ. Although the party had lost much of its working class base – by mid 1947 workers constituted only one third of membership compared with 58% before the war – small businessmen still constituted under 7% of the total. The really big increase had been in office workers.[86] Moreover, the strong numerical working class presence was backed by great strength in the trade unions and in industry. In fact when, for reasons discussed later, Social Democrats wanted to assert more vigorously their independence from the KSČ, the main pressure seemed to come from Plzeň and Ostrava. In the latter case 50% of party members were working class.[87] It appears, then, that it was not the attempts to broaden the party's social base that led to a shift in the party's overall policy. As distinct from the National Socialists, the Social Democrats remained committed primarily to the nationalised industries and approaches to the petty bourgeoisie were generally incorporated within a conception of a multi-sector model of socialism.

This enabled the Social Democrats to present an election slogan distinct from the KSČ, 'Democracy is our road, socialism is our aim'. They were able to give this some real meaning as they developed sensible ideas for public control over the organs of power, especially the police force, but they never left any doubt about their general commitment to the revolution. They could therefore have made a very positive contribution to developing a Czechoslovak model of socialism, but they were never able to gain any initiative over the KSČ. On most issues they could not formulate their own distinctive policies and, in the election campaign, they presented no new specific proposals. The key to advertising an independent existence was great publicity for leading personalities, particularly Fierlinger and Laušman who, as Prime Minister and Minister of Industry, seemed to indicate that Social Democracy really was the leading force in the revolution. They hoped that this would win them a big vote and conducted their campaign with a minimum of demagoguery.

4 THE PEOPLE'S PARTY

The People's Party, closely linked to the Catholic church, was the only Czech party to proclaim itself to be non-socialist. It had only a negligible share in formulating the Košice Programme and for some months seemed to be left out on a limb on the right of Czech politics unable seriously to influence events. It had political and organisational difficulties so serious that Šrámek felt obliged to admit: 'we are not standing on our own legs – we have been [secretly given] these by the agreement of the four parties'.[88] This points to the fundamental dilemma confronting the party as it tried neither to isolate itself completely from the revolutionary changes nor to allow itself to be identified with them:[89] it hoped thereby to be able to win support from anti-socialists who opposed the revolutionary changes.

The key to a more active role in political life was the National Socialists' abandonment of the bloc of socialist parties. Even then the People's Party still had to comment on the revolution as a whole and seemed only able to tie themselves into knots. At their congress in April 1946, which ideally should have been presenting a consistent policy, Procházka could argue that the Košice Programme was predominantly socialist so that they could only accept it as a compromise.[90] At the same time it was denied that the programme was close to the aims of the two Marxist parties: 'that programme is closest to the secular programme and principles of the ČSSL [People's Party], which actually has not retreated in anything'.[91]

Only gradually did leading party members produce any programmatic or philosophical principles. Basing themselves to a great extent on papal encyclicals, they condemned both 'private capitalism' and 'state capitalism' and advocated a form of nationalisation making the worker into a 'joint-owner'.[92] The emphasis was always on *more* individual private ownership even to the extent of suggesting that the principle in agriculture of land belonging to he who works on it should be made to apply also to factories.[93] The fullest attempt to argue this through was a pamphlet by Chudoba[94] who argued for a return to the Romanesque and Gothic periods when, he claimed, everybody had been an owner: he thought that even modern technology could allow for big factories to be divided up giving a maximum size of 20–24 employees. There could be little relevance for this explicitly backward-looking thinking to contemporary problems. Moreover, even the talk about everybody owning some property was not consistently applied. In practice the People's Party defended those who already had the property on every possible occasion.

Just as no single individual or group within the party could formulate a convincing policy, so too none could enjoy unchallenged supremacy. There were references at the time, and subsequently, to three main trends within the leadership, although they cannot be exactly defined. There was said to be a large but diversified right wing including Procházka and many new recruits from former members of banned parties. A second trend was associated with the leadership headed by Šrámek. He represented continuity from the pre-war party and had been Prime Minister in the London government. He was, by 1945, too old to play a full role and in practice his place was taken by Hála. This leading group came under strong pressure from the right after the 1946 elections. The left, characterised by definite commitment to the revolution, was weak and often seemed to be on the verge of disappearance.[95]

The difficulties in formulating a clearly right-wing position were illustrated by the controversies around the journal *Obzory*. Its editors were Ducháček and Tigrid and its most controversial contributor was H. Koželuhová, the wife of Procházka. She in particular left little doubt of her opposition to the Košice Programme.

Obzory found itself moving to the right too quickly. When attacks on the Czechoslovak army were published there were even requests that the paper should be banned. Kopecký resisted this on the grounds that it was not at that time necessary.[96] Fierlinger raised the issue with Hála who implicitly accepted much of the criticism of *Obzory*,[97] which then claimed to have been defending the Košice Programme.[98] Even the National Socialists echoed many of the criticisms of Koželuhová.[99] This must have been a major factor preventing the whole party from openly stating a clearly right-wing position. It was left with confused and ambiguous policies that were

quite distinct from the cautious and subtle way in which the
National Socialists were trying to dissociate themselves from clear
commitment to the revolution.

So, with very little basis for clear policy proposals in their election
campaign, the People's Party even made a virtue of necessity: 'a
good enough advertisement for us is our programme as of the only
non-socialist political party'.[100] They therefore had no concrete
policy proposals and concentrated on advertising their general defence of 'the economic and social middle of the nation, the private
businessmen, small businessmen, shop-keepers'[101] against the threat,
allegedly from Communists and Social Democrats alike, of 'the
dictatorship of the proletariat'.[102] This effectively summarises their
contribution to the development of Czech society. They were
important primarily as allies of the National Socialists in defending
private enterprise and in preventing, for a time, the KSČ from
establishing a monopoly of power.

5 THE PARLIAMENTARY ELECTIONS

The elections were held on 26 May 1946 and the basic results for
the Czech lands are shown in Table 4.

Table 4 *Percentage votes of Czech parties in 1946*

	Bohemia	Moravia	Total Czech lands	Seats in Parliament
KSČ	43.25	34.46	40.17	93
LS	16.27	27.56	20.23	46
SD	14.96	16.74	15.59	37
NS	25.20	20.80	23.66	55
Blank	0.32	0.44	0.35	0

A comparison of votes between 1935 and 1946 gives an impression of the sources of the increases in the share of votes received by
the Communists and National Socialists. Table 5 shows the overall
picture.

In interpreting these results two points have to be borne in mind.
First, it was not a question simply of individuals changing their
voting behaviour: after the eleven year gap over two million people
were voting for the first time. Secondly, all 1935 figures record

Table 5 *Percentage votes of Czech parties in 1946*
compared with 1935[103]

	Bohemia		Moravia	
	1935	1946	1935	1946
KSČ	11	43	10	34
LS	9	16	13	28
SD	19	15	19	17
NS	17	25	16	21
Total	57	100	59	100

Czech votes only and KSČ figures are reduced by 23.24% to account for the votes of other nationalities.

Further analysis of these results shows that the Communist success was due to an enormous vote in frontier areas plus an increase in the formerly Agrarian Czech interior and in industrial areas where the Social Democrats had been strong. It is likely that, at the very minimum, the KSČ took one third of former Agrarian votes while the National Socialists took about a quarter. The Communists probably won votes from the former supporters of all other parties in rural areas[104] to make them the strongest party in the countryside although the People's Party also made gains, especially in the Moravian villages.

The Communists' achievement in industrial areas was not so unexpected but was still remarkable as it was associated with an actual decline in the Social Democrats' share of the vote. This was particularly dramatic in their solidest pre-war bases where they lost up to one third of their absolute 1935 votes.[105] Post-war elections in Europe generally showed an increase in the share of the vote for the traditional parties of the working class. Sometimes within that Communists gained from Social Democrats, but only in two cases were Communists definitely the stronger: they were France and Czechoslovakia. The latter case was all the more exceptional because Communist predominance was so much greater and associated with a general decline for the Social Democrats.

The National Socialists were particularly disappointed by the election results as, although they had increased their own vote, they had fallen way below their dream of coming first and holding a convincing majority together with the People's Party. Apparently even Beneš had shared some illusions, thinking that the Communists would be pushed into third place.[106] It had been taken for granted that, at a minimum, the Communists would lose some of their key government positions.[107]

Two lines were adopted to explain away this disappointment. One was to maintain that the votes were not for the Communist programme as such so that the support would vanish if they deviated from the 'democratic' path. It was certainly true that votes did not represent the same level of commitment everywhere: in the countryside particularly they were not backed up with membership and appeared to be less secure, but that applied to the National Socialists too. The second line, argued by Ripka and somewhat contradicting the first, was that the Communists did well because of their control over positions of power, meaning that the election results indicated respect for power and fear of the holders of power resulting from the long Nazi occupation.[108] Sometimes this was put in a less extreme form, attributing the Communist victory in the countryside simply to their holding the post of Minister of Agriculture.[109]

There were also more perceptive assessments. Drtina pointed out that the Agrarians had definitively disappeared. It was not just that the party was outlawed but that the ideas on which it had been based had been destroyed so that the Communist victory was not a freak event: its causes had to be sought in the preceding years and in the pre-Munich republic.[110] The same point was made by others who argued that the National Socialists had made a serious mistake in not seeing 'that the new organisation of political relations in our country is not just the result of the Moscow discussions but that it is the outcome of a mighty historical process'.[111] Or, as Peroutka put it, people were tired of the old world and wanted an end to 'the rule of one over another', to poverty, gloom and the threat of war. They wanted a new world and saw this in the Communists' programme.[112] He left unanswered the crucial question of why they did not see this in the Social Democrats or National Socialists, both of which claimed to be socialist parties. The comparative failure of those parties can only be explained against the background of their role within the pre-Munich republic, during the occupation and during the revolutionary events of 1945.

Journalistic investigations of the reasons for the peasants' voting behaviour certainly gave no support to Ripka's argument. Peasants seemed to have approached the elections in a very open-minded way and were attracted to the Communists for a whole range of reasons. These included the policies the government was implementing which were often linked with expressions of respect for Ďuriš. They commented on the straightforward and realistic policies of the Communists and the absence of demagogic or impossible promises. They saw the Communist campaign as the best organised and expressed respect for many individual Communists because of their integrity although this was sometimes balanced by references to dubious elements within the party. They also often referred to direct contacts with workers which had led to a definite feeling of a common interest. Sometimes they indicated general approval for the government believing that they would be secure in holding onto their land. There was no sign of any real knowledge of, or interest in, Marxism.[113]

A further possible general explanation for the Communists' electoral success was the prestige of the Soviet Union. This had not been an issue during the election campaign as no party could directly challenge so popular a principle as close friendship with the USSR. Nevertheless the National Socialists always seemed to be uncertain – more so than the People's Party – and tried to appeal at least to some extent to two opposing positions. They could firmly deny that there could be any Soviet intention to interfere in Czechoslovakia's internal affairs[114] and proclaim their loyalty 'for better or for worse, in life as in death with the Soviet Union'.[115] This was accompanied by a presentation of the elections as a choice between '*totalitarianism or democracy* . . . an independent Czechoslovak state or . . . subservience'.[116]

Even then, relations with the USSR could hardly have been a major question in the elections, as universal proclamations of a desire for a very close alliance predominated. Beneš himself could be identified with such a notion. It would therefore be unconvincing to trivialise the Communist victory as a reflection of 'gratitude' to the liberator.

Nevertheless, Soviet military successes did appear to many to indicate the general strength of the social order prevailing in the Soviet Union. Admiration for the USSR could be quoted as a fundamental reason for allegiance to the KSČ.[117] The point, however, was not just that the Soviet Union had been the liberator of most of Czechoslovakia – nobody disputed that at all – but that it had shown strength in the war when so many other states had been proved weak. It was not only Communists who pointed to the superiority in precisely those aspects that seemed to have been Czechoslovakia's weak points – the moral fibre of its political leadership and its nationalities policy.[118] Now, of course, Stalin's leadership does not seem so impressive to anyone, but things looked different in Czechoslovakia in 1946.

In Slovakia, however, such questions were less important and, as Table 6 shows, the Democrats did very much better than the Communists. This meant that there was only a small overall majority for the Communists plus the Czech Social Democrats and

Table 6 *Percentage of votes won by Slovak parties in 1946*

	Percentage of votes	Number of seats
KSS	30.48	21
DS	61.43	43
Freedom Party	4.20	3
Labour Party	3.11	2
Blank	0.78	0

Slovak Labour Party. The final result gave them 153 seats against 147 for all the other parties. An analysis of the Slovak results showed that the Democrats had won practically all the former votes of the HSL'S and its allies and the overwhelming majority of former Agrarian votes. This gave them a sweeping victory in agricultural areas backed up by quite remarkable gains in several big towns. In Bratislava, where the autonomists and Agrarians had won only 24% in 1935, the Democrats actually gained at the expense of the socialist parties to win 64%. In Košice the increase was from 21% to 68% while the KSS vote of 19% was hardly above the 18% of 1935.[119]

The KSS made only minimal gains in agricultural areas and most of Eastern Slovakia. Their real strength was in Central Slovakia where they had clearly gained new supporters. Even then, they very rarely ousted the Democrats from first place. The small villages around Brezno based on forestry, wood working and heavy industry were their only really safe base.

There were obviously several factors affecting changes in the KSS vote including the socio-economic structure, the impact of the revolution, the traditions from the uprising, party work over the whole preceding period, the religious complexion of the area and the influence of the clergy and even the quality of the KSS.[120] Industrialised areas were not automatically pro-Communist and agricultural areas with striking inequalities in land holdings very rarely gave solid support to the KSS.

Nationality problems may have been extremely important in the Communist failures in Košice and Bratislava where there were significant Hungarian populations. By contrast, in some rural Eastern areas with Ukrainian populations the KSS did exceptionally well. It appears that the Democrats won in Catholic Ukrainian villages and the Communists in predominantly Orthodox villages.[121]

The outstanding fact remains the Democrats' achievement in restricting all the three other parties to 37½% of the vote. This compares with 28% for all the socialist parties in 1935 or 53% in 1920.[122] Moreover, the Democratic Party's vote was remarkably consistent in practically all of Slovakia, despite the country's diversity in levels of development and social and religious complexion. This suggests an achievement unparalleled in previous Slovak electoral history: it can hardly be explained in total by just one factor alone such as the April Agreement. The Democrats must have appeared as the best representative of the Slovak nation by somehow reconciling and combining the nationalist, but not pro-German, ideas of the Slovak state with the spirit of the uprising.

6

The Gottwald government

The first year after the 1946 elections was of great importance for the possibilities of developing a new model of socialism in Czechoslovakia. It was a period in which the Communist Party was clearly transcending, in much of its practice and to some extent in its ideas, the conception of the national democratic revolution as centring on a struggle against 'reaction'. The most prominent feature in the development of their policy was the Two Year Plan for economic recovery. This was of immense importance for the development of Czechoslovak society generally as it became the focal point for social conflicts and discontent. It was also matched by a recognition within the party that new realities required theoretical advances. This led to the hesitant development of the concept of the Czechoslovak road to socialism.

The starting point for this was the recognition by the KSČ leadership that, despite their good electoral performance, they could still only govern in a coalition with all the other Czech parties. They had expected no more. In fact, Gottwald could point out that their vote of 40% in the Czech lands was barely short of the 41% expected on the basis of predictions by basic organisations. This he saw as further evidence of how closely they were in touch with the people's thinking:[1] by contrast, the other parties held grossly exaggerated views of their own likely votes.

Communist satisfaction was restricted by three sources of unease. The first stemmed from the Democrats' victory in Slovakia which reduced the overall majority for the KSČ together with the Social Democrats to almost the narrowest possible. The second point was that even in many districts in the Czech lands there was no left majority, and the third was that the election campaigns of the right-wing parties led Gottwald to conclude that they really might want to reverse the achievements of the previous year:[2] Gottwald therefore implicitly concluded that the bloc of socialist parties was finished.

He argued that the only way to take full advantage of the post-election possibilities, while also minimising the dangers, was for the KSČ to orientate itself towards *all* the Czech parties without any differentiation. The hope and expectation was that this would give the best conditions for the development of left oppositions within the National Socialist and People's Parties. At the same time, Gottwald concluded that the KSČ had to increase its own strength and challenge the National Socialists' position among the urban middle strata. Although he did not state definitely what this would lead to, he already began hinting that the KSČ could aim for an absolute majority in the next elections.[3]

Following this assessment of the situation, the KSČ set about negotiating for a new government. They presented a comprehensive draft government programme which was soon accepted by the National Front. It appeared, like the Košice Programme, as a compromise with some very definite commitments alongside some vague or ambiguous formulations that gave plenty of scope for disputes over the ensuing months. More immediately, there were lengthy arguments over the allocation of particular ministries. The KSČ exercised the right, as the party with the most votes, to take the positions of Prime Minister and Agriculture: the latter was then formally conceded to the KSS. The National Socialists insisted on being given better representation in important posts, but eventually had to content themselves with control over Education. The KSČ remained adamant that no other party would take the Ministry of the Interior. For reasons explained below it was the Social Democrats who were the most demanding, wanting both Agriculture and the Interior, but eventually they had to accept much less. They still continued for a long time to demand that the Intelligence service should be taken away from the Ministry of the Interior and put under the Government Presidium. Agreement was finally reached on the new government on 2 July 1946.[4]

Much of the new government programme was concerned with completing and consolidating the revolutionary changes and then incorporating them into a new constitution. Although there were to be wide differences of opinion over these issues,[5] political life over the following year was dominated by a different question and a different aspect of the government programme: that was the question of economic consolidation and the KSČ proposal for a Two Year Plan. This followed a confused history of the idea of a plan from the time of liberation. Although there had been an almost universal belief that 'planning' would replace the liberal capitalist economy, the official KSČ position had been that it would be premature. Instead, they argued that priority should be given to solving problems of individual key industries. They therefore encouraged plans for individual products, but the persistence of shortages and bottlenecks led to variable results. Leading economists therefore began to recognise that, even if there were good arguments against a comprehensive plan on the Soviet model, there were also economic problems that could be overcome more quickly if there were some overall coordination.[6]

Nevertheless, it still came as a surprise to the KSČ economists when Gottwald, only three weeks before the election date, suggested that they should prepare an outline for a plan aiming to restore the pre-war production level in two years. They overcame their initial scepticism and soon became convinced of the ingeniousness of the idea[7] as it took into account the realities of both the economic and, perhaps more important, the political situations. By the autumn of 1946 the Communist press was devoting enormous publicity to preparations for the plan, which was to begin in January 1947. It became the central axis of their economic and social policies for the immediate future.

They combined their vigorous initiative with a tactful approach towards the other parties. They accepted from the start that it would require the good will of the private sector and therefore agreed to include in the government programme a specific assurance that no further nationalisations were planned. They also demonstrated their determination to secure cooperation between parties on economic policy by making a major concession to National Socialist thinking when a government resolution of 16 July 1946 created a new unique body by-passing all existing economic organs and incorporating directly leading economists from all the parties in proportion to their electoral strength. This later became known as the ÚPK (Central Planning Commission) and developed into the effective advisory organ to the government on all economic questions. In practice it always reached unanimous agreement and seemed to be a major factor holding the parties together while other issues were dividing them.[8] It could therefore be argued that Czechoslovak experience clearly refuted the theoretical proposition that the need for a single will in planning could not be achieved with a plurality of parties.[9]

Moreover, although there was some interest in the Soviet planning system, Communist economists emphasised the need to take specifically Czechoslovak conditions into account. Although they certainly believed that the Two Year Plan could be a transitional stage on the way to something much closer to the Soviet model,[10] their approach was still flexible and pragmatic. They thereby avoided alienating those for whom the plan was just 'to accelerate the return to normal conditions'[11] and not an attempt to build the basis for a later more comprehensive plan.

So in its actual form the first Czechoslovak plan was not based on any pre-existing model. It was not a full plan as many important questions were simply omitted. Investment was only planned in the broadest possible way. Foreign trade was not incorporated into the plan either and neither were long-term questions of Czechoslovakia's international orientation. There was no attempt to coordinate with other planned economies.[12]

It was often described as a 'partial' plan because of these and other omissions and, above all, because of the way it was formulated. There was not felt to be time, reliable information or adequate personnel to go through the whole complex process involved in plan formulation in the USSR. The so called 'counter plans' were not presented. Instead the centre, having set its aim, divided economic activity into individual tasks for enterprises. Perhaps one third of industry was given definite tasks while otherwise the main contact with the plan was through rigid allocations of raw materials, equipment and labour, and enterprises were simply asked to produce as much as they could. This could provide an optimistic target towards which economic activity could be directed. Even if not a precise prediction of what would happen the plan could still hope to encourage 'a new idealism' and 'a great productive effort of the broad masses of town and country'.[13]

With their tactful approach, the KSČ were able to ensure government approval for a draft plan and parliament unanimously accepted it as law in October. It set the target of raising industrial production above the 1937 level by 10% while agriculture was aiming to reach the pre-war level.

This proved very important in ensuring that the Social Democrats remained close allies of the KSČ. They had been doubly disappointed at the time of the elections. After their low vote the Communists insisted on taking nine ministries, thereby implicitly dismissing the Social Democrats as just another defeated party. Under these circumstances criticisms of the leadership and of its policies were inevitable. Fierlinger had to acknowledge the widespread desire for a clearly separate identity from the KSČ. This, however, was a tactical point and did not mean acceptance of the National Socialists' line that the principal danger came from the KSČ. It was, however, suggested that there should be, and should have been, firmer criticisms of the Communists when they based their policies on the exploitation of positions won during the first revolutionary weeks.[14] It was noticeable over the following months that the Social Democrats blew their own trumpet more but they were unable to create a full alternative to the KSČ and their assertions of independence often appear artificial or as only minor adjustments.

The National Socialists too, despite their lasting ideological reservations about state intervention in the economy, could not oppose the plan: perhaps, as was suggested at the time, they were frightened of isolating themselves from it when it could be a success.[15] Instead, they presented a string of six 'moral' preconditions for their cooperation. The most specific of these were an 'unbiased' purge and a speedy end to the period of validity of the special laws covering it, an end to 'undemocratic' methods in the police and in the Ministry of Information and the 'democratic' representation of all parties within trade unions and economic institutions.[16] They were evidently trying to shift the centre of political discussion away from purely economic questions and to concentrate on their notion of democracy.

The issue of the purge was, in fact, pushed into the centre of the political arena on several occasions and the Communists were always critical of its conduct. In the end 132,509 people were investigated, 40,000 were not even brought to trial and only 21,340 were tried and punished. A very large number of those accused seem to have escaped punishment by one means or another.[17] Not surprisingly, the Communists' concern was shared by the organisations which represented participants in the resistance and there were even calls for a renewal of all trials that were deemed to have had an un-satisfactory outcome.[18]

The National Socialists took a very different position. They favoured a general amnesty on the grounds that the prospect of the purge was creating 'fear' in the nation: in time they linked this with claims of 'gestapism' in the police force.[19] Authentic looking documentary evidence, published very quickly after the February events, suggests that even before that Drtina was using his position as Minister of Justice to help at least a few minor collaborators who he expected to become solid National Socialists.[20]

More generally, there were immense difficulties in proving guilt as decisive evidence was often dependent on the testimonies of people who themselves could be brought to trial and were therefore of very doubtful trustworthiness. Even this, however, could not explain the outcome of the trial by the National Court of the Protectorate Ministers. It was to be the implicit test-case and example for smaller processes elsewhere, and could obviously be taken as a precedent affecting the whole further course of the purge. It lasted from April until the end of July 1946 and none of these Czechs received more than a prison sentence: one of them was found guilty but given no sentence. This caused an outcry from the KSČ and from resistance organisations but the National Socialists insisted that the sentences could not be altered. They very firmly insisted on the principle of the independence of the courts, and added that they felt the sentences were satisfactory as they amounted to a condemnation by an independent court of the whole Protectorate system.[21] This attitude drew a bitter response. Those who had fought, suffered and even died in the resistance had not felt it necessary to sit around and wait for an independent court to tell them how they should judge the Protectorate. If that was the only aim of the legal processes then they were an unnecessary charade. This only strengthened fears that something was wrong in the legal system.

Nevertheless, a viable compromise was reached in the government. It was accepted that the sentences were too mild and contravened the Košice Programme. They were not to be used as a precedent for a soft line in other trials of war criminals. This much was the Com-munists' view, but the National Socialists could feel satisfied that the result of the trial was confirmed as being final.[22]

Generally, however, attention centred on economic issues and the National Socialists had to present some sort of position. They therefore expressed general support for the plan, but paid far less attention to it than did the Communists. They also continued to plug the dangers of 'totalitarian monopolisation', stemming from the centralised organisation of nationalised industries, and presented themselves as the protectors of private enterprise: this however, always appeared as a defensive position and never led to a full-scale attack on nationalised industries. Even a cautious attempt by Zenkl to argue that nationalised industries were economically less successful than the private sector backfired.[23] It appeared that he had misinterpreted the statistics and he was forcefully condemned in specialist journals.[24] The National Socialists' main emphasis was therefore rather on maintaining the equal status within the plan between state, cooperative and private forms of ownership – as was implicitly accepted by the government programme – although it was never made clear what this could mean in practice.

The People's Party were even less able to present a clear position on the plan. They suffered from sharp internal disputes after their electoral disappointment and it seemed possible that an emergency congress might be called to defeat Šrámek's leadership. This danger was pre-empted and the National Front policy definitely reaffirmed after the expulsion of Koželuhová.[25] They were, however, reserved in their support for the idea of the plan and generally preferred to avoid comment on economic questions which were not directly related to agriculture.

2 THE CZECHOSLOVAK ROAD TO SOCIALISM

Although the KSČ's electoral success presumably further strengthened the leadership's dominance within the party, it also posed a new question of how that electoral success was to be used. One possibility would have been to aim as quickly as possible for the 'dictatorship of the proletariat'. Gottwald, as has been argued, had no such intention and preferred instead to continue with the national front strategy that had already brought the party such success. This, however, made clarification of the theoretical basis of KSČ policy all the more pressing both because of the distrust within the other parties and because of the need for genuine conviction from Communists if it was to be successful.

Although a formally independent party, the KSČ was still unable to make major theoretical innovations without approval, or even an initial suggestion, from Stalin. It was therefore crucially important for the KSČ when, in a discussion with British Labour Party leaders, Stalin suggested that there were two roads to socialism – the Russian and the British. The former was apparently shorter but involved bloodshed and should not be regarded as the only possibility. These ideas were repeated to Gottwald when he visited Moscow after his appointment as Prime Minister and their clarification and application to the Czechoslovak situation was the special task for a Central Committee meeting in September 1946.

Gottwald pointed cautiously to the possibility, but only the possibility, of another 'road to socialism' apart from that via 'the dictatorship of the proletariat and soviets'. He pointed out that the road would be 'longer, more complicated and sometimes more roundabout too. But the basic changes in the economic and social structure of the new Czechoslovakia give us faith and self-confidence that we will get there.' He went beyond Stalin's formulation when he suggested that Czechoslovakia had already traversed 'a little bit' of the road,[26] later expanding it to a' pretty large bit',[27] but he did not fully elaborate on what possibilities this presented for the future.

He did, however, firmly link the notion of a Czechoslovak road to socialism with the Two Year Plan which, he argued, could serve as a practical demonstration of the superiority of planning, and hence of socialism. He hoped that it could succeed in raising production and then in translating that into a better life for the people.[28] It would then serve both as a start to planning, providing valuable basic experience for fully socialist planning, and as part of a political contest between different conceptions of economic activity. Calling on the whole party to work for its success Gottwald maintained that after its fulfilment 'we will be able to say that we are over the hill and that it will go more quickly to socialism'.[29]

As the Czechoslovak road to socialism was so closely linked to economic policy, it is not surprising that its social and economic implications were given further elaboration. There was, however, a continuing weakness in that the relationship between democracy, in the sense of the methods of exercising political power, and the road to socialism was hardly elaborated at all.

Only Bareš, responding directly to Peroutka, discussed the issue. He insisted that the Communists' loyalty to democracy was 'not accidental, nor tactical, nor temporary'.[30] Instead, he claimed, Czechoslovakia's road to socialism was based on the country's traditions and therefore involved taking 'everything positive from Masaryk's democracy' and giving its 'democratic forms . . . a far more real content'.[31] This was all extremely vague, and references to democracy were far more cautious than, for example, among French Communists.[32] Perhaps the Czechoslovak Communists, with their hold on certain key organs of power, did not feel the need to consider such issues. Their attitude towards the democratic control of the police force certainly suggests that, although their conception of a road to socialism involved broad participation in the execution of economic policies, it was not to be based on a general expansion of public control in all spheres.

Moreover, further development of ideas for a democratic road to socialism were hampered by bitterness between parties. This continued throughout the autumn of 1946 and Communists in roughly half the Districts felt that there were clear signs of the other parties forming a bloc against them.[33] Even if this was an exaggeration, the general atmosphere encouraged scepticism among Communists about the feasibility of lasting cooperation. The extent of this was revealed when the leadership opened an internal discussion on the idea of a Czechoslovak road to socialism: their objective was to win genuine conviction for Gottwald's line and thereby ensure that the party could behave as a single, united, constructive force within society. Above all, they hoped to encourage real commitment to the Two Year Plan.[34] Inevitably, such a discussion gave the ordinary members a chance to express their doubts and uncertainties and this was probably the principal pressure on the leadership for a further clarification of policy.

There evidently were some strong doubts which could be linked with ideas derived from the Comintern. There were also those much vaguer and more widespread doubts that indicated a degree of distrust towards other parties and a desire to make clear the separate identity of the KSČ.[35] Such views were generally not expressed in a strongly critical way and amounted to calls for a clarification of the party's line. The leadership, however, could not dismiss these worries as, in Gottwald's words: 'almost at every meeting of our party's Presidium, we raise again the question of whether the road we have taken is leading us to our aim and of whether we have not deviated from the correct road'.[36] Given such doubts, Gottwald was likely to take seriously reservations expressed more widely within the party and he therefore accepted the need for a further clarification of party policy. This was the task he set himself at the Central Committee meeting in January 1947.

During the course of the discussion, it seemed that there were two attitudes within the party leadership. Gottwald maintained that, on the whole, things were going well. He pointed to difficulties that stemmed from political differences within the coalition, but he did not suggest that all cooperation was impossible or blame 'reaction' for all the difficulties. Neither did he suggest that a bloc had been created against the KSČ and he still thought that problems could be overcome by mobilising 'the broad public'.[37] 'Reaction', he claimed, was fighting a rearguard action and should not be overestimated, even though it still stood some chance of reversing the post-war changes. He felt that some contributors to the discussion were beginning to panic and could foresee only a repeat of the events of 1920. This he effectively ruled out.

The alternative position was put by Ďuriš, who believed that 'reaction' was consciously trying to prevent consolidation and that this was the *main* problem. Moreover, he felt that this was what lay behind the economic policies of the other parties and he accused them of opposition to reconstruction.[38] In the following weeks it was suggested that 'reaction' believed that the worse the economic situation the better their potential chances.[39]

The difference between these two approaches did not lead to open conflict at the time. Instead, Gottwald clarified his conception of the Czechoslovak road to socialism in such a way as to allow for a sharpening of the fight against other parties, while also not rejecting further cooperation with them for the time being. He proclaimed the aim of winning an absolute majority in the next parliamentary elections. This then stood alongside the Two Year Plan as the centre of the party's strategy. It was made clear that this was not the same as the infamous 50% that the 'Austro-Marxists' had longed for but never achieved. They, so Gottwald argued, had sat back and waited for it while the KSČ saw the majority as attainable only by 'an active struggle against reaction'.[40]

At first glance Gottwald's new policy looks ingeniously ambiguous. There was still no explicit or even implicit criticism of the heritage of the Comintern, but neither was there any need to alienate coalition partners with talk of abandoning the existing democratic political framework. All those party members who wanted a sharper fight against the other parties and also those who still hoped for close national unity seemed to be accommodated within one policy. Gottwald could therefore believe that the party would remain firmly united as it sought to broaden and increase its influence.

The problems arose from the responses of other parties, which highlighted the contradiction between the aim of electorally defeating all rivals and the aim of establishing close cooperation between parties. As Peroutka pointed out, a target of 51% 'cannot be . . . a common aim of the National Front and will therefore inevitably bring division and unrest into our life'.[41] Beneš made a practically unique intervention into disputes between parties with a condemnation of the aim of 51% in a pre-recorded radio broadcast. Apparently that part of his speech was not broadcast.[42] Even Fierlinger was definitely unhappy at aspects of Communist policy related to the aim of 51%, and the National Socialists soon equated it with 'totalitarianism'. Although Gottwald answered this by insisting that he had no intention of excluding the other parties from power,[43] he exacerbated their fears when he clearly predicted that development would lead to 'the creation of one party of the working people'. He added that no further revolution would be necessary and that development itself would 'determine the concrete form of this process which at the moment is difficult to foresee'.[44] This was met with expressions of the utmost disquiet from the National Socialists who insisted that Gottwald was openly advocating totalitarianism.

There is, of course, no reason to suppose that he saw from January 1947 onwards a Communist electoral victory leading immediately to a forced merger of parties. He probably simply did not know what the future would bring in terms of cooperation between parties. Nevertheless, in practical terms, winning an absolute majority would have made it possible for the Communists to deal with other parties in any way they wanted.

In social and economic policies, however, the KSČ went slightly further in developing the conceptual basis for a model of socialism quite distinct from that in the USSR. Apart from those policies that were intended to benefit all working people, there was specific consideration for the differing social groups to correspond with their differing interests. Alongside proposals for agricultural policy discussed later in this chapter, peasants were assured that they would be given more security on their land than had been possible under capitalism,[45] and there were plenty of vague reaffirmations that collectivisation was not intended.[46] It was also maintained that socialism was ultimately the only guarantee of security for the urban petty bourgeoisie. But for the nationalisations, so it was argued, big capital would gradually swallow them up.[47] Moreover, even if Communist economic policy did require some restrictions on the creation of new private businesses particularly because of the general labour shortage, it was clearly stated that their property was 'inviolable'.[48]

In interpreting KSČ policy in this period it is very easy to get lost in a search for clear cut and definite ideas or aims. Very frequently Communist leaders honestly admitted that they were treading a new road and confronting problems as they arose rather than trying to follow any particular example.[49] The few attempts at more abstract, theoretical articles reflected this. No convincing analogy could be found with Lenin's notion of 'state capitalism' or with the New Economic Policy (NEP) in the USSR in the 1920s when a large private sector had been tolerated: Czechoslovakia seemed to be far further advanced towards socialism.[50] This obviously ruled out any thought of an anology between 1945 and the revolution of February 1917.

Related to the flexibility of their policy and their uncertainty as to where it would lead them, was the narrowness of their time horizon. Nothing definite was considered beyond the Two Year Plan. There was therefore no renunciation, or even questioning of earlier ideas about socialism. This could lend support to the view that the conception of the Czechoslovak road to socialism was new only in the means whereby the long-standing aim of a monopoly of power was to be achieved.[51]

This probably overstates the case. Gottwald's comments, quoted above, certainly suggest that he could not conceive of a model of socialism with a genuine plurality of parties, but they also indicate just how vague his ideas were. The aim of winning a majority in the next elections was not at that time seen as an absolute necessity. Moreover, the nature of the KSČ's role in society meant that their practice was becoming very broad and flexible. It was much more than just a strategy for winning power. So, although no new aim had been formulated there were two clear developments that could create scope for the gradual evolution of new aims provided Czechoslovakia's internal political life was not disrupted by sharp conflicts. These were the clear renunciation of the notion that there could be no progress towards socialism without taking full and exclusive power, and the recognition that the road to socialism, at least from then on, could be slow and gradual.

3 THE TWO YEAR PLAN AND THE WORKING CLASS

The purpose of this section is to investigate the social implications of KSČ and government economic policies. Two questions are interwoven here. The first is the emerging model of economic management and the position of the KSČ within that. The second concerns the economic and social conflicts involving the working class that could be discerned during 1947 and which could contribute to the sharpening political struggle culminating in the events of February 1948.

Although the plan was intended to provide a perspective for the advancement of all economic sectors in cooperation with each other, it was in large-scale industry that the plan's operation was to be directed in the most detail. So industrial workers, often firm supporters or even members of the KSČ, were given a particularly important role. Trade union leaders made no attempt to hide the fact that workers would be asked to make sacrifices and that it would not be easy to convince them that they should forgo their own possible sectional advancement in favour of the state's economic and social policies.[52] Nevertheless, ÚRO accepted the challenge: to encourage workers generally to regard the plan as being in their own best interests, they presented a list of demands for the whole working class as part of their resolution supporting the idea of the plan.

Most prominent was a social insurance scheme which would give all employees the security enjoyed by civil servants. Further demands included a 48 hour and six day working week, a 'just' wages system with more piece rates, the incorporation of confiscates into nationalised industries and price reductions allowing for a rise in real wages. There was also an expression of opposition to excessive pay for managers in nationalised industries.[53] This was not identical to the KSČ economic programme and suggests that Communist trade unionists saw the need to accept some additional demands so as to ensure the loyalty of trade unionists.

Despite the importance of ensuring political loyalty, it alone could not be a complete solution to the serious labour problems following the expulsion of Germans. Despite an enormous increase in the employment of Czechs and Slovaks and an apparent improvement in labour morale,[54] there was still an acute shortage of labour in agriculture, mining and construction. The use of voluntary brigades in mining and agriculture therefore became more systematic and the People's Party in particular favoured importing labour from Italy, Bulgaria and Rumania to replace the Germans in agriculture. In fact, remarkably little was achieved apart from the forceful transportation of 11,642 Hungarian families from Slovakia to the Czech frontier.[55]

The problem could then only be solved by an increase in productivity. There was no immediate prospect of this in agriculture and the problem was accentuated by disappointments throughout industry as shown in Table 7.

Table 7 *Industrial production and productivity in 1947 compared with 1937 in selected industries (percentages of 1937 level)* [56]

Industry	Production	Employment	Productivity
All	87.0	98.0	88.8
Mining	104.3	139.6	74.7
Metal work	96.6	107.8	89.6
Textiles	59.6	74.5	80.0
Food	65.2	108.9	59.9

Although some of these disappointments resulted from the expulsion of Germans – about half the textile workers had been German in 1945 – there was evidently a really widespread problem of low productivity. This highlighted to the KSČ the importance of ensuring the political loyalty of the working class if its economic, and hence political, strategy was to have any chance of success. It also underlined the need for moral and material incentives that could raise productivity.

The KSČ therefore attached great importance to the Factory Councils as a means to win workers' commitment to the Two Year Plan. It was assumed by the ÚRO that elections delayed earlier in 1946 because of the parliamentary elections could be held quickly and followed by an all-state congress of Factory Councils: this was to be a demonstration of the unity of the working people around the Two Year Plan.[57] This, however, was further delayed by disagreements over the election system. The National Socialists wanted proportional representation for political parties while the Communists and ÚRO insisted that there should be no reference to party affiliations: beyond that they were willing to be flexible on the exact method of voting.

The outcome was a strange system, agreed to on 31 October 1946, whereby trade union groups were to propose a single list of candidates. This then had to be voted on as a single bloc and needed an 80% vote for its approval. If this target was not reached, then the list could be changed and needed only a two thirds vote for approval: after that ÚRO could appoint a substitute Factory Council (Náhradní orgán). The National Socialists had wanted unending repeat elections until a proposed list could finally win 80%.[58]

The point about this election system was that 20% opposing an official list could almost always be found where different political parties were organised, so that the election would then inevitably be fought on party-political terms. The National Socialists, and sometimes the Social Democrats too, therefore gave maximum publicity to the Factory Council elections, presenting the previous bodies and proposed lists as being totally Communist dominated. They made no attempt to raise wider issues like the actual role of Factory Councils.

At first trade union groups seem to have been over-confident[59] and in fact the overwhelming majority of work-places did elect their Factory Councils on the first round with some quite staggeringly good results. Soon, though, it was being pointed out that the recommended lists were being rejected in the biggest and economically decisive factories and mines in the main industrial centres. Of fifteen factories with over 3000 employees, the Factory Council was elected on the first round in only one – ČKD–Libeň.[60] This was particularly remarkable when compared with claims that 40% of employees in big factories in Prague were Communist Party members.[61]

These election results may to a certain extent have reflected worker's reservations about economic policies and social conditions. The key point, however, was that the elections were turned into a struggle between parties, or more precisely into a referendum for or against the KSČ, whose members generally did predominate in the proposed lists. Under these circumstances many employees with doubts about the Communists would naturally feel it best to take the safe course of voting against or abstaining.

The election results certainly indicated that the Communists did not enjoy complete and unquestioning authority within the working class, but the other parties had not gained much either. They had fought simply on whether the KSČ was not taking *too much* power and not on concrete policies of their own. Presumably their hope was to reach a deadlock forcing elections on their own terms, but in this they failed.

Nevertheless, the authority of the Factory Councils must have been dented and this probably made it harder for the Communists to win conviction for voluntary efforts to raise productivity, such as the Stakhanovite movement, and for the readjustment of the wage structure which generally coincided with the widespread introduction of piece rates. There were even several strikes in big engineering factories against the changes. The most important was in Tatra-Kopřivnice, and it seemed that the intensity of the discontent could be blamed not on the changes, nor on the management acting high-handedly but rather on the failure of the Factory Council to explain either these and other changes to the work-force or the workers' feelings to the management. The dispute was settled after a new Factory Council had been appointed and it negotiated the same agreement.[62]

An even bigger problem in ensuring firm loyalty from workers was their dissatisfaction over living standards and the KSČ was fully aware of this. There could be an identifiable enemy in the black marketeering small traders and in the businesses making profits down the distribution chain and the KSČ had no hesitation in pointing an accusatory finger at private enterprise. The issue of workers' living standards then became interwoven with the contentious issue of relations between the public and private sectors.

Black market prices fell gradually during 1946 relative to official prices until, in March 1947, they were less than double the latter. From then on they rose steadily to reach five times the official level in September 1948.[63] Nevertheless, it was in late 1946 that the Communists and Social Democrats began pressing for very much stronger laws against black marketeering with the death sentence as the maximum penalty.[64] They also advocated a tightening of the organisation of distribution to prevent 'leakages' of goods onto the black market. Textiles were in particularly short supply and a proposal was presented for the incorporation of confiscates in that sector into nationalised enterprises and for a drastic reduction in the number of wholesalers which had roughly doubled since 1937 even though production had declined.[65]

Although there was no agreement between parties on this issue, the fact of economic recovery meant that somebody's living standards could rise. To ensure that the benefits would not go to private traders, as many workers undoubtedly feared was happening, pressure built up for immediate implementation of the Communist promise of price reductions. Early in 1947 the trade unions, Social Democrats and Communists began systematically pointing to the possibility of achieving this at the expense of profits in the distribution system. It was, however, only after workers had defied their official leadership and staged protest strikes in several large engineering factories in Prague that, on 21 March 1947,[66] the government announced a range of price reductions. The KSČ claimed full credit for this and wanted their achievement widely publicised in 'a great agitational drive'[67] claiming, and subsequent statistics confirmed this, that there would be a 10% rise in living standards.[68] By contrast, prominent National Socialists opposed price reductions[69] and complained afterwards that they had been agreed too quickly,[70] although they had responded to the strikes by demagogically demanding really big price reductions.[71]

During this same period the parties clashed more seriously over the issue of the fate of the confiscates. There were three reasons for this becoming a major source of controversy; first, the plan seemed to be threatened by unimpressive results in construction and distribution which were almost entirely in private hands; secondly, the idea of nationalisations in general was still very popular and, thirdly, feelings were raised by attempts to transfer some confiscates back to private ownership.

Three sorts of enterprise were concerned. They were those previously German owned but too small to qualify for nationalisation, those previously belonging to collaborators and those confiscated because of the 'anti-social' behaviour of the former owner towards his employees. The real problems arose with sizeable factories (smaller enterprises, it was agreed, would be given to new private owners) which had been confiscated because their previous owners were accused of collaborating with the occupiers. Legal proceedings were often dropped or the accused found not guilty. This led to test cases of particular factories where the former owners claimed their property back and the workers responded with protest strikes.

Their case was always backed by ÚRO which had a standing policy of demanding incorporation of 'important' confiscates into nationalised industries.

The issue came to a head in the small frontier town of Varnsdorf. A textile factory there, which had been confiscated in May 1945, was to be handed back to its pre-war Jewish owner following a court decision: this was opposed by the Communist dominated District National Committee which supported the workers' view that he had been an anti-social employer. The conflict led to a strike in the area which apparently started spontaneously but was then supported by the trade unions and the KSČ. All the other parties dissociated themselves from it,[72] but other strikes and demonstrations around this period confirmed the strength of working class feelings on the issue. At a meeting of the National Front on 15–18 March 1947, the right-wing parties therefore conceded a lot to the demands of the Varnsdorf strikers. They accepted that confiscates could be incorporated into nationalised industries if it generally helped production, but that they could not be returned to private ownership by courts. Instead approval had to be gained from the government in consultation with trade union representatives.[73] This success seemed to confirm Gottwald's belief that the National Front framework did not seriously restrict the KSČ in pursuing their immediate aims. By mobilising public opinion and explaining policies in public, it was possible to convince others of their correctness.[74] To those who saw the machinations of 'reaction' behind every difficulty he could therefore insist that conditions in the National Front had actually improved and this strengthened his conviction that the road chosen was the correct one.[75]

Although no disagreements relating to labour problems were serious enough to contradict this view, there were considerably sharper conflicts over the related issue of pay and differentials for civil servants. These included all those, both manual and non-manual, working in state enterprises – railways, posts, airlines – those in public services such as education and the police and those in central offices and ministries. In all there were almost 899,000 people and they enjoyed special privileges in pension rights and job security.[76]

There was an almost universal belief that, following the relaxation of war-time controls on the labour market, there had been an economically damaging flight from heavier manual labour into more agreeable office jobs, especially civil service ones. There were, however, serious manpower shortages even in some sections of public administration[77] and one astute observer suggested that the growth in the numbers of office workers might be an inevitable part of the wider changes in the Czech economy, especially the centralised controls over the economy.[78] This view was supported in slightly modified form by a later study which provided very strong evidence that it went with the administration, control and planning of the economy, with the controlled organisation of labour, the expansion of the rationing system and other activities demanding comparatively unspecialised administrative personnel.[79]

Nevertheless, there was widespread agreement at the time that higher production could be achieved by transferring people back into directly productive activities. In fact the National Socialists were particularly keen to propagate the view that the administrative apparatus was overgrown,[80] although this might seem a disadvantageous argument as they were building support among workers in administration. For the Communists it was even easier to refer to the need to raise the status of manual as compared with mental labour and they saw in this a possible means to reverse the 'exodus' from manual work.[81]

It was therefore suggested that the civil servants' repeated requests for more pay could be met only after their numbers had been reduced by 100,000.[82] The argument then centred on how to achieve this, a point on which the government programme had said nothing. There was no problem in agreeing to encourage voluntary resignations, to attempt to halt further recruitment and to encourage older employees to retire early. The real problem arose when all these had failed and involuntary methods had to be found. Gottwald insisted that those sacked should not be those recruited since liberation but rather those whom the occupiers had trusted.[83] He thereby linked the proposal for a reduction in numbers with a thorough purge of the civil service. The National Socialists reacted strongly against this suggestion which they feared would lead to a repeat in public administration of what Factory Councils had achieved in industry.[84]

Naturally, this would have been feared by many senior civil servants, but the extent of the differences between the parties was still further accentuated as the National Socialists tried to secure their support among civil servants. In particular, they ruthlessly distorted a statement by Zápotocký at a conference of civil service unions where he advocated changes in their contract of employment. He argued that even the privileges it gave would soon be made irrelevant by the introduction of similar job security for all employees.[85] This was misquoted as indicating a desire to annul civil servants' job security.[86]

The National Socialists, portraying the plight of the civil servants as being particularly desperate,[87] even gave implicit support to one of the civil service unions which demanded a 30% pay rise, apparently to counter the effects of the wage and price revisions of 1945, and a full review of their pay in January 1948: these demands were backed with a threat of strike action.[88] The ÚRO Presidium was obviously embarrassed. They did not deny the civil servants' right to strike but still refused to support them.[89] They had been fully aware from the time of liberation onwards that the issue of civil servants' standing was a major threat to trade union unity.[90]

4 AGRICULTURAL POLICY AND LAND REFORM

The Communists' approach to workers and even to civil servants was closely related to their respective positions within the Two Year Plan. There was, however, no simple analogy for peasant policy, as the plan could offer little immediate benefit to agriculture and made no difference to the actual outputs achieved. If anything, peasants could feel themselves threatened as ambitious industrial projects accentuated their labour shortage. At the same time, the Czech peasants still seemed undecided in their political allegiances and there was no reason to suppose that they would again vote as they had in 1946.

So, particularly as the KSČ was turning its attention to ways of increasing its electoral support, a special approach was sought for the countryside. Although this was based within the general ideas of the specific Czechoslovak road to socialism, it was in the presentation of the policy for a new land reform that the KSČ deviated most markedly from the tactful approach with which they initiated the Two Year Plan.

For a time they even contemplated dropping any idea of a further land reform so as to minimise divisions and make easier the participation of the other parties in the Two Year Plan.[91] Then, following preparatory work within the Ministry of Agriculture, six draft laws were published. The most important of these were revision of the first, post World War I, land reform and a law enabling the consolidation of holdings to replace the existing scattered strips of land. Controversy quickly erupted after Ďuriš, in October 1946, bypassed the National Front and the government and sent his proposals first of all to JSČZ branches. The reason for this was the expectation of opposition from the right-wing parties which could only be overcome by mobilising peasant opinion. KSČ organisations were therefore asked to encourage discussions of the proposals:[92] other parties then had to present their positions in response to Ďuriš's six draft laws.

The People's Party, often with nothing much to say on other issues, left little doubt of its support for the biggest farmers and its opposition to a further land reform, but the National Socialists were more cautious. They opposed Ďuriš's proposals at first, but soon found it impossible to attack them openly.[93] Their problem was summarised by the former Agrarian Torn who 'was neither against them nor for them. He was not against because it is impossible to go against the tide.'[94] Increasingly they joined the People's Party in warning that land reform was just a step towards kolkhozes.[95]

The Social Democrats were naturally more approving towards Ďuriš's proposals, and their principal reservation was at Ďuriš's method of initiating the discussion. Fierlinger argued that, in bypassing the National Front structure, the KSČ was using its control over the Ministry of Agriculture to push through its proposals without any regard for the other parties. By going *at once* to the public, the discussion *had* to take the form of one proposal against all the other parties who had not even had a chance to state their positions.[96]

The other two Czech parties soon made this the central issue so that the actual content of the proposed laws could be pushed into the background. Then even the People's Party could suggest that the laws as such were not controversial but that presenting them for discussion in villages was an 'undemocratic and terrorist method',[97] and a majority in the Agricultural Committee of parliament condemned the minister. There was even an unconvincing attempt to argue that he had acted unconstitutionally although, as he made absolutely clear, the ultimate decision was to be taken by parliament.[98]

The course of the discussions in the villages on Ďuriš's draft laws quickly made it clear that outright opposition would have been politically suicidal. Over one third of Czech villages, many of which had voted overwhelmingly for the National Socialist or People's Parties, sent in resolutions supporting the proposals while only 2% definitely opposed them.[99] Ďuriš, however, was still convinced that 'reaction' was pinning its main hopes on agriculture as he believed that attempts to persuade peasants to refuse to fulfil quota obligations were finding a response.[100]

So, at the same time as the KSČ was adopting the aim of winning 51% in the next elections, Ďuriš proposed a broadening and sharpening of the six laws.[101] He still made no attempt to work out a long-term policy for Czech agriculture, but placed new emphasis on egalitarian land reform. At a JSČZ meeting in April 1947 in Hradec Králové, attended by 4000 peasants, Ďuriš added the aim of buying up and allocating to poorer peasants all land held by any one family in excess of 50 ha. Holdings up to that size were then to be constitutionally guaranteed,[102] so that this implied a definitive solution to the question of private property, thereby answering the incessant rumours about kolkhozes.

Although Ďuriš argued that the enemy was 'reaction', this policy was evidently intended as part of a sharp fight against other Czech political parties. He hoped for a political mobilisation of peasants around deputations to parliament in Prague. He even worked out the timing of the campaign such that a militant peasant congress could be held in Prague prior to the elections. The peasants could then call a demonstration to parliament, possibly with working class support, and refuse to disperse until their demands were met. This would thereby decide 'the defeat of reaction and . . . the elections even before the elections'.[103] He seemed already to be equating his political opponents with reaction and to assume that they would stubbornly refuse to allow the passing of his proposed laws.

Ďuriš's proposal for a further land reform became the central part of his so-called Hradec Programme. Its announcement was followed by tense debates in parliamentary committees and then in parliament itself over his original six laws. The People's Party and the Slovak Democrats, in particular, filibustered with masses of counter-proposals but never expressed outright opposition. Nevertheless, as Ďuriš's proposals had been well received in villages, it was not difficult to organise deputations of peasants, who came throughout June and July to lobby their MPs and to follow the debates. Naturally, the People's Party regarded this as a 'terrorist' measure, but were embarrassed to discover that some deputations were even formed on a parity basis.[104] This pressure forced the People's Party to clarify their own agricultural policy. At a rally on 13 July 1947 on Kunětická hora near Pardubice they presented a set of general peasant demands. The only reference to land reform was a strong insistence on private property without any constitutional stipulation of a ceiling for the size of holdings,[105] which they argued would be a step towards the abolition of all private property leading to 'the slavery of the kolkhoz'.[106] It certainly was true that the KSČ never renounced their belief that large-scale farms are the most efficient, but the Hradec Programme was in no sense a preparation for that. They seem not to have considered at all how such a transformation of agriculture could be achieved. Instead, their ideas reflected a subordination of systematic, long-term thoughts to the immediate needs of the struggle against other parties.

The Social Democrats, by contrast, broadly supported the Hradec Programme. They differed from the KSČ by seeing the need to settle for good the question of kolkhozes with a clear *long-term* programme for the following twenty years.[107] They seemed no longer to believe that large-scale farming was necessarily more efficient and articles in their journals indicated a desire for holdings to fall within a 4–50 ha range of sizes.

The National Socialists did not present a clear policy of their own. They were still interested in incorporating prominent former Agrarians and it was the latter who became the centre of a major controversy in mid 1947. The issue was an attempt to reactivate the 'Selská jízda' which was an organisation for equestrian sport with a military style structure and apparently a past record as one of the most aggressively partisan of all pre-war Agrarian organisations.[108] It had, it was claimed, continued an illegal existence, and chose to renew its activities in July 1947 in the village of Nechanice near Hradec Králové. This, given the choice of venue, the political situation and the political pasts of the rich farmers supporting it, was obviously intended to be a political demonstration of strength.[109] The Ministry of the Interior decided that the event was illegal as it was organised by an illegal body. In this they overruled the District National Committee and enforced their decision with a massive police presence. Even Fierlinger was disturbed by this. Although no actual clashes took place it was described as 'the first armed offensive by the security organs against the peasantry'.[110] By contrast, the Communists described the incident as an 'Agrofascist' provocation and would accept no criticisms of the police.[111] Even though agricultural policy was the subject of such tension and controversy, agreement on many points was possible and the Communists were able to push some of Ďuriš's draft laws through parliament. It therefore caused surprise when Ďuriš suddenly accused his political opponents of trying to defend the interests of large landowners.[112] The implication was that he resented any compromise at all.

Moreover, the KSČ clearly demonstrated their belligerence when, following a compromise on the organisational principles of JSČZ in the autumn of 1947, they placed great emphasis on reviving and expanding Peasant Commissions. These were bodies which had been formed out of those entitled to benefit from the 1945 land reform with the task of allocating confiscated land. Soon they were appearing again in many villages and creating structures covering whole districts.[113]

5 SLOVAKIA

The political atmosphere became even more tense in Slovakia where the Communists were deeply worried by the election results, which they interpreted as indicating the successful re-emergence of the same bloc as had been behind the Žilina Agreement. Their fears were strengthened when an investigating team, sent by the Ministry of the Interior, revealed that the election campaign had been marred by the exploitation of religion, the active involvement of priests and the glorification of the Slovak state and its leaders. There were even Democratic Party parliamentary candidates who had previously been photographed in SS uniform and some MPs were still awaiting trial before People's Courts.[114]

This, of course, was an expression of only one of the trends within the Democratic Party, but within the KSS there were already strong doubts about continuing with the National Front strategy. Gottwald and Široký, however, were quick to point to the weaknesses in alternatives. Administratively dissolving the Democratic Party, they argued, would have amounted to dissolving the newly elected parliament in which the KSČ was the dominant force. Dissolving the Democratic Party while leaving its parliamentary representation was also felt to be wrong because it could only have led to disorder in Slovakia with blame ultimately going to the Gottwald government. Even keeping the Democrats out of the government would have been very dangerous as they could then behave as a purely opposition party: the resulting heightened tension could even have resulted in civil war. Under certain circumstances that might invite intervention from the West.[115]

These possibilities were felt to be dangerous and also unnecessary as they overlooked the dominant fact of the election results: that was the KSČ victory. Moreover, although the April Agreement had helped the Democrats to 60% of the votes, it also increased the potential for conflicts within their party.[116] There was therefore no point in flatly refusing to form a government with the Democratic Party as that would help unite the party rather than encourage divisions within its ranks.[117]

The ideal strategy, therefore, was to expose and intensify this potential division and Gottwald believed that that could best be done by placing certain conditions before the Democrats could join the government. In particular, he demanded a clear statement from them on their attitude towards Tiso and also an acceptance of the definite subordination of the SNR to the Prague government.[118] It would then be possible to accept a reorganisation of the SNR in line with the election results.

Such tough conditions could be imposed because of the continuing 'Czechoslovakism' of the National Socialists who shared many of the Communists' fears. Moreover, the differences within the Democratic Party did limit its ability to resist. This became apparent when HSL'S supporters, openly interpreting the election results as their own victory, staged public demonstrations in Bratislava. The Slovak trade union leadership called a counter-demonstration and then print workers bluntly refused to print the Democratic Party's daily *Čas* until the party's leaders made clear their approval for the uprising and the Košice Programme and publicly dissociated themselves from the pro-fascist demonstrations.[119]

Following this the Slovak situation was discussed at a National Front meeting on 12 June 1946 and the outcome was the 'Third Prague Agreement' of 28 June 1946. The SNR accepted that its legislative powers and the appointment of Commissioners were subject to the approval of the government,[120] and agreement was then reached on a new Board of Commissioners containing representatives of the two biggest Slovak parties in proportion to their electoral performances. The Democrats took the key posts of Agriculture and Information. The KSS even had to concede control over the Interior to the non-party soldier Lt. Col. Ferjenčík. Husák, however, took the important position of chairman.

Some Slovak Communists saw the Third Prague Agreement as a regrettable necessity which they hoped would not be permanent. Nevertheless, in practical terms, the only way they could overcome their electoral setback was to pursue those policies that would be given backing from the majority of Czech parties. They therefore could not advocate general land reform, although some prominent Slovak Communists did want to raise the issue again. Instead, they placed great emphasis on the benefits from the proposals in the Two Year Plan for a start to Slovak industrialisation. They were well placed for this as they controlled industrial affairs and were dominant within the managements of nationalised industries.[121] Moreover, although the objective of raising Slovakia to the economic level of the Czech lands could certainly not be achieved within two years, the Communists did believe that a firm rejection of economic separatism could quickly bear fruit. Above all, they saw the possibility of transferring industrial equipment from the depopulated Czech frontiers – where the shortage of labour had led to factory closures – into backward parts of Slovakia. Laušman discussed the idea in Bratislava in June 1945 but no real initiatives were taken until after the 1946 elections when, jointly with Široký, he proposed a plan to relocate existing industry to bring 24,000 jobs to Slovakia. They hoped all this would be completed by March 1947.[122]

Unfortunately, there were continual delays because of political opposition, especially from the right. Even in 1947 all four parties in Cheb and their representatives in the District National Committee opposed the removal of industrial equipment which, they claimed, was important to the local economy. There was even a brief protest strike which the trade union leadership vigorously condemned.[123]

These delays enabled the Democrats to gain political capital by portraying the operation as a failure. They pointed to its slow progress, to the obsoleteness of the equipment and to the minimal impact in Eastern Slovakia.[124] The KSS tried to make capital out of what was being achieved claiming, in the summer of 1947, that 188 factories had already been shifted and provided employment for 12,000 workers: more were coming to provide another 14,000 jobs.[125] There is no doubt that the policy could have been very popular as there were appeals from all sides for factories,[126] but it was still only a drop in the ocean and of itself could not significantly change the complexion of Slovak society.

This made the Democrats' task much easier. The ideas and policies they evolved were far less specific than those of the KSS but, by presenting themselves as the only genuinely Slovak party and as the representative of all the peasants, they were able to hold together the diverse interests that they represented. As long as the central government did not bring major social advances to Slovaks through industrialisation or a general land reform, their consistent opposition to the 'centralism' of the Third Prague Agreement could probably assure them of continued strength. In fact, this was the basis of their economic thinking too as they made great play of advocating 'decentralism' as opposed to 'centralism'. Beyond that their social and economic policy often appeared to be essentially a peasant policy centring, according to Kvetko, on the defence 'of the private property of all farmers irrespective of the area of land'.[127] In practical terms, this meant opposition to further land reform and defence of larger farms, which were said to be more productive.[128] To the mass of peasants, then, their appeal hinged on fears of collectivisation and on those issues, such as the price scissors, that could unite all those working on the land. Their position there was hardly threatened at all by the KSS, at least until mid 1947. Only then, following the announcement of the Hradec Programme, could the issue of further land reform finally be raised.

The Democrats even saw a chance to expand their influence among the working class as they knew that many workers had voted for them. There were also signs of demoralisation in the trade unions as membership slumped by 65% between April 1946 and the end of the year.[129] The Democrats responded to this situation with violent attacks on the trade unions and Lettrich even seriously threatened that, if the unions were not 'depoliticised', the Democrats would establish their own trade union organisation.[130] The real test of strength was the Factory Council elections. The Democrats could point with satisfaction to a considerable number of abstentions,[131] but they could not oust the KSS from its leading position.

Nevertheless, the KSS could not fail to recognise the precariousness of their position in Slovakia. They therefore decided to change their approach and to concentrate on a political offensive against the Democratic Party. The central issue in this, by early 1947, was the trial of Tiso, which was to be given maximum publicity so as to 'influence public opinion'.[132] It was a natural issue for the KSS to choose as the centre of their campaign as, apart from the possible danger former fascists could represent to Czechoslovakia, there was every chance of the National Socialists supporting tough measures. Moreover, it was the most natural way to strike at the fundamental weakness of the April Agreement which had brought together elements who fought on opposing sides during the war.

The public trial of Tiso, Ďurčanský, who had emigrated, and Mach lasted from 2 December 1946 to 19 March 1947 and ended with Tiso and Ďurčanský sentenced to death while Mach received thirty years imprisonment. The accusations included their roles in the Munich crisis, their general help for the German war effort, their role in inviting foreign troops against the uprising and crimes against humanity including their policy towards Jews.[133] The strongest defence argument was that the leaders of the Slovak state had done the best they could and chosen the 'lesser evil': they could also derive support for milder sentences from the verdicts against the Protectorate Ministers in Prague.[134]

The trial was accompanied by considerable activity from the HSL'S underground, including leaflets calling for an uprising to save Tiso. Controversy was heightened when Archbishop Kmet'ko was called as a witness in early January. He insisted that Tiso, who was a priest, was not a 'sinner' and even described him as 'the second Slovak leader' after the legendary figure Svatopluk.[135]

Following the sentence a plea for clemency was sent to Beneš. He referred the issue to the government where the Communists, Social Democrats, National Socialists, Svoboda and Masaryk were all strongly for implementing the death sentence.[136] It was carried out on 18 April 1947 and its announcement in Slovakia was met with no visible unrest.

This inevitably created acute difficulties for the Democratic Party's leadership as one more of the promises of the April Agreement had not been fulfilled. There was from then on a greater emphasis among HSL'S elements on underground work and considerable disillusionment with the legal party framework.

Nevertheless, the Democrats did not split or change their publicly stated policy. Instead they pushed a decree through the SNR Presidium, within which they had a majority, removing Daxner from his post as chairman of the National Court in Bratislava.

Although the ostensible reason was the mild sentence for Mach, the move was generally interpreted as a veiled revenge for Tiso's execution. The government therefore overruled the SNR Presidium on the grounds that their action had been unconstitutional and had threatened the independence of courts by giving precedence to political judgements.[137] The Democrats did not accept this and even accused the government of acting unconstitutionally: they thereby finally succeeded in isolating themselves – at least for a time – from all Czech ministers.[138] The way seemed to be open for the Communists to transform the political situation in Slovakia.

7

Deepening divisions

As has been made clear throughout the preceding chapters, post-war Czechoslovak society was by no means free from conflicts. There were unmistakable social tensions that could find expression in the differing social policies of the parties. There were continuing conflicts over the general issue of nationalisations and tension was generated by the natural rivalry between parties.

Nevertheless, at least until mid 1947, there did not appear to be an unbridgeable gulf. Even the Communist Party's stated aim of winning an absolute majority and of ultimately establishing effectively a one-party state need not have been totally disruptive of the existing coalition. Aims could have changed, or been postponed indefinitely, in line with the practical realities of politics and so as to keep political tensions at a low enough level in the interests of cooperation on other issues.

It is possible to conceive of Czechoslovakia developing, broadly under Communist leadership, with a gradual extension of economic planning and some further nationalisations. This would have involved some sharp disagreements, but not necessarily a fierce struggle for power. Ideas on the future of the private sector and of agriculture could then have evolved gradually, in line with the possibilities opened up by the reconstruction and further development of industry. Collectivisation of agriculture could have been encouraged considerably later, when justified by the potential for mechanisation.

This process would have been reinforced by an increase in the Communist vote, but to hope for 51% as early as 1948 was probably both over-ambitious and unnecessary. Czechoslovakia seemed at the time essentially safe from the machinations of 'reaction' and the Social Democrats were helping and enriching rather than opposing the general direction of development.

There were, of course, other possible lines of development for Czechoslovakia to follow, but the conflicts within Czechoslovak society do not seem adequate to explain the sudden change that took place after mid 1947. From then on tension mounted rapidly: disagreements on individual points multiplied, culminating in a struggle for power.

This chapter is concerned with identifying the origins and course of this change. The crucial point was not the gradual aggregation of disagreements, but a conscious decision by political parties. Instead of working to reconcile the various conflicting interests they were trying to represent, they switched to intensifying those conflicts as part of a new strategy of fighting for – at the minimum – a much greater share of power.

This partly reflected exasperation at the number of issues on which they disagreed, but the principal cause of this change in strategies was the international situation. The division of Europe encouraged the belief that the existing National Front could not last much longer. Czechoslovak politics began to divide roughly into three trends. One was firmly for the Soviet Union. One was for the United States, but was unable to say so openly. The third could see no satisfactory policy for Czechoslovakia if Europe was to be divided and could therefore only look on in horror.

I BEGINNINGS OF THE COLD WAR

There were for a time no major disagreements among Czechoslovak politicians over foreign policy. The continuing good relations between the victorious great powers – universally believed to provide the best basis for Czechoslovakia's security – obviated the necessity to choose an exclusive allegiance to any bloc. Even the first signs in the West of open hostility towards the USSR – an example being Churchill's speech in Fulton – met with unanimous condemnation from Czech politicians.[1] This unity was maintained at the time of the Paris peace conference in the autumn of 1946, where it appeared that a minority of states that had suffered most during the war – including Czechoslovakia – were being repeatedly outvoted by the West. This was felt to be a very bad omen for the future as the most difficult and crucial of all issues – the German question – was still to be discussed.

Czechoslovak views on this were totally uncompromising, and Beneš insisted that Germany had to be disarmed for ever.[2] The closeness of Soviet and Czechoslovak foreign policies therefore followed from a basic common interest: accusations in the West that they were already a Soviet satellite were firmly rejected by all prominent Czechoslovak politicians.[3] A forceful reminder of their dependence on the USSR was the realisation that the expulsion of Germans had only partially solved the problem. Those same Germans now hated Czechoslovakia more than ever before and they were being allowed to organise legally in the US zone.[4]

Against this background the US suddenly announced that it was cancelling a loan because Czechoslovakia had allegedly joined, 'in its press and at the peace conference with the unjustified accusations of the Soviets that the US is pursuing an imperialist economic policy'.[5] This reflected a new attitude within the US State Department where it had been decided to end economic assistance to those who 'are opposing the principles for which we stand'. Czechoslovakia clearly came within that category and Secretary of State Byrnes feared that aid could be 'subsidising the Communist control of Czechoslovakia'.[6]

Within Czechoslovakia the unilateral US action was universally condemned. Other accusations, which included questions of compensation for nationalised industries, were carefully refuted. Although nothing was known of Byrnes's new policy, it seemed increasingly likely that the United States had just picked on any available pretext to break with Czechoslovakia. Their objective could then be to use their economic strength to force a major change in the direction of Czechoslovakia's development leading to a 'return to the liberalistic economy as practised before the last war'.[7] Fears of this were further raised when it was announced that UNRRA's activities were to end. Instead there were to be bilateral agreements between states which would effectively give the US government greater control over international aid policies.

Nevertheless, Gottwald apparently made a serious attempt to comply with all the US wishes. This, however, did not prevent the US from stopping effectively all economic assistance by the late spring of 1947.[8] At the same time, the US announced aid to Turkey and Greece as part of the so-called Truman doctrine. An examination of the US press provided quotes indicating that a major reason for this new policy could be the excellent military bases within easy striking distance of important centres in the USSR. It certainly seemed clear that US policy was no longer concerned with co-operation between the great powers.[9] Even if the analysis of this presented by the Communists and Social Democrats may not appear complete today, the fact remains that they alone could confront and attempt to analyse developments. By contrast, the right wing faced an acutely embarrassing situation. They would have liked closer relations with the West, but this was impossible if a Western bloc supporting German revival was created against the Soviet Union.

The Truman doctrine, however, seemed to reveal the start of a major division inside Czechoslovakia. The left were vigorous, articulate and expansive in their condemnations. The People's Party press, after earlier expressing deep concern at US policy which they had seen as the cause of renewed tension in Europe,[10] effectively ceased analysing the international situation. The National Socialists, however, actually welcomed the new US policy. They did not even report Soviet comments on it, preferring to quote only the enthusiastic responses of Churchill and the Greek government.[11] They did not elaborate on this later to explain in full how they understood US policy but presumably the point was that the US had shown a definite will to intervene in European politics. Presumably they still hoped that this would not lead to the creation of two opposing blocs and that the US would still allow Czechoslovakia to retain a close alliance with the USSR. The key to this had to be US *economic* strength. Apparently Ripka had convinced US Ambassador Steinhardt of how important economic aid could be.[12]

This became more obvious as enough time passed for post-war economic trends to be discernible. At first it had been possible to boast of a rapid economic recovery when compared with other countries directly affected by the war. Unfortunately, a great deal more had changed in the world and exports did not seem to be recovering rapidly enough. This pointed to the need to compare with those countries that had suffered no war damage, and then there was nothing to be pleased about.[13] Moreover, it was of doubtful benefit to Czechoslovakia that some other countries were facing difficulties as it led them to reduce imports. Following a spring trade fair in 1947 the heads of nationalised industries made no secret of their disappointment and concern. To be able to export successfully, Czechoslovakia needed to improve dramatically the competitiveness of its products in terms of quality and price.[14]

These worries were given greater urgency after the reappearance of a trade deficit in mid 1947. The immediate cause was the need to pay for imports that had previously been donated by UNRRA,[15] but monthly figures showed enough fluctuations for a review of 1947 as a whole to suggest that all was well.[16] Nevertheless, two particular worries were mentioned. The first was an absolutely persistent deficit with the £ and $ areas.[17] The second was the failure of traditional pre-war exports such as textiles, leather, ceramics, wood and paper. The new leading exports were machinery and heavy capital equipment.[18] This was a consequence of changes in the world economy including the development of industries in many previously backward countries. It meant that, even when raw materials had become available, exports of textiles remained below one third of their pre-war level.[19]

All this seemed to strengthen the argument, which had become popular among Communist and Social Democrat economists, for trying to replace Germany's role as the industrialised state serving Eastern and South-Eastern Europe. The potential seemed enormous as those countries were embarking on industrialisation plans while also establishing close political links with Czechoslovakia. KSČ economists therefore worked out a proposal for a Five Year Plan based on a structural transformation of the economy to give greater weight to heavy engineering.[20]

Unfortunately, even that could not be a complete solution because, when firm long-term trade agreements were negotiated with Eastern European countries, it was realised that those agreements could not be honoured without raw materials available only from the £ and $ areas. For this a significant loan from the West would be almost essential.[21]

It would have been quite indispensible to the National Socialists' conception of economic policy which excluded any detailed future plan and also any specific international orientation. In practical terms the Czechoslovak economy could then only have stood any chance after a massive programme of industrial modernisation.

So there was a growing awareness inside Czechoslovakia of a long-term economic problem just at the time when discussions were starting around Marshall's proposal to aid European economic recovery. It was not immediately clear what strings would be attached, but Communist suspicions about US intentions had already been aroused by the Truman doctrine. Naturally, the

National Socialists were very pleased as they saw it as a chance to reverse Czechoslovakia's gradual isolation from the West.

Nevertheless, before real discussions could begin, Czechoslovakia announced its withdrawal. The decisive factor had been an insistence from the Soviet leadership, in private, that they believed Marshall's offer to be part of the US strategy of isolating the Soviet Union. They would therefore regard participation in the Marshall Plan as an unfriendly act towards the USSR.[22] Czechoslovakia had no choice but to comply with this as 'the German question has not been solved'.[23] The National Socialists could not indicate any public opposition to the government's decision, but they were extremely disappointed.[24]

Judging from their later actions they must have been hoping to be able to accept a loan from the West. It is not clear how far they had worked out their position or how far they were drifting in response to events, but for their hope to become a reality it would have been necessary, at the very least, for the Czechoslovak government to find the courage to call what might just have been Stalin's bluff. In practical terms that presumably required a weakening of the Communists. The National Socialist leadership apparently concluded at this point that the KSČ were the main enemy and that, if possible, a bloc of parties should be formed against them.

In September Ripka and Drtina informed Beneš of a plan to start a more active and energetic campaign against the Communists.[25] Although this was an immediate response to internal tensions, it could have been partly aimed at winning friends in the United States. There is ample evidence that US ambassador Steinhardt encouraged the National Socialists to pursue a clearly anti-Communist policy.[26]

Nevertheless, the party leaders proved unable to formulate a coherent position on the world situation, and seemed to be looking two ways at once. They still tried to insist that they were as loyal to the Soviet Union as were the Communists but, although they published nothing rigorous or analytical, they did print plenty of satirical attacks on the Soviet Union and they reproduced many comments from the Western press. They also showed a revealing predilection for giving ample coverage to reports of the alleged military supremacy of the USA and to its preparedness to provide economic assistance around the world.

Their offensive was crucially weakened from the start because the Soviet leaders had no intention of yielding to the economic or military strength of the USA. Instead, US involvement in Europe, the Truman doctrine, the exclusion of Communists from Western governments, disagreements over Germany and then the Marshall Plan caused them to rethink their foreign policy. Fearing that, as before World War II, they would be internationally rejected and isolated, the Soviet leaders abandoned any hope of an all-European approach and instead concentrated on strengthening relations with Eastern European states.

This was achieved through treaty arrangements, through economic agreements and by direct pressure on smaller states to weaken their links with the West. Then, in September 1947, a new agency for the consolidation of a 'Soviet bloc' was created in the form of the Information Bureau of nine Communists Parties.

This new body differed from the old Comintern as it did not issue explicit directives to its constituent organisations and neither was it directly concerned with world revolution. Nevertheless, its influence on its members was enormous from its first meeting which accepted the new Soviet analysis of the European situation. The central thesis was that the division of Europe was a fact and had been caused by the application of a US strategy aiming for world domination. This involved destroying democracy and supporting reactionary forces everwhere in the world in preparation for a new war.[27] Although the KSČ did not greatly publicise the Informbureau, they certainly accepted this deep concern at the fluid and seemingly dangerous international situation. There were lengthy discussions of the international situation and of the dangers of war at KSČ and KSS Central Committee meetings, and Gottwald indicated the possibility of unfriendly acts from the USA. Little of this was published either at the time or in the relevant edition of Gottwald's works.[28]

Communist involvement within the Informbureau had two important consequences for internal Czechoslovak politics. The first was to arouse suspicion from the right wing. It was claimed that the KSČ had deviated from the Košice Programme by associating itself with outright attacks on Britain and the US,[29] and the People's Party, in particular, portrayed it as a coordinating centre for plotting seizures of power. The evidence they produced to back this up was flimsy, but they could justifiably be concerned that Communist policy was changing and becoming less predictable.

The second consequence was in encouraging a more systematic political offensive from the KSČ. Far from yielding to the National Socialists' desire for the alliance with the USSR to be loosened by friendly relations with the West, the KSČ began insisting that the Informbureau had to be the basis for Czechoslovakia's foreign policy. Any attacks on the USSR or on Slavonic states were equated with treason and with aid to 'foreign reaction' which was accused of preparing 'a new Munich'.[30] In effect this meant that the previously stated aim of winning 51% in the next elections was not just a vague target, but was becoming an absolute necessity. Only then could Czechoslovakia's incorporation into a 'Soviet bloc' be firmly guaranteed.

2 THE MILLIONAIRES' TAX

Despite the enormous importance of changes in the international situation in increasing divisions inside Czechoslovakia, the first really sharp, open conflict arose in connection with internal economic problems. That does not mean that the division of Europe was of secondary importance. On the contrary, it was a major factor encouraging the KSČ to respond to these economic problems with a vigorous political offensive, as it seemed that the Two Year Plan would not yield sufficient benefits to guarantee victory in the next elections.

Throughout the first half of 1947 it had seemed that the plan was succeeding. Those sectors most directly planned were doing best while failures or shortcomings were most serious in agriculture, construction and foreign trade: all of these were predominantly private. There were disappointments in the whole economy because of delays in investment projects and a striking failure for productivity to rise as hoped,[31] but this did not threaten the credibility of planning as such. Arguments that the plan was unrealisable or that it merely predicted what would have happened anyway seemed to have been refuted.[32]

Agriculture, though, was in difficulties from the start and all hopes of reaching the plan targets were shattered by an exceptional drought which was particularly severe in the most productive agricultural areas. The harvest yielded less than it had in 1945 and only about 60% of the pre-war level. This represented a major threat to the Communists' strategy. Living standards would inevitably fall and the leading party in the government could hardly fail to take some of the blame. Expecting the National Socialists to try to exploit everything available to discredit them, the Communists did not hesitate to take the initiative. This indicated a major change in their approach: the international situation converted the aim of 51% into an ˚absolute necessity while the domestic economic situation made it effectively impossible to achieve on the basis of the Two Year Plan. The KSČ therefore began to use their vast organisational strength more clearly than ever before *against* the other parties rather than concentrating on winning their cooperation in the economy.

The initial issue was compensation for the losses suffered by the peasants. This was proposed first by the Social Democrats and quickly taken up by Communists who added that compensation should be financed from a special millionaires' tax which, it was claimed, would raise 2500 million Kčs.[33] The idea was not at this stage worked out in detail: even the numbers to be taxed varied from an early high of 100,000 down to 35,000. It was clearly intended primarily to have a political impact.

When the question of compensation for the peasants was discussed in the government, it was agreed that there should be a special tax on luxury goods, but the idea of the millionaires' tax was rejected by a majority vote. The only Social Democrat present was Laušman and he abstained. Instead of accepting defeat the Communists seized the opportunity to launch a campaign against their political rivals and published details of how individual ministers had voted. On top of this clear break from previously accepted coalition procedure, they threatened to bring the issue before parliament and there were suggestions that the debate might be broadcast live over the radio.[34] All this was part of a wider campaign to portray the other parties as the defenders of the millionaires. It found a ready response in big factories where meetings were organised by the trade union bodies.

There seems no reason to doubt that Communists were making headway with members and supporters of the other parties. The available reports of factory meetings suggest that they were orderly but effectively unanimous in supporting resolutions which called, in very general terms, for 'millionaires and exploiters' to pay for the compensation to the peasants.[35]

This compelled the various party leaderships to state publicly their attitudes to the Communist proposal. The People's Party were the most negative, dismissing any idea of a special tax and suggesting that the financial imbalance could be solved by allowing inflation.[36] The Social Democrats expressed concern at the conversion of the issue into a mass campaign. They wanted a calmer discussion within the National Front and tried to discourage their own members from supporting meetings and resolutions by pointing out that Majer, Fierlinger, Svoboda and Masaryk all opposed the Communists' suggestion.[37] They supplemented this with concrete proposals of their own including the early introduction of a progressive income tax system and the immediate revival of 'tax commissions' to help track down the 'nouveau riche' who had profited from black marketeering.[38] This was not very far from the Communists' position. The tax changes desired had even been proposed long before by the KSČ. The main reason for doubting the proposed millionaires' tax was that it might not raise enough.

The National Socialists, as usual, had difficulty in formulating a consistent position. They tried to stop the growth of the campaigning and to discredit in any way possible the resolutions being sent in from factories. Their verbal attacks on the KSČ intensified: above their references to 'terror' in factories were enormous headlines condemning 'communo-fascism'.[39] Tension between themselves and the Communists reached an unprecedented level as illustrated by the responses of the two parties to the announcement that bombs had been sent through the post to the three government ministers J. Masaryk, Drtina and Zenkl. The National Socialist view was that, irrespective of what the police investigations might reveal, the culprits were the Communists because of the campaign they were conducting at the time.[40] Slánský rivalled this by implying that the perpetrators were trying to divert popular criticism away from the National Socialists and onto the Communists.[41]

At the same time the National Socialists tried to discredit, rather than openly oppose, the Communists' proposal. They did not deny the existence of millionaires but said there were not 35,000 but between 7000 and 8000.[42] They tried to suggest that the tax would hit 'all middle farmers and small businessmen',[43] meaning 100,000 tax payers or 400,000 people in all.[44] The aim could even be to liquidate all private property.[45]

When actually forced to present their proposals it was clear that they differed fundamentally from the Communists and Social Democrats. They did not want millionaires to cover the full cost but argued instead: 'A lower national income will bear a lower burden of public and investment outlays. *It is therefore necessary to search for part of the essential compensation in savings in the state budget.*'[46] This, of course, was precisely what the Communists wanted to avoid as it would have meant cutting the living standards of their own supporters or abandoning projects within the Two Year Plan.

As political tension mounted so all parties seemed to be going separate ways. The Social Democrats, in fact, seemed to be more vociferous than ever before in denouncing 'Communist terror'. The Communists in turn seemed to be making ever more general attacks on the other parties for allegedly harbouring reactionaries. Then, suddenly, they called for a renewal of the bloc of socialist parties.[47] They even seemed to be on the point of achieving their objective when an agreement was announced between the Communists and leading Social Democrats. The KSČ presented this as a major step towards rebuilding cooperation between the two parties starting with a common platform on the question of compensation for peasants.[48]

Most leading Social Democrats at first welcomed this attempt to restore the bloc but Majer, who had not even been consulted before the agreement was reached, tried to resign from the government in protest. The National Socialists expressed even stronger opposition. Although the Communists may well have had no clear aims beyond a propaganda victory when they initiated the campaign, it seemed to the National Socialists that the aim might be to create a real government crisis.[49] The assassination attempts could fit into such a strategy, which could culminate in a new government firmly dominated by the KSČ through the Socialist Bloc.

Whatever Fierlinger's original intentions had been, the agreement was then reinterpreted as an attempt to restore cooperation in the National Front. It started with the KSČ only because that was the biggest party. Then the Social Democrats held talks with the leaderships of the other two Czech parties and afterwards claimed considerable credit for the subsequent calming of the political atmosphere.[50] They seemed to have been the only bridge between the two sides. Finally, at a government meeting on 21 October 1947, the proposals presented by Dolanský, the Communist Minister of Finance, were accepted

The Communists could then claim a victory because the principle of taxing millionaires to pay the compensation had been accepted.

The National Socialists also claimed to have been proved right as there seemed to be only 12,000 and not 35,000 millionaires.[51] The Social Democrats could be even happier as several of their suggestions had been accepted by Dolanský. The People's Party seemed the least content, still verbally opposing the idea.[52]

Perhaps as important as this outcome were the lessons learnt by the various parties. The National Socialists and many Social Democrats were deeply disturbed, but the Communists had discovered that after being isolated in the government they could still mobilise working class opinion. No other party could either stop them or mobilise support around an alternative position. Instead, the other parties had become confused and disunited: there was certainly no sign of them forming a bloc as each was determined to put forward its own distinctive proposal.

It must also have been clear that mass mobilisation alone could not ensure a complete victory and, although this had not necessarily been the Communists' intention, neither could it change the composition of the government. Although there is no evidence of the KSČ leadership making a clear and thorough assessment of all this, it is hard to believe that they did not learn a great deal for their tactics in early 1948. This was probably even more true of the events in Slovakia in the autumn of 1947, which were finally to convince the KSČ leadership that they had to strike a direct blow against the National Socialists.

3 THE SLOVAK CRISIS

It must have seemed to the Slovak Communists in June 1947 that they would be able to win enough Czech support to press home their advantage and perhaps even force the humiliated Democrats to announce the reversal of the April Agreement. Gottwald certainly believed that a major offensive was possible and necessary. He advocated demanding from the other Czech parties cooperation in removing, and perhaps even imprisoning, the HSL'S trend within the Democratic Party.[53]

Attacks were directed against the Catholics within the party leadership and as early as May 1947 the prominent Catholics Kempný, Bugár and Staško were accused of working for the HSL'S underground.[54] Evidence of direct involvement was not clear and the National Socialists were already nervous of the Communists' intentions. Nevertheless, the Czech parties generally accepted that the permanent crisis in the Slovak National Front was a consequence of the April Agreement and the Czech and Slovak National Fronts agreed to establish a parity committee to investigate the situation within the Democratic Party.[55]

Shortly after this Gottwald delivered a major speech at Devín on 5 July 1947 in which he emphasised the dangers to Slovakia from 'remnants of the old fascist regime'. He maintained that they had become a serious threat because they had gained important positions in political life, in the state administration and in the economy. He therefore argued that it was essential to complete the purge in Slovakia.[56] There was no explicit attack on the Democratic Party but, obviously aware of how best to win support in the West and in the Czech lands, the Democrats portrayed Gottwald's speech as an attack on their party as a whole.

In this increasingly tense situation the next initiative came from the Communist dominated Union of Slovak Partisans who opened a conference on 19 August 1947. They demanded measures 'to fight against leading compromised figures who are obviously receiving orders from abroad and are hindering the successful development of our state',[57] and passed a resolution calling for the removal by 20 September 1947 of all functionaries of the former regime who held important positions in the state.[58] They also demanded arms to fight against 'Banderovci'. These were right-wing Ukrainian nationalist guerrillas who were causing some disorder in Slovakia as they tried to make their way to the West. The army seemed for a brief period to be losing control of the situation and, although subsequent evidence did not confirm this, the partisans claimed that the Banderovci had established links with underground supporters of the Slovak state.[59] They might therefore be planning to stay in Slovakia to make the government's position more difficult.[60]

Although in some respects the partisans may have over-dramatised the situation, there is no reason to doubt the genuineness of their concern. They were still suffering discrimination, including possible imprisonment, for their wartime activities.[61] Moreover, their demands were supported by other resistance organisations. Even the Democrats accepted that a further purge was needed, but they insisted that the problem affected all political parties equally and that any purge should adhere to normal legal methods.[62]

The partisans then stepped up their campaign, holding

demonstrations in many parts of Slovakia on 14 September 1947. Lettrich even addressed a rally in Lučenec, where he pledged himself to the fulfilment of the partisans' 'justified demands'.[63] Shortly afterwards the Board of Commissioners agreed to establish special commissions to check employees' past records on the basis of evidence presented by partisans. Undecided cases were submitted to a commission headed by Ferjenčik.[64]

Apparently nothing was done where Democrat Commissioners were in control, but former officials of the Slovak state were removed from the office of the Commissioner of the Interior.[65] Then the Communists' hand was suddenly strengthened by the announcement of the discovery of another conspiratorial organisation of former supporters of the Slovak state. The typical conspirators were, apparently, those former activists who had either gone unpunished or received laughably low sentences and had worked their way back into high positions after the April Agreement.[66] The eventual plan seemed to be an uprising against the Czechoslovak state which could be helped by cooperation with Banderovci.[67] More was revealed over the following days and it appeared that the organisation was extensive. It was not, however, proven that it was linked directly with the Democratic Party's leadership and it certainly did not have the means to take power alone.

Nevertheless, its discovery seemed to underline the urgency of a really thorough purge and pressure was stepped up at a joint conference of resistance organisations on 21 September 1947. On the following day a meeting of the Slovak National Front accepted their demands as justified and soon there were reports of suspensions from the National Committees in line with the resolution of the resistance organisations.

It must then have seemed to the Communists that they had firmly taken the initiative into their own hands. Perhaps if they had concentrated solely on the issue of known prominent officials of the former Slovak state, then they could have achieved some sort of reversal of the April Agreement. By the autumn of 1947, however, they sought a more fundamental change. The Informbureau undoubtedly had an influence: Slánský and Bašťovanský, who attended its first meeting, advocated sharpening the general fight against 'reaction' by means of a mass mobilisation of the Slovak people against conspirators.[68]

As in the Czech lands, however, they had to face immense

economic difficulties and it was an open question who the population would blame. The drought forced the inadequacy of rations, always prominent in workers' complaints, right to the front of the political arena. Some areas apparently had no flour at all[69] while it was later claimed, without elaboration, that workers were being forced to buy 80% of the necessities of life on the black market.[70] Nevertheless, the trade union leaders continued to reject pressure for wage increases which could have enabled workers to buy food and other consumer goods on the black market. Instead they directed activity towards campaigning for a better organised supply system with strict controls and quotas throughout the production process, like those that had been inherited in the Czech lands from the Nazi war economy.

This, however, was opposed by the Democratic Party. They were always touchy about criticisms of the supply system as their Commissioners were in charge of food supplies and agriculture: the former, Filo, was a Catholic while the latter, Kvetko, had participated in the uprising. Generally accusations against them were carefully worded. Sometimes, however, militant workers had no hesitation in accusing them not just of incompetence but of 'deliberately provoking chaos so as to reverse the gains of our national and democratic revolution'.[71]

Such attitudes were reflected in a more militant mood among trade union leaders too as they indicated their growing disillusionment with the idea of the National Front. When Zápotocký visited Slovakia in July he argued strongly against them maintaining that the existing government policies would lead to success in Slovakia as in the Czech lands.[72] Nevertheless, he made no attempt to smooth over differences between the Slovak Communists and the Democrats and he analysed the Slovak situation in the same way as had Gottwald at Devín. His visit even seemed to have heightened tension when *Čas* described it as an unwelcome interference in Slovakia's internal affairs and maintained that Zápotocký had no more in common with the Slovak people than had Karmasin,[73] the leader of the Nazis in wartime Slovakia.

Slovak trade union organisations, without any directives from above, then began preparing for strike action in response, they said, to the insulting attacks on Zápotocký and to the Democrats' statements that they were going to establish 'democratic' trade union organisations. The leadership then tried to calm the atmosphere somewhat with reassurances that normal methods could still bring results so that 'extreme revolutionary measures' were not yet necessary. Anger was diverted into protest meetings in factories on 21 July 1947 which sent resolutions to the SNR Presidium.[74]

It was against this background that the KSS Presidium decided, on 29 September 1947, to step up their campaigning and to link together the issues of collaborators, the millionaires' tax, food supplies and peasants' demands.[75] They still left flexible their precise immediate aim, but there was no doubt that they hoped 'to change the whole political structure of Slovakia'. This could have meant expelling the Democrats from the government, dissolving their party completely, or placing firm conditions on their continuing in the government.[76] Presumably it was assumed that the National Socialists could be persuaded to support such a perspective after the discovery of the conspiracy, but in practice the strength and breadth of the KSS offensive itself alarmed them.

The central point in the Communists' plan was to be mass mobilisation of the organised working class involving meetings and rallies and a Congress of Factory Committees. The details and even the precise demands were left open until the KSS Presidium meeting of 18 October 1947 when it was decided to place the main emphasis on economic and social questions, especially the supply difficulties. The issue of traitors and collaborators was to be secondary.[77]

Nevertheless, the Communists missed no opportunity to imply that the influence of former fascists in supply and agriculture policies could go some way towards explaining disappointments in those spheres. Moreover, considerable publicity was given to the revelations about the conspiracy and the KSS leadership made sure that the legal investigation did not slip into the hands of the Commissioner for Justice. They insisted that members of the KSS dominated Seventh Section of the police were present during all investigations. They also worked out how to use their strength within the radio in Prague so as to play up the importance of what was discovered,[78] and the Ministry of the Interior published, with amazing haste, a booklet presenting the evidence against the conspirators.[79]

The Democrats responded to this offensive by portraying themselves as great defenders of parliamentary democracy, as opponents of Prague centralism and as full supporters of the government programme. They made no references to inner-party differences so that KSS activities could appear as attempts to destroy the whole Democratic Party and establish a monopoly of power. This was the basis of their appeal to the Czech right wing.

In practical terms they had somehow to discredit the revelations about the conspiracy and they therefore pointed from the start to the suspicious fact that the revelations had come at a remarkably convenient time.[80] The necessity for such an argument was increased as the Democratic Party leaders Kempný and Bugár may have had at least some contact with the conspirators.[81] There was also incriminating evidence against O. Obuch, who was in charge of Ursíny's office, and Party General Secretary F. Hodža was involved in an attempt to cover up for him at the last minute.[82]

Within a few weeks they were claiming that the real conspiracy originated in the KSS: the Communists, they claimed, were unscrupulously exploiting their strength within state security organs as part of an alleged plot to bring about the dissolution of the Democratic Party.[83] The objectivity of the police was, however, defended by Ferjenčík who insisted, both in a parliamentary committee and in the Board of Commissioners, that neither agents provocateurs nor false documents were used.[84] Lt Col. Polák, a member of the Democratic Party's Presidium and chairman of the largest of the resistance organisations (ZVOJPOV – Union of Soldiers of the Uprising), felt obliged to praise the sober and objective way Ferjenčík reported the investigations: the problem of HSL'S remnants was not necessarily linked with the Democratic Party but the Democrats' claim that it was 'a conspiracy to order' was implicitly rebutted.[85]

Soon there seemed to be clear evidence that Obuch had used his position to get information on secret government meetings, and on political, military and economic questions, which had then been sent to Ďurčanský.[86] When this became clear, Ursíny resigned without attempting to suggest that the charges might be untrue.[87] Lettrich still tried to save something by claiming that Obuch had been forced to confess by police brutality, but Ferjenčík and Nosek visited the prison and convinced themselves that Lettrich's claim was untrue.[88]

It would appear, then, that the evidence for illegal groups with some contacts in the Democratic Party leadership was undeniable. It was a very different situation from the trials of the early 1950s as this time confessions were very subsidiary parts of the evidence and there was plenty of documentary material that could be published. Moreover, although the KSS did make every effort to exploit the conspiracy in the interests of their political aims, links were not as clear as they would have liked. Ferjenčík, in fact, continued to insist that the political allegiances were not known of all the conspirators.[89] Moreover, it proved impossible to show the links between the conspirators and either economic difficulties or the Banderovci which could have made them a far more serious threat to the state.

Nevertheless, the Czech right wing had no hesitation in accepting the Democrats' explanation that the real issue was the Communist aim of 'the total Communisation of Czechoslovakia'[90] and that the KSS aimed to outlaw the Democratic Party and seize power.[91] Implications of leading Democrats' involvement in the conspiracy were dismissed and the Czech right wing was united in its defence of the Democratic Party.

It is quite possible that in October and November 1947 the National Socialists were not fully convinced either way, but that they were far more disturbed by the Communists' possible intentions than by the presence of former fascists in Slovakia, who presented no immediate threat to the Czechoslovak state or to the policies the National Socialists wanted to pursue in the government. They therefore swallowed whatever doubts they had about the Democratic Party, although Ripka had apparently known in advance that there was strong evidence against Obuch,[92] who later pleaded guilty and was sentenced to thirty years imprisonment. The involvement of Kempný and Bugár, who received six year and one year sentences respectively, is far from clear: Ripka believed they could have been the victims of agents provocateurs. There is no serious doubt that fabricated evidence was later used to implicate Ursíny in the conspiracy. He refused to admit anything and was given a seven year sentence: in 1964 his innocence was publicly acknowledged.[93]

The National Socialists' attitude proved to be crucial when the crisis reached its climax following the Congress of Factory Committees in Bratislava on 30 October 1947. The resolution adopted indicated a deep concern at the supply situation and at the increase in black marketeering and expressed firm support for the demands of the resistance organisations. It concluded with a categorical demand for the resignation of the existing Board of Commissioners. This was supported by the resistance organisations and led to the resignation of the KSS representatives on the board and of Ferjenčík.

The Democrats, however, refused to be bound by the views of the main mass organisations and, already assured of National Socialist support if they rejected all the Communists' demands,[94] took the issue to the full Czech and Slovak National Front. During the discussions that followed the two sides tried to demonstrate their popularity inside Slovakia. Meetings were held in work-places on 5 November 1947 expressing enthusiastic support for the resolution from the Congress of Factory Committees. There were even some factories beginning preparations for a general strike.[95] In the countryside too the KSS could at last claim some active support when an all Slovak Congress of District Organisations of JZSR and of Peasant Commissions was held on 14 November 1947 with over 2000 delegates in attendance. It expressed support for the Hradec Programme and for the demands of the Factory Committees.

Although there can be little doubt that the KSS was gaining more influence in the countryside, it remains unclear how representative the conference really was. Communists were therefore still nervous that the Democrats might be able to mobilise peasant support for demonstrations on 15 November 1947 to oppose the alleged KSS attempt to take power. The Democrats claimed that 30,000 answered their call in Bratislava and that there were also big and successful demonstrations in Košice and Zvolen.[96] Obviously, the KSS presented them as a complete fiasco, but in private too the Communist leaders seemed to be pleased that the Democrats had mobilised less support than they claimed and that the demonstrations were not big enough to affect the negotiations within the National Front.[97]

Nevertheless, Gottwald could make little headway in Prague. Then, on 5 November 1947, a government meeting entrusted him with the task of going to Slovakia to form a new Board of Commissioners. The Democrats, however, still refused to concede the key posts of Agriculture, Supply and Justice even when Gottwald suggested that the first two of these could be given to the two smaller parties while Justice could go to the KSS in exchange for another post.[98]

The new Board of Commissioners was finally formed after two days of discussion in the Czech and Slovak National Front on 17 and 18 November 1947. The Democrats were deprived of their overall majority and the key position of Justice went to Búza, a Social Democrat who was presented as a non-party specialist.[99] They retained the other two controversial posts even though their Catholic representatives were removed. The Communists' position remained unchanged but the two smaller parties were each given one comparatively unimportant post.

Although the Democrats seemed only to have made small concessions, they had in fact suffered a serious blow. Already prior to this, while never openly admitting that the April Agreement had been one of the causes of the crisis, and certainly never making public its contents, they had quietly announced: 'the famous internal agreement in the Democratic Party of 31 March 1946 is no longer an inner-party factor . . . the party's Executive Committee will make it the subject of discussion at the meeting it has already called with the intention of *announcing it invalid and non-binding*'.[100] Whether this was meant genuinely or not, Catholics were already losing key positions as many were implicated in the conspiracy and the Democrats later joined in a unanimous resolution of the new Board of Commissioners on 7 January 1948 expressing full confidence in Ferjenčík: this was an implicit repudiation of the charges made against the security forces by Lettrich on 16 November 1947.[101] It seemed that the party, and especially its Catholic wing, had no strength at all to present an independent position. It owed its existence entirely to the protection of the National Socialists in Prague.

Within the KSS too there was plenty of cause for dissatisfaction at the outcome of the Slovak crisis. Although the Democratic Party had been weakened, the aims set by Široký had in no way been achieved. Nevertheless, at the KSS Central Committee meeting of 4 December 1947, he insisted that there was no alternative to accepting and supporting the new Board of Commissioners. Not surprisingly, doubts appeared about this within the party leadership. The trade unionists Zupka and Kušík indicated that they felt no need to express confidence in the personal composition of the Board. Šmidke even proposed abandoning the existing National Front for a political structure analogous to those in Yugoslavia and Bulgaria.[102] Although he argued for it on slightly different grounds, this would in practice have enabled the KSS to become the leading force in Slovak politics even without winning a majority in the forthcoming elections.

Both of these proposals were firmly rejected. They anyway did not mean that the party was splitting. They rather reflected disappointment that the Democratic Party had not been split and totally humiliated as a result of their offensive. In practical terms, the majority in the KSS leadership had to recognise that there was no way to change things within Slovakia alone. It was a major lesson for the Communist leaders in Prague too that Slovakia provided no easy road to a transformation of the all-state political situation. On the contrary, the Slovak situation could only be changed by means of a major confrontation in Prague with the National Socialists.

8

Prelude to February

I SOCIAL DEMOCRATS

The tense atmosphere created by the international situation, the Communist campaign over the millionaires' tax and the Slovak crisis forced all Czech parties to reassess their policies. Among Social Democrats this meant, particularly after the agreement signed by the party's leadership with the KSČ, a growing belief that only the removal of Fierlinger and election of a new leadership could give their party a new and distinctive identity. The only credible alternative chairman was Laušman. He could command support throughout the party thanks to his role in the nationalisation of industries, and he seemed more committed to an independent identity for the party than was Fierlinger. At the party's congress in November 1947 Fierlinger refused to resign voluntarily and the issue was taken to a vote. Laušman received 283 votes, Fierlinger 182 and the outsider John only got one. The significance of this change was not immediately obvious as there had been no open division over policies and it could even be presented as a change of personalities only. Moreover, both Fierlinger and Laušman resigned from the government and were replaced by Tymeš, who had supported Laušman, and Jankovcová, a firm Fierlinger supporter.

The greatest obstacle to the formulation of a non-Communist but not anti-Communist policy was the international situation. In practice the Social Democrats had been looking to the East. They were suspicious of ideas of reviving the Second International which had been anti-Communist and contained pro-Munich elements.[1] They could not ally with German Social Democracy because of its vague position on the expulsion of Germans and its support for the Truman doctrine.[2] They rejected the French Socialists whose vote had declined after they lacked the courage to implement socialist policies.[3] Instead, they placed their emphasis on building unity with Socialists and Social Democrats in Eastern and Central Europe, where there was agreement for cooperation with Communists and for friendship with the USSR. Later this ground was to be knocked from under their feet as those parties merged with Communist Parties. There seemed, however, to be no viable alternative. Some on the party's right wing hesitantly praised the British Labour Party,[4] but they could never associate themselves with – or even publicise – the foreign policy being advocated by Bevin. In a speech mentioned in the Czechoslovak press only in *Rudé právo*, he effectively blamed the Soviet Union for all Europe's troubles: he showed no interest in the existence or problems of Eastern Europe and called instead for the consolidation of a Western bloc. This was presented as the first official admission of the existence of such a bloc.[5]

Domestically too there was still plenty of common ground between Communists and Social Democrats. The obvious point of division was the so called 'Communist terror' in factories, examples of which were given publicity in the journal of the Social Democrats' factory organisations especially after the results of the Factory Council elections suggested that there might be scope for a working class base in opposition to the Communists.

Reference to unpleasant 'tactics and methods' by the Communists was made even by E. Erban,[6] and the Executive Committee had unanimously expressed the hope that 'KSČ terror' would stop.[7] Nevertheless, the term 'terror' often appeared as an exaggeration: there were only very occasional allegations of employees being sacked for their political affiliations. Moreover, it was very difficult to evolve a consistent theoretical position out of this to really differentiate Social Democracy from the KSČ.

An attempt was made by Veltruský who stood on the far left of Social Democracy.[8] There were many weaknesses in his position, which evidently owed a great deal to Trotskyism, and he even convinced himself that the KSČ stood on 'the extreme right' of the National Front. His most credible argument was that the KSČ were intent simply on winning positions of power for themselves by controlling managements and Factory Councils: he claimed that beyond this they had no interest in the working class. The serious elaboration of this position proved extremely difficult as he had to ignore the economic thinking of the KSČ which undeniably went beyond a crude desire for power. Neither could he deny or explain away the great strength of the KSČ within the working class. Moreover, the Social Democrats could not use this theoretical starting point as the basis for an independent policy as they too were accused of having taken disproportionately many leading positions within the economy and of helping Communists to get where they were.[9] References to 'Communist terror' could therefore never appear as more than individual complaints about mistakes by individual Communists.

There was, however, another arena in which Social Democrats could try to present a distinct alternative. Tension between parties led to a debate on the role of trade unions at the ÚRO plenum in November 1947.[10] A number of Social Democrats, including Kubát, argued for a restriction of activities to 'trade union' questions, especially wages. Potentially divisive issues, like the question of compensation for the peasants, were to be evaded.

Zápotocký, however, had little difficulty in winning support for his view that such questions quite obviously directly affected the workers' most basic interests and could therefore not possibly be avoided. The debate ended with a reaffirmation of trade union unity around a resolution expressing exasperation with the supply situation and the distribution system: this, it should be added, was already a politically controversial issue.

2 NATIONAL SOCIALISTS

The National Socialists too were deeply affected by the KSČ offensive: it gave greater urgency to their decision to adopt a more vigorous line. They still believed that the Communists intended to fight the elections rather than trying to seize power beforehand, but they were very worried as the Communists seemed to be deliberately and unnecessarily raising the political temperature.[11] They feared that provocative incidents could become a normal part of KSČ behaviour in what they believed would be a desperate bid for 51% of the votes.

To counter this danger the National Socialists evolved a strategy for a political counter-offensive. Apart from vigorous propaganda against the KSČ, they decided to strengthen their organisation and reinforce their own support in preparation for the next elections: above all they pursued a conscious policy of trying to create alliances with anybody available who would oppose the KSČ. Presumably they thereby hoped to prevent the struggle from going beyond their purely parliamentary conception of politics. This was not an unrealistic hope as even Fierlinger, to judge from his attitudes towards the millionaires' tax and towards land reform proposals, could be expected to oppose the more aggressive aspects of KSČ policy.

They placed great emphasis on winning support and establishing party organisations among workers in factories, but their economic and social policies could provide little basis for this. In fact, they still evaded references to economic questions and did not even try to represent the interests of all workers. Instead they claimed that their organisations were just to protect their own members against 'KSČ terror'[12] with the eventual perspective of 'breaking the terror in factories' and 'a purge of the trade unions'.[13] Against this background, and as their own organisational structure was still very loose,[14] it is impossible to believe extraordinary statements about their working class strength: they even claimed to have more members in Prague factories than the KSČ.[15]

They could, however, win support elsewhere. In alliance with the People's Party they won sweeping victories in student elections.[16] They also made a determined effort to consolidate support among civil servants. During the crisis over the millionaires' tax they publicly advocated a 30% pay rise to be backdated to January 1947 for all civil servants. Even the People's Party characterised this as cheap agitation aimed purely at winning votes[17] but, to avert the threatened strike, ÚRO had to do something definite: they started by accepting that a comparison should be made of pay between civil servants and equivalent employees in the 'economic sector'. The comparison showed that civil servants were worse paid, especially in higher grades,[18] and ÚRO responded by proposing an immediate financial gift to civil servants.[19] This was a pretty small gesture as the comparison indicated the justifiability of a large pay rise. Zápotocký, however, had never been interested in this procedure. He wanted a comparison with workers' wages,[20] which averaged out slightly below those of civil servants. A comparison of pensions was even more helpful to him as civil servants received on average twice as much as miners and three to four times the average for workers as a whole.[21] The point was therefore not just the exact cost of a substantial pay rise for civil servants but also its likely impact on much wider wage demands and hence on the ability of ÚRO to remain united around a policy of considerable wage restraint.

The National Socialists also tried to win more solid support in the countryside. This led them once more to try to exploit the alleged prestige of former Agrarians, who increasingly dominated the party's agricultural policy.[22] A congress of National Socialist farmers even ended by laying a wreath at Švehla's grave.[23] This, however, did not mark a shift to an aggressively right-wing agricultural policy as they were at the time accepting the need to allow through parliament some of Ďuriš's laws.

Their defence of the Slovak Democrats, both during and after the Slovak crisis, was perhaps the most obvious real change in National Socialist policies, but even in their attempt to portray the roots of the Slovak crisis entirely in the KSČ offensive, they suffered from some indecision and confusion. They were apparently divided in the parliamentary vote on whether to remove parliamentary immunity from Kempný and Bugár[24] and may well have encouraged the Democratic Party to renounce the April Agreement.

So, even as their propaganda against the KSČ became more powerful, the National Socialists remained uncertain on several important aspects of policy. Nevertheless, their attitude was interpreted by the KSČ as indicating that the character of their party had been changed by non-socialist members shifting it markedly to the right.

3 COMMUNISTS

The KSČ leadership, and party activists generally, therefore felt that they had plenty of cause for concern. Several possible options confronted them when the Central Committee met at the end of November but, before taking any precipitate action, the leadership wanted to be sure of the situation in the country. Information had therefore been gathered and collated from the party's basic organisations. It left no doubt that the centre of public attention absolutely everywhere was the shortage of basic necessities of life. This was hardly surprising as bread rations had been reduced by almost 40%.[25] There were even signs of developing panic with those in towns making accusations against villages.[26] Very often, though, Communists were held responsible as they dominated the government. This did not necessarily mean growing support for the other

parties as, particularly among workers in big towns and big factories, discontent was expressed in the belief that the government was
being too soft: strong measures against speculators and black
marketeers were demanded.

Gottwald's speech to the Central Committee took its ideas on
the supply crisis more or less exactly from these contributions from
lower levels within the party. There was, however, a marked
tendency to emphasise those ideas that could help the campaign
against political opponents, thereby implying that difficulties could
be overcome if the KSČ had more power. It seemed that the needs
of party-political propaganda were dominating in considering the
impact of the drought. Everybody was trying to attribute at least
some degree of blame to their political opponents. Majer, the
Minister in charge of food supply, was an obvious target and he
was vigorously condemned for relying too much on imports and
not paying enough attention to domestic sources.[27] He wasted no
time in counter-attacking by blaming the Ministry of Agriculture
and by pointing out that it had been the Communists who had for
so long optimistically denied that anything drastic needed to be done
about food supplies.[28]

Thus attacks on other parties were increasingly linked to their
attitudes towards the economic difficulties which were causing discontent. The KSČ had even tried to accuse their political rivals of
not opposing, and hence of implicitly supporting, politically motivated economic sabotage which, it was claimed, was being carried
on by 'reaction'. It would have been perfectly valid to argue that
the National Socialist and People's Parties were lukewarm in their
support for the Two Year Plan and that they were happy to exploit
politically economic difficulties so as to discredit the Communists'
economic policies. It was also true that several sectors dominated
by private enterprise were performing badly, and that could be
used later as an argument for further nationalisations. There was,
however, no justification for accusing 'reaction' – by this time
effectively equated with private enterprise – of consciously organising
economic chaos and hence of causing the serious and immediate
difficulties. Frejka, the leading Communist economist, even had to
admit that it was 'necessary to determine concretely' how capitalists
were 'disrupting' the economy.[29]

While trying to direct some of the popular anger about the economic situation onto their political rivals the KSČ also tried to

blame them for the rising political tension. The National Socialists were accused of capitulating to 'reaction' in their attitudes towards the international situation and Slovakia, and by their advocacy of impossible demands on civil servants' pay.[30] It certainly was true that they were becoming more aggressively anti-Communist, and they were trying to unite all other political forces against the KSČ, but this was to a great extent in response to the determination with which the Communists pursued their own offensive. The KSČ analysis that the National Socialists, or 'reactionaries' who were dominating their policies, were responsible for political tensions was at best an exaggeration in the interests of political propaganda.

Nevertheless, it did undoubtedly reflect a genuine fear on Gottwald's part that the National Socialists might prove capable of launching a real political offensive and creating a bloc of parties around demands that the KSČ simply could not accept. This could lead to a crisis, a vote of no confidence and hence the resignation of the government followed by a 'government of officials' analogous to the one in 1920.[31] The danger of this was increased both by the changes in Social Democracy which Gottwald expected to lead to a fundamental shift in that party's policies[32] and by the belief – derived from the Informbureau's analysis of the international situation – that the US would somehow try to intervene in Czechoslovak politics.[33] His fears on both these points were probably exaggerated.

Neither is there evidence of a plan at that time to exclude Communists from the government prior to the elections, but they could very realistically fear that they might fail to substantially increase their vote and they might then find themselves isolated within the government. In public, however, the KSČ indicated every confidence in their ability to win an absolute majority. On 24 August 1947 Gottwald had set the target of one and a half million members expecting that, given the previous ratio of members to voters, this would lead to over 50% of the votes.[34] This target certainly did not seem impossible and in early 1948 there was still greater emphasis on election campaigning. At least as early as February local organisations were being encouraged to work out which individuals' votes would be needed for a majority in their locality – or even within their small block of flats – and then persistent personal agitation was to ensure those votes.[35]

There were still serious and justified doubts within the leadership about the party's ability to win in the elections and some even

contemplated taking power by extra-parliamentary means. Gottwald, however, still thought that the elections could be the decisive
arena of struggle, but he implicitly accepted that the KSČ alone
was unlikely to win an absolute majority. He therefore advocated,
as 'an essential part of the preparation of the election campaign
and of our electoral victory',[36] creating a broader platform to
include left elements from *all* parties. Approaches were in fact made
to likely participants in this electoral front.[37]

This Gottwald referred to as a 'new' National Front, to replace
the old framework which had apparently become unworkable, and
he fully expected a strong trend to develop within the National
Socialists to change the course of their party's policy or to ally with
the KSČ.[38] The new National Front was also to include the left
Social Democrats who had supported Fierlinger. They, however,
were criticised for lack of initiative as they seemed to see nothing
disastrous in the change in their party's leadership.[39] Communists
were therefore expected to help develop a more belligerent left
wing. Gottwald even saw fit to set its tactical aim which was to
regain control of the party and work closely with the KSČ. Communists were obviously to be closely involved in developing this
left as they were to 'advise and support' it and to 'create organisational and technical possibilities for direct contact with the left
from top to bottom.'[40]

In public statements Gottwald still argued that 'the system of
cooperation of the parties in the National Front government' was
'the most advantageous for the prosperous and peaceful development of the state',[41] but news of preparations for the 'new' National
Front appeared in some Czech papers[42] and tension between parties
was still further aggravated when Kopecký made an ambiguous
public reference to the idea.[43] Fears seemed to be confirmed that
the KSČ in fact wanted an absolute majority so as to be able to
dispense with their existing coalition partners, and that they were
prepared to break the understandings underlying the existing
National Front so as to achieve their aim.

At the same time, there were still reassurances that Czechoslovakia was to follow 'a peaceful, non-violent road and on no
account the road of the dictatorship of the proletariat'.[44] Kopecký
explained it as follows: '*We have no reason to resort to other means for
power than people's democracy.* We have a great share of power which
the people have given us and we are convinced that the people will

give us still more power. It is reaction that is cultivating putschist plans . . . *We stand by the law, the law of the new republic.*'[45] In the Central Committee meeting he amplified his meaning in the only way that seemed consistent with the new KSČ attitude towards the other parties: 'We will choose the moment to apply that strength such that nobody can criticise us for abandoning the democratic road.'[46]

In other words, even if the KSČ leaders were still firmly opposed to putschist methods, they did recognise that they could hardly achieve a political transformation leading to a new National Front without a major struggle. Moreover, Kopecký's comments leave little doubt that they were prepared to use all the strength of their immense organisation plus their positions within the police and the media: it was to be a development of their tactics in the campaign for the millionaires' tax and during the Slovak crisis.

Even if they could not definitely be accused of 'totalitarianism', as they were still prepared to face contested elections and said nothing that could rule out the existence of a legal opposition afterwards, they certainly had changed their approach. The idea of the 'new' National Front and the determination with which they began to work for it indicated that they could see no future in continuing cooperation and compromise within the existing National Front. Even if opposition was not necessarily to be totally suppressed, it was certainly to be excluded from effective decision-making. The Communists were determined to assure themselves of an absolutely firm grip on power within the next few months.

The key to any political transformation remained the economy and the question of who could be held most responsible for difficulties that were largely due to objective causes. The Central Committee meeting presented a list of measures with the principal emphasis on overcoming supply difficulties and putting order into the distribution system.[47] These could have been the centre of a purely Communist election campaign or that campaign could have led to the creation of a broader front following divisions within other parties.

While still keeping these options open, Gottwald called for very strong measures against black marketeers and also demanded a new distribution system for textiles. They had become extremely scarce partly because exports were being increased to finance essential food imports and partly, it was claimed, because the diffuse distribution system allowed possibly as much as 30% of production to be illegally smuggled out of the country.[48] The proposal was to replace completely the mass of wholesalers by a system of central and local centres ensuring control from the factories right down to the shops.[49] The National Socialists opposed this and advocated instead a reduction in the number of wholesalers but the Social Democrats' support ensured that the KSČ proposal was accepted in the government against the other parties' opposition.[50] The new system began operating within a few days.

A solution to the supply shortages also depended on the peasants and the Communists were aware of the difficulties this presented. They needed peasant votes but their firmest supporters desperately needed food. This obviously made any relaxation of the strict quota system impossible, but that amounted to asking peasants to surrender even essential reserves that they needed for their own consumption and for the next sowing.[51] By early 1948 calls to fulfil quota obligations were being ignored by poor as well as rich peasants.[52] The Communists were therefore effectively forced to do everything they could to win back some sympathy in the countryside. The crucial weapon was the proposed new land reform.

The National Front, meeting on 11 and 12 December 1947, agreed to a very rapid parliamentary timetable for the discussion of Ďuriš's remaining proposals.[53] There was soon surprisingly quick progress after the earlier delays, and the revision of the first land reform took place during January and February.[54] Only the People's Party and Slovak Democrats had voted against this in the government[55] so that, again, both total deadlock and a solid bloc against the KSČ had been averted.

Perhaps Gottwald really believed that the other parties would do everything to block the measures he felt were necessary and was surprised to find that there was still some scope for agreement. It certainly appears that he would have welcomed deadlock in the government if that gave the KSČ a chance to use their extra-parliamentary strength.

4 DEADLOCK IN THE GOVERNMENT

Nevertheless, there was no denying the widening gulf between the Communists and the National Socialists. Particularly serious was the apparent standstill over the principal task set for parliament, the formulation and passing of a new constitution. Broadly speaking, there were two sides, with the National Socialists advocating only a few modifications to the 1920 constitution, while the KSČ wanted to codify and incorporate many of the post-war changes without restricting the scope for further socialist change.[56]

An important discussion that had reached deadlock was that of the powers and organisational structure of National Committees. Although they had quickly receded from the centre of political debates after liberation, the KSČ continued to hope that they could provide the basis for a more democratic form of local administration. They therefore wanted to see them incorporated into the new constitution and took the opportunity to propose a number of further changes to the structure of local government. Among these was the controversial proposal to dissolve the Regional National Committees and decentralise their powers into a number of smaller units. This would, it was claimed, strengthen the position of elected over unelected workers.[57] Unfortunately, the embittered political atmosphere meant that, after a great deal of equivocation, the National Socialists opposed the proposal. Although they accepted that in principle it was a good idea, they feared that 'units would be created which would be under Communist influence'.[58] This could have been said of almost any elected organ, but it was less true of the large and fairly powerful Regional National Committees. The National Socialists, and also the Social Democrats, were determined to defend these: by doing so they could hope to exercise at least some control over the strength of the Communist dominated Ministry of the Interior.

If the political atmosphere made agreement on a new constitution impossible, then the government could not complete its programme. The National Socialists were unconcerned by this and joined with the People's Party in advocating early elections while the Communists and Social Democrats did not want them before 23 May 1948. The timing of the elections could have a great bearing on their outcome because the Communists needed time to build up their campaign and could expect to gain prestige from the completion of the government programme. The Social Democrats found themselves pulled both ways: they feared a KSČ victory, but they definitely wanted the programme completed. Moreover, as Laušman sensibly pointed out, there was no reason to suppose that agreement could be reached more easily after the elections.[59]

Despite some nervousness the National Socialists seem to have been generally confident of markedly reducing the KSČ vote and their optimism was shared by Beneš and J. Masaryk.[60] There was support for this view in a powerful rumour that a public opinion poll, highly embarrassing for the KSČ, had been suppressed by Kopecký. The claim in numerous Western sources is that the KSČ vote was expected to drop from 38% to 29%.[61]

In fact it seems that, although there was an opinion poll, its results were never even calculated.[62] Anyway, it would have been of limited value in so fluid a political situation. The Communists conducted a survey of their own which suggested that they would win 55% of the votes in the Czech lands. This, however, was not a firm prediction, but only an estimate of what could be achieved after vigorous campaigning.[63]

Changes in the membership of parties do not give a definite indication for the elections either. All the parties were growing as political conflicts became sharper. The National Socialists made some losses in re-registration of members over the new year so that their total was 602,056 on 31 January 1948 compared with 593,982 in September 1946.[64] The KSČ, with no re-registration to disrupt the impression of uninterrupted growth, drew near to the target of one and a half million: they were claiming more members than all the other parties put together. They may, however, have been recruiting mostly their former supporters: they still lacked a firm membership base among peasants, office workers and the urban petty bourgeoisie.[65]

In this fluid and uncertain situation the National Socialists were surprisingly confident. Ripka could foresee a KSČ victory only if the Soviet Union actively intervened. He convinced himself that, owing to their cautious attitude on the situation in Greece, the Soviet leaders were scared to go too far in offending the West and would therefore hesitate to send troops into Czechoslovakia.[66] It was also particularly encouraging for him that the leaders of other parties were becoming more nervous about the Communists' possible intentions. Scope was therefore created for an anti-KSČ bloc which, as it could unite a majority of MPs, could have the strength to block the development of the Communists' campaign and force an early election. Towards this end, discussions were held between Drtina and Lettrich in January 1948 on a possible common approach between their two parties. The KSČ were able to expose this to the public,[67] and the National Socialists, having previously expressed total opposition to any 'blocs', were acutely embarrassed.

Even more encouraging for the National Socialists was Laušman's fear of KSČ victory in the elections which he thought would be 'a jump into the dark'. This led him to welcome secret contacts with Zenkl which, unfortunately for them, were publicised by the KSČ albeit with exaggerated claims about the extent of agreement.[68] The Social Democrats had particular cause for concern as, following the Communist Party's November Central Committee meeting, an organised left wing was taking shape within their own party. Although its policies differed from those of the KSČ – it opposed further nationalisations and gave great prominence to allegiance to the heritage of T. G. Masaryk – its existence could certainly justify Laušman's fears that it would join the KSČ in a 'new' National Front. He therefore agreed fully with Zenkl that only the existing parties, with the same titles, could take part in the elections.

The National Socialists evidently hoped to exploit this nervousness to create a bloc against the KSČ and they achieved a major success in the government meeting on 10 February 1948 when they defeated the Communist backed ÚRO proposal on civil servants' pay. The National Socialists dropped their initial proposal of a 25% wage increase and backed a Social Democrat proposal for a smaller overall rise but with more for the highest paid and an increase in pensions too. When this won a majority in the government the trade union leaders were furious. They claimed that it had been extremely difficult to present a united position on civil servants' pay. All the civil servants' unions had wanted an increase in pensions, but had accepted the Presidium's objections that there could be no case for the preferential treatment of one group of employees.[69] The ÚRO proposal was not held up as an ideal solution but rather as a difficult compromise that left plenty of other unions in the embarrassing position of holding back their own members because of the serious economic situation. Zápotocký therefore argued that to accept the civil servants' wishes would open the way for a free for all with disastrous consequences for the economy. He also began hinting at the need to find a means to finance pay increases and he referred ominously to 'a road of struggle' and to a possible congress of Factory Councils.[70]

This rebuff to the trade unions was not seen by the KSČ as a disastrous setback. Instead, the KSČ Presidium meeting of 9 February 1948 reckoned that it gave the maximum scope for a broadly based offensive against the other parties around the general demand for further nationalisations.[71] A second government rejection of the ÚRO proposal therefore led not to a retreat but to a statement from Zápotocký that an all-state congress of trade union groups and Factory Councils was to be called as soon as possible to discuss *all* the questions worrying the trade unions and to discuss a new suggestion for further nationalisations. This could be assured of particularly solid backing from the workers in big nationalised factories as it was presented as a solution to supply problems and as a definitive end to attempts to secure the return of nationalised factories to private ownership: this issue had suddenly been thrust back into the centre of attention in early 1948 by a controversial Supreme Court ruling handing back the nationalised Orion chocolate factory to private owners.

The build up to the congress was coordinated between the trade union and KSČ leaderships. It was also reinforced by the Communist press which prominently publicised the extent of capitalists' profits. Moreover, their papers devoted great attention to the proposals for a comprehensive social insurance scheme that were raised by KSČ ministers in the 13 February 1948 government meeting. Its benefits were to be available to *all* employees and must have been viewed very favourably, especially by manual workers.

It is still unclear exactly what results the KSČ expected from the Congress of Factory Councils, but Gottwald later implied that the aim was to repeat the experience of the campaign over the millionaires' tax when, by carefully choosing and presenting the issue, many people who had previously wavered were rapidly convinced that the National Socialist leaders really were 'reactionaries'.[72] The congress could therefore have been part of a longer campaign or it could have coincided with an immediate attempt to create a 'new' National Front or to change the composition of the government.

Even the Social Democrats, who were likely to support demands for further nationalisations, were nervous. They opposed the calling of the Congress of Factory Councils which they saw as creating a situation of 'dual power' with the trade unions arrogating for themselves the right to watch over and judge the government.[73] They viewed with similar apprehension the apparent determination of the KSČ to force a confrontation over agricultural policy. The

Agricultural Committee of parliament refused to accept in full the Hradec Programme at its meeting on 11 February 1948 and the KSČ Presidium then decided to call a congress of Peasant Commissions through the 'Kladno Regional Action Committee of Peasant Commissions'. The response from villages was extraordinarily rapid,[74] but the Social Democrats joined the National Socialists in condemning the congress as illegal.[75] Their argument, backed by the majority of the JSČZ leadership, was that the JSČZ was the only legitimate representative body for peasants. Nevertheless, the congress was held at the end of February.

Despite this opposition, preparations for the Congress of Factory Councils went ahead very rapidly. Resolutions from factory meetings were soon flooding in at a faster pace than during the dispute over the millionaires' tax.[76] There were only a few resolutions from office workers opposing the congress and the ÚRO received only 96 resolutions from civil service union branches supporting Majer's proposal while 137 agreed with the trade union leadership's position.[77] Nevertheless, the National Socialists could feel reassured that precisely this situation was making even the Social Democrats nervous. They believed that they had the strength to deflate the impact of the Congress of Factory Councils, achieve the isolation of the KSČ in the government and thereby force early elections,[78] but they had first somehow to take the initiative. The key to this was to be the issue of Communist domination of the police force.

They had attacked the police force persistently throughout 1946 and 1947, giving great publicity to alleged instances of improper practices by policemen which they labelled 'gestapism': it must be added that most of the specific cases were easily answered. Moreover, when presenting concrete proposals, the National Socialists were extremely vague. The Social Democrats were both more constructive in their suggestions and more serious in their criticisms. Following the 1946 elections they publicised a small number of cases which seemed to amount to the police helping the KSČ to search other parties' premises.[79] They complained more vigorously when it was decided that the police should be present at political meetings and rallies but they never implied that the police in the pre-Munich republic had been free from criticisms.[80] Consequently their proposals looked for means to ensure what they saw as a further democratisation of the police force to give it more trust from the public. This was to include *full* control by the Regional National

Committees rather than the Ministry of the Interior.[81] This particular suggestion would, obviously, have given them more power over the police at the expense of the Ministry of the Interior. It was unacceptable to the KSČ.

Bitter arguments continued until September 1947 when a law was finally agreed to and passed laying out the role and organisational structure of the new police force. Despite some concessions, it broadly followed the Communists' ideas. They claimed to be seeking a reconciliation of the two opposite conceptions of a centralised military organisation and of maximum power to decentralised National Committees. Within this, they insisted absolutely that the Ministry of the Interior should head an independent police organisational structure and thereby retain full control over personnel questions.[82]

Shortly afterwards, as political tension mounted, the National Socialists stepped up their attacks and began warning of an imminent police state.[83] They, in fact, did not believe that the KSČ had the strength to stage a coup against the existing government. Beneš even thought that half the police and effectively the whole army would follow him rather than the KSČ.[84] This was hardly an accurate assessment, but there certainly was a significant anti-Communist presence within the union representing the police.[85] The union's journal often expressed concern about the conditions of work and the need for higher pay for policemen, who were classified as civil servants.[86]

The army, with 140,000 men compared with 40,000 in all the different sections of the police force, was potentially far more powerful. Although there was a definite Communist presence, the typical army officer probably vacillated somewhere around the middle of the Czechoslovak political spectrum. Even Svoboda showed an unmistakable tendency to dissociate himself from the Communists' campaigning methods. Disagreements became open when, evidently in the expectation of a major power struggle, the KSČ began calling for a purge of army officers on the grounds that many had been indisputably pro-German during the war.[87] Svoboda sharply rejected such suggestions.[88]

Even if this made a 'police coup' an improbable eventuality, there were three new factors which made the National Socialists' case more serious. These were the personnel policy of the Ministry of the Interior, the course of investigations into the assassination attempts on three government ministers and the behaviour of the security forces in early 1948.

Nosek naturally continued to maintain in public that appointments were not made on party terms, but the true situation is clear from his speech to Communist policemen in Prague on 19 January 1948. He revealed there that half the Prague police force had joined the KSČ but that this was still inadequate. His aim was to continue with reorganisations and personnel changes 'so as to have the leading posts and commanding positions in our hands'.[89] This was apparently justified because only Communists were 'the best and most reliable patriots'. So, although Nosek was definitely trying to ensure Communist domination of the police, it was still not clear what role this would play in party-political struggles.

It seemed, however, that the National Socialists could demonstrate direct police partisanship in investigations of the attempted assassinations. The police believed that the boxes containing the bombs had been made in Prague. They were uninterested when a carpenter in the Moravian village of Krčmáň boasted while drunk that he had been involved in the assassination attempt, although he apparently never altered his story afterwards.[90] The National Socialists used their strength within the Ministry of Justice to continue investigations and Drtina presented the findings to parliament: it was then publicly revealed that five people held under suspicion in Moravia were all KSČ members.[91] He even tried to implicate the whole party by linking up the assassination attempt with a discovery of arms apparently stored by the Communist MP Jura-Sosnar who denied any knowledge of the offence.[92]

The evidence Drtina presented on the assassination attempts was very strong. Gottwald, however, had already dismissed it at the November Central Committee meeting as a serious provocation against the Ministry of the Interior and the KSČ.[93] It is therefore quite possible that Nosek was using his position to close off a line of investigation that could prove embarrassing to the KSČ. This certainly indicated the politically partisan nature of the police force and Drtina could provide further support for this with an even more serious accusation. This concerned the behaviour of the security organs in the so-called Most spy affair. He claimed that agents provocateurs had been used to show links between a spy group, allegedly working for the West, and leading National Socialists.[94]

He certainly could not in any way prove the connivance of the

KSČ leadership, but the allegations were still very serious. It seems likely that the Communist leaders were not aware of everything that was happening in the security organs. Initiatives may have been taken by party members who had been placed in key positions. Doubting the party's ability to win by elections alone, they could have been looking for other means to transform the political situation.[95] The KSČ leadership, however, refused to accept any criticism of the organs they officially controlled. This was a significant change from their attitude in 1946. They were no longer prepared to make any concessions at all.

The National Socialists were justifiably concerned by all this, but it also seemed to give them an opportunity to raise still more forcefully the issue of Communist domination of the police and security forces.

In fact, they chose to stage a confrontation over personnel changes in the Prague police. During the government meeting of 13 February 1948 a report reached the National Socialist ministers of further changes which they believed transferred eight senior police officers out of Prague into provincial posts. It proved possible, even though Nosek was absent, to create a bloc against the KSČ and demand the reversal of these most recent changes. The National Socialists then refused to attend another government meeting until this resolution was carried out. When the decisive meeting was to take place on 20 February 1948, *Svobodné slovo* published a lengthy article under the title 'We will not allow a police regime'. The content was less sensationalist than usual: the essential message was that 80% of decisive positions in the police were held by the KSČ.[96] Irrespective of the truth of the article's claims – and it probably was exaggerating[97] – it can hardly be expected that a windy and controversial account in a highly partisan paper could have transformed the political situation so completely as to push into the background questions of completing the government programme, of ration shortages and of the international situation. Ripka, however, later even suggested that KSČ proposals for a social insurance scheme were intended purely to divert attention from the issue of the police;[98] he even implied that a virtue of the *Svobodné slovo* article was that it was the first time the public had been informed of the situation in the Ministry of the Interior.[99]

Under these circumstances, the KSČ were more than willing to invite a confrontation. Nosek was even preparing a reply which would prove that the National Socialists had received an inaccurate enough account of the changes in the police force to make the government's resolution meaningless.[100]

Before attending the next government meeting, the National Socialist ministers asked whether the preceding meeting's resolution had been implemented. On hearing only that Nosek was preparing a statement, they felt their own inside information to have been confirmed. They therefore handed in their resignations to the President and to the Prime Minister. The People's and Democratic Parties followed.

9

The February crisis

After handing in their resignations, the leaders of the National Socialist, People's and Democratic Parties sat back and waited. It is not clear exactly what they expected to gain: although the action had been discussed beforehand there were strong doubts about it within the leaderships of the three parties and there had been no attempt to gain the prior approval of the Social Democrats or of the non-party Ministers.[1] Although the ideal outcome for the National Socialists would have been exclusion of the KSČ from the government, they probably only expected that the KSČ would give way rather than face a government crisis: apparently Beneš generally encouraged this belief.[2] They could then have hoped for the reversal of the most recent changes in the police and for early elections without any political involvement from the security forces.

This, however, can only have been based on a woefully inaccurate assessment of the Communists' strength, of their intentions and of their willingness to face a final confrontation and of how the mass of the population – especially the working class – would respond to a major political crisis. Far from yielding at once the KSČ took very vigorous and decisive action. Their aim, it very quickly became clear, was not simply to 'expose' their political opponents. Instead, they saw and seized upon the opportunity that had suddenly been created to stage the decisive power struggle *before* the elections.

They could see a chance for the National Socialists' plan to succeed. Should the Social Democrats join the others in resigning the government could fall: Gottwald would be entrusted by Beneš to form another government but would be unable to persuade the other parties to join it. The only possibility then would be a government of officials. Alternatively, if the KSČ tried to maintain the

government, then Beneš could refuse to accept the resignations and
the resigning Ministers would return with Presidential approval so
that the government majority could block the activities of KSČ
Ministers one after another.[3]
    Nevertheless, the resignations were a blunder. They left the KSČ
holding positions of power while seeming to confirm precisely what
the Communists had wanted to prove, i.e. that the three resigning
parties were opposed to the completion of the government programme and were scared of the Congresses of Factory Councils and
Peasant Commissions. The police, the KSČ believed, was for most
ordinary people not a central issue, so that the Communists were
left with 'more or less all the trumps' in their hand.[4] They therefore
took an absolutely firm stand from the start, portraying the resignations in the most dramatic terms possible as an abandonment of
the National Front and transition to the opposition. Gottwald
claimed that, although the immediate aim behind the resignations
was not the expulsion of the KSČ from the government, they were
still part of a plan 'to gradually annul everything that has been
brought to the people by the national revolution and liberation'.[5] A
call was therefore issued for the mobilisation 'of all the strength of
the working people' and for the creation of a 'firm National Front'
in support of the Gottwald government.[6]
    Gottwald insisted that a solution to the crisis had to be found on
the basis of the existing parliamentary and constitutional structure.
This allowed him to argue that the resignations need not lead to the
immediate dissolution of the government as the chairman and a
majority of the Ministers were still in office. Even the President had
no constitutional right to demand its resignation unless parliament
passed a vote of no confidence. Gottwald presented this view to
Beneš adding that he could not accept back those who had resigned.
This was the crucial point as it meant that he was seizing the
opportunity to demand a complete change in the character of the
government. Beneš, however, refused to accept the Ministers'
resignation.[7]
    It was a pleasant surprise for Communist activists that they found
no difficulty in mobilising support for Gottwald's position:[8] huge
demonstrations took place in all major towns on 21 February 1948
and enthusiastic meetings were held in factories. Very occasionally
there was support for the Social Democrats' position expressed in the
call for parties to reach agreement within the existing National

Front.[9] There was, however, no sign of real mobilisation among the supporters of the other parties. Instead, it seemed that their members doubted the correctness of the resignations.[10]

The paralysis of the right-wing parties came into the open at the Congress of Factory Councils on 22 February 1948. This was attended by 8030 delegates and referred to at the time as a great parliament of the working people. There was, however, no direct representation for those in enterprises employing under fifty as they had no Factory Councils. The congress opened with addresses from Gottwald, Zápotocký and E. Erban. There then followed a fairly wide-ranging discussion around a draft resolution prepared by the trade union leadership apparently on the basis of resolutions received from basic organisations over the preceding days. The government's crisis was naturally at the centre of attention, and there were several very militant expressions of the Communists' view of its origins. Nevertheless, it was remarkable how many contributors evaded *directly* taking sides in the crisis, and concentrated on the social issues more typically associated with trade unions.

It was also remarkable that the expected opposition, which could conceivably have been supported by one third of the delegates, proved quite incapable of presenting a coherent position. A. Vandrovec, a member of the ÚRO Presidium who supported National Socialist policy, produced an ambiguous speech: he claimed to support unconditionally the proposed social insurance scheme and further nationalisations, but then referred to reservations on some further unspecified points. He therefore wanted to be able to vote on the final resolution in parts rather than taking it as a whole.[11] Šplíchalová, his ally, was even more vague. This contrasted pathetically with Ripka's attempt only a few days before to argue to the National Socialist delegates to the congress that all the ÚRO suggestions were either bad or somehow unreasonable. He had particularly opposed the idea of further nationalisations.[12] Presumably it would have been politically suicidal to say that in public.

The congress resolution included a preamble analysing the political situation and stating that 'reaction' was trying to reverse the development of People's Democracy. This was put in a fairly general way and did not contain direct references to the government crisis. The core of the resolution was a set of five demands: the passing of the social insurance law without delay, passing the new constitution, accepting the ÚRO proposal on civil servants' pay, further nationalisations and rejection of any attempts to denationalise nationalised firms. There was also a general expression of support for peasants' demands concerning land reform and finally a definite proposal for a one-hour stoppage of work on 24 February 1948 in all factories and offices so that all employees could be informed of the results of the congress.[13] It was voted on as a single resolution and according to the official account only ten votes were cast against.

Attention then turned to the one-hour general strike which proved to be extraordinarily successful. In Prague 200,300 took part, there were only 98 strike breakers: 96% then voted for the Congress resolution.[14] Similar figures were produced for other parts of the country although they are difficult to calculate with accuracy as it is not always clear what resolutions were passed. One estimate suggests that 4% voted against while 5% voted for resolutions not containing all the demands.[15] It is at least clear that, alongside the effective unanimity of the working class, many offices joined in too.

This appeared to confirm the disappearance of any organised force opposing the KSČ. Behind this apparent unanimity, however, was considerable differentiation: office workers were by no means as definite as manual workers and could be expected to view some of the Congress's demands with suspicion, particularly on the question of civil servants' pay. They often reached their decisions in the presence of delegations of workers from big factories who seem to have been pretty blunt in expressing their views on the situation.[16] The response from many office workers therefore probably stemmed from fear, confusion and disorientation rather than firm commitment.

Nevertheless, the Communist leaders felt themselves strong enough to demand that, if Beneš did not accept the proposals for a new government which Gottwald had by then prepared, there would be a full general strike.[17] They firmly opposed a subtle compromise solution whereby different representatives of the same parties would be accepted into the government and, claiming that the old National Front had been abandoned by the resigning ministers, they set about preparing a new National Front which was to be a solid support for the Gottwald government and its programme.

Action Committees, presented as the organs of this new National Front, began appearing on 23 February 1948. That evening a Central Action Committee was established following an initiative from ÚRO – the idea had been proposed and accepted at the Congress of Factory Councils[18] – and the KSČ. It is not clear who was invited but a number of mass organisations and the left within the People's Party were present. The Social Democrats sent observers, but no National Socialists were present. Perhaps most important of all, the commanders of the army attended.

After this it appeared that the KSČ had enough support from groups within the National Socialist and People's Parties, and also from Šrobár's Freedom Party, to guarantee a parliamentary majority. There was therefore no opposition to delaying the meeting of parliament scheduled for 24 February 1948.[19]

The Communists must by then have been confident of some sort of victory. They had no compunctions about using their positions in the police to ensure that the National Socialists, rather than suffering a single major setback, were completely defeated. They were even less restrained in exploiting control of the radio. This was an extremely useful instrument for encouraging mass mobilisation as events such as the Congress of Factory Councils or Gottwald's speeches could be given maximum publicity. Laštovička also had no hesitation in preventing anyone likely to oppose the KSČ view of events from broadcasting,[20] and a whole number of employees of the radio simply received dismissal notices through the post.[21]

The press was more difficult to control, but the KSČ Presidium on 21 February 1948 discussed ways for the union of print workers to limit the amount of paper for some newspapers. The initiative had apparently already been taken by workers in paper mills stopping the paper supplies so that National Socialist and People's Party publications would have been stopped within a week.[22]

A pretext for more direct measures was the discovery of what organs of the Ministries of Defence and of the Interior described as a plot to seize power. Their evidence suggested that National Socialists in the army and police were preparing to distribute arms to reliable party members.[23] The police used this as a reason for searching offices of both the National Socialist and People's Parties on 23 February 1948. They took away some written material,[24] but made no arrests.[25] The National Socialists, previously full of rhetoric, responded very meekly: the police were accused of illegal actions in searching premises and confiscating documents, but the charge that some sort of plot had existed was not denied. Instead, the party's Presidium expressed its inability to comment and gave an assurance that nobody would be defended who could be proven by a proper court to have committed an offence. They did, however, reject any attempt to link the party as a whole, or its leadership, with any anti-state activities.[26]

Legal proceedings were later started against the National Socialist MPs Krajina, Hora and Čížek. Accusations included the establishment of an intelligence network in the police and army and a plan to make arms available to members of their party.[27] These accusations are in no sense ridiculous: there obviously was a rudimentary intelligence network providing inside information on the police force, and Ripka seems to have been fully aware of plans to organise serious defensive actions should the KSČ attempt to stage a coup.[28]

At the time, though, the KSČ willingly exaggerated the significance of the police discoveries so as to accuse the National Socialists of preparing a putsch. The Ministry of the Interior, taking advantage of the atmosphere created by these allegations, acted on 24 February 1948 to ban public meetings of all the parties whose ministers had resigned because, it was claimed, such meetings were being used to attack the government.[29] On the same day the Ministry of the Interior ordered, 'in the interest of law and order', that measures should be taken 'to stop the further systematic spreading of lies and false reports' by the National Socialists' publishing house: this involved removing the senior editorial staff.[30]

Although the Communists were able to achieve their aims without any armed clashes, their position within the police force was certainly a great help. They were in a position to direct particularly reliable units into Prague where the decisive struggle was taking place. Already before the crisis had broken a special unit that had been formed out of frontier guards to fight the Banderovci was brought from Eastern Slovakia to locations near Prague.[31] On 20 February 1948 they were brought into Prague itself and on 23 February 1948 they took up positions guarding communications, public places and members of the government.[32] This must have further demoralised any potential opposition.

At the same time, the unquestioning loyalty of the ordinary police, who were armed with rifles and small machine guns, was assured by the way the crisis developed. They were simply asked to stand by the country's legal government which seemed to be quite capable of maintaining the loyalty of the population. Moreover, many policemen could interpret the National Socialist accusations as an attack on all of them while workers' resolutions often expressed 'solidarity with the police'.

The possibility was always present that the army could intervene against the KSČ, particularly if the latter became politically isolated and then attempted a putsch. This, however, was not how the political situation developed. Nevertheless, the KSČ did fear the possibility of part of the army answering a call to move against them,[33] but believed that they too could rely on some army units.[34] Among these was a tank brigade located close to Prague.[35] It therefore appears that any direct intervention, even if ordered by Beneš, could only have led to a bloody clash with no certainty of success and no guarantee of a stable political future afterwards. This would have been a type of action very distant from Beneš's conception of politics and with extremely dangerous international implications. It is therefore not surprising that he made no actual approaches to the army[36] but instead insisted on a peaceful solution to the crisis.

So, instead of intervening decisively on either side, the army commanders gave an emphatic order that the army should keep out of internal political disputes and remain loyal to its supreme commander – Beneš – and to the alliance with the USSR.[37] This did not prevent the same commanders from attending the founding meeting of the Central Action Committee and there is also evidence of army officers being involved at lower levels in the creation of Action Committees.[38] The exact reasons for Svoboda's actions have never been explained as he soon buried his differences with the KSČ. His reasoning could well have been similar to that of the left-wing Social Democrats.[39] It meant that rather than trying to decisively influence the situation, the army confirmed its inability to play a role independent of the general political tide.

Alongside the police and army the KSČ created a further armed body on which they could rely completely. This was the People's Militia which appeared as a small force of reliable KSČ members and was given the task of policing, and ensuring control in factories. Militia groups seem to have been very hastily organised,[40] and generally made their first public appearances on 23 February 1948. Their task then was to ensure unanimity in the general strike and the mere sight even of a few armed men in factories was enough to silence any potential opposition.[41] They were also concerned in Prague with ensuring physical dominance in the centre of town and preventing 'larger gatherings of reaction'.[42]

They must have strengthened the tendency towards demoralisation and resignation among anti-KSČ forces, but as a real military force they were insignificant. Outside the capital they had great difficulty acquiring arms and over the whole country they probably numbered only 15,000–18,000 with 6550 in Prague.[43] On the night of 24–25 February 1948 the KSČ leadership called on them to arm themselves and simultaneously presented Beneš with a full proposal for the composition of the new government.[44]

The President, faced with yet another huge demonstration of public support for KSČ policy, finally yielded. The crisis ended with the formation of a government in which the parties that had resigned lost posts to the KSČ, ÚRO and the Freedom Party. The Social Democrats and Slovak Communists retained exactly the same positions as before, but the Government Presidium was fundamentally altered. The precise situation is shown below.

The KSČ had even maintained the existing constitutional frame-

Czechoslovak Government from 25 February 1948

Prime Minister	K. Gottwald	(KSČ)
Deputy Prime Minister	V. Široký	(KSS)
	A. Zápotocký	(ÚRO)
	B. Laušman	(SD)
Foreign Affairs	J. Masaryk	(non-party)
National Defence	L. Svoboda	(non-party)
Foreign Trade	A. Gregor	(KSČ)
Interior	V. Nosek	(KSČ)
Finance	J. Dolanský	(KSČ)
Education	Z. Nejedlý	(KSČ)
Justice	A. Čepička	(KSČ)
Information	V. Kopecký	(KSČ)
Industry	Z. Fierlinger	(SD)
Agriculture	J. Ďuriš	(KSS)
Internal Trade	F. Krajčír	(KSČ)
Transport	A. Petr	(LS)
Posts	A. Neuman	(NS)
Social Security	E. Erban	(ÚRO)
Health	J. Plojhar	(LS)
Food Supply	L. Jankovcová	(SD)
Technology	E. Šlechta	(NS)
Unification of Laws	V. Šrobár	(Freedom Party)
State Secretary for Foreign Affairs	V. Clementis	(KSS)
State Secretary for National Defence	J. Ševčík	(Party of Slovak Revival)

work, although it became a common theme of émigré writers that the takeover was unconstitutional. This can hardly be argued for the overall solution to the crisis, but it does have considerable validity in relation to aspects of Communist tactics that went beyond the mobilisation of opinion. Examples were the activities of Action Committees and the creation of the People's Militia: these were only legalised retrospectively.

Nevertheless, the controversies around the constitutionality of February can lead to evasion of the central issues on both sides. The *general* constitutionality of the solution to the crisis can be used as a cover for the real essence of the change which was the complete transformation of the political power structure. Alternatively, unconstitutional acts can be presented as the explanation for the defeat of the resigning ministers thereby diverting attention from their political weaknesses without which the Communists' victory could not have been so simple.

Their easy victory must have been partly a consequence of their own tactics and of their ability to mobilise massive support. It must also be seen as a consequence of the failure of any potential opposition to raise significant support and then of the conscious decisions by army commanders, Social Democrats, elements of the National Socialist and People's Parties and ultimately Beneš himself to accept the Communists' demands. The reasons for this, it is argued below, must be sought in the restrictions imposed on the various potentially anti-Communist forces by the international situation and by the weaknesses in their own political philosophies which the Communists were able to exploit.

2 THE FAILURE OF POTENTIAL OPPOSITION

It was a major obstacle particularly for the National Socialists that they could not pose, and mobilise support around, a practical alternative to the implicit KSČ line of incorporation into the developing Soviet bloc. They still clung to hopes of better relations with the USA and they must have been encouraged when the US Ambassador Steinhardt arrived in Prague just as the crisis broke. Unfortunately for the National Socialists he could offer nothing concrete and only expressed the continuing hope that Czechoslovakia would reconsider its decision about the Marshall Plan.[45]

Although the US government did want to influence the political situation in Czechoslovakia, they stuck to their policy of giving no economic aid. Their reasoning was that any offer of assistance would only help solve the Two Year Plan's problems. Moreover, they regarded Czechoslovakia as already effectively a Soviet satellite under firm Communist domination. To give aid would therefore imply that such a government could still expect Western assistance and this, they feared, would be beneficial to Communists generally.[46] Their strategy was therefore to *refuse* any economic assistance in the hope that it would strengthen the anti-Communist forces. The trouble with this was that the National Socialists, for reasons already explained, were not in a position to advocate removing the KSČ from the government. Accepting realities, they had to maintain that Czechoslovakia could retain a strong Communist influence and a close alliance with the Soviet Union while still remaining friendly with the West. They were therefore placed in an awkward position by US strategy and seemed to be left clutching at straws. An example was their enthusiastic report that US Ambassador Steinhardt had indicated that, under certain conditions, it just might be possible to reconsider a Czechoslovak request for a small loan for the purchase of cotton.[47]

Steinhardt in fact did have some understanding for their predicament and argued for some comparatively cheap gestures to improve cultural relations. He also suggested that documents relating to the US role in the liberation of Prague should be declassified. This could have had some impact as the Communist press was claiming that US reluctance to advance beyond Plzeň in May 1945 indicated their indifference to the fate of the Czech people. The truth, as already indicated, was more complicated, but the KSČ line could appear especially credible in view of the US refusal to give economic assistance. The State Department, however, took no speedy action. Perhaps this reflected Marshall's doubts about the significance of events in Czechoslovakia. He later argued that the February events merely confirmed the existing situation as Czechoslovakia had for three years been a close ally of the USSR in international affairs.[48] A political gesture that could help prevent the KSČ from winning 51% of the votes, and hence possibly a monopoly of power, would therefore be of little interest to him. He was concerned only with measures that could swing Czechoslovakia firmly back towards the West. This, of course, was not the National Socialists' stated position and it therefore contributed to their inability to formulate a positive policy.

The United States' refusal to offer economic assistance contrasted strikingly with the Soviet position. This was represented by Deputy Foreign Minister Zorin who arrived in Prague at the same time as Steinhardt. He was offering to conclude a deal for supplying wheat which had been negotiated during the autumn of 1947. This was certainly not a gift: the wheat had to be paid for with industrial goods and this meant that shortages were simply shifted elsewhere.[49] Nevertheless, it could be presented as a very good omen for the future because firm long-term trade agreements with other Slavonic states were to guarantee 40% of Czechoslovakia's exports and imports.[50]

Zorin also made clear that Soviet interest went beyond trade agreements as he expressed concern over allegedly anti-Soviet articles appearing in part of the Czechoslovak press.[51] It is also possible that Soviet concern over Czechoslovakia was so great that Stalin positively wanted the KSČ to ask for Soviet military assistance to establish a full monopoly of power. He was, apparently, well informed of doubts within the KSČ about the chances of winning an electoral victory. This raises further unanswered questions about Zorin's possible role as he might well have been putting pressure on Gottwald to seek a speedy definitive solution to the question of political power rather than waiting for the elections.[52] In view of the situation within his own party, Gottwald could hardly have ignored such pressure and this would certainly help explain why the Communists pursued their aim so vigorously and with so little thought for any possible compromise. It is, however, unlikely that this was the principal explanation for what happened. In the light of their thinking over the previous months, KSČ behaviour was a logical reaction to the marvellous opportunity they were given to settle for good the question of political power.

In practice, of course, Soviet assistance was definitely not requested. Instead, the crisis was ended by Beneš's acceptance of the resignations and approval of the new government. This has even led to some attempts among later émigré writers to place some blame on him for the outcome. Following claims that he knew of and approved the resignations beforehand, he could even be accused of selling out. It certainly is difficult to believe that he was not consulted, but he may well have been ignorant of the risks and uncertainties involved, particularly concerning the likelihood of the Social Democrats also resigning from the government.[53]

In any case, there was soon a clear difference between Beneš and the National Socialist leaders who were surprised when he did not demand the resignation of the whole government.[54] It would anyway have been a pointless gesture as the constitution did not allow him such power and if *he* abandoned the constitution then the KSČ too would feel free to do so.

His position was expressed concisely to a delegation of workers' representatives who argued that he had to yield to the massive demonstrations of support for the KSČ position. Beneš was apparently visibly shaken and snapped back: 'We have not reached the stage yet when the street decides whether I as President should or should not accept the resignations.'[55] He followed this with an insistence that a solution to the crisis must be reached by compromise. He said that he understood when the workers' representatives suggested that they were willing to confront civil war rather than retreat, but maintained that he would 'not accept anything in any situation that would mean excluding one or other group from participation in the government.'[56]

He seems to have hoped that a compromise would still be possible with Gottwald accepting the renewal of a similar sort of government at least as a temporary expedient,[57] but this was tantamount to leaving the initiative in Gottwald's hands. Already on 22 February 1948 he was becoming increasingly aware of the seriousness of the situation and expressed to Laušman fears that there could be civil war: he was beginning to conclude that he had to accept the Communists' demands.[58]

The point, then, was not just the mobilisation of public opinion, but the way in which the KSČ heightened the crisis into a struggle for power. This left Beneš ultimately with the choice between conceding or using every means available to fight them. The latter course seemed hopeless: at the very best, given the realities of the international situation, it could only hope to force active Soviet intervention. To Beneš that would be a disaster as he could see no future for Czechoslovakia *against* the USSR. Ripka, however, seems to have been quite willing to base his hopes on yet another war in which he thought the USSR would be defeated. He suggested that he would have succeeded if it could be shown that a Communist regime could be instituted only by violence,[59] and that if there were

Soviet intervention then it would be clear that external aggression had happened. He could once more go into emigration and await a later victory. Beneš dismissed this as totally unrealistic.[60] Instead, as the KSČ heightened their campaigning and demonstrated their ability and willingness to utilise organs of power, he lost interest in talking to the National Socialist leaders, accepted the resignations and approved Gottwald's new government.

Perhaps Beneš would have resisted the KSČ demands far more stubbornly if there had been any sign of active mass support for the National Socialists. They, however, seem to have assumed that the crisis would remain confined within the government and restricted to the single issue of the police. They therefore made no attempt to mobilise support, although they apparently planned to hold public meetings on 24, 25 and 26 February 1948, when they believed negotiations would be taking place for a new government.[61] By that time, however, they were split internally, divided from potential allies, subjected to police repression and generally in a state of total demoralisation.

This paralysis stemmed in the first instance from the weaknesses in the National Socialist Party, which were brought into the open by the Congress of Factory Councils and by the vigorous activities of the KSČ. The crisis was then posed to the mass of the population as a far more general one. To mobilise any widespread support the National Socialists had to be able to formulate convincing and realistic aims. This, owing to the international situation and to the fact that they had to a great extent initiated the crisis precisely so as to avoid commenting on the issues raised at the Congress of Factory Councils, the National Socialists were unable to do. Instead, they soon found themselves playing down the breadth and scope of the crisis.

Behind this lay crippling contradictions in their position. On the one hand they had refused to come to a National Front meeting and had even resigned from the government: this seemed to suggest that they saw conflicts as becoming irreconcilable. On the other hand they could not seriously advocate a government without Communists – apart from any other considerations that would expose them without question as disrupters of the National Front – and that meant that they could only advocate a return to the previous National Front. If they called for immediate elections, and they had previously advocated this if agreement could not be reached on the constitution, that still left the same unanswered questions about their future intentions. Did it mean that they opposed completion of the government programme? Did it mean that they thought co-operation between parties would be ended after the elections? Why, if they did not oppose the workers' demands, could they not have continued in the government or, as a minimum gesture, expressed full support for them? Finally why, if they really feared a police state, had they chosen to resign from the government? If they really believed the Communists wanted to seize power it would be hard to think of any more naive act.

Instead of clarifying their position and answering the questions that had been raised by their own actions, they unconvincingly asserted: 'we have it firmly assured that the only cause of the critical situation in the government is the question of the security and police forces', adding 'We beg the public not to believe that we want to defend capitalists, landowners and reactionaries.'[62] As their power-ful anti-Communist rhetoric of earlier months gave way to meek-ness – while not advocating anything they even announced that they would not oppose participation in the general strike 'in the interests of peace in the factories and work places'[63] – their whole attitude appeared at best confused and at worst hypocritical.

There were some attempts to mobilise support in Prague but the biggest was a student demonstration which, according to the most optimistic account, had a total strength of 9000.[64] It presented no positive proposals, did not emphasise the original National Socialist demands concerning the police and instead just expressed its loyalty to President Beneš. Two days later a similar demonstration led to a confrontation with the police and during this a policeman's machine gun was accidentally fired lightly wounding a student. Apparently this was the only serious violence during the whole crisis.[65]

This suggests that the great majority of National Socialists could find no counter to the Communists' position. It is therefore not surprising that many people who had been unconvinced a few days before, when the *Communists* had been arguing that disagreements represented conflicts between two fundamentally different concep-tions of development, should suddenly be forced to rethink their ideas.[66] Those Communists who had for months been fruitlessly seeking firm allies in other parties, but had been unable even to convince Social Democrats that Zenkl would betray socialism, suddenly found that their work had been done for them by the resignations.[67] Not surprisingly, some National Socialist leaders began to accept the inevitability of complying with the KSČ desires. One such group was represented by the trade union leaders Koktán and Mátl who followed through the logic of the whole party's compliance with the general strike to argue: 'In the interests of peace and order in the factories we recommend that trade unionists of the National Socialist Party should join the Action Committees and cooperate with members of the other political parties.'[68] They joined with A. Neumann and the economist Šlechta to form, on 24 February 1948, an Action Committee inside the National Socialist Party:[69] they thereby supported Gottwald's efforts to create a new government.

This confusion among National Socialists made it quite impossible for them to act in unity with the People's Party who were just as vague about their aims and even evaded comment on the issues brought before the Congress of Factory Councils. Finally, in a letter to Beneš, the party's Executive Committee made it clear that they wanted early elections while: 'the present government, in a state of resignation, would be trusted with conducting the normal course of government until after the elections. That is the road known to our constitution.'[70] Presumably this meant that the government programme was not to be completed and that Beneš, even though he lacked the constitutional right to do so, should formally dissolve the government.

Alongside the general confusion in the People's Party there seems also to have been wider differentation in interpretations of the likely outcome of the resignations. A number of prominent figures simply disappeared and reports, which were not denied, began to appear suggesting that Tigrid had left for West Germany even before the crisis started. This made it very easy to portray him and his political associates as agents of Western imperialism.[71] It must also have further strengthened feelings of resignation and defeatism in the People's Party and thereby helped the small left-wing group that approached Gottwald on 20 February 1948 with an offer of cooperation.[72] By 25 February 1948 they had been able to assume control of the party's publishing house.[73]

The Social Democrats found it quite as difficult to formulate a clear position. They were unable to accept the full implications of resigning and rejected thoughts of a government of officials. They also turned down a Communist offer to join a majority government and insisted instead on continuing with the 'existing' government until the elections.[74]

The point was that, although even many on the left of the party viewed with apprehension the aims of the KSČ, the Social Democrats disagreed with the National Socialists on many other issues and therefore had grounds for dreading a Communist defeat just as much as a Communist victory. So, instead of joining one side or the other, they condemned both. The resignations were described as over-hasty while the Communists' vigorous response was criticised for making further cooperation more difficult. They set themselves the task of bringing the two sides together 'on the platform of the hitherto existing National Front'.[75]

This was fully consistent with their approach over the preceding months and was the only basis for preventing the fragmentation of the party. Majer, on the right wing, favoured joining the resignations. On the left were voices for negotiating with the KSČ on the basis of the proposal for a governemnt without the parties that had resigned.[76] At first both of these positions were easily outvoted, but even the more cautious 'centrist' position gradually became untenable as the initiatives the KSČ was taking made the renewal of cooperation in the old National Front inconceivable. At the party's Executive Committee meeting on 23 February 1948 it was decided not to participate in the Central Action Committee. Nevertheless, the voting indicated that the left was gaining ground. It was effectively argued that a special agreement had to be reached with the KSČ in view both of the dangerous international situation and of the alleged internal threat to the general direction of Czechoslovakia's post-war development.

On 24 February 1948 the party's Presidium again discussed Gottwald's proposals and other possible solutions to the crisis. Fierlinger could then win a decisive majority for negotiating with Gottwald, but the precise terms were still unclear. Then, as discussion continued, the Social Democrats' Central Secretariat in Prague was occupied by left wingers, who were carrying out a decision reached at a meeting of factory organisations in Prague: they were apparently helped by KSČ students. Laušman called for the police, but they would not help him.[77]

Late that evening Fierlinger led the majority of the Presidium out of the meeting and announced their willingness to accept Gottwald's terms, which included the removal from the government of Tymeš and Majer. The statement read over the radio indicated to some extent how it had been possible to win over the party's centre as it suggested that Social Democracy was to be an equal partner with the KSČ in creating a new government.[78] Even if such a hope was highly optimistic, there no longer seemed to be any serious alternative. Gottwald had mobilised enough support to ensure that joining the resignations would only divide the party without altering the outcome of the crisis. To the party's centre it probably seemed wiser to follow the dominant tide of events and thereby try to retain some party unity and a significant mass base even after the defeat of the two Czech right-wing parties.

In fact even Laušman, after he had been left in a minority in the Presidium, outmanoeuvred Fierlinger by going to Gottwald to discuss the composition of the new government, in which he became Deputy Prime Minister. In view of this failure of all potential Czech opposition to the KSČ, Beneš really had little choice but to yield.

Even in Slovakia there was very little resistance to the Communist victory. The Democratic Party seemed to collapse more readily than the Czech parties after Husák, on 21 February 1948, effectively dissolved the existing Board of Commissioners by informing all its Democratic Party members that their party had resigned from the National Front.[79] Two days later replacements were appointed and the headquarters of the Democratic Party was occupied.[80] On 27 February 1948 the consolidation of power was made more complete as Ferjenčík resigned, apparently not for political reasons, and then Búza too was replaced.[81] Meanwhile, an Action Committee was formed within the Democratic Party. It soon became the nucleus for the much smaller Party of Slovak Revival which was given two minor posts in the new Board of Commissioners.

Nevertheless, it was still not absolutely clear that the KSČ had won undivided power. Beneš remained as President although he intended to resign at once and was only dissuaded from doing so by Gottwald. His actions in the remainder of his life suggest confusion and deep depression as he could neither approve of the KSČ actions nor could he see any point in seriously opposing them. So, despite various fluctuations in his position, he never openly opposed the new government's policies and finally resigned on 7 June 1948. Gottwald was then quickly elected President and Beneš died shortly afterwards.[82] Although the KSČ may have felt somewhat constrained during those months by Beneš's continued presence, they were generally very pleased that he did not resign at once. His presence seemed to indicate that they were still working within the constitution.

Probably the same applied to J. Masaryk who remained as Foreign Minister in the new government. His death on 10 March 1948 was officially described as suicide. This explanation was widely accepted by informed sources even if they were aware of the political capital to be gained from encouraging rumours that there might have been 'some other' cause.[83] No credible evidence for such a view has ever come to light and it is hard to see any motive for anybody associated with the new government wanting to murder him. Had they wanted to remove him from the government he could have been sacked as were Majer and Tymeš. Neither did they need to fear voluntary emigration which for them was a harmless form of protest: suicide was a very powerful one in the period when they wanted the appearance of maximum continuity with the previous constitutional forms.

They were also eager to win approval for the new government and its programme from parliament which met on 10 March 1948. Out of the 300 elected MPs 230 attended and none voted against. The Communists seem at first to have expected an opposition group to emerge in parliament but all its possible leaders either fled or capitulated. Perhaps they feared that some pretext would be found for their arrest. By emigrating however, they made it very easy for the Communists to discredit them.

It is not even obvious what émigrés hoped to achieve in the West: some seem to have always assumed that they would have to go. Apparently about 3000 left by 21 May 1948[84] and by mid 1950 there had been 20,450 attempts and successes. Surprisingly, the overwhelming majority were not members of any party and neither were there any leading figures from cultural, economic or scientific life.[85] The defeated political leaders are of special interest as they still hoped to influence the domestic stituation by starting political activities in emigration. They were hampered in this because the US government, while wanting to encourage their organisation,[86] also believed that by emigrating they reduced to zero the chance of any anti-Communist opposition inside Czechoslovakia.[87] This meant, particularly as Beneš refused to denounce the new government, that there was no point in supporting a full government in exile which would lead inevitably to a break in diplomatic relations. US concern, then, was not primarily or immediately with influencing events inside Czechoslovakia, but rather with ensuring that the easy Communist victory there would not help Communists in Western Europe and, in particular, in the elections that were about to take place in Italy.[88] For this purpose émigrés could obviously be a great help as they could appear as the most convincing support for propaganda against Communism.

They fitted into the developing cold war atmosphere in the West and this provided their main field of influence in ensuing years. They could add authenticity to the extremely strong condemnations of the new Czechoslovak government from the press and official circles in the West where the February events were later quoted even as a major justification for the establishment of NATO.

Inside Czechoslovakia, however, they made the Communists' task of consolidating power a very comfortable one. That, of course, does not mean that the final outcome would have been substantially different if a serious attempt had been made to create an opposition movement.

I O

Post-February Czechoslovakia

I CONSOLIDATION OF POWER

Changes in power throughout society were brought about to a great extent by Action Committees. They were presented as the organs of the new National Front, but the practical details of their size, exact composition and relationship to other institutions were all left vague. Only the essential principle was made clear and directives from the Ministry of the Interior left little doubt that they were to be formed, and to remain, under Communist control: their immediate role was to reflect and consolidate the Communist Party's newly won power regardless of any normal democratic procedures.

They were not to be elected organs and control was to be exercised only from above – even the calling of public meetings was discouraged. Nevertheless, they were apparently the 'authorised' spokesmen of the will of the Czechoslovak people[1] and had enormous powers of discretion: they were assured that decisions, provided they had been 'correct', would be retrospectively approved by law.

Their first task was to implement a purge. At some levels, however, this was done by direct administrative measures. The Communist mayor of Prague simply requested the removal of *all* representatives of the other three parties from the National Committee and the Ministry of the Interior quickly approved the measure![2] Changes then went down to lower levels. The official figures suggest that of 9419 employees in the political administration, 526 were removed, while out of 5600 in Regional administration only 28 were sacked.[3] Overall, in all spheres of life, the immediate post-February purge probably affected 20,000–30,000, including those demoted or prematurely pensioned off.[4]

Apart from public administration, the purge was also concerned with political parties and mass organisations. This, naturally, did not affect the KSČ, and the trade unions too were felt to be capable of carrying out necessary internal changes themselves. Action Committees were, however, established inside the parties of the ministers who had resigned thereby effectively giving the KSČ the power to decide their fate.

In economic life the purge was probably considerably milder than in the political and public administration spheres. It was also implemented more quickly, particularly in factories, and Action Committees were generally not necessary where Factory Councils were firmly Communist dominated. Instead, the KSČ leaders found themselves holding back their followers who wanted to use political doubts about the new regime, or even general feelings of personal dislike, as grounds for discrimination against qualified personnel. This was resisted on the grounds that it would unnecessarily damage production. The KSČ still believed that there was no need to create a 'new intelligentsia' to replace the existing body of qualified manpower, as had been done in the USSR.[5]

Nevertheless, there was no restraint in the speediest possible takeover of those firms set by previous KSČ policy for nationalisation. When the government announced the further nationalisations on 6 April 1948, it probably did little more than confirm the existing situation. By the beginning of May it was claimed that $68\frac{1}{2}\%$ of industrial enterprises and 95% of employees were in the public sector.[6]

At the same time, it was promised that businesses employing up to 50 and landholdings of up to 50 ha would be constitutionally guaranteed. This, it was claimed, meant that the Hradec Programme provided 'a final solution to the land question'.[7] This was made equally explicit at the Congress of Peasant Commissions held in Prague on 28 February 1948, where it was stated that the new constitution would 'refute for once and for all' the stories 'about somebody wanting to establish some sort of kolkhozes'.[8]

This indication of KSČ intentions was not as unambiguous as claimed. Gottwald, following Stalin, made clear that a constitution was not a programme for the future but rather 'a codification of results so far achieved'.[9] It was therefore perfectly possible for the KSČ to constitutionally guarantee private property while still believing that it would ultimately disappear. Nevertheless, there certainly was no rush by the KSČ after February to alter their general conception of social and economic policies for the immediate future. Alongside vague references to 'faster' progress towards socialism, it was made clear that they were still not 'following the Soviet example to the Soviet system'.[10] The laws that were rushed through parliament in those months seemed to confirm that view. Particularly important was the passing of the constitution as the KSČ had wanted it. Undoubtedly the rapid formulation and acceptance of the new social insurance scheme, including a free health service and adequate pensions, also had a great political impact. The necessary apparatus for the revision of the pre-war land reform was created and Peasant Commissions were established, as the KSČ had wanted, from those demanding land. There was even a new law extending security of employment to more in the civil service, thereby appearing to make nonsense of previous claims that the KSČ wanted to abolish their security.[11]

Continuity with previous KSČ policy on social and economic questions could even lead to a generally favourable assessment of February from those who had vacillated or doubted the KSČ before. This was a further reason for the absence of any active opposition in the immediate aftermath of February. There could still be doubts about the future development of the political structure and many could not believe that Zenkl, Drtina and Stránský were outright traitors. It nevertheless could be accepted that 'they were not especially progressive people',[12] and that their removal enabled the government to implement popular measures.

It was then only a short step to accept the argument that, far from being a guarantee of democracy, the previous system with vigorously competing parties had been a purely negative encumbrance. It could even be hoped, as there was no immediate limitation to discussion in non-party specialist journals, that February would lead not to a limitation of discussion in general, but only to the elimination of negative and destructive criticisms and of petty politicking between parties.[13]

While such hopes may have further disoriented potential opposition, similar views seem neither to have been held nor discussed in the KSČ leadership. All attention there was devoted to confirming the party's grip on political power. The first step towards this, although one which still left plenty of ambiguities about the future political structure, was the encouragement of a massive influx of new members into the party. Having previously set a target of one and a half million members by 1 May 1948, Gottwald announced that, with membership already over 1,400,000, the target could be raised to two million.[14]

This could appear as a continuation of the previous policy of winning the maximum number of new members as a basis for the biggest possible vote. It also acquired new features in the post-February situation. Analysis of the 856,657 new members gained by August shows that a quarter of them were members of other parties, including a total of over 116,000 former National Socialists. As the party grew to contain almost 26% of the total Czech population,[15] so it changed its social base: the percentage of workers among members sank from 57% in March 1946 to 49% in late 1947 and then below 40% in August 1948.[16] By contrast, post-February mass recruitment led to an increase in the representation of office workers from 5.6 to 20.6%.[17]

There is no reason to doubt that many of the new recruits had previously been supporters of the KSČ. This, however, was improbable for most former National Socialists, for many office workers and for the technical intelligentsia. It was the recruitment of these people that was particularly important in confirming the new position of the KSČ within the power structure.

There was, in fact, considerable resistance within the KSČ to recruiting former National Socialists. Apparently many of them had supported the resigning ministers, but then suddenly rushed to join the KSČ so as to save their jobs. The leadership argued in reply that even those who were not convinced Communists should be allowed to join as they did not represent a threat inside the party and could be won over and re-educated in time.[18] The immediate aim, however, was to immobilise the potential opposition parties without having to resort to open and direct administrative measures.[19]

The second important category of new recruits, which probably contains many of the same people as the first, was made up of those holding positions of power and influence in the state and economy. For the KSČ, subordination of such people to party discipline was a logical corollary to the great power the party was acquiring. It could either completely purge all power structures – and in the process lose valuable specialist abilities – or, as was done, ensure compliance with some help from the visible threat of a purge by the Action Committees. Criticisms were, in fact, soon being made by the KSČ leaders of the practice whereby office workers were given application forms for the party and limited periods in which to fill them in.[20] Even if such warnings were heeded, every encouragement was still given to many of those who wanted to retain high positions to hastily join the KSČ. Warnings against allowing 'careerists' into the party were revealingly balanced by reassurances that they were no more of a threat than former National Socialists.[21]

In this situation neither the National Socialist nor the People's Parties were able to argue when Slánský insisted that they could never be allowed as mass parties again. Fears of their continuing potential for support led him to insist that they should remain small and be thoroughly purged of 'reactionaries'.[22] That left only the Social Democrats as a potentially serious opposition to the KSČ. Their future was not immediately clear as they had vacillated through the February events and their final commitment to the Gottwald government did not necessarily represent full subordination to the KSČ. The decision had been reached by a hastily formed coalition between the 'centre' and Fierlinger's left wing, and this still left open the old question of how far the Social Democrats should differentiate themselves from the KSČ. Moreover, a new twist was added to the old problem by an influx into the party of former National Socialists.

At first the leadership seems to have felt that February gave the party tremendous prospects. There were references to being 'an equal partner with the Communist Party'[23] and Fierlinger later said that the response at meetings was quite sufficient to justify hopes of building a real mass party.[24] There were, however, a number of obstacles if the Social Democrats were to avoid basing their expansion on former National Socialists who were simply seeking a more respectable base to pursue their former policies.

The first problem was that there was even less scope for finding a credible international orientation as other Socialist or Social Democratic parties in Eastern Europe were merging with Communist Parties on terms that left the new party as a member of the Informbureau. Moreover, the British Labour Party firmly turned its back on the Czechoslovak Social Democrats through a strong statement on the February events.[25]

It was also accepted throughout the party that the Social Democrats had been found wanting during the February crisis. This encouraged, particularly among the left, an inferiority complex towards the KSČ leading naturally to thoughts of a merger. Many

Social Democrats saw this as inevitable either at once after February or in the near future.[26]

Very probably it was the uncertainties about the future course of Social Democracy and the continued scope for the other parties to develop into real opposition forces that led to a change in KSČ policy on the conduct of the elections and on the overall future party structure. Immediately after the February events, they had still assumed that the elections would be contested between all the legal parties. The aim was for the most convincing possible victory as a confirmation of February. An overall target of 75% was set and this was broken down into targets for individual areas.[27] Lower levels in the party responded enthusiastically to this with assurances that there would be little difficulty in winning a quite enormous vote.[28] There were, however, sobering voices at a meeting of KSČ regional secretaries suggesting that only 55–60% of the vote would go to the KSČ. February, as was recognised at the Central Committee meeting on 9 April 1948, had been so easy because the opposition had been disorientated and immobilised. Its social base still remained intact, especially in the countryside. The Peasant Congress, it was pointed out, had by no means expressed the feelings of the whole peasantry.[29] It can be added that neither small businessmen nor employees in many smaller enterprises had really had an opportunity to express any opinion during the February events.

This led to the fear in the KSČ leadership that, despite the organisational weaknesses of the other parties, the KSČ still might not win enough votes to justify a monopoly of power.[30] Moreover, looking further into the future, 'reaction' could re-emerge within the same parties as before. It could find support among those with reservations about government policy as it had before February. It was therefore decided at the party's Presidium meeting on 5 April 1948 that all legal parties would stand on the same platform. This was not a decision to ban all opposition outright as any candidate who succeeded in the formidable task of collecting 1000 signatures could stand. Gottwald even toyed with the idea that there should be a party which 'reaction' could join so that it would not need to penetrate the KSČ,[31] but none of the regime's potential opponents showed any interest in openly oppositionist activities. This is hardly surprising as to do so would automatically encourage the epithet 'reaction' and mean definitive exclusion from the developing power structure. This, of course, was precisely what Gottwald wanted.

The elections themselves were held on 30 May 1948 and 93.5% of those eligible voted with 89.3% expressing approval for the single list of National Front candidates. It is always difficult to know how seriously to take the results of uncontested elections because there is no opposition to confirm whether they are conducted fairly, but such a convincing victory is not impossible when there was no credible alternative and therefore little point in voting against. This was particularly true as it became the general practice to cast one's vote openly in favour. Anybody voting against could thereby easily be identified and could fear later discrimination. This obviously contravened the principle of the secret ballot.

There can anyway be no question that the elections, which passed without the slightest hint of any disorders, were a great success for the KSČ. Soon afterwards Beneš – depressed, demoralised and soon to die – resigned and was replaced by Gottwald. The question of the continued existence of other parties alongside the KSČ was then purely a tactical one.

It had already been decided in early April that the Social Democrats would merge into the KSČ. This was presented as a fulfilment of the belief that the split in the workers' movement after World War I would one day be reversed. More immediately, it was a tactical expedient to prevent the re-emergence of a strong Social Democracy that could challenge Communist supremacy. The decision was taken by the KSČ leadership alone and they also laid down the terms of the merger which were unquestioningly accepted by the Social Democrats. It was made quite clear that the two parties could not approach each other as equals and that, despite the mass recruitment of office workers and National Socialists, by no means all Social Democrats could be accepted into the KSČ.[32]

The process of merging took place from the end of June and the leading left Social Democrats were given good representation in the KSČ leading organs. At lower levels individual KSČ branches were able to choose who they would accept. It is pretty clear that they excluded any who had spoken against them before. The merger thereby effectively eliminated the legal political platform for about half the Social Democrats.[33]

The attitude towards the other two parties was different partly because a merger would not have succeeded in easily absorbing the majority of their former members into the KSČ. Moreover, their continued independent existence was advantageous both domestically, as had been shown in the elections, and internationally as the appearance of a multi-party system was still maintained.[34] It was therefore decided, so as to avoid the risks of serious opposition and the need for excessive administrative measures, that they would be allowed to continue a legal existence within the National Front under firm Communist supervision.[35]

This stabilisation of the new party structure and the completion of the post-February purge meant that there was no further work for the Action Committees. They could have existed as coordinating committees between the various parties and mass organisations of the National Front, but such a role was made unnecessary by the enormous growth and power of the KSČ, and by the complete irrelevance to serious decision-making of the remnants of the other parties. So, rather than a political structure in which the KSČ could exercise its influence through a system of 'transmission belts', the Communist Party was big enough and influential enough to exercise its authority to an increasing extent directly. Action Committees therefore played no further significant role in political life.

2 THE END OF THE CZECHOSLOVAK ROAD?

The consolidation of the Communists' monopoly of power created for the party a completely new situation. It opened up new possibilities but also confronted them with bigger tasks than ever before as, instead of just being the dominant force in the government, they had implicitly taken responsibility for all aspects of the development of Czechoslovak society. This quickly defined the types of conflicts that would determine the future direction of society's development.

There is a highly plausible argument that, in an advanced socialist society, there is a tendency towards the democratisation of the power structure. It is, according to Medvedev, 'an objective necessity'.[36] Brus similarly concludes that social advance has led in Eastern Europe to a 'growing complexity of the object and methods of decision-making',[37] such that there is an 'indisputable need for democratism'.[38] He even concludes that economic needs will ultimately determine 'the democratic evolution of the political system under socialism'.[39]

Czechoslovak experience in the immediate post-war period gives some support to the view that democratisation was a 'need' of society, but could be taken to contradict the argument that evolution will inevitably lead in that direction.

There certainly were signs that many party members felt they could express in public some mildly critical and controversial views, and they were being allowed to do so by the leadership. The initial impetus for this was probably slightly different from that implied by Brus. Before February, when other parties were continually criticising the KSČ, it had been natural to avoid giving their arguments any credence at all. After February, however, restraining one's views in the interests of a display of unanimity around the leadership's policies and actions no longer seemed necessary and there was a small but significant change in several party journals. Particularly interesting were the large number of recommendations on the reorganisation of the National Committee structure. Generally they agreed with the KSČ pre-February proposals, but many seemed to want more genuine decentralisation of powers. One party Area Committee even criticised the criminal and state security branches of the police force for evading any contacts with the National Committee members concerned with police affairs.[40]

There was enough genuine discussion to indicate the feasibility of an alternative line. It could have involved a less rigid interpretation of the 'leading role' of the party such as to allow for differences within its own ranks and also for criticisms and contributions from outside. There certainly was a definite desire to continue with the pre-February notion of a *slower* road to socialism avoiding the dictatorial imposition of major social changes.

Hopes for any real democratisation of political life were a very partial and short-lived consequence of February. The party leadership did not see the need to tolerate diversity and discussion. Their attitude could also be seen as following logically from the February events, which eliminated the need to seek compromises so as to maintain power. Nevertheless, they could only adopt such an approach if they believed, in contrast to Brus' more recent argument, that the new tasks for a ruling party were essentially simple. Under such circumstances there was no need for a full discussion on how to proceed or for an increase in broad participation in decision-making.

Ideas for any degree of democratisation could only become strong and coherent within the Communist movement some years later, when the approach accepted in the early 1950s had demonstrably led to disaster. In 1948, however, any development in that direction was made far more difficult when, presumably as part of Stalin's determination to consolidate a Soviet bloc around his own leadership, the Informbureau's meeting of June 1948 produced a firm condemnation of the Yugoslav leadership. The relevance for Czechoslovakia of the specific criticisms made was not at first clear: above all there was no doubting Czechoslovakia's close relationship with the USSR so that criticisms of 'anti-Sovietism' were felt to be irrelevant.

Nervousness within the KSČ was gradually increased by changes in other Eastern European parties. The central question was always the policy towards the private sector, particularly in agriculture, and the most important case from Czechoslovakia's point of view was Poland where Gomulka resigned after being accused of a right deviation in peasant policy and of a nationalist position amounting, it seemed, to too much independence from the Soviet Union.[41] Around this time the Informbureau's journal suddenly began insisting that Stalin's basic works were of supreme importance for Eastern Europe and great prominence was given to his theory that during socialist construction the class struggle would intensify.

This had not been verified by any empirical method nor had it been validly deduced from other theoretical notions. Essentially it was a bland assertion that proved capable of giving practical meaning to the condemnation of the 'right deviation' in the late 1920s and of the notion of 'nationally specific' roads to socialism in the late 1940s. Ultimately it led to a conception of social development reduced entirely to terms of class struggle. All conflicts with the holders of supreme power were seen as examples of class struggle. Ultimately even economic difficulties, due largely to objective causes, were blamed on the conscious activity of class enemies.

Stalin's theories inevitably had a powerful influence on the KSČ. There had been an apparent theoretical vacuum over the preceding years, and suddenly party journals were full of ideological articles which could appear to provide a sounder basis for policies than had the earlier pragmatism. Nevertheless, their exact implications for policy measures only became clear against a background of setbacks at home combined with the fear of direct interventions from Stalin himself.

The most important setback for the Communists was the failure of industrial productivity to rise significantly. It seems that the February events were expected to unleash initiative from ordinary workers and there were some signs of this happening with the announcement of 'counter plans'. These were effectively promises to reach the Two Year Plan targets by the end of October. At first it was claimed that they were collective agreements reached by workers, engineers and managers in individual factories.[42] It seems, however, that enthusiasm gripped only a few of the workers who were willing to put in a great effort, including working extra shifts, to reach the ambitious new targets. These comparatively small voluntary brigades had a very limited impact.[43] Moreover, their enthusiasm soon ran up against bottlenecks in supplies of raw materials. A particularly serious problem was the mining industry where considerable labour indiscipline persisted.[44] During the summer it became clear that some important factories could not even expect to reach the plan targets by the end of the year[45] and that could only encourage further disillusionment with voluntary labour.

There can be little doubt that workers' attitudes were more diversified and complex than the KSČ had expected. This, however, was not subjected to a detailed investigation. Instead, completely contradicting earlier claims, the failure to achieve an upsurge in plan over-fulfilment was 'blamed' on the failure of counter-plans to go beyond the work of a few specialists.[46] Gradually the responsibility was placed on party organisations to ensure genuinely broad participation in the counter-plan movement and failures were then attributed to weaknesses in party organisation.[47] Objective difficulties were thereby pushed into the background and the success of the economy was increasingly seen as dependent on the ability of the KSČ to raise workers' morale.[48]

This had been one element in KSČ economic thinking before February but suddenly it became the dominant element. Factory Councils were also to concentrate on raising morale and there was little further mention of any other role they could play: they were certainly not given any greater say over economic decisions. In effect, a new model of economic management was beginning to take shape. The supreme organs formulated a plan with ambitious targets and organisations at lower levels had only the limited task of persuading the work-force to try to reach, or pass, those targets.

Unfortunately, increased effort could not be rewarded with immediate improvements in living standards. Initial optimism had obscured this as it was believed that the pre-war production level had been passed even with a smaller population so that real wages should have been 40% above the 1937 level. It was therefore claimed that Czechoslovakia could soon become a 'shop window of socialism'.[49] Unfortunately, the calculation was done in such a way as to ignore the shortages in basic necessities and the need to pay high black market prices which became even more necessary throughout 1948. A more recent estimate suggested that consumption for those who had been socially the weakest in the pre-Munich republic could have been somewhat higher than ever before in 1948 while for the better off there was a marked decline.[50] There was certainly no cause for any sort of complacency as it was a long time before bread rations could be raised again to their pre-November 1947 level.

In fact, shortages and black market prices were increasing throughout 1948 and at least one Communist leader believed that living standards were dropping to 'the lowest possible level'.[51] So, instead of responding with an immediate voluntary commitment to work harder, workers began to translate their increased selfconfidence into insistent demands for improvements in their social conditions. There were some strikes in the late summer of 1948[52] and voices were heard criticising the softness or 'liberalism' of the party leadership.[53] There had, of course, been discontent before February too, but it had generally remained muted or been expressed in hostility towards other parties. February, however, was regarded by many workers as *their* victory and they were unwilling to be fobbed off with promises for the future. The leadership was therefore confronted with a potentially very dangerous situation as they had implicitly taken full responsibility for all aspects of government policy.

Moreover, workers' demands for a social standing commensurate with their self-assurance were accompanied by a sceptical attitude towards other social groups that were less firm in their commitment to the new government. Above all there was suspicion from Communist workers towards the 'intelligentsia'. This term was as vaguely defined as ever, sometimes referring to leaders in the cultural field but very often to those technically qualified people that workers encountered in their work. The depth of the problem was revealed in a lengthy discussion in *Tvorba*. The common theme of practically all the workers who participated in the discussion was *not* that the intelligentsia was acting against or really damaging the regime, but rather a deep distaste for those who could enjoy higher incomes or better working conditions and positions of power and influence while remaining lukewarm or even, as many workers saw it, hypocritical in their commitment. There were even calls for training up ordinary workers to quickly take over top positions.[54]

The leadership was at first perfectly willing to resist such ideas, just as they had resisted calls for a more thorough purge in factories during February, but late in 1948 they suddenly became extremely compliant towards working class attitudes towards intellectuals and towards the private sector of the economy. This could appear as a 'class' line that could be hoped to raise the morale of the working class and also as a re-interpretation of the implications of the Informbureau's resolution on Yugoslavia. An important further factor indirectly encouraging this change was the reappearance of an active opposition which first showed itself in public at the Sokol festival in July and then more forcefully in connection with Beneš's funeral in early September.

Irrespective of the source of opposition or of its strength, and it hardly seems likely that the regime was genuinely threatened,[55] a warning was given by the Central Action Committee that an attempt was about to be made to hold a major demonstration against the regime and to reverse the results of February. Meetings in factories were quickly held and resolutions passed calling for tough measures.[56] Soon there was evidence of 'reaction's' plots in the form of leaflets. One in Tábor allegedly called for the occupation of KSČ offices, National Committees and police stations wherever strength permitted.[57] The distributors of these leaflets later received sentences of up to seven years imprisonment.

The crucial question here is not the measures used against the opposition but the way in which the workers in factories had previously been presented with a dramatised account of the dangers. The strong police measures could then be used with their apparent approval and help overcome their ambivalence on other issues. This appears to have been the principal purpose of the factory meetings as otherwise the police force proved perfectly capable of handling the situation. It indicated a marked shift from earlier policies. Aware of a possible narrowing of their social base, the party leadership chose to rely increasingly on manipulated demonstrations of support from the industrial working class instead of the previous broader approach of trying to win support from all social groups.

Slánský almost admitted as much when he said: 'In the months of July and August over the holiday period hardly anything was mentioned apart from the supply difficulties. By our course of action we have succeeded in changing the mood at once. *We have experience that as soon as the question of the regime is posed so everything else recedes.* Also from the telegrams coming from factories it can be seen that the workers want a vigorous course against reaction.'[58] This was of paramount importance in giving meaning to the theory that the class struggle would intensify during socialist construction. Thanks to such ideas, working class discontent could lead to a hardening rather than a liberalisation of the regime.

Suddenly Stalin's theory was repeated on every possible occasion and there was a willingness to draw sweeping conclusions. In effect all difficulties were attributed to a class struggle in the sense of a conscious effort by 'reaction' to destroy the regime. This was accompanied by the beginnings of a self-critical approach from the KSČ leadership: it was suggested that difficulties had been caused by a complacent view that 'reaction' was completely defeated.[59] This view had, in fact, never been held: the real change was not the acceptance of 'reaction's' continued existence but rather the attribution of economic difficulties to conscious sabotage by 'reaction'. A possibly unique attempt to prove this empirically revealed a vague correlation between the votes cast against the National Front in the elections in agricultural areas and the number of litres of milk delivered per cow. There then followed the sweeping claim that nonfulfilment of delivery obligations was 'primarily a component of reaction's political struggle against our people's regime'.[60]

Such arguments could hardly have withstood serious public criticism. They could only be accepted and allowed to influence KSČ economic policies because of the realities of the new political power structure. Instead of seeking serious empirical evidence, the Communist leaders repeated on every possible occasion Stalin's theory of the inevitable intensification of the class struggle. They found a new and easy explanation for difficulties from the assertion 'the more we weaken the positions of the bourgeoisie, the more they will resist and use all possible means, even criminal ones, to reverse our development to socialism'.[61] This was, of course, a complete reversal from the argument, which had been presented so often before, that the bourgeoisie was cripplingly weakened by the revolutionary changes of 1945.

Stalin's theory was extremely important in the formulation of the whole new direction of KSČ policy. The first and most direct point was that vague and diverse discontent or apathy could suddenly be redirected against a single identifiable enemy. Related to this, a very simple answer was given to the question of what the general direction of KSČ activity was to be. New theoretical concepts did not need to be formulated despite the immense changes in society: instead the central concept was still the old, familiar class struggle.

3 CLARIFICATION OF THE NEW LINE

This change in approach was accentuated when, on 11 September 1948, Gottwald left Czechoslovakia for consultations with the Soviet leadership. There was little doubt that questions of internal policy would be discussed and it seemed likely that the KSČ would be criticised. The possible line of such a criticism appeared in an article written by the philosopher Kolman who was himself a Soviet citizen. His criticisms, presented at party meetings and in an article that was never published, were pretty sweeping: he described the 'specific road' as a retreat from Leninism and argued that an 'all-national' as opposed to a 'class' spirit had been allowed to dominate. He blamed what he described as the effective leadership of the party – Slánský, Švermová and Bareš – for preventing development towards a fully 'Marxist–Leninist' party.[62] Although publication of this article was prevented, there was evidently a fear that Kolman might have been speaking with the authority of the Soviet leadership and Slánský, at a meeting of area secretaries on 22–23 September 1948, accepted that Gottwald's return from the Soviet Union would be followed by a major revision of party policy based on the recognition that a 'period of sharpening class struggle' was beginning.[63]

A Central Committee meeting was therefore called for November and preceded by vigorous condemnations of the view that there could be a road to socialism without a 'dictatorship of the proletariat'. It was even argued that seeking major differences from the Soviet road was a 'dangerous nationalist deviation' aiming to separate Czechoslovakia from the Soviet Union.[64] Instead, specificity was reduced to no more than the fact that the Red Army had liberated Czechoslovakia. Remarkably, there were still some prepared to repeat the old arguments that nobody should lose his head at the continuing presence of 'reaction': the Czechoslovak road, it was repeated, was 'more complicated, in a certain sense more difficult'.[65]

Gottwald stood somewhere between these two positions. Perhaps Stalin had been persuaded that a full self criticism was not necessary

as there were no influential 'anti-Soviet' tendencies in Czechoslovakia. He was able to argue for a continuing element of specificity in
the sense of a slower and more cautious approach albeit within
Stalin's general conception of socialist construction. He warned
against excessive haste – particularly in the collectivisation of
agriculture – opposing any public references to kolkhozes although
they certainly were to be organised in the future. Stalin had approved of this.[66]

Nevertheless, the KSČ leadership increasingly returned to a 'pure
class' line, in some respects similar to the attitudes of the 1928–34
period, and this reinforced a number of tendencies that were making
themselves felt after the post-February consolidation of power.
Above all, the 'class' approach quickly penetrated into inner-party
affairs as the political core of the party reacted against the largely
indiscriminate recruitment of earlier months. That had made sense
when it had been necessary to compete with other legal parties, or to
prevent their revival as serious opponents. It was, however, a
logical corollary of the immense power acquired by party officials
and leading activists after February that they should no longer see
any need to make apparent compromises in favour of these newer
recruits. Such attitudes could clearly have a great deal in common
with those of manual workers towards intellectuals.

So, following persistent signs of distaste towards the whole
practice, mass recruitment was officially stopped in early August and
the KSČ Presidium admitted that serious mistakes had been made.[67]
Simultaneously, new recruitment principles were announced with an
emphasis on the need to be more selective when recruiting peasants,
small businessmen and intellectuals and to see recruiting workers as
the primary aim.[68] Only shortly beforehand, *broadening* the party's
social base had been a definite objective in recruitment policy.[69]

Officially the change was not intended to be particularly dramatic.
The proposals for a screening of all party members, announced
shortly afterwards, appeared to be essentially in harmony with the
stated justification for the post-February recruitment. Although it
was felt that some 'alien elements' would have to be removed,[70] the
principal aim was to be the education of new members.[71] Shortly
before the start, which was to be on 1 October 1948, there were
strong warnings against the assumptions of 'many comrades' who
'wanted to get rid of the so-called "February and post-February
members" which they see as nothing more than ballast'.[72]

Nevertheless, such attitudes were at least partly accepted at the Presidium meeting of 9 September 1948. It was argued, albeit improbably in view of the realities of the party's organisational structure plus the nature of the opposition the regime was facing, that feelings of uncertainty and even panic had been able to penetrate more easily because of the party's social breadth.[73] It was even suggested that bourgeois attitudes and petty bourgeois elements were causing the trouble, so that many members would have to be expelled.[74] Then in early November the party screening was made more rigorous so as to correspond to the 'class' approach. Workers were given something of a privileged status while for others there was to be a very close examination of what had motivated them to join the KSČ.

The fears generated in this new atmosphere inevitably stunted genuine discussion, but a still more ominous deterioration of inner-party life was the growth of a new phenomenon described as 'dictatorialism'. In a sense it was no more than an extension inside the party of the methods that were being used against other parties and against active opponents of the regime. It appeared during the autumn of 1948 when a number of party officials were accused of shunning cooperation with party organisations: instead they exercised power alone.[75] The problem came into the open over the so-called Karlovy Vary case where party members were expelled or even imprisoned for voicing criticisms.[76] There were plenty of similar cases in other areas with officials consciously restricting internal discussions that could lead to criticisms of themselves. Perhaps most revealing of the immense and largely uncontrolled power they had gained after February, they sometimes used the security organs to silence criticisms from within the party.[77]

The leadership naturally condemned such practices, but did not see in them a consequence of the new power structure. Instead, in line with Marxist theory as they understood it, power was seen as no more than the expression of the will of a class. Problems of its control and regulation and of the role and activities of the ruling party had not been seriously considered before and were raised only in a very uncertain, pragmatic and unsystematic way. Gottwald did at least once indicate that there could be advantages in the legal existence of another party, but he never pressed the point.[78] Zápotocký felt that trade unions could act as a control, pointing out that external criticisms had served a purpose in making party members aware of the need to defend their policies before the public.[79] In practice, the trade unions were given a role within society fully subordinated to the party so that they could not possibly perform this function.

Systematisation of these observations into a recognition of the need for a continuing mechanism of control over power was impossible in the prevailing atmosphere. Advantages of the pre-February system were never mentioned and there was never any suggestion that anything could be learnt from the pre-Munich republic. Instead, alongside the condemnation of 'specificity' went condemnation of 'the remnants of bourgeois liberalism and pseudo-democracy'.[80] There was no longer any suggestion that there had been anything positive in previous democratic forms and instead only their negative features were emphasised – such as the restrictions on freedom of expression particularly for Communists[81] – as if that were sufficient to justify the post-February system.

So the leadership's condemnations of 'dictatorialism' could only imply that the phenomenon was no deeper than the mistakes and transgressions of a few specific individuals. They, in fact, had no compunctions about using similar methods. In investigating the Karlovy Vary case, security organs were used and the leading party official in the area was condemned as a 'class enemy who had wormed his way into our party to do deliberate harm'.[82]

Still more serious was the treatment of Kolman. Evidently, he was felt to be a real danger and he was expelled from the party, apparently without his own knowledge, and transported to imprisonment in the USSR.[83] So, paradoxically, it was the man who wanted the most consistent application of the 'class' line who was the most harshly suppressed. Nevertheless, the scope for more general abuses of power was undoubtedly greatly increased by the spread of attitudes and ideas that were broadly in line with Kolman's critique. Above all it justified the notion that there was a dangerous enemy within the party thereby terrorising into silence anyone who might have wanted to advocate a more democratic model of socialism.

The leadership went at least halfway towards accepting those attitudes. They too saw the problem not as the need for a democratisation of political life, but as the need to take a strong line against alleged enemies within the party. This could be supported by Stalin's theories and could even appear as a means to win back solid working class commitment. Moreover, within such a conception 'dictatorialism' appeared just as another reason for distrusting party members at lower levels.

It was suggested that the introduction of secret ballots in inner-party elections could be a useful restraint on party officials, thereby restricting these abuses of power. This was strongly favoured as a principle within the leadership, but it was rejected as premature owing to the alleged immaturity of members and to the prevalence of internal conflicts between groups.[84] Control over the abuses of power was therefore left in the hands of the leadership who, of course, had more scope than anyone else to abuse power.

The importance and practical meaning of the 'class' approach was quickly becoming clear. It could justify distrust towards much of the membership which in turn justified an increasingly dictatorial regime within the party. It backed this up with answers to the questions of the conception of social development and the content of the work of a party holding a monopoly of power. Instead of seeing the complexity of the problem, everything was reduced to a continuing and fierce political struggle. The party therefore had all the more reason for rigid and disciplined unity and for paranoia about maintaining the purity of its ranks.

This 'class' approach also became the basis of the new social and economic policies which were developed and clarified by the KSČ in the autumn of 1948. They centred on the so-called 'sharp course' against 'reaction'. This was justified by Stalin's theory of the intensifying class struggle. In pragmatic terms it was an attempt to stifle opposition while simultaneously responding to immediate economic difficulties in such a way as to maintain working class loyalty.

The most obvious and immediate practical expression of the 'sharp course' was a strengthening of the powers of the police. Also, apparently in response to demands from factory meetings, labour camps were established for 'loafers and disrupters.'[85] They were soon used for those whose transgressions were so mild that even new repressive laws could not touch them: this included the mere spreading of rumours which were alleged to be a conscious part of 'reaction's' activities.[86] It was a further novelty that no court sentence was needed. Even National Committees, it was felt, might be biased one way or the other, so that decisions were to be taken by the Ministry of the Interior alone. It is hard to imagine any other action that could more clearly illustrate their failure to understand the need for a mechanism of control over organs of potential repression. The argument that workers responded positively to strong measures in no way alters this.

Another element of the 'sharp course' was the introduction of 'class rationing'. This involved the establishment from 1 January 1949 of a dual market whereby about one fifth of the population (capitalists, small businessmen and those peasants owning over 15 ha or not fulfilling their obligations to the state) were excluded from the ration system for some goods. In one sense this was just a practical solution to a real economic problem as the imbalance between supply and demand on the market could only be corrected at the expense of some or all of the population. It was felt to be quite impossible to lower workers' living standards so that the chosen alternative hit very hard at much of the private sector. It was hoped that in time market equilibrium could be re-established and rationing abolished completely.[87]

The wider changes in the thinking of the KSČ pushed this pragmatic conception into the background. Instead, class rationing was increasingly interpreted as a permanent blow against the private sector and hence as a firm renunciation of the previous 'all-national' policy. It could be justified by the belief that the private sector was essentially hostile to the government and that only among the working class was there solid support. It could therefore appear as the start to rapid administrative measures aiming to eliminate quickly the private sector.[88]

This was even incorporated into the conception of economic planning. Not only was the economic contribution of the private sector ignored, it was argued that the pre-condition for economic success was 'unceasing, untiring and even intensifying struggle against the remnants of capitalist elements in our economy and a striving to replace backward small-scale production with socially higher forms'.[89] This view was probably encouraged by the feeling expressed by Gottwald that, as the Two Year Plan had failed to raise living standards, planning in general was discredited among part of the population.[90] Presenting the plan as a political struggle and blaming political opponents for all difficulties could make it easier to mobilise support and even enthusiasm.

In agricultural policy a new element was introduced with expressions of the need to 'restrict and suppress' capitalist elements who were allegedly subtly sabotaging the economy.[91] This was the beginning of an approach which ignored Gottwald's earlier calls for caution and justified collectivisation on purely political grounds, ignoring the need for a high technical level if it was to raise agricultural productivity. Not surprisingly, talk of this aroused suspicions among peasants.

Small businessmen were also becoming nervous, particularly after the introduction of class rationing, and the intelligentsia's fears were aroused by further aspects of policy. Their concern stemmed from the purge, the restriction of opposition and discussion, the changes in the party demanding more positive commitment and, perhaps most frightening of all, serious talk of creating a 'new intelligentsia' which followed Gottwald's return from Moscow. Part of the aim was to provide a new cadre force for the army and police. There is nothing remarkable in this as any regime would want maximum loyalty from its armed forces. More surprising and significant was the great emphasis Gottwald gave to the rapid development of young workers so that they could quickly acquire the necessary qualifications for high positions in industry. This was justified by unsubstantiated claims that workers' enthusiasm had encountered 'a lack of sympathy, bordering sometimes even on sabotage, from part of the technical intelligentsia'.[92] It appeared as an interpretation of the policy of creating a new intelligentsia which amounted to a capitulation to the attitudes of at least the politically vocal workers. It also linked up with the developing ideas on economic management as expressed by Slánský. He broke completely from his earlier calls 'to deepen the comradely and friendly cooperation of managers, technicians and workers, irrespective of political affiliation'[93] and argued instead that a successful manager had to be 'a politically educated Marxist–Leninist': apparently he would otherwise suppress socialist competition and be unable to support 'the development of the initiative and labour elan of the work-force'.[94]

All these new elements in social and economic policy must have caused apprehension among much of the population, but it could find no legal means of expression. Instead, owing to the nature of the new power structure plus the atmosphere within the KSČ, its existence could encourage more repressive measures. Slánský effectively argued that there was no longer any point in trying to broaden the party's support: 'What has remained outside our ranks we will probably never win for the policy of People's Democracy, they are outright enemy elements.'[95]

This again reveals how far the KSČ had moved from their implicit pre-February conception of social development. At that time broad national unity had been a conscious aim whereby as much as possible of the population could be involved in economic construction. By late 1948, direct planning, political commitment and the working class alone were felt to be all that was necessary for Czechoslovakia's social and economic development. There was no need for wide ranging discussion or debate, or for compromises between conflicting interests. Even the specific problems of Slovak development were denied within a distorted and oversimplified view of what was happening there.

In the aftermath of February, leading Communists in Slovakia seemed to expect a relaxation of the degree of centralisation of authority in Prague. Their reasoning was analogous to that of the Czech Communists who expected a liberalisation of conditions within the KSČ, but it was not understood by the leadership in Prague. In fact, as there appeared to be more opposition to the regime in Slovakia than in the Czech lands, Gottwald and Kopecký could see only risks and no possible gains from devolving more power.[96] The KSČ Presidium decided, at its meeting on 26 July 1948, for a full merger with the KSS: this effectively ensured the elimination of a potentially independent Slovak party.[97] Široký implicitly justified this with references to 'petty bourgeois nationalism' within the leading organs of the KSS.[98] Totally misunderstanding the case for a degree of independence for Slovak organs, he even insisted that any attempt to maintain the distinctness of Slovakia was essentially no more than an attempt to prevent 'the acceptance of progressive ideas from more advanced nations'.[99]

Already the pattern for Czechoslovak development in the early 1950s was taking shape. The KSČ leadership had taken a monopoly of power after February 1948 and therefore had to take the full brunt of discontent stemming from the failures of their economic policies. Their response was not to liberalise the regime but, on the contrary, to centralise power still more. This, it must be emphasised, does not in any way point to a theory of a 'new class' or even of a clearly defined ruling 'bureaucracy'. Such notions obscure the point that 'dictatorialism' came to affect all levels of the party and therefore cannot be seen as a rational expression of a definite interest within society. The crucial issue was the precise mechanism of decision-making and of exercising political power, which was such as to prevent the formulation of policies corresponding to the needs and possibilities of Czechoslovak society at the time.

The regime can hardly be described as a 'dictatorship of the proletariat', although that rapidly became the official view, as workers had no direct control over it. Nevertheless, consolidation of a monopoly of power was legitimised by social gains to the working class in the very first weeks after February. Moreover, workers certainly gained over the following years compared with the pre-Munich republic and the model of socialism that developed in Czechoslovakia could claim credit for overcoming the more extreme social inequalities and injustices of capitalism. This justifies reference to a 'social' conception of socialism, which could consolidate a political power structure by its ability to give benefits to at least a part of the working class, but which could not satisfy all the other needs of an advanced society.[100]

Its failings were to become glaringly apparent in the show trials of the early 1950s. They were not simply individual abuses of power, or reflections of the disruption of earlier legal norms. Although both those set the scene, the real point was the conversion of the use of the security forces into a systematic element in the leadership's method of governing society.

In the autumn of 1948 there were still some vestiges of external opposition that could serve as a scapegoat. In February 1951, however, as economic difficulties and working class discontent mounted again, Šling, Švermová and Clementis were arrested and accused by the Central Committee of treason. Bareš commented as follows: 'We are not exaggerating when we say that to a certain extent the spirit inside the party and the response to the resolution of the Central Committee resembles the atmosphere of February 1948. And this is not accidental . . . because as in February 1948, at a different stage of development, we have crushed the enemy which tried to turn back the wheel of history.'[101] So, again, the identification of an alleged enemy diffused developing discontent and converted it into enthusiastic support.

It is impossible to avoid the conclusion that, although the February events did confirm that there would be no return to capitalism, they led to a model of socialism which was quite unsuitable for Czechoslovakia at the time. That does not mean that it would necessarily have been ideal to continue with exactly the same National Front structure that had developed after May 1945. There were plenty of difficulties within that and divisions inevitably intensified after the first real beginnings of the cold war. That, however, is no argument in favour of the post-February political structure. The KSČ could have considered at least three general alternatives to what was done. They could have made a far more determined effort to maintain the old National Front; they could have accepted the inevitability of a major political struggle but still not insisted on totally silencing all other parties; or, even after February, they could have allowed for the continuing expression of alternative and critical views both within and outside the party. The last alternative would, of course, have been to some extent internally contradictory as the Communists' behaviour during February itself indicated that they did not appreciate the benefits of diversity. Moreover, it certainly can be argued that, without the right to organise and coordinate their activities, those who want to criticise a regime are almost impotent. The party leadership certainly had no trouble in silencing any alternative views whenever they wanted to.

In any case, all of these alternatives were ruled out by the application of ideas derived from the oversimplified version of Marxism that had been propagated within the Comintern and again by the activities of the Informbureau. These led to the belief that the problems of leading society are simple enough to be solved adequately by a single, hierarchically organised party enjoying a monopoly of power.

Only years later, when the realisation of failure had grown even among some party leaders, did the tendency towards democratisation referred to by Brus begin to assert itself. It meant that the party leaders had to accept that they did not have a monopoly of truth and that they therefore could not afford to silence all critical views. It did not, however, point automatically to any single ideal political structure. All that can be said is that, for all its faults, the National Front system established after May 1945 provided a possible basis for the development of socialism in Czechoslovakia. Even if difficulties were mounting towards the end of 1947, a party theoretically equipped to be aware of the dangers that lay ahead would have avoided crushing all opposition, diversity of opinions and effective public participation.

Notes

INTRODUCTION

1 K. Kaplan, *Znárodnění a socialismus* (Prague, 1968).
2 J. Opat, 'K metodě studia a výkladu některých problémů v období 1945–8', *Příspěvky k dějinám KSČ*, 1965, 1.
3 J. Belda, 'Československá cesta k socialismu', *Příspěvky k dějinám KSČ*, 1967, 1.

I. THE DEVELOPMENT OF THE COMMUNIST PARTY OF CZECHOSLOVAKIA

1 For accounts of these events see F. Peroutka, *Budování státu* (4 vols., Prague, 1933–6), F. Soukup, *28 října 1918* (2 vols., Prague, 1928), Vol. II, T. G. Masaryk, *The Making of a State. Memoirs and Observations 1914–18* (London, 1927), and E. Beneš, *My War Memoirs* (London, 1928).
2 Peroutka, *Budování*, Vol. II, pp. 777–8.
3 J. Křížek, *Říjnová revoluce a česká společnost* (Prague, 1967).
4 Peroutka, *Budování*, Vol. II, pp. 534–5.
5 Peroutka, *Budování*, Vol. IV, pp. 2338–9.
6 Z. Kárník, *Za československou republiku rad* (Prague, 1963), and J. Kolejka, *Revoluční dělnické hnutí na Moravě a ve Slezsku 1917–1921* (Prague, 1957).
7 V. Mencl, J. Menclová, 'Náčrt podstaty a vývoje vrcholné sféry předmnichovské československé mocensko-politické struktury', *Československý časopis historický*, XVI, 3 (1968).
8 Peroutka, *Budování*, Vol. II, p. 1164.
9 Peroutka, *Budování*, Vol. II, pp. 1141–2.
10 Z. Kárník, *Habsburk, Masaryk či Šmeral* (Prague, 1968), esp. Chapter 1.
11 K. Gorovský, 'Bohumír Šmeral', *Revue dějin socialismu*, 1970, 1, pp. 119–22.
12 Peroutka, *Budování*, Vol. I, p. 517.
13 Gorovský, 'Bohumír'.
14 See the view of the Hodonín delegate at the Social Democrats' congress in November 1918; *Protokol XII, řádného sjezdu čs. sociálně demokratické strany dělnické* (Prague, 1919), pp. 119–20.
15 Kárník, *Habsburk*, p. 169.

16 Z. Kárník, *První pokusy o založení Komunistické strany v Čechách* (Prague, 1966), pp. 22–4.

17 *Protokol XII*, pp. 209–10.

18 e.g. *Protokol XII*, p. 197.

19 For detailed figures see Otáhal, *Zápas o pozemkovou reformu* (Prague, 1963), pp. 196 and 199–200.

20 Peroutka, *Budování*, Vol. II, pp. 1363–5 and Kárník, *Za československou*, p. 133. See also the resolution of 26 November 1919 from striking miners in Most, *Boj o směr vývoje československého státu* (2 vols., Prague, 1965–9), Vol. II, p. 208.

21 *Sociální demokrat* 21 January 1920, p. 1.

22 *Sociální demokrat* 18 March 1920, p. 2.

23 *Boj o směr*, Vol. II, p. 114.

24 Peroutka, *Budování*, Vol. III, pp. 1699–1707.

25 *Sociální demokrat* 29 April 1920, p. 1.

26 Peroutka, *Budování*, Vol. III, pp. 1744–58.

27 Accounts of his discussions with Lenin, Trotsky, Zinoviev and Radek were published in B. Šmeral, *Pravda o sovětovém Rusku* 2nd edn (Prague, 1966).

28 They are reproduced in J. Degras (ed.), *The Communist International 1919–1943: Documents* (3 vols., London, 1956–65), Vol. I, pp. 168–72. Šmeral's full speech appeared in *Sociální demokrat*, 30 September 1920 pp. 1–5.

29 Peroutka, *Budování*, Vol. III, p. 2098 and Kolejka *Revoluční*, p. 209.

30 For information on the role of the Comintern in this period, see Z. Kárník, 'Založení KSČ a Kominterna', *Revue dějin socialismu*, 1969, 2, p. 182 and K. Gorovský, 'O založení KSČ – dražd'anská konference v dubnu 1921', *Revue dějin socialismu*, 1968, 3, p. 444.

31 *Protokol II řádného sjezdu Komunistické strany Československa* (Prague, 1925), p. 32.

32 Gorovský, 'O založení', p. 444.

33 e.g. Jesen, *Sociální demokrat* 4 March 1921, pp. 1–2.

34 Čerešňák, *Dělnické hnutí na jihovýchodní Moravě v letech 1917–1921* (Brno 1969), p. 131.

35 *Protokol prvního řádného sjezdu Komunistické strany Československa* (Prague, 1923), p. 52. See also M. Hájek, 'K problému levičáctví v Komunistické internacionále' *Příspěvky k dějinám KSČ*, 1965, 5.

36 From the Founding Congress of the KSČ in May 1921: *Protokoly sjezdů KSČ, I. svazek Ustavující a slučovací sjezdy KSČ roku 1921* (Prague, 1958), pp. 83–7.

37 An explanation of how they were led to this position is given by Z. Požárský, *Založení komunistické strany v Severních čechách*, Ústí nad Labem, 1971.

38 For figures, see H. G. Skilling, 'Gottwald and the Bolshevization of the Communist Party of Czechoslovakia 1929–1939', *Slavic Review*, XX, 4 (December 1961).

39 M. Klír, 'Úloha B. Šmerala při vypracování strategicko-taktické orientace KSČ', *Příspěvky k dějinám KSČ*, 1965, 1, p. 12.

40 J. Choráz, *Komunismus* 15 August 1923 and 4 September 1923. See also the draft for a party programme: *Komunismus* 4 October 1923, pp. 391–393.
41 *Protokoly sjezdů*, pp. 363–80.
42 J. Haken, *Komunista* 28 October 1921, p. 2 and Vajtauer in *Protokoly sjezdů*, pp. 411–17.
43 *Protokoly sjezdů*, p. 481.
44 *Protokol prvního*, p. 11.
45 Z. Hradilák, 'Československá sociální demokracie a zmocňovací zákon v roce 1933', *Příspěvky k dějinám KSČ*, 1967, 1, esp. pp. 29–30.
46 J. Harna, 'Československá strana socialistická ve vládě a v parlamentě (1918–1923)' *Československý časopis historický*, xx, 3 (1972).
47 M. Hájek, *Jednotná fronta* (Prague, 1969), pp. 91–3.
48 See *Protokol II.*
49 See J. Koudelková 'Rudý den 1928', *Revue dějin socialismu*, 1969, 3.
50 V. Kopecký, *Vlast v nebezpečí?* (Prague, 1931), p. 24.
51 See the resolution of the KSČ Sixth Congress in March 1931, *Program komunistické internacionály a usnesení VI. sjezdu KSČ* (Prague, 1931), p. 80.
52 For an account of the unemployed workers' movement, see K. Kořalková, *Hnutí nezaměstnaných v Československu v letech 1929–1933* (Prague, 1962).
53 For a brief account, see Z. Fröhlichová, *Mostecká stávka* (Most, 1967).
54 e.g. *Rudé právo* 26 March 1932, editorial.
55 Hájek, *Jednotná* p. 186.
56 Z. Hradilák, 'On the Process of the Constitution of the "Definitive" Form of the Communist Party of Czechoslovakia (1929–1936)' *History of Socialism Yearbook 1968* (Prague, 1969), pp. 51–3.
57 P. E. Zinner, *Communist Strategy and Tactics in Czechoslovakia 1918–1948* (London, 1963), Chapter 3.
58 H. G. Skilling, 'The Comintern and Czechoslovak Communism 1921–1929', *American Slavic and East European Review* xix, 2 (April 1960), p. 247.
59 Hájek, *Jednotná*, p. 240, and Hradilák, 'On the Process', pp. 65–7.
60 Hájek, 'K problému', p. 715. See also 'Místo VII. Kongresu Kominterny v dějinách mezinárodního a československého dělnického hnutí', *Příspěvky k dějinám KSČ*, 1966, 1.
61 G. Dimitrov, *For a United and Popular Front*, Sofia, p. 175.
62 Dimitrov, *For a United*, p. 140.
63 Hradilák, 'On the Process', pp. 78–9.
64 K. Gottwald, *Spisy* (15 vols., Prague, 1951–60), Vol. vii, pp. 30–3.
65 *Protokol VII. sjezdu Komunistické strany Československa* (Prague, 1936), pp. 34–5.
66 *Protokol VII*, pp. 32–3.
67 e.g. Klíma in *Protokol VII*, p. 71.
68 *Protokol VII*, p. 82.
69 *Protokol VII*, p. 33.
70 e.g. P. Vilemský, *Přítomnost* 1 June 1938, pp. 346–8.
71 e.g. O. Berger, *Nová politika KSČ* (Prague, 1936), esp. p. 3.

72 *Přítomnost* 9 June 1937, p. 354.
73 *Přítomnost* 2 October 1935, p. 610.
74 *Prehl'ad dejín KSČ na Slovensku* (Bratislava, 1971), p. 234 and p. 235.

2. WAR AND OCCUPATION

1 For detailed accounts see V. Král, *Zářijové dny* (Prague, 1971), and J. Křen, *Do emigrace: západní zahraniční odboj 1938–1939*, 2nd edn (Prague, 1969).
2 Accounts in English are V. Mastný, *The Czechs under Nazi Rule: The Failure of National Resistance, 1939–1942* (New York, 1971), and J. Doležal, J. Křen, *Czechoslovakia's Fight 1938–1945* (Prague, 1964).
3 *Dokumenty z historie československé politiky* (2 vols., Prague, 1966), Vol. II, pp. 602–3.
4 Documentary evidence of Nazi plans is collated in *Chtěli nás vyhubit* (Prague, 1961).
5 See below, pp. 29–30.
6 *Chtěli*, p. 161.
7 *Chtěli*, p. 159 and pp. 187–8.
8 For a detailed account of economic and social issues see V. Král, *Otázky hospodářského a sociálního vývoje v českých zemích 1938–1945* (3 vols., Prague, 1957–9).
9 F. Mainuš, *Totální nasazení* (Brno, 1970), pp. 95–6.
10 *Národní fronta a komunisté* (Prague, 1968), p. 31.
11 *Stručný hospodářský vývoj Československa do roku 1955* (Prague, 1969), p. 273.
12 For a succinct account of his aims and activities see Táborský's chapter in V. Mamatey, R. Luža, *A History of the Czechoslovak Republic 1918–48* (Princeton, 1973). More exhaustive are J. Křen, *Do emigrace* and *V emigraci: západní zahraniční odboj 1939–1940* (Prague, 1969).
13 See J. Eliášová, T. Pasák, 'Poznámky k Benešovým kontaktům s Eliášem ve druhé světové válce', *Historie a vojenství* XVI, 1 (1967).
14 *Dokumenty z historie*, Vol. II, p. 613.
15 J. Křen, 'Beneš – problém politického vůdcovství (1939–1940)', *Revue dějin socialismu*, 1968, 2, pp. 188–9.
16 See the messages to London in *Dokumenty z historie*, Vol. II, pp. 553–4 and p. 578. See also V. Kural, 'Cesta k programu nacionálního odboje', *Revue dějin socialismu*, 1968, 1, pp. 72–3.
17 E. Beneš, *Demokracie zítra a dnes* (Prague, 1946), p. 245.
18 See Beneš's discussion with Ripka on 8 May 1942: *Cesta ke Květnu* (Prague, 1965), pp. 44–5.
19 E. Beneš, *Úvahy o slovanství* (Prague, 1947), Second Edition, p. 335.
20 R. H. B. Lockhart, *Comes the Reckoning* (London, 1947), p. 269, and C. Mackenzie, *Dr. Beneš* (London, 1946), p. 261.
21 Mackenzie, *Dr. Beneš*, p. 296, and Z. Fierlinger, *Ve službách ČSR* (2 vols., Prague, 1948), Vol. II, p. 101.
22 Mackenzie, *Dr. Beneš*, p. 296 and E. Táborský, 'Beneš and Stalin; Moscow 1943 and 1945' *Journal of Central European Affairs*, XIII, 2 (July 1953), p. 155.

23 See his comments of 28 September 1943, *Dokumenty z historie*, Vol. i, p. 378.
24 Táborský's record of these discussions appeared in 'Záznam o rozhovoru s maršálem Stalinem v divadle v Moskvě dne 12. 12. 43', *Svědectví*, xii, 47, pp. 479–89.
25 A record of these discussions from the Communist side was published in *Cesta ke Květnu*, pp. 40–59.
26 See Beneš's speech of 3 February 1944; E. Beneš, *Šest let exilu a druhé světové války* (Prague, 1946), esp. pp. 394–5.
27 R. Vetiška, *Skok do tmy* (Prague, 1966), p. 63.
28 Křen, *Do emigrace*, pp. 494–5.
29 O. Janeček, 'Zrod politiky Národní fronty a Moskevské vedení KSČ', *Revue dějin socialismu*, 1969, 6, pp. 808–12.
30 See Šverma's conversation with Beneš in the autumn of 1939; Beneš, *Memoirs, From Munich to New War and New Victory* (London, 1954), pp. 140–1.
31 J. Fučík, *Reportáž psaná na oprátce* (Prague, 1957), p. 134.
32 The radio messages were published in 'Depeše mezi Prahou a Moskvou 1939–1941', *Příspěvky k dějinám KSČ*, 1967, 3.
33 Křen, *V emigraci*, pp. 558–60, and F. Janáček, J. Novotný, A. Hájková, 'Nová orientace', *Historie a vojenství*, xviii, 4, (1969).
34 V. Kopecký, *Gottwald v Moskvě* (Prague, 1946), esp. p. 16.
35 Janeček, 'Zrod', pp. 808–12.
36 Janeček, 'Zrod', esp. p. 831. See also 'Vojensko-politická linie KSČ a domácí odbojová fronta v okupovaných českých zemích (červen 1941 – duben 1944)', *Historie a vojenství*, xxiii, 4 (1974).
37 For a comparison between the conditions in these three countries see *Národní fronta*.
38 This is reproduced in *Slovenské národné povstanie: dokumenty* (Bratislava, 1965. Henceforth *SNP*), p. 65.
39 K. Gottwald, *Spisy*, Vol. xi, pp. 289–96.
40 R. Slánský, *Za vítězství socialismu* (2 vols., Prague, 1951). Vol. i, pp. 370–7.
41 J. Šverma, *Za socialistickou vlast* (Prague, 1949), pp. 399–408.
42 See the Comintern resolution of 5 January 1943, *SNP*, p. 42. See also notes prepared by Gottwald in April 1944; *Cesta ke Květnu*, p. 106.
43 e.g. S. Falťan, *Slovenská otázka v Československu* (Bratislava, 1968), pp. 153–4. Kopecký's articles in *Československé listy* are reproduced in *SNP*.
44 Fierlinger, *Ve službách*, Vol. ii, p. 219.
45 Kopecký in *SNP*, p. 151.
46 Gottwald, *Spisy*, Vol. xii, p. 80.
47 cf. K. Bartošek, 'Antifašistická revoluce v Československu 1944–1945', *Revue dějin socialismu*, 1969, 5.
48 F. J. Kolár *Zestátnění průmyslu a peněžnictví* (Prague, 1945), p. 21.
49 K. Kaplan, 'Poznámky ke znárodnění průmyslu v Československu', *Příspěvky k dějinám KSČ*, 1966, 1, p. 9.
50 e.g. Slánský, *Za vítězství*, Vol. i, p. 382.
51 Gottwald, *Spisy*, Vol. xii, pp. 13–19.

52 Gottwald, *Spisy*, Vol. XII, p. 21.
53 Kopecký, speaking at the KSČ Central Committee meeting of 6 February 1946; J. Belda, M. Bouček, Z. Deyl, M. Klimeš *Na rozhraní dvou epoch* (Prague, 1968), p. 30.
54 For an account of their activities, see V. Mencl, O. Sládek, *Dny odvahy* (Prague, 1966).
55 *Cesta ke Květnu*, p. 149.
56 *Cesta ke Květnu*, pp. 134–5.
57 See his comments of 28 September 1943 in *Dokumenty z historie*, Vol. I, pp. 378–9.
58 Jaroslav Stránský's view of 3 May 1944, *Cesta ke Květnu*, p. 137.
59 Fierlinger, *Ve službách*, Vol. II, p. 207.
60 For general coverage see F. Beer, A. Benčík, B. Graca, J. Křen, V. Kural, J. Šolc, *Dějinná křižovatka* (Prague, 1964). Also useful are G. Husák, *Svědectví o Slovenském národním povstání* (Prague, 1970), and two accounts by supporters of the Slovak state; J. Kirschbaum, *Slovakia: Nation at the Crossroads of Central Europe* (New York, 1960), and J. Mikuš, *Slovakia in the Drama of Europe* (Milwaukee, 1963).
61 L'. Lipták, 'Slovenský štát a protifašistické hnutie v rokoch 1939–1943', *Historický časopis*, XIV, 2 (1966), pp. 194–5.
62 Husák in *SNP*, p. 949 and L'. Lipták, *Slovensko v 20. storočí* (Bratislava, 1968), pp. 203–4.
63 See the message to London of 12 March 1943 in *SNP*, p. 67, and L'. Lipták, *Slovensko*, pp. 203–4.
64 L'. Lipták, *Slovensko*, pp. 204–5.
65 For an account of KSS activity, see *Prehl'ad*, Chapter 9, and Beer, et al, *Dějinná*, esp. pp. 74–80.
66 For a full account, see M. Tichý, *Z bojov komunistov banskobystrickej oblasti* (2 vols., Bratislava, 1966), Vol. II.
67 V. Král, *Osvobození Československa* (Prague, 1975), esp. pp. 43–4, and 64.
68 Letter from Slánský to Gottwald, 12 August 1944, quoted in Beer et al, *Dějinná*, p. 278.
69 *SNP*, pp. 320–1.
70 The only full account of this is in Husák, *Svědectví*.
71 J. Jablonický, *Z ilegality do povstanie* (Bratislava, 1969), p. 203, and J. Lettrich, 'Odboj a povstanie' in *Zborník úvah a osobných spomienok o Slovenskom národnom povstaní* (Toronto, 1976), pp. 74–5.
72 See Gottwald's note to Molotov, 2 September 1944, *SNP*, p. 404.
73 Beneš, *Memoirs*, p. 253. See also Král, *Osvobození*, pp. 151–8.
74 P. Drtina in *SNP*, p. 865.
75 For accounts of this, see Husák, *Svědectví*, pp. 221–2, and M. Kvetko, 'Na prelome dvoch epoch: V ilegalitě a v povstání' in *Zborník úvah*, esp. pp. 118–20 and 132–3.
76 *SNP*, pp. 798–9 and 806–10.
77 *SNP*, p. 460.
78 For accounts of its beginnings see Lettrich, 'Odboj' and Kvetko, 'Na prelome'.
79 Uhlíř's report of 14 December 1944 in *SNP*, pp. 898–9.

80 Husák, *Svědectví*, p. 226.
81 *Nové slovo*, 24 September 1944, p. 1.
82 Husák, *Svědectví*, p. 273 and *Pravda*, 17 October 1944.
83 See Kubáč's reports to the SNR meetings of 14 September 1944 and 19 September 1944 in *SNP* p. 496 and p. 529. See also Šverma's report to Moscow on 14 October 1944 in *SNP*, p. 690.
84 *Pravda* 17 October 1944, p. 1.
85 M. Falt'an, *Nové slovo*, 15 October 1944, p. 60, and Husák, *Svědectví*, p. 285.
86 *Cesta ke Květnu*, pp. 267–8.
87 E. Friš, *Československé listy*, 15 April 1944, reproduced in *Za nové Československo* (Moscow, 1944), p. 112.
88 Friš, *Československé listy*, 15 July 1944, reproduced in *Za nové*, p. 89.
89 The relevant documents are in Fierlinger, *Ve službách*, Vol. II, F. Němec, V. Moudrý, *The Soviet Seizure of Subcarpathian Ruthenia* (Toronto, 1955), and *Cesta ke Květnu*.
90 For accounts see J. Jablonický, *Slovensko na prelome* (Bratislava, 1965), and S. Cambel, 'Vzt'ahy Červenej Armády a slovenských národných orgánov po oslobodení', *Příspěvky k dějinám KSČ*, 1965, 2.
91 M. Bouček, M. Klimeš, M. Vartíková, *Program revolúcie* (Bratislava, 1975), pp. 195–7.
92 Král, *Osvobození*, p. 229.
93 The best account is J. Nedvěd, *Cesta ke sloučení sociální demokracie s komunistickou stranou v roce 1948* (Prague, 1968).
94 *Cesta ke Květnu*, p. 359.
95 Fierlinger, *Ve službách*, Vol. II, pp. 588–9.
96 *Cesta ke Květnu*, pp. 585–7.
97 e.g. H. Ripka, *Czechoslovakia Enslaved* (London, 1950), Chapter 3.
98 The full dialogue is in *Cesta ke Květnu*, pp. 391–453.
99 *Cesta ke Květnu*, p. 519.
100 Husák, *Svědectví*, p. 523.
101 Beer et al, *Dějinná*, pp. 486–7.
102 Fierlinger, *Ve službách*, Vol. II, p. 592, and *Cesta ke Květnu* pp. 441–2.
103 Jan Stránský, *East Wind over Prague* (London, 1950), p. 196.
104 See his comments in March 1945 to Harriman, the US Ambassador to the Soviet Union, *Foreign Relations United States 1945*, Vol. IV (Europe) (Washington, 1968), pp. 432–3.
105 The best account is in J. Doležal *Jediná cesta* (Prague, 1966).
106 Two leading members of the group have both written excellent accounts: K. Veselý-Štainer, *Cestou národního odboje* (Prague, 1947), and J. Grňa, *Sedm roků na domácí frontě* (Brno 1968).
107 O. Machotka, 'Česká národní rada za revoluce' and J. Kotrlý, 'Moje účast v Pražském povstání', both in *Pražské povstání 1945* (Washington DC, 1965).
108 See the ČNR statement of 5 May 1945, *Cesta ke Květnu*, p. 685.
109 Belda et al, *Na rozhraní*, p. 40, and Král, *Osvobození*, p. 360.
110 Grňa, *Sedm*, p. 308 and pp. 282–3 and Veselý-Štainer, *Cestou*, pp. 280–2.
111 *Dnešek*, 9 January 1947, p. 659.

112 This claim is made in O. Machotka, 'Vznik České národní rady a její předrevoluční činnost', *Pražské povstání*, pp. 20-1.
113 Král, *Osvobození*, p. 252.
114 *Foreign Relations United States 1945*, Vol. IV, *Europe* (1974), pp. 446-7 and p. 451.
115 For a fuller discussion, see Král, *Osvobození*, pp. 304-7.
116 Král, *Osvobození*, p. 329.
117 Král, *Osvobození*, pp. 359-60.
118 Král, *Osvobození*, p. 307, and K. Bartošek, *Pražské povstání* (Prague, 1960), p. 88.

3. THE NATIONAL REVOLUTION

1 K. Gottwald, 'Projev soudruha Gottwalda na 1. aktivu KSČ v osvobozené Praze', *Příspěvky k dějinám KSČ*, 1961, 3, p. 408.
2 *PL*, 23 May 1946, p. 2, and *PL*, 4 April 1946, p. 1.
3 *SS*, 17 June 1945, p. 1, and *RP*, 17 June 1945, p. 1.
4 For an account of how the National Front functioned, see M. Bouček, M. Klimeš, 'Národní fronta Čechů a Slováků 1946-1948', *Sborník historický*, 20 (1973).
5 *Stručný*, p. 331.
6 Decree No. 109/1945 of 27 October 1945, *Sbírka zákonů a nařízení*, 1945, pp. 255-6.
7 See V. Majer, *UNRRA a Československo* (Prague, 1946).
8 *Stručný*, pp. 377-8.
9 *PL*, 12 December 1945, p. 2.
10 O. Mrázek, *Nové hospodářství*, II, 9 (1946), p. 129.
11 This is argued by H. Seton-Watson, *The East European Revolution* (London, 1950), p. 181.
12 E. Dvořáková, P. Lesjuk, *Československá společnost a komunisté* (Prague, 1967), p. 37.
13 Slánský, *RP*, 9 September 1945, pp. 1-2.
14 Dvořáková, Lesjuk, *Československá*, p. 41, and J. Navrátil, T. Hochsteiger, 'K otázkám demokratizace velitelského sboru čs. armády v letech 1945-1948', *Historie a vojenství* XI, 3 (1962).
15 Dvořáková, Lesjuk, *Československá*, p. 42.
16 J. Lipták, M. Špičák, 'Únor 1948 a československá armáda' in *Únor a československé ozbrojené síly* (Prague, 1973), p. 153.
17 Beneš's comments to US Ambassador Steinhardt, *Foreign Relations 1945*, Vol. IV, p. 490-1.
18 Cambel, 'Vzťahy', p. 279.
19 J. Lettrich, *A History of Modern Slovakia* (London, 1956), p. 230.
20 *Čas*, 3 July 1947, p. 1.
21 *Foreign Relations United States, The Conference of Berlin 1945* (Washington, 1960), Vol. I, p. 831.
22 *Foreign Relations 1945*, Vol. IV, p. 456.
23 Nosek speech, 16 October 1946 in *Cesta k lidové bezpečnosti* (Prague, 1975), p. 102.

24 Nosek, *RP*, 19 January 1946, p. 1.
25 Dvořáková, Lesjuk, *Československá*, p. 43.
26 K. Bertelmann, *Vývoj národních výborů do ústavy 9. května (1945–1948)* (Prague 1964,), p. 95.
27 *Cesta k lidové*, p. 148 (my emphasis).
28 *PL* 17 February 1946, p. 2, and *SS* 20 February 1946, p. 1.
29 J. Žižka, 'Únorová politická krise a státní aparát lidové demokracie', *Československý časopis historický*, XXI, 5 (1973), p. 664.
30 *SS*, 22 November 1945, p. 1, and *RP*, 22 November 1945, p. 1.
31 e.g. *PL*, 4 December 1945, p. 4.
32 *RP*, 15 February 1946, p. 1.
33 Ripka, *Czechoslovakia*, pp. 113 and pp. 156–9.
34 e.g. Gottwald's speech at the Eighth Congress of the KSČ, *Spisy*, Vol. XII, p. 358.
35 Decrees No. 16/1945 and 17/1945, both 19 June 1945, *Sbírka zákonů a nařízení*, 1945, pp. 29–33.
36 *Lidová správa*, 21 October 1945, p. 6.
37 Decree No. 138/1945 of 27 October 1945, *Sbírka zákonů a nařízení*, 1945, p. 338.
38 Dvořáková, Lesjuk, *Československá*, p. 44.
39 *RP* 1 March 1946, p. 2.
40 *SS* 15 March 1947, p. 2. In the ministry the figure was 46%; Žižka, 'Únorová', p. 664.
41 e.g. *Svobodný zítřek*, 18 October 1945, p. 1.
42 P. Tigrid, *LD*, 3 October 1945, p. 1.
43 In the Information Committee of Parliament, *RP*, 22 November 1946, p.1.
44 *SS*, 22 November 1946, p. 2.
45 Decree No. 6/1945 of 17 May 1945, *Sbírka zákonů a nařízení*, 1945, p. 11.
46 Decree No. 71/1945 of 19 September 1945, *Sbírka zákonů a nařízení*, 1945, pp. 121–2.
47 Decree No. 126/1945 of 27 October 1945, *Sbírka zákonů a nařízení*, 1945.
48 *RP*, 8 September 1945, p. 1. Judgement on this was left to National Committees.
49 *SS*, 3 January 1946, p. 3, and *SS*, 6 January 1946, p. 2.
50 Dvořáková, Lesjuk, *Československá*, p. 84.
51 *Lidová správa*, 1 June 1948, p. 169–70.
52 Calculated from *Statistická příručka ČSR* (Prague, 1948), p. 11.
53 This was referred to by G. Kliment, *RP*, 30 August 1945, p. 1. See also the resolution of 18 August 1945 in *Sjezd národních správců z Čech, Moravy a Slezska ve dnech 17. a 18. srpna 1945 v Praze* (Prague, 1945), p. 70.
54 The proportion of Germans employed in mining actually increased to almost one third of the labour force in the spring of 1946; for figures see *Československý průmysl v prvním pololetí roku 1946* (Prague, 1946), Chapter 1.
55 *PL*, 5 October 1945, p. 2, and *RP*, 19 October 1945, p. 2.

56 *Stručný*, p. 341.
57 *SS*, 12 June 1945, p. 1.
58 e.g. R. Slánský, *Nedopustíme přípravu nového Mnichova* (Prague, 1945).
59 *SS*, 10 April 1946, p. 1.
60 J. Ďuriš, *Odčiňujeme Bílou horu* (Prague, 1945).
61 *RP*, 20 November 1945, p. 2.
62 For a general description of the atmosphere, see R. Cílek, J. Fabšic, *Vlkodlaky kryje stín* (Prague, 1968).
63 Cílek, Fabšic, *Vlkodlaky*, p. 191.
64 Danubius, 'Tézy o vysídlení československých nemcov', *Svědectví*, xv, 57 (1978), p. 119.
65 See below pp. 237–8.
66 J. Kot'átko, *Tvorba*, 26 July 1945, p. 18.
67 J. Kot'átko, *Zemědělská osidlovací politika v pohraničí* (Prague, 1946), p. 7.
68 e.g. F. Kostiuk, *Cíl*, 15 February 1946, pp. 82–3.
69 K. Jech, *Probuzená vesnice* (Prague, 1963), pp. 57–8 and 60–1.
70 Kot'átko, *Zemědělská*, p. 46.
71 Kot'átko, *Zemědělská*, pp. 75–6.
72 For figures see L. Stejskal, *Statistický zpravodaj*, ix, 3 (March, 1946).
73 *RP*, 7 June 1945, p. 4.
74 *Práce*, 24 May 1945, p. 3.
75 e.g. B. Kozelka, *Vzpomínky* (Prague, 1968), pp. 163–5.
76 See J. Sátora, *Svobodné noviny*, 4 October 1945, p. 1.
77 *ÚRO*, 13 September 1945, p. 3.
78 *RP*, 31 May 1945, p. 2 and *RP*, 16 June 1945, p. 4 give the cases of Škoda and Bat'a respectively.
79 Z. Bradáč, *Lidové milice v Severomoravském kraji* (Ostrava, 1968), p. 98.
80 e.g. *Obzory*, 8 December 1945, p. 210.
81 e.g. E. Erban, *ÚRO*, 24 January 1946, p. 6.
82 *RP*, 29 November 1945, p. 2, and *Jiskra*, 30 March 1946, p. 6.
83 Zápotocký, *Práce*, 23 October, 1946 p. 1.
84 J. Benedikt, *Národní bezpečnost*, 5 May 1947, p. 76.
85 For conflicting accounts of Veltruský's contribution, see K. Růžička, *ROH v boji o rozšíření moci dělnické třídy (1945–1948)* (Prague, 1963), p. 44, and K. Kovanda, 'Works Councils in Czechoslovakia', *Soviet Studies*, xxix, 2 (April 1977). A general account of the whole conference is given in *Práce*, 17 July 1945, p. 2, while further detailed information on disagreements within the trade union leadership is given in J. Bloomfield, *Passive Revolution. Politics and the Czechoslovak Working Class 1945–1948* (London, 1979), esp. p. 96.
86 G. Kliment, *ÚRO*, 20 September 1945, p. 3.
87 *Věstník závodních rad*, June 1945, pp. 1 and 2.
88 Kaplan, *Znárodnění*, p. 105.
89 e.g. J. Kolský, *Československé listy*, 15 February 1945, reproduced in *Z dejín odborového hnutia na Slovensku (1944–1946)*, (Bratislava, 1970), pp. 54–7.
90 Růžička, *ROH*, p. 230.
91 See Zápotocký's comments to the KSČ Central Committee on 30 May

1945 quoted in V. Jarošová, I. Škurlo, M. Vartíková, *Odbory na ceste k Februáru* (Bratislava, 1967), pp. 86–7.
92 B. Tvrdoň, *Dnešek*, 11 December 1947, pp. 573–4.
93 *Stručný*, p. 313.
94 *RP*, 10 July 1945, p. 1.
95 Kaplan, *Znárodnění*, p. 22.
96 *RP*, 13 July 1945, p. 2.
97 Opat, *O novou demokracii* (Prague, 1966), p. 108.
98 Zápotocký, *RP*, 28 September 1945, p. 1.
99 e.g. Jan Stránský, *SS*, 16 October 1945, p. 1.
100 *Práce*, 4 October 1945, p. 1.
101 O. Mrázek, 'Course and Results of the Nationalisation of Industry' in *The Czechoslovak Economy 1945–1948* (Prague, 1968), p. 98.
102 *Svobodné noviny*, 15 January 1948, p. 2.
103 See M. Klimeš, M. Zachoval, 'Příspěvek k problematice únorových událostí v ČSR', *Československý časopis historický*, VI, 2 (1958), pp. 195–6.
104 The relevant decree is reproduced in *Cestou května* (Prague, 1975), pp. 282–301.
105 It is reproduced in *Cestou května*, pp. 302–18.
106 F. Dvorín, *Věstník závodních rad*, October, 1946, p. 1.
107 *Průmyslový věstník*, 1 September 1947, p. 655.
108 See the reports of regular Factory Council meetings in the Malé Svatoňovice coal mines in *Jiskra*. For evidence from large factories see Kozelka, *Vzpomínky* and P. Roušar, *Dějiny národního podniku SVIT: národní podnik Baťa* (Prague, 1967), esp. pp. 70–3.
109 J. Hříbek, *K úloze KSČ ve vývoji ekonomiky Ostravska v letech 1945–1948* (Ostrava, 1974), pp. 60–3.
110 e.g. J. Šťastný, *Funkcionář*, October 1945, p. 11.
111 *Fakta a cifry*, 31 October 1946, p. 16 and p. 17.
112 L. Strada, *Nové hospodářství*, II, 4 (April 1946).
113 F. J. Kolár, *RP*, 13 January 1946, p. 1.
114 *Fakta a cifry*, 5 November 1947, pp. 54–9.
115 J. Kárný, *Funkcionář*, 10 January 1946.
116 Slánský, *RP*, 14 November 1945, p. 2.
117 e.g. J. Zeman, *Praga*, 17 December 1946, p. 147.
118 *RP*, 10 August 1945.
119 J. Maňák, 'Problematika odměňování české inteligence v letech 1945–1948', *Sociologický časopis*, 1967, 5, p. 535.
120 See below pp. 230–1 and p. 239.
121 For figures see *Statistický zpravodaj*, VII, 3, (September 1945), p. 62, and *Statistická příručka*, p. 56.
122 *Student*, 11 October 1945, p. 8.
123 e.g. *Věstník závodních rad*, July 1946, p. 8.
124 B. Kozelka, *Vzpomínky*, p. 172.
125 J. Čepelák, V. Čech, *ÚRO*, 3 July 1947, p. 7.
126 For a full account see Hříbek, *K úloze*, esp. pp. 74–6.
127 Pelnář, *Nové hospodářství*, II, 3 (March 1946), p. 36, and Hříbek, *K. úloze*, p. 77.

128 V. Kadlec, *Přebytek kupní síly a jeho odstranění* (Prague, 1945), pp. 8 and 298–9.
129 *Statistická příručka*, pp. 79, 80 and 81.
130 Fierlinger broadcast, quoted in *RP*, 17 November 1945, pp. 1–2.
131 O. Mrázek, *Jak zvýšit životní úroveň pracujících* (Prague, 1947), p. 6.
132 e.g. his speech on 16 August 1945, Gottwald, *Spisy*, Vol. xii, p. 118.
133 J. Krblich, *Stará a nová zemědělská politika* (Prague, 1946), and A. Volavka, *Zásady nové cenové politiky v zemědělství* (Prague, 1946).
134 *Hospodář*, 25 July 1946.
135 *RP*, 8 September 1945, p. 3.
136 e.g. *Rolnické hlasy*, 13 April 1947, p. 1.
137 Nepomucký in *Sněm*, p. 143.
138 Jech, *Probuzená*, pp. 201–2.
139 Kaplan, *Znárodnění*.
140 Kaplan, *Znárodnění*, p. 75.
141 Calculated from Kaplan, *Znárodnění*, pp. 68–97, and Z. Deyl, 'Naše cesta k socialismu a ekonomické problémy drobné buržoazie měst 1945–1948', *Československý časopis historický*, xiii, 4 (1965), p. 501.
142 J. Hejna, *Jiskra*, 14 December 1946, p. 2. See also T. Svatopluk's report on his conversations with miners in Kladno, *Tvorba*, 19 September 1945, p. 136.
143 *Statistický zpravodaj*, xi, 3 (March 1948), p. 104.
144 e.g. at the ÚRO plenum of 13 December 1946, in A. Zápotocký: *Nová odborová politika* (Prague, 1948), p. 468.
145 e.g. the letter from a worker in Ostrava, *Funkcionář*, 10 December 1946, pp. 30–2. The issue was raised repeatedly, to judge from Gottwald's comments at the Central Committee meeting of 25 September 1946; *RP*, 26 September 1946, p. 1.
146 *Svět práce*, 8 May 1947, p. 5. Ministers' salaries are given in Decree 57/1945, *Sbírka zákonů a nařízení*, 1945, p. 97. For further details, see J. Maňák, 'K problematice struktury a postavení československé inteligence v letech 1945–1953', *Revue dějin socialismu*, 1968, *Zvláštní číslo*, p. 1007.
147 *Stručný*, p. 550.
148 For figures see *Hospodář*, 25 July 1946, p. 3.
149 *RP*, 24 July 1945, p. 3.
150 *Svobodný zítřek*, 27 September 1945, p. 9.
151 Deyl, 'Naše', p. 503.
152 Kaplan, *Znárodnění*, p. 89.
153 J. Maňák, 'Početnost a struktura české inteligence v letech 1945–1948', *Sociologický časopis*, 1967, 4, p. 400.
154 Kaplan, *Znárodnění*, p. 93, quoting *Veřejné mínění*, 1946.
155 Belda et al. *Na rozhraní*, p. 52.
156 M. Bouček, M. Klimeš, *Dramatické dny února 1948* (Prague, 1973), p. 28.
157 *What is Your Opinion?* (Prague, 1947), p. 14.
158 *What is Your Opinion?*, p. 11.
159 Kaplan, *Znárodnění*, pp. 111 and 110.
160 Bertelmann, *Vývoj*, pp. 181–2.

161 *Průběh národní revoluce na Kladně* (Kladno, 1945), pp. 11–12.
162 *What is Your Opinion?*, p. 33.
163 *What is Your Opinion?*, p. 29.
164 A. Gramsci, *Selections from the Prison Notebooks of Antonio Gramsci* (London, 1971), p. 238.
165 W. Brus, *Socialist Ownership and Political Systems* (London, 1975), p. 2.
166 Michels, *Political Parties, a Sociological Study of the Oligarchical Tendencies of Modern Democracy* (London, 1915), p. 174.
167 Michels, *Political*, p. 401.

4. THE NATIONAL REVOLUTION IN SLOVAKIA

1 The best account is in Jablonický, *Slovensko*. Also invaluable is the report of a meeting of prominent Slovak Communists in Košice in April 1945, 'Záznam z konference (aktivu) funkcionářů KSS 8. 4. 45 v Košicích', *Československý časopis historický*, XIV, 2, 1966.
2 *Cesta ke Květnu*, p. 485.
3 P. Plánovský, 'Odbojová činnost' na Východnom Slovensku za II. svetovej vojny' in *Zborník úvah*, p. 258.
4 Bednár in 'Záznam', pp. 246–7.
5 Čulen in 'Záznam', p. 245.
6 Husák in 'Záznam', p. 248.
7 See the circular from the KSS Central Committee, 10 April 1945, *Cesta ke Květnu*, pp. 600–1.
8 Jablonický, *Slovensko*, p. 208.
9 See Husák's speech at the KSS conference in Košice on 28 February 1945 in *Komunistická strana Slovenska. Dokumenty z Konferencií a plén 1944–1948* (Bratislava, 1971. Henceforth *KSS*), p. 87.
10 Jablonický, *Slovensko*, pp. 213–14.
11 See Jablonický, *Slovensko*, pp. 336–50.
12 See the report of the KSS conference in Bratislava, 20 May 1945, *Cesta ke Květnu*, p. 625.
13 S. Falt'an, *Slovenská*, pp. 233–4.
14 S. Falt'an, *Slovenská*, p. 213.
15 V. Prečan, *Slovenský katolicizmus pred Februárom 1948* (Bratislava, 1961), pp. 169–71.
16 V. Prečan, *Slovenský*, pp. 214–16.
17 *Nové slovo* 20 July 1945, p. 3.
18 Kaplan, *Znárodnění*, p. 131.
19 *Výstavba Slovenska*, II, 3, p. 6 quoted in Jarošová, et al., *Odbory*, pp. 66–7.
20 See Jarošová, et al., *Odbory*, esp pp. 18 and 42.
21 I. Laluha, *Február 1948 a stredné Slovensko*, Banská Bystrica, 1967, p. 141.
22 Jarošová, et al., *Odbory*, pp. 15–16.
23 S. Cambel, *Slovenská agrárna otázka 1944–1948* (Bratislava, 1972), Chapter 1.
24 Laluha, *Február*, pp. 140–1.

25 *Cesta ke Květnu*, p. 593.
26 Cambel, *Slovenská*, pp. 114–15.
27 e.g. A. Fabián at the Žilina conference of the KSS on 11 August 1945 in *KSS*, p. 210.
28 See Bašt'ovanský's criticisms of this view at the KSS Central Committee meeting of 26 October 1945 in *KSS*, p. 315.
29 *Cesta ke Květnu*, p. 487.
30 D. M. Krno, *Nové slovo*, 1 June 1945, p. 5.
31 Cambel, *Slovenská*, pp. 84 and 88.
32 Cambel, *Slovenská*, pp. 61 and 102.
33 For a basic factual account see L'. Lipták 'The Role of the German Minority in Slovakia in the Years of the Second World War', *Studia historica slovaca*, 1 (1964), pp. 150–78.
34 *Documents on the Expulsion of the Germans from East Central Europe*, Vol. IV (Bonn, 1960), p. 163.
35 Cambel, *Slovenská*, pp. 76–7.
36 See the messages from underground organisations to Beneš in March 1943 and March 1944, *SNP*, pp. 66–7, and 173.
37 *SNP*, p. 457.
38 *KSS*, p. 73.
39 *Cesta ke Květnu*, pp. 491–2.
40 Cambel, *Slovenská*, p. 310.
41 See the London government's memorandum to the great powers on 23 December 1944, quoted in J. Purgat, 'Niektoré otázky mad'arskej menšiny v Československu', in *Východné Slovensko pred Februárom* (Košice, 1968), p. 93.
42 Husák, *Svědectví*, p. 525.
43 Purgat, 'Niektoré', p. 107.
44 J. Purgat, 'Čo predchádzalo Dohode o výmene obyvateľstva medzi Československom a Mad'arskom?', *Revue dějin socialismu* 1969, 4, p. 511.
45 Purgat, 'Čo predchádzalo', pp. 516–17.
46 Purgat, 'Čo predchádzalo', pp. 524–6.
47 J. Zvara, *Mad'arská menšina na Slovensku po roku 1945* (Bratislava, 1969), p. 62.
48 Čulen in the KSS Central Committee's Peasant Commission on 7 June 1945 quoted in Cambel, *Slovenská*, p. 141.
49 Čulen at a KSS conference in Bratislava on 20 May 1945, quoted in Cambel, *Slovenská*, p. 149.
50 M. Falt'an, *Prvá časť pozemkovej reformy* (Trnava, 1945), esp. pp. 16 and 13.
51 S. Falt'an, *Slovenská*, p. 215, and *Prehľad*, p. 350.
52 For an account of how the criticisms took shape, see *KSS*, pp. 153–6.
53 *KSS*, pp. 233–6. See also I. Škurlo, 'Celoslovenská konferencia KSS v Žiline roku 1945 a čo jej predchádzalo', *Historický časopis*, XIX 2, (1971), pp. 145–75.
54 *KSS*, p. 155.
55 *KSS*, pp. 188–9.
56 *KSS*, p. 223.

57 *KSS*, p. 228.
58 See Ďuriš's comments to the KSS Central Committee, in October 1945, *KSS*, p. 271.
59 Calculated from figures in Jech, *Probuzená*, p. 447, and *Stručný*, p. 551.
60 Cambel, *Slovenská*, pp. 184–8.
61 See Ďuriš's speech in the Agricultural Committee of Parliament on 28 November 1945, in J. Ďuriš, *Přítomnost a budoucnost československého zemědělství* (Prague, 1946).
62 *KSS*, p. 173.
63 *KSS*, p. 215.
64 Purgat, 'Niektoré', p. 120.
65 Purgat, 'Čo predchádzalo', pp. 515–16.
66 Zvara, *Maďarská*, pp. 57–8.
67 V. Jarošová, O. Jaroš, *Slovenské robotníctvo v boji o moc (1944–1948)* (Bratislava, 1965), p. 110.
68 *Svobodné noviny*, 2 December 1945, editorial.
69 Cambel, *Slovenská*, p. 260.
70 Jarošová, Jaroš, *Slovenské*, p. 110.
71 *PL*, 9 March 1946, p. 1.
72 Prečan, *Slovenský*, pp. 85–6.
73 *RP*, 7 March 1946, p. 1.
74 Prečan, *Slovenský*, p. 96.
75 Prečan, *Slovenský*, pp 100–3.
76 e.g. Cambel, *Slovenská*, p. 204.
77 See his speech to a Democratic Party conference in Žilina 15–17 February 1946 quoted in M. Vartíková, *Roky rozhodnutia – k dejinám politického boja pred Februárom 1948* (Bratislava, 1962), p. 107.
78 Cambel, *Slovenská*, p. 203.
79 *RP*, 7 March 1946.
80 Vartíková, *Roky*, p. 108, and Prečan, *Slovenský*, p. 107.
81 V. Adámek, *Boj KSČ za přerůstání národně demokratické revoluce v socialistickou v letech 1945–1948* (Prague, 1970), pp. 34–5.
82 *RP*, 19 April 1946, p. 3.

5. CZECH POLITICAL PARTIES

1 Dvořáková, Lesjuk, *Československá*, p. 70.
2 e.g. the figures in Hříbek, *K úloze*, p. 15.
3 Hříbek, *K úloze*, p. 27.
4 J. Zhor, *Dnešek*, 25 April 1946, p. 66.
5 *Život strany*, 22 November 1947, p. 11.
6 *Funkcionář*, 21 February 1947, p. 32.
7 *Co má vědět desítkový důvěrník* (Prague, 1947), and the letter in *Funkcionář*, 8 May 1947, pp. 23–4.
8 e.g. Gottwald's speech of 2 September 1945, Gottwald, *Spisy*, Vol. XII, p. 142.
9 See L. Frejka, *25. únor v československém hospodářství* (Prague, 1949), p. 61.
10 Frejka, *RP*, 15 July 1945, p. 1.

11 Gottwald, *RP*, 17 July 1945, p. 1.
12 e.g. Gottwald's speech at the Eighth Congress of the KSČ, Gottwald, *Spisy*, Vol. XII, p. 355.
13 J. Horn in *Sněm budovatelů: Protokol VIII. řádného sjezdu KSČ* (Prague, 1946), p. 179.
14 *Sněm*, p. 39.
15 Slánský in *Sněm*, p. 46.
16 Slánský in *Sněm*, p. 39.
17 e.g. *Svobodný směr*, 21 May 1946, p. 3.
18 e.g. Slánský, *RP*, 14 November 1945, p. 1. The full election programme was published in *RP*, 12 May 1946.
19 Gottwald, at the KSČ Central Committee meeting on 18 December 1945, *Spisy*, Vol. XII, p. 218.
20 Speech to leading party officials 4 February 1946, Gottwald, *Spisy*, Vol. XII, p. 253.
21 *Zemědělské noviny*, 24 April 1946, p. 1.
22 See above pp. 13 and 17.
23 J. Kozák, 'Význam vnitrostranické diskuse před 8. sjezdem KSČ: aktivní účast členů strany na vypracování sjezdových usnesení', *Příspěvky k dějinám KSČ*, 12 (1960). See also Gottwald's speech of 4 February 1946 Gottwald, *Spisy*, Vol. XII, p. 250.
24 Discussion centred around a letter from the Central Committee sent on 15 January 1946 and reproduced in *Sněm*, pp. 7–13.
25 Kozak 'Význam', esp. pp. 28–32.
26 Gottwald, *Spisy*, Vol. XII, p. 253.
27 A. Kolman, *RP*, 25 January 1946, p. 1.
28 K. Kaplan, M. Reiman, 'Naše revoluce a myšlenky o socialismu', *Plamen*, VII, 12 (1965), pp. 113–14.
29 Speaking on 17 August 1945, *Sjezd národních správců*, p. 37.
30 *RP*, 3 January 1946, p. 2.
31 *Dnešek*, 18 April 1946, p. 50.
32 The fullest argument was from Dr J. Dočekal, *Dnešek*, 2 May 1946, pp. 86–7.
33 G. Bareš, *Rozhovor s Ferdinandem Peroutkou* (Prague, 1947).
34 Bareš, *Rozhovor*, p. 29.
35 See below pp. 138–9 for more on the debate.
36 See Krajina, *SS*, 1 March 1947, p. 4.
37 *SS*, 7 October 1945, p. 1.
38 See Zenkl's speech, *SS*, 11 December 1945, p. 4.
39 e.g. Drtina at the party's Central Executive Committee, 6 June 1946, *Cestou k Únoru* (Prague, 1963), p. 162.
40 *SS*, 12 November 1945, p. 2.
41 e.g. Krajina, *SS*, 1 March 1947, p. 4.
42 J. Petráš, *SS*, 2 August 1945, p. 1.
43 J. Zhor, *Dnešek*, 25 April 1946, p. 65, and Cato, *Dnešek*, 22 May 1947 p. 118.
44 Drtina, *SS*, 2 March 1947, p. 2.
45 Zenkl, *SS*, 11 December 1945, pp. 2–3.

46 V. Bušek, *Vzdělavatel* (May 1947), pp. 154–5.
47 Zenkl, *SS*, 11 December 1945, p. 3.
48 *Cesta ke Květnu*, pp. 585–7.
49 *Česká pravda*, 12 May 1945, p. 1.
50 J. Hejda, *SS*, 19 November 1946, pp. 1–2.
51 Drtina, *SS*, 22 May 1946, p. 3.
52 cf. Ripka's speech quoted in *ÚRO*, 22 November 1945, p. 3.
53 Ripka speech, *SS*, 9 October 1945, p. 2.
54 Růžička, *ROH*, p. 79.
55 Kaplan, *Znárodnění*, p. 105.
56 See the report of the National Socialists' youth rally, *SS*, 4 December 1945, p. 1. See also Krajina, *SS*, 10 December 1945, p. 4.
57 *SS*, 8 May 1946, p. 1, and *SS*, 12 May 1946, p. 1.
58 *RP*, 14 February 1946, p. 2.
59 *Tvorba*, 27 February 1946, p. 132.
60 L. K. Feierabend, *Pod vládou Národní fronty* (Washington DC, 1968), pp. 66–7.
61 *PL*, 23 March 1946, p. 1.
62 *SS*, 28 March 1946, p. 2.
63 Feierabend, *Pod vládou*, pp. 25 and 24.
64 *RP*, 21 May 1946, p. 3, and *RP*, 24 May 1946, p. 6. Feierabend later brought a successful libel case against a provincial KSČ paper in which he claimed these accusations started. This, he believed, cleared his name (*SS*, 4 June 1947, p. 2). Those accusations, however, seem to have been nowhere near as comprehensive as the ones in *Rudé právo* (see *Palcát*, 6 April 1945, p. 2.) Moreover *Rudé právo's* accusations were repeated even after the court case (e.g. *Práce*, 31 January 1948, p. 1 and *RP*, 31 January 1948, p. 1) but Feierabend has continued to deny them (Feierabend, *Pod vládou*, p. 118).
65 *SS*, 12 May 1946 quoted in Jech, *Probuzená*, p. 207. See also Feierabend, *Pod vládou*, pp. 79–81.
66 Koucký, *RP*, 10 April 1946, p. 1.
67 e.g. *SS*, 7 April 1946, p. 3.
68 *Dnešek*, 30 May 1946, p. 145.
69 V. Bernard, *Cíl*, 25 January 1946, p. 34–5 and *PL*, 2 March 1946, p. 1.
70 *Svobodný směr*, 20 May 1946, p. 1.
71 Nedvěd, *Cesta*, p. 41.
72 *Protokol XX. manifestačního sjezdu československé sociální demokracie* (Prague, 1946), pp. 249–50.
73 e.g. V. Erban in *Protokol XX*, p. 84.
74 e.g. Fierlinger's analysis of the party's history in *Protokol XX*, pp. 41–55.
75 e.g. Vilím in *Protokol XX*, p. 121.
76 e.g. Berger's questionable account of the party's independent role during the occupation in *Protokol XX*.
77 e.g. Bernard, *Cíl*, 17 May 1946, p. 291.
78 V. Erban in *Protokol XX*, pp. 80 and 83.
79 *Cíl*, 29 April 1946, pp. 241–3.
80 e.g. O. Mrázek, *Lidovláda v hospodářství* (Prague, 1945).

81 Laušman in *Protokol XX*, p. 228.
82 P. Sajal, *PL*, 7 December 1945, p. 2.
83 e.g. J. Bubník, *PL*, 1 December 1945, p. 1. and Sajal in *Protokol XX*, pp. 169–75.
84 *Protokol 1. pracovního sjezdu živnostnictva čs. sociální demokracie 6–7/4/46* (Prague, 1946).
85 *Protokol 1. pracovního*, p. 68.
86 Nedvěd, *Cesta*, p. 52, and Dvořáková, Lesjuk, *Československá*, p. 64.
87 Hříbek, *K úloze*, p. 61.
88 Speaking to People's Party MPs on 13 November 1945, quoted in Opat, *O novou*, p. 75.
89 cf. Šrámek's speech of 13 November 1945, Opat, *O novou*, p. 125.
90 *LD*, 3 April 1946, p. 4.
91 J. Řehulka, *LD*, 5 April 1946, p. 3.
92 Hála, *LD*, 19 May 1946, p. 2.
93 *Obzory*, 11 January 1947.
94 B. Chudoba, *Co je křest'anská politika* (Prague, 1947).
95 Dvořáková, Lesjuk, *Československá*, p. 60: *PL*, 16 January 1948, p. 1, and J. Plojhar, *Vítězný únor 1948 a Čs. strana lidová* (Prague, 1958), esp. pp. 25–31.
96 *PL*, 11 December 1945, p. 2.
97 *PL*, 15 December 1945, p. 2.
98 *Obzory*, 15 December 1945, p. 225.
99 *SS*, 5 March 1946, p. 5.
100 *Obzory*, 11 May 1946.
101 *LD*, 5 May 1946, p. 1.
102 *LD*, 26 May 1946, p. 1.
103 *Zprávy státního úřadu statistického*, 1947, p. 329.
104 *Zprávy státního úřadu statistického*, 1947, pp. 335 and 336.
105 *Zprávy státního úřadu statistického*, 1947, p. 335.
106 *Cestou k únoru*, p. 33, and V. Adámek, *Boj*, p. 63.
107 Jaroslav Stránský, *SS*, 25 May 1946, p. 3.
108 e.g. Ripka, *SS*, 2 June 1946, p. 1.
109 V. Bolen, *SS*, 7 June 1946, p. 1.
110 At the National Socialists' Central Executive Committee meeting on 6 June 1946, *Cestou k Únoru*, p. 167.
111 L. Khás, *Svobodné noviny*, 24 August 1946, p. 1.
112 *Dnešek*, 30 May 1946, p. 146.
113 M. Mareš, *Dnešek*, 13 June 1946, pp. 181–3 and 20 June 1946, pp. 195–197, and J. Hudec, *Dnešek*, 4 July 1946, p. 230.
114 e.g. Ripka's speech, *SS*, 18 April 1946, p. 1.
115 F. Klátil, *SS*, 20 April 1946, p. 1.
116 Zenkl's speech, *SS*, 16 April 1946, p. 3 (his emphasis).
117 e.g. F. Trávníček, *Zemědělské noviny*, 15 May 1946, p. 2.
118 *Cíl*, 6 December 1946, p. 757.
119 *Zprávy státního úřadu statistického*, 1947, pp. 336–8.
120 Laluha, *Február*, p. 28.
121 Cambel, *Slovenská*, p. 221.
122 *Zprávy státního úřadu statistického*, 1947, p. 342.

6. THE GOTTWALD GOVERNMENT

1 Gottwald, *Spisy*, Vol. XIII, pp. 76–7.
2 At the KSČ post-election Central Committee meeting 30 May 1946, Gottwald, *Spisy*, Vol. XIII pp. 75–6.
3 His words were: 'so that we can wash it clean in one go', Gottwald, *Spisy*, Vol. XIII, p. 89.
4 Belda et al., *Na rozhraní*, pp. 84–6.
5 See below, Chapter 8, section 4.
6 R. Očenášek, *První hospodářský plán v Československu* (Brno, 1947), and Mrázek, *Nové hospodářství* II, 1 (January 1946), p. 11.
7 Frejka, *RP*, 23 November 1946, p. 4.
8 See Očenášek, *První* and D. Fišer, *Teoretické otázky vrcholných plánovacích orgánů* (Prague, 1965).
9 cf. J. Sommr, *Nové hospodářství*, III, 7 (July 1947), pp. 134–5, and K. Maiwald, *Hospodář*, 11 December 1947, p. 3.
10 See especially Frejka in *SSSR dnes* (Prague, 1946), p. 45.
11 Klimek, in parliament, *LD*, 22 September 1946 p. 1. For a similar view see *SS*, 15 October 1946, p. 1.
12 All this is discussed in the official booklet, *Základy československé dvouletky* (Prague, 1946).
13 *Základy*, p. 25.
14 Kojecký, *Cíl*, 7 June 1946, p. 339.
15 *Cíl*, 14 February 1947, p. 65.
16 *SS*, 15 October 1946, p. 1.
17 A. Čepička, *RP*, 26 March 1948, p. 1 and Dvořáková, Lesjuk, *Československá*, p. 44.
18 *RP*, 3 October 1947, p. 1.
19 e.g. Hora, quoted in *Tvorba*, 25 June 1947.
20 *RP*, 4 March 1948, p. 1: *RP*, 9 March 1948, p. 1: *RP*, 20 March 1948, p. 3.; *RP*, 27 March 1948, p. 5. He apparently left all the information easily accessible in his office when resigning because he assumed that the resignation would not be accepted.
21 *SS*, 1 August 1946, p. 2.
22 *RP*, 7 August 1946, p. 1, and *SS*, 7 August 1946, p. 1.
23 *SS*, 12 August 1947, p. 2.
24 e.g. E. Šlemar, *Statistický zpravodaj*, x, 4 (April 1947), pp. 142–5, or K. Pány, *Průmyslový věstník*, XXXIV, 34 (25 August 1947), pp. 633–5.
25 Belda, et al., *Na rozhraní*, p. 76.
26 *RP*, 26 September 1946, p. 1. and 27 September 1946, p. 1.
27 *RP*, 5 October 1946, p. 1.
28 *RP*, 27 September 1946, p. 1.
29 *RP*, 5 October 1946, p. 1.
30 Bareš, *Rozhovor*, p. 39.
31 Bareš, *Rozhovor*, pp. 37–8.
32 P. Hervé, *Nové slovo*, 1 March 1947, p. 129.
33 Nedvěd, *Cesta*, p. 53 and J. Kozák, 'K objasnění postupu ÚV KSČ v

boji za získání většiny národa v období před únorem 1948', *Příspěvky k dějinám KSČ,* 2 (1958), pp. 11–12.

34 Resolution of the Central Committee meeting of September 1946 in *Funkcionář,* 7 November 1946, p. 10.
35 J. Kozák, 'K objasnění'.
36 Gottwald, *Spisy,* Vol. xiii, p. 282.
37 Gottwald, *Spisy,* Vol. xiii, p. 301.
38 Adámek, *Boj,* p. 86.
39 e.g. V. Nový, *RP,* 26 January 1947, p. 1.
40 Gottwald, *Spisy,* Vol. xiii, p. 292.
41 *Svobodné noviny,* 12 October 1947, p. 1.
42 *SS,* 9 May 1947, p. 2.
43 Gottwald, *Spisy,* Vol. xiv, p. 66.
44 *RP,* 28 September 1947, p. 1.
45 Nepomucký in *Sněm,* esp. pp. 144–5.
46 e.g. J. Ďuriš, *Scelením půdy a mechanisací výroby k zvelebení československého zemědělství* (Prague, 1946), p. 21.
47 *Živnostenské noviny,* 16 November 1947, p. 1.
48 Slánský, speaking at a congress of KSČ small businessmen, *RP,* 18 March 1947, p. 1.
49 e.g. Zápotocký, *Nová,* p. 384.
50 Pexa, *Tvorba,* 15 January 1947, p. 52.
51 This is argued in Belda, 'Československá'.
52 e.g. L. Cígler, *Práce,* 15 January 1947, p. 1.
53 *ÚRO,* 26 September 1946, p. 1.
54 L. Ruman, *Statistický zpravodaj,* x, 3 (March 1947), p. 92, and *Fakta a cifry,* 31 October 1946, p. 33.
55 Z. Nejedlý, *O vyšší životní úroveň* (Prague, 1947), pp. 19–20 and Cambel, *Slovenská,* p. 318.
56 Figures from *Statistický zpravodaj,* xi, 7–8 (July–August 1948), p. 279.
57 *ÚRO,* 26 March 1946, p. 2.
58 Zápotocký, *ÚRO,* 29 January 1948, p. 5 and Růžička, *ROH,* pp. 179–181.
59 See the report of an ÚRO plenum meeting, *ÚRO,* 19 December 1946, p. 6.
60 *Praga,* 1947, p. 50. For a full breakdown of figures see *ÚRO,* 17 April 1947, p. 2 and Růžička, *ROH,* pp. 188–9.
61 M. Bouček, *Praha v únoru 1948* (Prague, 1963), p. 54.
62 *Tatra,* 1948, 2, pp. 6–7, 3 pp. 6–7 and 5, pp. 6–7.
63 *Statistický zpravodaj,* xi, 2 (December, 1948), p. 427.
64 e.g. *PL,* 10 December 1946, p. 1.
65 *Fakta a cifry,* 25 April 1947, p. 19.
66 For reports of workers' feelings, see *RP,* 28 February 1947 p. 1, *SS,* 26 February 1947 p. 1, and *SS,* 28 February 1947, p. 4. For the trade unions' position, see Zápotocký, *Práce,* 6 March 1947, p. 1.
67 *Funkcionář,* 7 March 1947, front cover.
68 *RP,* 29 March 1947, p. 1.
69 e.g. Hejda, *Svobodné noviny,* 1 January 1947, p. 10.

70 Žáčková-Batková, speaking in parliament, *SS*, 2 April 1947, p. 1.
71 *SS*, 28 February 1947, p. 4.
72 For accounts see Růžička, *ROH*, pp. 158–64, and *Práce*, 18 March 1947, pp. 1–2 and 22 March 1947.
73 *RP*, 19 March 1947, p. 1.
74 cf. his comments to the January Central Committee meeting, Gottwald, *Spisy*, Vol. XIII, p. 301.
75 See his speeches to KSČ conferences in Plzeň and Zlín, Gottwald, *Spisy*, Vol. XIII, pp. 384–97.
76 *Fakta a cifry*, 31 May 1947, pp. 2–5.
77 Nosek, *RP*, 1 February 1946, p. 2.
78 Ruman, *Statistický zpravodaj*, IX, 7–8 (July–August 1946), p. 238.
79 Maňák, 'Početnost', esp. p. 403.
80 e.g. the speeches in parliament on two budgets; J. Firt, *SS*, 28 November 1946, pp. 1–2, and Krajina, *SS*, 13 December 1946, p. 1.
81 e.g. Gottwald speaking on 31 August 1946: Gottwald, *Spisy*, Vol. XIII, p. 195.
82 *RP*, 7 December 1946, p. 1.
83 Speaking on 24 April 1947, Gottwald, *Spisy*, Vol. XIII, pp. 401 and 405.
84 *SS*, 19 January 1947, p. 2.
85 His speech was printed in full in *ÚRO*, 30 January 1947, p. 2.
86 *SS*, 19 January 1947 p. 2, and *Obzory*, 25 January 1947, p. 53.
87 *SS*, 27 July 1947, p. 1.
88 *SS*, 30 August 1947, p. 2.
89 *ÚRO*, 4 September 1947, p. 2.
90 e.g. *ÚRO*, 19 February 1946, p. 2.
91 Jech, *Probuzená*, pp. 233–4.
92 Jech, *Probuzená*, p. 248.
93 K. Kaplan, 'Rolnické hnutí za prosazení 6 zákonů a popularizaci Hradeckého programu' in *Vznik a vývoj lidově demokratického Československa* (Prague, 1961), pp. 143–4.
94 *Život strany*, 31 May 1947, p. 6.
95 e.g. *Život strany*, 31 May 1947, p. 5.
96 *PL*, 10 January 1947, p. 1.
97 *Vývoj*, 15 January 1947, p. 51.
98 *RP*, 9 January 1947, p. 1.
99 Kaplan, 'Rolnické', 154–8.
100 Ďuriš, *Dvouletka v zemědělství* (Prague, 1947), esp. p. 3.
101 Kaplan, 'Rolnické', 160.
102 *RP*, 5 April 1947, p. 3.
103 Jech, *Probuzená*, p. 321.
104 *Funkcionář*, 16 March 1947, p. 1.
105 *Obzory*, 26 July 1947, p. 426.
106 Rozehnal, *LD*, 13 September 1947, p. 2.
107 See Z. Fierlinger, *Zemědělská politika čs. sociální demokracie* (Prague, 1947), esp. p. 18.
108 Jech, *Probuzená*, p. 314.
109 Jech, *Probuzená*, pp. 315–16.

110 J. Smetáček, *Svět práce*, 7 August 1947, p. 1.
111 *RP*, 8 July 1947, p. 1.
112 *RP*, 4 October 1947, pp. 1–2.
113 Jech, *Probuzená*, p. 351.
114 *RP*, 9 June 1946, p. 1. *Nové slovo*, 7 June 1946, p. 5. See also Laluha, *Február*, pp. 24–5.
115 Široký speaking at the KSS Central Committee meeting of 1 August 1946 in *KSS*, pp. 479–80. This was essentially an expansion of Gottwald's argument at the KSČ Central Committee meeting of 30 May 1946; Gottwald, *Spisy*, Vol. xiii, pp. 80–1 and p. 85.
116 Široký, 1 August 1946, in *KSS*, p. 478.
117 *KSS*, p. 430.
118 *KSS*, p. 424.
119 Jarošová, et al., *Odbory*, pp. 109–10.
120 S. Falt'an, *Slovenská*, p. 222.
121 Laluha, *Február*, p. 65.
122 J. Bušniak, *Výstavba Slovenska*, ii, 3 (March 1947), pp. 13–14.
123 *Dnešek*, 6 February 1947, p. 723, and G. Kliment, *Práce*, 11 February 1947, p. 1.
124 e.g. *Čas*, 20 July 1947, p. 3.
125 *Pravda*, 22 August 1947, p. 1.
126 Laluha, *Február*, p. 94.
127 Cambel, *Slovenská*, p. 335.
128 Cambel, *Slovenská*, p. 165.
129 Jarošová, et al., *Odbory*, pp. 138–9.
130 *Čas*, 14 January 1947, quoted in Jarošová et al., *Odbory*, p. 162.
131 *Čas*, 13 July 1947, p. 8.
132 Resolution of the joint meeting of the Presidia of the KSČ and KSS on 2 December 1946 in Prague, *KSS*, p. 492.
133 I. Daxner, *L'udáctvo pred národným súdom 1945–1947* (Bratislava, 1961), pp. 168–9.
134 Daxner, *L'udáctvo*, p. 188.
135 Prečan, *Slovenský*, p. 141.
136 Belda et al., *Na rozhraní*, p. 172.
137 *RP*, 4 June 1947, p. 1.
138 Belda et al., *Na rozhraní*, p. 175.

7. DEEPENING DIVISIONS

1 e.g. *PL*, 15 March 1946, p. 1, or Ducháček, *Obzory*, 23 March 1946, p. 183.
2 *PL*, 21 November 1946, p. 1.
3 e.g. Ripka, *SS*, 7 November 1946, p. 1.
4 Zenkl, speech, *SS*, 4 April 1947, p. 1.
5 *SS*, 18 October 1946, p. 1.
6 W. Ullmann, *The United States in Prague 1945–1948* (New York, 1978), pp. 44 and 43.

7 *PL*, 17 November 1946, p. 2.
8 Ullmann, *The United States*, pp. 45-7.
9 *Svět práce*, 10 April 1947 p. 1. *RP*, 15 April 1947, p. 2 could quote from
   Walter Lipmann. See also the carefully documented articles by A.
   Simone, *Světové rozhledy*, I, 3 (April 1947), pp. 215-20 and I, 4 (May
   1947), pp. 312-13.
10 e.g. *Obzory*, 19 October 1946, pp. 657-8.
11 *SS*, 15 March 1947, p. 1, and *SS*, 16 March 1947 p. 1.
12 Ripka, *Czechoslovakia*, p. 44.
13 S. Řezný, *Statistický obzor*, XXVII, 1 (25 March 1947), pp. 95-7.
14 R. Šimáček, *Hospodář*, 15 May 1947, p. 6.
15 Ruman, *Hospodář* 10 July 1947, p. 4. For figures on the extent of their
   aid, see *Statistická příručka*, p. 97.
16 e.g. *Hospodář*, 1 January 1948, p. 1.
17 For details see *Statistický zpravodaj*, XI, 3 (March 1948), p. 132.
18 *Hospodář*, 4 September 1947, p. 1.
19 *Hospodář*, 2 October 1947, p. 1.
20 Goldmann, *Hospodář*, 16 October 1947, p. 5, and K. Kaplan 'Úvahy o
   první pětiletce,' *Příspěvky k dějinám KSČ*, 1967, 5.
21 L. Chmela, *Problémy československého hospodářství* (Prague, 1948), p. 7.
22 J. Belda, M. Bouček, Z. Deyl, M. Klimeš, 'K otázce účasti Československa na Marshallově plánu', *Revue dějin socialismu*, 1968, 1, esp. pp.
   96-7.
23 *Dnešek* 17 July 1947, p. 242.
24 Ripka, *Czechoslovakia*, p. 47.
25 Ripka, *Czechoslovakia*, pp. 110 and 102.
26 Ullmann, *The United States*, esp. p. 95.
27 *Funkcionář*, 15 October 1947, p. 1.
28 See Gottwald, *Spisy*, Vol. XIV, p. 174. Interesting information on the
   KSS Central Committee meeting of 4 December 1947 is provided in
   KSS, pp. 617-20.
29 *SS*, 7 October 1947, pp. 1-2, and *SS*, 9 October 1947, p. 2.
30 V. Kopecký, *Zápas o nové vlastenectví* (Prague, 1948), p. 26 and p. 27.
   See also G. Bareš, *SSSR a naše samostatnost* (Prague, 1947), p. 31.
31 *Průběh plnění hospodářského plánu roku 1947* (Prague, 1948), p. 47.
32 See J. Goldmann, J. Flek, *Planned Economy in Czechoslovakia* (Prague,
   1949), esp. pp. 36-7.
33 *RP*, 24 August 1947, p. 1.
34 *RP*, 10 September 1947, p. 1.
35 *RP*, 4 September 1947 p. 1. See also the account of the meeting in
   Zbrojovka-Brno, *Svobodné noviny*, 7 September 1947, p. 2.
36 *LD*, 12 September 1947, p. 1.
37 *PL*, 6 September 1947, p. 1.
38 V. Erban, *Hospodář*, 11 September 1947, pp. 3-4.
39 e.g. *SS*, 6 September 1947, p. 1.
40 *SS*, 12 September 1947, p. 1.
41 *RP*, 12 September 1947, p. 1. Much more came to light about the
   bombs in the following months. See below, p. 197.

42 See the report of the government meeting of 2 September 1947, *Cestou k Únoru*, pp. 220–1.
43 Ripka, speech, *SS*, 9 September 1947, p. 2.
44 *SS*, 10 September 1947, p. 1.
45 *Svobodný zítřek*, 18 September 1947, p. 4.
46 Firt, *Hospodář*, 11 September 1947, p. 3 (emphasis in the original).
47 Slánský, speech, *RP*, 9 September 1947, p. 1.
48 *RP*, 12 September 1947, p. 1.
49 See *SS*, 23 September 1947, p. 1.
50 Laušman, *Svět práce*, 2 October 1947, p. 1.
51 *SS*, 22 October 1947, p. 1, and *LD*, 22 October 1947, p. 1.
52 V. Mixa, *LD*, 26 October 1947, p. 1.
53 Speaking at the KSČ Central Committee meeting of June 1947, *KSS*, pp. 586–7.
54 L. Holdoš, *RP*, 21 May 1947, p. 1.
55 *RP*, 21 June 1947, p. 1.
56 Gottwald, *Spisy*, Vol. xiv, p. 87.
57 S. Falt'an, speech, *Pravda*, 21 August 1947, p. 1.
58 *Pravda*, 21 August 1947, p. 1.
59 For more information see I. Bajcura, *Ukrajinská otázka v ČSSR* (Košice, 1967), pp. 99–102, and J. Fiala, 'Banderovci a politická krise v Československu v roce 1947', *Revue dějin socialismu*, 1969, 5, p. 709.
60 *Pravda*, 23 August 1947, p. 1.
61 V. Huml, 'Svaz slovenských partizánů a jeho úloha ve slovenské společnosti v předúnorovém období', *Historie a vojenství*, xx, 4 (1971) pp. 550–1 and 554–5.
62 *Čas*, 23 August 1947, p. 1.
63 *Pravda*, 16 September 1947, pp. 1–2.
64 S. Falt'an, *Pravda*, 21 September 1947, p. 1.
65 See S. Falt'an's account of the course of the purge, *Pravda*, 21 September 1947, p. 1.
66 Belda et al., *Na rozhraní*, p. 176.
67 *RP*, 16 September 1947, p. 1.
68 Jarošová, Jaroš, *Slovenské*, p. 232.
69 *Pravda*, 13 July 1947, p. 3.
70 F. Zupka, speaking to the ÚRO plenum of 16 October 1947, *ÚRO*, 18 December 1947.
71 Resolution from Čierny Balog, *Čas*, 29 June 1947, p. 3.
72 Jarošová et al., *Odbory*, p. 185.
73 *Čas*, 19 July 1947, p. 1.
74 *Pravda*, 23 July 1947, p. 1.
75 *KSS*, p. 609.
76 Široký, speaking at the KSS Presidium meeting of 11 October 1947, *KSS*, p. 610.
77 Jarošová et al., *Odbory*, pp. 203–4, and *Pravda*, 23 October 1947, p. 2.
78 This was discussed at the KSS Presidium meeting of 11 October 1947, *KSS*, p. 611.
79 *Spiknutí proti republice* (Prague, 1947).

80 *Čas*, 17 September 1947, p. 1.
81 See *Spiknutí*.
82 *RP*, 23 October 1947, p. 1.
83 *Čas*, 5 October 1947, p. 1, and 7 October 1947, p. 1.
84 *Spiknutí*, p. 6.
85 *RP*, 23 October 1947 p. 1; Polák's comments were reported in *Pravda*, 24 October 1947, p. 1, and then in *Čas*, 25 October 1947, p. 1.
86 Ferjenčík, speaking in a parliamentary committee, *Čas*, 28 October 1947, p. 3.
87 *Čas*, 1 November 1947, p. 1.
88 *Pravda*, 21 November 1947, p. 1 and 27 November 1947, p. 1.
89 *RP*, 13 January 1948, p. 1.
90 e.g. K. Fára, *Obzory*, 4 October 1947, pp. 591–2.
91 *SS*, 5 October 1947, p. 2.
92 Ripka, *Czechoslovakia*, pp. 112–14.
93 J. Jablonický, M. Kropilák, *Slovník Slovenského národného povstania* (Bratislava, 1970), p. 302.
94 Ripka, *Czechoslovakia*, p. 116.
95 Jarošová, et al., *Odbory*, p. 211.
96 *Čas*, 18 November 1947, p. 1.
97 *KSS*, p. 615.
98 *Čas*, 12 November 1947, p. 1, and *Pravda*, 12 November 1947, p. 1.
99 *Pravda*, 20 November 1947, p. 1.
100 *Čas*, 11 November 1947, p. 1.
101 *Pravda*, 9 January 1948, p. 1.
102 *KSS*, pp. 668–73.

8. PRELUDE TO FEBRUARY

1 e.g. J. Hájek, *Cíl*, 18 January 1946, p. 18.
2 *PL*, 18 June 1947, p. 1.
3 Laušman, speech, *PL*, 26 January 1947, p. 1.
4 e.g. Bernard, *PL*, 16 November 1947, p. 3.
5 *RP*, 23 January 1948, p. 1. For the full text of Bevin's speech, see *Hansard*, Vol. 446, esp. columns 395, 396, 397 and 402.
6 Speaking to a congress of Social Democrat railwaymen, *Sociální demokrat*, 17 October 1947, p. 1.
7 *PL*, 17 September 1947, p. 2.
8 See his articles in *Cíl*, 27 September 1946 and 30 May 1947.
9 e.g. Krajina, at the National Socialists' Fourteenth Congress, *SS*, 2 March 1947, p. 2, or Cato, *Dnešek*, 22 May 1947, p. 117.
10 Contributions were printed in *ÚRO* in the following weeks.
11 e.g. Zenkl, speech, *SS*, 16 September 1947, pp. 1–2.
12 *Život strany*, 15 October 1947, p. 15.
13 *SS*, 5 October 1947, p. 2.
14 See the critical report from the Central Executive Committee meeting of 21 September 1947, *Život strany*, 27 September 1947, pp. 1–3.
15 *Život strany*, 27 October 1947, p. 3.

16 For the full results, see *Dnešek*, 18 December 1947, p. 592.
17 F. Matýsek, *LD*, 20 September 1947, p. 1.
18 J. Laube, *Svobodné noviny*, 25 October 1947, p. 2.
19 See the account in *Sociální demokrat*, 12 February 1948, p. 1.
20 Speaking to civil servants' representatives on 15 January 1948, Zápotocký, *Jednota odborů oporou bojů za socialisaci* (Prague, 1951), p. 711.
21 Speaking on 15 January 1948, Zápotocký, *Jednota*, p. 723.
22 For details, see *Fakta a cifry*, 19 September 1947, p. 46.
23 *SS*, 23 November 1947, p. 2.
24 *RP*, 17 October 1947, p. 1.
25 Bouček, Klimeš, *Dramatické*, p. 25.
26 Kozák, 'K objasnění', pp. 25–6.
27 Gottwald, *Spisy*, Vol. xiv, p. 197.
28 *PL*, 30 November 1947, p. 1.
29 Frejka, *25 Únor*, p. 26.
30 Slánský, speech, *RP*, 12 October 1947, p. 1.
31 Gottwald, *Spisy*, Vol. xiv, p. 190.
32 Gottwald, *Spisy*, Vol. xiv, pp. 182–4.
33 Gottwald, *Spisy*, Vol. xiv, p. 174.
34 Gottwald, *Spisy*, Vol. xiv, p. 103.
35 *Funkcionář*, 10 February 1948, esp. p. 2.
36 Gottwald, *Spisy*, Vol. xiv, p. 192.
37 V. Pavlíček, *Politické strany po Únoru. Příspěvek k problematice Národní fronty* (Prague, 1966), p. 100, and Belda et al., *Na rozhraní*, p. 198.
38 Gottwald, *Spisy*, Vol. xiv, pp. 187–8.
39 Gottwald, *Spisy*, Vol. xiv, p. 183.
40 Gottwald, *Spisy*, Vol. xiv, pp. 185–6.
41 *RP*, 25 December 1947 in *Spisy*, Vol. xiv, p. 221.
42 e.g. *Obzory*, 24 January 1948, p. 34.
43 Laušman, *Kdo byl vinen?* (Vienna, 1953), p. 92.
44 Kopecký, *Zápas o nové vlastenectví* (Prague, 1948), p. 41.
45 Kopecký, *Zápas*, p. 43.
46 Belda, et al., *Na rozhraní*, p. 196.
47 Gottwald, *Spisy*, Vol. xiv, pp. 205–6.
48 Weberová, *RP*, 19 December 1947, p. 3.
49 *RP*, 25 October 1947, p. 1.
50 *SS*, 10 January 1948, p. 1.
51 *Stručný*, p. 354.
52 K. Jech, A. Václavů, 'Některé problémy československého zemědělství v letech 1944–1948' in *Československá revoluce*, pp. 244–5.
53 Jech, *Probuzená*, pp. 411–12.
54 Jech, *Probuzená*, pp. 415–17.
55 Kaplan, 'Úloha', p. 494.
56 Bouček, Klimeš, *Dramatické*, p. 44.
57 The arguments were persuasive and repeated many times. See esp. *Lidová správa*, 1 March 1947, p. 3, and *Fakta a cifry*, 28 December 1948, pp. 88–94.
58 *Život strany*, 15 October 1947, pp. 5–6.

59 Speech, *PL*, 15 January 1948, p. 1.
60 R. H. B. Lockhart, 'The Czechoslovak Revolution', *Foreign Affairs*, xxvi, 4 (July 1948), p. 632.
61 R. E. Black, 'The last free poll in Czechoslovakia', *Public Opinion Quarterly*, xiv, 2 (Summer 1950), p. 384. See also O. Friedmann, *The Break-up of Czech Democracy* (London, 1950), p. 68.
62 Belda et al., *Na rozhraní*, pp. 206–7.
63 Belda et al., *Na rozhraní*, pp. 204–5.
64 Pavlíček, *Politické*, pp. 101–2.
65 J. Kašpar, 'Clenská základna Komunistické strany Československa v letech 1945–1949', *Československý časopis historický*, xix, 1 (1971) p. 11.
66 Ripka, *Czechoslovakia*, pp. 137 and 141.
67 *RP*, 28 January 1948, p. 1.
68 *RP*, 17 February 1948, p. 1, and Bouček, Klimeš, *Dramatické*, pp. 91–2.
69 *Práce*, 25 January 1948, p. 1.
70 *Práce*, 23 January 1948, p. 1.
71 Růžička, *ROH*, p. 253.
72 Gottwald, *Spisy*, Vol. xiv, p. 358.
73 *Cíl*, 20 February 1948, p. 81.
74 Kaplan, 'Úloha'.
75 *PL*, 18 February 1948, p. 1, and *SS*, 18 February 1948, p. 1.
76 *RP*, 19 February 1948, p. 1, and following days.
77 See *LD*, 20 February 1948, pp. 1–2, and Bloomfield, *Passive Revolution*, p. 222.
78 Ripka, *Czechoslovakia*, esp. p. 208.
79 *PL*, 1 August 1946, p. 1.
80 *PL*, 23 March 1947, p. 1. See also the report of their Central Executive Committee meeting of 14 April 1947, *PL*, 15 April 1947, p. 1.
81 For a full discussion see Jeřábek, *PL*, 15 February 1947, p. 2.
82 *Lidová správa*, 21 October 1945, pp. 2–3, and subsequent issues of the same journal.
83 e.g. Hora, *SS*, 18 December 1947, pp. 1–2.
84 J. Korbel, *The Communist Subversion of Czechoslovakia 1938–1948; the Failure of Coexistence* (London, 1959), p. 199.
85 V. Kroupa, 'Únor 1948 a Sbor národní bezpečnosti' in *Únor a československé*, pp. 85–6. See also Belda, et al., *Na rozhraní*, p. 220.
86 *Národní bezpečnost*, 10 December 1946, and later issues.
87 *RP*, 30 November 1947, p. 2.
88 *PL*, 21 January 1948, p. 1.
89 *Cesta k lidové*, p. 147.
90 *SS*, 21 November 1947, pp. 1–2 and 25 November 1947, p. 1, and *RP*, 22 November 1947, p. 1.
91 *SS*, 22 January 1948 p. 1 and 28 January 1948, p. 1.
92 *PL*, 22 January 1948, pp. 1 and 2 and 24 January 1948, p. 2.
93 *KSS*, p. 616.
94 cf. J. Švec, 'Únor 1948', unpublished manuscript, 1975, p. 405.
95 See the Ministry of Justice statement, *SS*, 22 February 1948, p. 3.

96 *SS*, 20 February 1948, pp. 1–2.
97 See Žižka, 'Únorová', p. 664.
98 Ripka, *Czechoslovakia*, pp. 193–4.
99 Ripka, *Czechoslovakia*, p. 223.
100 Bouček, Klimeš *Dramatické*, p. 120. See also Gottwald's speech to the Central Committee meeting of 9 April 1948, Gottwald, *Spisy*, Vol. xiv, p. 361.

9. THE FEBRUARY CRISIS

1 For summaries of the confused situation, see Belda et al., *Na rozhraní*, p. 230 and J. Švec, 'Únor', p. 440.
2 Ripka, *Czechoslovakia*, pp. 217–19.
3 Gottwald, *Spisy*, Vol. xiv, p. 362.
4 Gottwald, speaking at the KSČ Central Committee meeting of 9 April 1948, Gottwald, *Spisy*, Vol. xiv, p. 363.
5 Gottwald, *Spisy*, Vol. xiv, p. 251.
6 Resolution of the KSČ Presidium meeting of 20 February 1948, *RP*, 21 February 1948, p. 1.
7 Bouček, Klimeš, *Dramatické*, pp. 130–1.
8 Bouček, *Praha*, pp. 123–4.
9 e.g. in ČKD-Karlín, *PL*, 21 February 1948, p. 2.
10 Bouček, Klimeš, *Dramatické*, pp. 169–70.
11 L. Lehár, *Sjezd velkého rozhodování* (Prague, 1968), pp. 72–3, and *SS*, 24 February 1948, p. 3.
12 Bouček, *Praha*, pp. 139–40.
13 Lehár, *Sjezd*, pp. 104–6.
14 *Práce*, 25 February 1948, p. 1.
15 Bouček, *Praha*, p. 231.
16 Bouček, Klimeš, *Dramatické*, p. 270.
17 Bouček, Klimeš, *Dramatické*, pp. 287–8.
18 Bouček, Klimeš, *Dramatické*, p. 191.
19 Bouček, Klimeš, *Dramatické*, pp. 238–9.
20 Bouček, Klimeš, *Dramatické*, p. 143.
21 *PL*, 22 February 1948, p. 2.
22 Bouček, Klimeš, *Dramatické*, p. 165.
23 *RP*, 24 February 1948, p. 1.
24 *Svobodné noviny*, 24 February 1948, p. 2.
25 Bouček, Klimeš, *Dramatické*, p. 230.
26 *SS*, 24 February 1948, p. 1.
27 *RP*, 19 March 1948, p. 2.
28 Ripka, *Czechoslovakia*, p. 262.
29 Bouček, Klimeš, *Dramatické*, p. 213.
30 *RP*, 25 February 1948, p. 1, and *RP*, 26 February 1948, p. 3.
31 Bouček, Klimeš, *Dramatické*, p. 133, and Kroupa 'Únor', p. 96.
32 Bouček, Klimeš, *Dramatické*, pp. 212–13.
33 J. Pavel, 'Hlavní štáb Lidových milicí v Únoru' in *Pražské milice v Únoru* (Prague, 1964), pp. 24–5.
34 Pavel, 'Hlavní', pp. 21–2.

35 J. Lipták, Špičák, 'Únor' pp. 161–2.
36 J. Liptak, Špičák, 'Únor', p. 167.
37 *PL*, 25 February 1948, p. 1.
38 J. Lipták, Špičák, 'Únor' pp. 159–60.
39 See below pp. 214–16.
40 See Pavel, 'Hlavní'.
41 Bradáč, *Lidové*, p. 92.
42 Bouček, Klimeš, *Dramatické*, p. 216.
43 Belda, et al., *Na rozhraní*, p. 251.
44 F. Sova, 'Lidové milice – věrná stráž revolučních vymožeností pracujícího lidu' in *Únor a československé*, p. 30.
45 *SS*, 21 February 1948, p. 3.
46 Ullmann, *The United States*, p. 134. See also *Foreign Relations United States 1948*, Vol. IV (Washington DC, 1974), p. 733.
47 *SS*, 11 February 1948, p. 1.
48 *Foreign Relations 1948*, p. 736.
49 *Stručný*, p. 355.
50 *Hospodář*, 18 December 1947, p. 1.
51 Bouček, Klimeš, *Dramatické*, p. 107.
52 Švec, 'Únor', pp. 201–2.
53 See Ripka, *Czechoslovakia*, pp. 219–20.
54 Ripka, *Czechoslovakia*, p. 236.
55 Kozelka, *Vzpomínky*, p. 183.
56 Kozelka, *Vzpomínky*, p. 184, and *SS*, 22 February 1948, p. 1.
57 Bouček, Klimeš, *Dramatické*, p. 156, quoting from Smutný's account.
58 Bouček, Klimeš, *Dramatické*, pp. 206–7, quoting from Smutný's account.
59 Ripka, *Czechoslovakia*, p. 203.
60 Ripka, *Czechoslovakia*, p. 257.
61 Ripka, *Czechoslovakia*, p. 247.
62 *SS*, 21 February 1948, p. 2 and p. 1.
63 *SS*, 24 February 1948, p. 1.
64 *SS*, 24 February 1948, p. 2.
65 Bouček, Klimeš, *Dramatické*, p. 311.
66 Bouček, *Praha*, pp. 134–5.
67 J. Nosek in *Cesta k vítězství* (Brno, 1963), pp. 16–17.
68 *PL*, 25 February 1948, p. 2.
69 Bouček, Klimeš, *Dramatické*, p. 277.
70 *LD*, 24 February 1948, p. 1.
71 *Mladá fronta*, 22 February 1948, p. 1, and *RP*, 25 February 1948, p. 1.
72 Bouček, Klimeš, *Dramatické*, p. 137.
73 *LD*, 25 February 1948, p. 1.
74 Resolution of their Presidium meeting of 19 February 1948, *PL*, 20 February 1948, p. 1.
75 Resolution of the Presidium meeting of 20 February 1948, *PL*, 21 February 1948, p. 1.
76 Nedvěd, *Cesta*, p. 61.
77 Bouček, Klimeš, *Dramatické*, pp. 279–80, and Belda et al., *Na rozhraní*, p. 242.

78 Bouček, Klimeš, *Dramatické*, pp. 280–1.
79 *Pravda*, 24 February 1948, p. 2.
80 Bouček, Klimeš, *Dramatické*, p. 240.
81 Bouček, Klimeš, *Dramatické*, p. 321.
82 K. Kaplan, *Utváření generální linie výstavby socialismu v Československu* (Prague, 1966), pp. 55–60.
83 See Ripka, *Czechoslovakia*, pp. 301–2, and Steinhardt's message to Washington on 30 April 1948, *Foreign Relations 1948*, p. 751.
84 Veselý, speaking at a press conference, *Věstník ministerstva vnitra československé republiky*, xxx, 11 (15 June 1948), p. 2.
85 Maňák, 'K problematice', pp. 689 and 699.
86 R. A. Lovett's comments on 25 October 1948, *Foreign Relations 1948*, p. 433.
87 Steinhardt's message of 30 April 1948, *Foreign Relations 1948*, p. 752.
88 e.g. Marshall's message to the US Ambassador in Paris on 24 February 1948, *Foreign Relations 1948*, p. 736.

10. POST-FEBRUARY CZECHOSLOVAKIA

1 Circular from the Ministry of the Interior, 8 March 1948, *Věstník ministerstva vnitra československé republiky*, xxx, 3–4 (15 March 1948), p. 60.
2 Bertelmann, *Vývoj*, pp. 256–7.
3 *Lidová správa*, 1 May 1948, p. 138.
4 L. Kalinová, 'K poúnorovým změnám ve složení řídícího aparátu', *Revue dějin socialismu*, 1969, 4.
5 See Kopecký, *Zápas*, p. 48, and Frejka, *25 únor*, p. 53.
6 *Statistický zpravodaj*, xi, 7–8 (July–August, 1948), p. 282.
7 *Fakta a cifry*, iii, 1–2 (1948), p. 34.
8 *Zemědělské noviny*, 29 February 1948.
9 Speaking on 4 February 1946, Gottwald, *Spisy*, Vol. xii, p. 258.
10 Gottwald, 6 March 1948 quoted in Kaplan, *Utváření*, p. 138.
11 *Lidová správa*, 1 April 1948, p. 102.
12 This widespread attitude was commented on in *Tvorba*, 1948, 11, p. 201.
13 See *Hospodář*, 11 March 1948, p. 1.
14 *RP*, 29 February 1948, p. 1.
15 Kaplan, *Utváření*, p. 100.
16 J. Fulka, 'Růst členské základny KSČ a únor 1948', *Nová mysl*, xxiv, 3 (1970), p. 355.
17 Kaplan, *Utváření*, p. 99.
18 *Funkcionář*, 6 April 1948, pp. 32–3.
19 See Slánský, *Funkcionář*, 10 March 1948, p. 24.
20 Slánský, *RP*, 7 March 1948, p. 2.
21 e.g. *Funkcionář*, 6 April 1948, p. 33.
22 Pavlíček, *Politické*, esp. pp. 185–6.
23 *PL*, 29 February 1948, p. 1.
24 Speaking on 17 April 1948, quoted in Nedvěd, *Cesta*, p. 66.
25 See the reply sent by Laušman and Lindauer, *PL*, 7 March 1948, p. 1.
26 Kaplan, *Utváření*, p. 70.

27 J. Belda, 'Mocensko-politické změny v ČSR po únoru 1948', *Revue dějin socialismu*, 1969, 2, p. 236.

28 Kaplan, *Utváření*, p. 41.

29 M. Reiman, 'Únor a československá cesta k socialismu' in *K politickým a sociálně ekonomickým přeměnám v ČSR v letech 1948–1953* (Prague, 1967), p. 14.

30 Belda, 'Mocensko-politické', p. 236.

31 Nedvěd, *Cesta*, p. 69.

32 Gottwald, speaking at the Central Committee meeting of 9 April 1948, quoted in Nedvěd, *Cesta*, p. 74.

33 Nedvěd, *Cesta*, p. 76.

34 See Gottwald's comments to the Central Committee on 9 June 1948, quoted in Kaplan, *Utváření*, p. 67, and Belda, 'Mocensko-politické', p. 234.

35 Pavlíček, *Politické*, p. 203.

36 R. Medvedev, *On Socialist Democracy* (London, 1977), p. 311.

37 Brus, *Socialist*, p. 188.

38 Brus, *Socialist*, p. 197.

39 Brus, *Socialist*, p. 207.

40 *Lidová správa*, 15 August 1948, p. 253.

41 *For a Lasting Peace. For a People's Democracy*, 15 September 1948, p. 4.

42 e.g. *Tvorba*, 1948, 10, p. 261.

43 E. Jukl, 'Rozvoj tvořivé iniciativy pracujících na našich průmyslových závodech v období počátků socialistické výstavby' in *Vznik a vývoj*, pp. 334 and 335.

44 J. Neuls, *Tvorba*, 1948, 25, p. 495.

45 *Tatra*, 1948, 10, p. 1.

46 e.g. Z. Valouch, *Funkcionář*, 14 June 1948, p. 23.

47 e.g. Z. Valouch, *Funkcionář*, 7 July 1948, p. 34.

48 Kliment, *Tvorba*, 1948, 27, pp. 521–2.

49 *RP*, 6 April 1948, p. 1.

50 *Stručný*, p. 383.

51 J. Frank, at the KSČ Presidium meeting of 9 September 1948, quoted in V. Brabec, 'Vztah KSČ a veřejnosti k politickým procesům na počátku padesátých let', *Revue dějin socialismu*, 1969, 3, p. 376.

52 Brabec, 'Vztah', p. 377.

53 M. Reiman, *Nová mysl*, XXII, 8 (1968), p. 1081.

54 e.g. A. Uher, *Tvorba*, 1948, 19, p. 379.

55 cf. M. Reiman, 'Únor', p. 32.

56 *RP*, 9 September 1948, p. 1.

57 *RP*, 12 September 1948, p. 1.

58 Speaking at the KSČ Presidium meeting of 9 September 1948, quoted in Brabec, 'Vztah', p. 377.

59 Gottwald, speaking at the Central Committee meeting of November, 1948, quoted in K. Kaplan, 'Třídní boje po únoru 1948', *Příspěvky k dějinám KSČ*, 1963, 3.

60 *Lidová správa*, 1 October 1948, p. 295.

61 G. Kliment, speech, *RP*, 12 September 1948, p. 1.
62 M. Reiman, *Nová mysl*, xxii, 8 (1968), p. 1082.
63 *RP*, 24 September 1948, p. 1.
64 Bareš, *Tvorba*, 1948, 38, pp. 741–2.
65 'O.H.', *Funkcionář*, 23 September 1948, pp. 1 and 2.
66 Kaplan, *Utváření*, p. 247.
67 *Funkcionář*, 7 August 1948, p. 1.
68 *Funkcionář*, 7 August 1948, p. 1.
69 e.g. H. Lomský, *Funkcionář*, 14 June 1948, pp. 19–20.
70 *Funkcionář*, 14 June 1948, pp. 12–13.
71 *Funkcionář*, 21 August 1948, pp. 1–9.
72 *Funkcionář*, 7 September 1947, p. 5.
73 Kaplan, *Utváření*, p. 131.
74 Kaplan, 'Třídní', p. 339.
75 Císař, *Tvorba*, 1948, 35, p. 684.
76 Kaplan, *Utváření*, pp. 177–8, and Tausigová, *Tvorba*, 1949, pp. 458–9.
77 Kaplan, *Utváření*, pp. 183–4.
78 See above p. 224.
79 Speaking on 9 April 1948 quoted in Kaplan, *Utváření*, p. 182.
80 E. Bolgár, a Hungarian referring to Czechoslovak developments, quoted in *Světové rozhledy*, ii, 10 (October 1948), p. 773.
81 *Fakta a cifry*, iii, 8 (10 August 1948), pp. 2–11.
82 Tausigová, quoted in Kaplan, *Utváření*, p. 190.
83 See the letter from Kolman in *Nová mysl*, xxii, 8 (1968), pp. 1079–80.
84 Kaplan, *Utváření*, p. 185.
85 *RP*, 14 September 1948, p. 2.
86 Široký at the KSS Central Committee meeting of 27 September 1948, *KSS*, p. 709.
87 Kaplan, *Utváření*, pp. 212–13, and *Stručný*, pp. 372–3.
88 Kaplan, *Utváření*, p. 213.
89 F. J. Kolár, *Tvorba*, 1948, 40, p. 781.
90 Quoted in Kaplan, *Utváření*, p. 202.
91 *Funkcionář*, 29 November 1948, p. 30.
92 Kliment, *RP*, 9 October 1948, p. 1.
93 *RP*, 23 November 1947, p. 2.
94 Slánský, *Za vítězství*, Vol. ii, pp. 220–1.
95 Speaking on 11 October 1948, quoted in Kaplan, 'Trídní', p. 343.
96 Kaplan, *Utváření*, pp. 34–40.
97 S. Falt'an, *Slovenská*, pp. 260–1.
98 Speaking on 27 September 1948, *KSS*, p. 710.
99 Speaking to the KSS Central Committee on 27 September 1948, *KSS*, p. 710.
100 See K. Kaplan, 'Historické místo akčního programu', *Nová mysl*, xxii, 5 (May 1968).
101 Brabec, 'Vztah', p. 379.

Bibliography

I NEWSPAPERS AND PERIODICALS IN CZECH AND SLOVAK

Budovatel' (1947), Builder. Slovak economic journal.
Budovatel národního podniku (1948), Builder of the Nationalised Enterprise. Paper of the Schicht factory in Ústí nad Labem.
Cíl (1945–8), The Aim. Social Democrat theoretical journal.
Čas (1947–8), Time. Daily paper of the Democratic Party.
Česká pravda (1945), Czech Truth. See *Svobodné Slovo*.
Československý časopis historický (1958, 1964–6, 1968–9, 1971–5), Czechoslovak Historical Journal. Bimonthly of the Institute of Czechoslovak and World History of the Czechoslovak Academy of Sciences.
Dnešek (1946–7), Today. Non-party weekly edited by Peroutka.
Fakta a cifry (1946–8), Facts and Figures. Periodical providing basic information for Communists to use as political propaganda.
For a Lasting Peace For a People's Democracy (1948–9).
Funkcionář (1945–8), Functionary. Communist Party journal for active and leading members.
Historický časopis (1966, 1971), Historical Journal.
Historie a vojenství (1960–2, 1966, 1967, 1969, 1971, 1974–5), History and the Military. Bimonthly of the Institute of Military History.
Hospodář (1946–8), Economist. Czech weekly on economic questions.
Jiskra (1946, 1947), The Spark. Paper of the Malé Svatoňovice miners.
Katolícke noviny (1947, 1948), Catholic Newspaper. Slovak paper of the Catholic church.
Komunismus (1922, 1923), Communism. Communist Party theoretical journal.
Komunista (1921), Communist. Successor to *Sociální demokrat*.
Komunistická revue (1924), Communist Review.
Lidová demokracie (1945–8). People's Democracy. Daily paper of the People's Party.
Lidová správa (1945–8), People's Administration. Communist Party journal on local government questions.
Mladá fronta (1945, 1946, 1948), Young Front. Daily paper of the Czechoslovak Union of Youth.
Národní Bezpečnost (1947), National Security. Journal of the trade union organisation in the police force.

Naše doba (1930, 1934, 1936), Our Time. Journal of political and other commentary generally close to T. G. Masaryk.

Nová mysl (1947, 1968, 1970), New Thought. Communist Party theoretical journal.

Nové hospodářství (1946, 1947), New Economy. Semi-theoretical economic journal.

Nové slovo (1944–7), New Word. Slovak Communist journal owned by Husák.

Obzory (1945–7), Horizons. People's Party weekly.

Plamen (1935), The Flame. Communist Party discussion journal.

Plamen (1965), The Flame.

Práce (1945–8), Labour. Daily paper of the trade unions.

Praga (1946, 1947). Journal of the ČKD engineering combine.

Pravda (1944, 1947, 1948), The Truth. Daily paper of the Slovak Communists.

Právo lidu (1920, 1931, 1932, 1936, 1938, 1945–8), Right of the People. Daily paper of the Social Democrats.

Průmyslový průkopník (1946), Industrial Pioneer. Journal produced by Bat'a concerned primarily with marketing.

Průmyslový věstník (1947), Industrial Bulletin.

Příspěvky k dějinám KSČ (1958, 1960–7), Contributions to the History of the Communist Party of Czechoslovakia. Bimonthly of the Institute of History of the Communist Party of Czechoslovakia.

Přítomnost (1935–8), The Present. Journal of political commentary edited by Peroutka.

Rádkyně (1946), Counsellor. Communist Party journal for women.

Revue dějin socialismu (1968, 1969), Review of the History of Socialism. Successor to *Příspěvky k dějinám KSČ*.

Rolnické hlasy (1947), Peasant Voices. Communist Party journal for peasants.

Rudé právo (1920, 1921, 1932, 1938, 1945–8), Red Right. Daily paper of the Communist Party of Czechoslovakia.

Sbírka zákonů a nařízení (1945), Digest of Laws and Statutes. Annual containing all laws passed in the preceding year.

Sborník historický (1973), Historical Miscellany. Annual containing diverse historical articles.

Směr (1948), The Direction. Journal of the left within Social Democracy.

Sociální demokrat (1919–20), Social Democrat. Weekly of the left within Social Democracy.

Sociální demokrat (1947–8), Social Democrat. Journal of the Social Democrat factory organisations.

Sociologický časopis (1967), Sociological Journal. Bimonthly of the Philosophy and Sociology Institute of the Czechoslovak Academy of Sciences.

Statistický obzor (1947), Statistical Horizon. Journal of commentary and information on economic and social statistics.

Statistický zpravodaj (1946–8), Statistical Reporter. Journal of commentary and information on economic and social statistics.

Student (1945–6), Student. Journal of the union of students.

Svědectví (1957, 1974), Testimony. Czech language quarterly produced in the West and edited by Tigrid.

Svět práce (1945–8), World of Labour. Social Democrat weekly.
Světové rozhledy (1947–8), World View. Communist Party journal on international questions.
Svobodné noviny (1945–8), Free Newspaper. Independent daily edited by Peroutka.
Svobodné slovo (1945–8), Free Word. National Socialists' daily.
Svobodný směr (1946), Free Direction. National Socialist local paper in Olomouc.
Svobodný zítřek (1945–8), Free Tomorrow. National Socialist weekly.
Škodovák (1946–8), Škoda Worker. Paper of the Škoda engineering combine.
Tatra (1948). Paper of the Tatra engineering combine.
Tvorba (1945–8), Creation. Communist Party journal for culture and politics.
ÚRO (1945–8). Journal of the Central Council of Trade Unions.
Věstník komunistické oposice (1927), Bulletin of the Communist opposition. Trotskyist paper.
Věstník ministerstva spravedlnosti (1946), Bulletin of the Ministry of Justice.
Věstník ministerstva vnitra československé republiky (1946, 1948), Bulletin of the Ministry of the Interior of the Czechoslovak Republic.
Věstník ROH (1947), Bulletin of the Revolutionary Trade Union Movement.
Věstník závodních rad (1945–6), Bulletin of the Factory Councils. Name changed to *Věstník ROH* at start of 1947.
Výstavba Slovenska (1947), Construction of Slovakia. Slovak Communist periodical on economic questions.
Vývoj (1946, 1947), Development. People's Party journal.
Vzdělavatel (1946, 1947), Educator. National Socialist journal for inner-party education.
Zemědělské noviny (1946, 1948), Farmers' Newspaper. Daily paper of the Czech Union of Farmers.
Zprávy státního úřadu statistického (1947), Reports of the State Statistical Office. Annual with diverse statistical information and commentary.
Živnostenské noviny (1946–8), Small Businessmen's Newspaper. Communist Party weekly for small businessmen.
Život strany (1947), Life of the Party. National Socialist journal on party organisation.

2 BOOKS AND ARTICLES

Adámek, V. *Boj KSČ za přerůstání národně demokratické revoluce v socialistickou v letech 1945–1948*, Prague, 1970.
Bajcura, I. *Ukrajinská otázka v ČSSR*, Košice, 1967.
Bareš, G. *Naše cesta k socialismu*, Prague, 1948.
Bareš, G. *Rozhovor s Ferdinandem Peroutkou*, Prague, 1947.
Bareš, G. *SSSR a naše samostatnost*, Prague, 1947.
Bartošek, K. 'Antifašistická revoluce v Československu 1944–1945', *Revue dějin socialismu*, 1969, 5.
Bartošek, K. 'Československá společnost a revoluce' in *Československá revoluce*.
Bartošek, K. *Pražské povstání*, Prague, 1960.
Bechyně, R. *Pero mi zůstalo*, Prague, 1947.

Beer, F., Benčík, A., Graca, B., Křen, J., Kural, V., Šolc, J. *Dějinná křižovatka*, Prague, 1964.

Belda, J. 'Československá cesta k socialismu', *Příspěvky k dějinám KSČ*, 1967, 1.

Belda, J. 'Mocensko-politické změny v ČSR po únoru 1948', *Revue dějin socialismu*, 1969, 2.

Belda, J. 'Some Problems Regarding the Czechoslovak Road to Socialism' in *History of Socialism Yearbook 1968*.

Belda, J., Bouček, M., Deyl, Z., Klimeš, M. 'K otázce účasti Československa na Marshallově plánu', *Revue dějin socialismu*, 1968, 1.

Belda, J., Bouček, M., Deyl, Z., Klimeš, M. *Na rozhraní dvou epoch*, Prague, 1968.

Beneš, E. *Demokracie zítra a dnes*, Prague, 1946, Second Edition.

Beneš, E. *Memoirs. From Munich to New War and New Victory*, London, 1954.

Beneš, E. *My War Memoirs*, London, 1928.

Beneš, E. *Šest let exilu a druhé světové války*, Prague, 1946.

Beneš, E. *Úvahy o slovanství*, Prague, 1947, Second Edition.

Berger, O. *Cesta za mírem*, Prague, 1947.

Berger, O. *Československá průmyslová delegace ve SSSR*, Prague, 1946.

Berger, O. *Nová politika KSČ*, Prague, 1936.

Berger, O. *Velké dílo*, Prague, 1946.

Bertelmann, K. *Vývoj národních výborů do ústavy 9. května (1945–1948)*, Prague, 1964.

Bertelmann, K. *Vznik národních výborů*, Prague, 1956.

Black, R. E. 'The last free poll in Czechoslovakia', *Public Opinion Quaterly*, XIV, 2, Summer 1950.

Bloomfield, J. *Passive Revolution. Politics and the Czechoslovak Working Class 1945–1948*, London, 1979.

Boj o směr vývoje československého státu, 2 vols., Prague, 1965–9. Documents from July 1919 to May 1921 prepared for publication by A. Kocman, V. Pletka, J. Radimský, M. Trantírek, L. Urbánková.

Bouček, M. *Praha v únoru 1948*, Prague, 1963.

Bouček, M., Klimeš, M. *Dramatické dny února 1948*, Prague, 1973.

Bouček, M., Klimeš, M. 'Národní fronta Čechů a Slováků 1946–1948', *Sborník historický*, 1973, 20.

Bouček, M., Klimeš, M., Vartíková, M. *Program revolúcie*, Bratislava, 1975.

Brabec, V. 'Vztah KSČ a veřejnosti k politickým procesům na počátku padesátých let', *Revue dějin socialismu*, 1969, 3.

Bradáč, Z. *Lidové milice v Severomoravském kraji*, Ostrava, 1968.

Brown, J. *Who's Next? The Lesson of Czechoslovakia*, London, 1951.

Brus, W. *Socialist Ownership and Political Systems*, London, 1975.

Brus, W. *The Economics and Politics of Socialism*, London, 1973.

Cambel, S. *Slovenská agrárna otázka 1944–1948*, Bratislava, 1972.

Cambel, S. 'Vzťahy Červenej Armády a slovenských národných orgánov po oslobodení', *Příspěvky k dějinám KSČ*, 1965, 2.

Cesta ke Květnu. Prague, 1965. Documents from December 1943 to May 1945 selected and annotated by M. Klimeš, P. Lesjuk, I. Malá, V. Prečan.

Cesta k lidové bezpečnosti, Prague, 1975. Documents on the post-war police selected by V. Kroupa.

Cesta k vítězství, Brno, 1963. Memoirs from the 1945–8 period edited by L. Bednařík.

Cestou k Únoru, Prague, 1963. Documents on the National Socialists selected and annotated by V. Král.

Cestou května, Prague, 1975. Documents from April 1945 to May 1946 selected and annotated by J. Soukup.

Chmela, L. *Hospodářská okupace Československa; její metody a důsledky*, Prague, 1946.

Chmela, L. *Problémy československého hospodářství*, Prague, 1948.

Chtěli nás vyhubit, Prague, 1961. Documents on the German occupation of the Czech lands selected and annotated by V. Král.

Chudoba, B. *Co je křest'anská politika*, Prague, 1947.

Cílek, R., Fabšic, J. *Vlkodlaky kryje stín*, Prague, 1968.

Clementis, V. *The Czechoslovak–Magyar Relationship*, London, 1943.

Co má vědět desítkový důvěrník, Prague, 1947.

The Curtain Falls, London, 1951. Articles on post-war Eastern Europe edited by D. Healey.

The Czechoslovak Economy 1945–1948, Prague, 1968, edited by K. Jech.

Čerešňák, B. *Dělnické hnutí na jihovýchodní Moravě v letech 1917–1921*, Brno, 1969.

Černá kniha kapitalistického hospodaření před únorem 1948, Prague, 1948.

Československá revoluce v letech 1944–1948, Prague, 1966. Contributions to a conference of historians in 1965, edited by J. Kladiva and V. Lacina.

Československá sociální demokracie v exilu. Osmdesát let československé sociální demokracie 1878–1958, London, 1958. Articles on the history of Czechoslovak Social Democracy edited by A. Mokrý.

Československý průmysl 1948, Prague, 1949.

Československý průmysl v prvním pololetí roku 1946, Prague, 1946.

Danubius, 'Tézy o vysídlení československých nemcov', *Svědectví*, XV, 57 (1978).

Daxner, I. *L'udáctvo pred národným súdom 1945–1947*, Bratislava, 1961.

Degras, J. (ed.) *The Communist International 1919–1943 Documents*, 3 vols., London, 1956–65.

Dějiny Komunistické strany Československa, Prague, 1961. Written by a collective under P. Reiman.

'Depeše mezi Prahou a Moskvou 1939–1941', *Příspěvky k dějinám KSČ*, 1967, 3.

Deyl, Z. 'Naše cesta k socialismu a ekonomické problémy drobné buržoazie měst 1945–1948', *Československý časopis historický*, XIII, 4, (1965).

Deyl, Z., Snítil, Z. 'K některým problémům hospodářské politiky KSČ v letech 1945–1948', *Příspěvky k dějinám KSČ*, 1965, 5.

Dimitrov, G. *For a United and Popular Front*, Sofia, undated.

Documents on the Expulsion of the Germans from Eastern Central Europe, Vol. IV, Bonn, 1960.

Dokumenty z historie československé politiky 1939–1943, 2 vols., Prague, 1966. Documents prepared for publication by L. Otáhalová and M. Červinková.

Doležal, J. *Jediná cesta*, Prague, 1966.

Doležal, J., Křen, J. *Czechoslovakia's Fight 1938–1945*, Prague, 1964.
Drška, P. 'Boj KSČ za upevňovanie l'udovodemokratického charakteru armády (1945–1948)', *Historie a vojenství*, XXI, 2–3 (1971).
Dubský, V. *KSČ a odborové hnutí v Československu na počátku dvacátých let*, Prague, 1966.
Dubský, V. 'Utváření politické linie KSČ v období šmeralova vedení', *Příspěvky k dějinám KSČ*, 1967, 5 and 6.
Ďuriš, J. *Čo pripravuje ministerstvo zemedelstva pre slovenských rolníkov*, Prague, 1947.
Ďuriš, J. *Dvouletka v zemědělství*, Prague, 1947.
Ďuris, J. *Jak pomáhá vláda a ministerstvo zemědělství rolníkům poškozeným suchem*, Prague, 1947.
Ďuriš, J. *Odčiňujeme Bílou horu*, Prague, 1945.
Ďuriš, J. *Přítomnost a budoucnost československého zemědělství*, Prague, 1946.
Ďuriš, J. *Scelením půdy a mechanisací výroby k zvelebení československého zemědělství*, Prague, 1946.
Ďuriš, J. *Směrnice pro národní výbory o nejnutnějších opatřeních v zemědělství*, Prague, 1945.
Dvořáková, E., Lesjuk, P. *Československá společnost a komunisté v letech 1945–1948*, Prague, 1967.
Eliášová, J., Pasák, T. 'Poznámky k Benešovým kontaktům s Eliášem ve druhé světové válce', *Historie a vojenství*, XVI, 1, (1967).
Erban, E. *Základní problémy demokracie*, Prague, 1946.
Erban, E., Dvořák, A. *ÚRO v Pražském povstání*, Prague, 1946.
Falt'an, M. *Prvá čast' pozemkovej reformy*, Trnava, 1945.
Falt'an, S. *Slovenská otázka v Československu*, Bratislava, 1968.
Feierabend, L. K. *Pod vládou Národní fronty*, Washington DC, 1968.
Fiala, J. 'Banderovci a politická krise v Československu v roce 1947', *Revue dějin socialismu*, 1969, 5.
Fierlinger, Z. *Národní fronta – vychovatelka revoluce*, Prague, 1945.
Fierlinger, Z. *Ve službách ČSR*, 2 vols., Prague, 1948.
Fierlinger, Z. *Zemědělská politika čs. sociální demokracie*, Prague, 1947.
Fischer. E. *An Opposing Man*, London, 1974.
Fišer, D. *Teoretické otázky vrcholných plánovacích orgánů*, Prague, 1965.
Foreign Relations United States, The Conference of Berlin 1945, Vol. I, Washington, 1960.
Foreign Relations United States 1945, Vol. IV, *Europe*, Washington, 1968.
Foreign Relations United States 1948, Vol. IV, *Europe*, Washington, 1974.
Foustka, R. *Sociální demokracie a KSČ*, Prague, 1946.
Fraštacký, R. 'Zo Slovenska cez Freya' in *Zborník úvah*.
Frejka, L. *25. únor v československém hospodářství*, Prague, 1949.
Friedmann, O. *The Break-up of Czech Democracy*, London, 1950.
Fröhlichová, Z. *Mostecká stávka*, Most, 1967.
Fučík, J. *Reportáž psaná na oprátce*, Prague, 1957.
Fulka, J. 'Růst členské základny KSČ a únor 1948', *Nová mysl*, XXIV, 3 (March 1970).
Glos, B. *Hospodářské plánování v ČSR*, Prague, 1946.
Goerlich, L. *Demokracií k socialismu*, Prague, 1946.

Goldmann, J. *Czechoslovakia – test case of nationalisation*, Prague, 1947.

Goldmann, J., Flek, J. *Planned Economy in Czechoslovakia*, Prague, 1949.

Gorovský, K. 'Bohumír Šmeral', *Revue dějin socialismu*, 1970, 1.

Gorovský, K. 'O založení KSČ – dražd'anská konference v dubnu 1921', *Revue dějin socialismu*, 1968, 3.

Gottwald, K. 'Projev soudruha Gottwalda na 1. aktivu KSČ v osvobozené Praze', *Příspěvky k dějinám KSČ*, 1961, 3.

Gottwald, K. *Spisy*, 15 vols. Prague, 1951–60.

Gramsci, A. *Selections from the Prison Notebooks of Antonio Gramsci*, London, 1971.

Grigoriev, A. *Nové formy socialistické práce*, Prague, 1945.

Grňa, J. *Sedm roků na domácí frontě*, Brno, 1968.

Grňa, J. *Svaz národní revoluce – jeho program a úkoly*, Brno, 1945.

Hájek, M. *Jednotná fronta*, Prague, 1969.

Hájek, M. 'K problému levičáctví v Komunistické internacionále', *Příspěvky k dějinám KSČ*, 1965, 5.

Halbhuber, J. *Hospodářská politika nového Československá*, Prague, 1946.

Harna, J. 'Československá strana socialistická ve vládě a v parlamentě (1918–1923)', *Československý časopis historický*, xx, 3 (1972).

History of the Communist Party of the Soviet Union (Bolsheviks), Moscow, 1939.

History of Socialism Yearbook 1968, Prague, 1969.

Holub, O. *Boj o stranu*, Prague, 1971.

Hradilák, Z. 'Československá sociální demokracie a zmocňovací zákon v roce 1933', *Příspěvky k dějinám KSČ*, 1967, 1.

Hradilák, Z. 'Josef Guttmann – konflikt rozum a svědomí', *Revue dějin socialismu*, 1968, 4.

Hradilák, Z. 'On the Process of the Constitution of the "Definitive" Form of the Communist Party of Czechoslovakia (1929–1936)' in *History of Socialism Yearbook 1968*.

Hradilák, Z. 'Třídní boje československého proletariátu v roce 1933 a taktika KSČ', *Příspěvky k dějinám KSČ*, 1964, 3.

Hříbek, J. *K úloze KSČ ve vývoji ekonomiky Ostravska v letech 1945–1948*, Ostrava, 1974.

Huml, V. 'Svaz slovenských partizánů a jeho úloha ve slovenské společnosti v předúnorovém období', *Historie a vojenství*, xx, 4 (1971).

Husák, G. *Svědectví o Slovenském národním povstání*, Prague, 1970.

Jablonický, J. *Slovensko na prelome*, Bratislava, 1965.

Jablonický, J. *Z ilegality do povstanie*, Bratislava, 1969.

Jablonický, J., Kropilák, M. *Slovník Slovenského národného povstania*, Bratislava, 1970.

Janáček, F., Novotný, J., Hájková, A. 'Nová orientace', *Historie a vojenství*, xviii 4 (1969).

Janeček, O. 'Boje o hegemonii v čs. vojsku v SSSR (1942–1945)'. *Příspěvky k dějinám KSČ*, 1964, 2.

Janeček, O. 'K otázce našeho přístupu k socializmu a k typu naší revoluce v letech 1944–1945' in *Slovenské národné povstanie roku 1944*.

Janeček, O. 'Kdy u nás začala socialistická revoluce' in *Československá revoluce*.

Janeček, O. 'Zrod politiky Národní fronty a Moskevské vedení KSČ', *Revue dějin socialismu*, 1969, 6.

Jarošová, V., Jaroš, O. *Slovenské robotnictvo v boji o moc (1944–1948)*, Bratislava, 1965.

Jarošová, V., Škurlo, I., Vartíková, M. *Odbory na ceste k Februáru*, Bratislava, 1967.

Jech, K. *Probuzená vesnice*, Prague, 1963.

Jech, K. 'Sociální pohyb a postavení čs. zemědělského obyvatelstva v letech 1948–1955', *Revue dějin socialismu*, 1968, *zvláštní číslo*.

Jech, K., Václavů, A. 'Některé problémy československého zemědělství v letech 1944–1948' in *Československá revoluce*.

Josten, J. *Oh my Country*, London, 1949.

Jukl, E. 'Rozvoj tvořivé iniciativy pracujících na našich průmyslových závodech v období počátků socialistické výstavby' in *Vznik a vývoj*.

Jukl, E. 'Z historie bojů o poválečnou obnovu a znárodnění plzeňské Škodovky', *Příspěvky k dějinám KSČ*, 1962, 4.

K politickým a sociálně ekonomickým přeměnám v ČSR v letech 1948–1953, Prague, 1967. Textbook with contributions by Z. Deyl, L. Kalinová, M. Reiman, Z. Snítil, A. Václavů.

Kadlec, V. *Přebytek kupní síly a jeho odstranění*, Prague, 1945.

Kalinová, L. 'K poúnorovým změnám ve složení řídícího aparátu', *Revue dějin socialismu*, 1969, 4.

Káňa, O. *KSČ na Ostravsku v bojích na obranu republiky proti nebezpečí fašismu a války (1934–1938)*, Ostrava, 1962.

Káňa, O. *Mnichov na Ostravsku – k událostem roku 1938 ve Slezsku a na Hlučínsku*, Ostrava, 1963.

Kaplan, K. 'Československá cesta k socialismu', *Československá revoluce*.

Kaplan, K. 'Historické místo akčního programu', *Nová mysl*, XXII, 5 (May 1968).

Kaplan, K. 'K počátkům první pětiletky', *Československý časopis historický*, XII, 2 (1964).

Kaplan, K. 'K výsledkům prvé pětiletky', *Československý časopis historický*, XIII, 3 (1965).

Kaplan, K. 'Poznámky ke znárodnění průmyslu v Československu', *Příspěvky k dějinám KSČ*, 1966, 1.

Kaplan, K. 'Rolnické hnutí za prosazení 6 zákonů a popularizaci Hradeckého programu' in *Vznik a vývoj*.

Kaplan, K. 'Třídní boje po únoru 1948', *Příspěvky k dějinám KSČ*, 1963, 3.

Kaplan, K. 'Úloha hnutí rolnických mas v procesu přerůstání národní a demokratické revoluce v socialitickou'. *Příspěvky k dějinám KSČ*, 1962, 4.

Kaplan, K. *Utváření generální linie výstavby socialismu v Československu*, Prague, 1966.

Kaplan, K. 'Úvahy o první pětiletce'. *Příspěvky k dějinám KSČ*. 1967, 5.

Kaplan, K. 'Zakotvení výsledků únorového vítězství', *Československý časopis historický*, X, 2, (1962).

Kaplan, K. 'Zamyšlení nad politickými procesy', *Nová mysl*, XXII, 6, 7 and 8 (June, July and August 1968).

Kaplan, K. *Znárodnění a socialismus*, Prague, 1968.

Kaplan, K., Reiman, M. 'Naše revoluce a myšlenky o socialismu', *Plamen*, VII, 12 (December 1965).

Kárník, Z. *Habsburk, Masaryk či Šmeral?*, Prague, 1968.

Kárník, Z. *První pokusy o založení Komunistické strany v Čechách*, Prague, 1966.

Kárník, Z. *Za československou republiku rad*, Prague, 1963.

Kárník, Z. 'Založení KSČ a Kominterna', *Revue dějin socialismu*, 1969, 2.

Kašpar, J. 'Členská základna Komunistické strany Československa v letech 1945–1949', *Československý časopis historický*, XIX, 1 (1971).

Katedra dějin KSČ a ČSR 'K syntéze našich novodobých dějin. Socialismus', *Příspěvky k dějinám KSČ*, 1963, 4.

Kirschbaum, J. *Slovakia: Nation at the Crossroads of Central Europe*, New York, 1960.

Klimeš, M., Zachoval, M. 'Příspěvek k problematice únorových událostí v Československu v únoru 1948', *Československý časopis historický*, VI, 2 (1958).

Klír, M. 'Úloha B. Šmerala při vypracování strategicko-taktické orientace KSČ', *Příspěvky k dějinám KSČ*, 1964, 5 and 1965, 1.

Kojecký, Z. *Československá sociální demokracie včera a dnes*, Prague, 1946.

Kolár, F. J. *Dvouletka a její příprava*, Prague, 1946.

Kolár, F. J. *Ke kapitalismu není návratu*, Prague, 1947.

Kolár, F. J. *Nastupujeme k dvouletému plánu*, Prague, 1946.

Kolár, F. J. 'Vzpomínky na komunistu', *Příspěvky k dějinám KSČ*, 1965, 2.

Kolár, F. J. *Zestátnění průmyslu a peněžnictví*, Prague, 1945.

Kolejka, J. *Revoluční dělnické hnutí na Moravě a ve Slezsku 1917–1921*, Prague, 1957.

Komunistická strana Slovenska. Dokumenty z konferencií a plén 1944–1948, Bratislava, 1971 (abbreviated to *KSS*). Documents from Slovak Communist conferences and Central Committee meetings annotated by M. Vartíková.

Kopecký, V. *ČSR a KSČ*, Prague, 1960.

Kopecký, V. *Gottwald v Moskvě*, Prague, 1946.

Kopecký, V. *Vlast v nebezpečí?* Prague, 1931.

Kopecký, V. *Zápas o nové vlastenectví*, Prague, 1948.

Korbel, J. *The Communist Subversion of Czechoslovakia 1938–1948: the Failure of Coexistence*, London, 1959.

Kořalková, K. *Hnutí nezaměstnaných v Československu v letech 1929–1933*, Prague, 1962.

Kot'átko, J. *Konfiskace rozdělování a osídlování půdy*, Prague, 1946.

Kot'átko, J. *30 let sovětského zemědělství*, Prague, 1947.

Kot'átko, J. *Zemědělská osidlovací politika v pohraničí*, Prague, 1946.

Kotrlý, J. 'Moje účast v Pražském povstání' in *Pražské povstání 1945*.

Kotyk, V. *Střední a jihovýchodní Evropa ve válce a v revoluci 1939–1945*, Prague, 1967.

Koucký, V. *Ilegální KSČ a Pražské povstaní*, Prague, 1946.

Koudelková, J. 'Rudý den 1928', *Revue dějin socialismu*, 1969, 3.

Kovanda, K. 'Works Councils in Czechoslovakia 1945–47', *Soviet Studies*, XXIX, 2 (April 1977).

Kozák, J. *How parliament can play a revolutionary part in the transition to socialism and the role of the popular masses*, London, 1961.

Kozák, J. 'K objasnění postupu ÚV KSČ v boji za získání většiny národa v období před únorem 1948', *Příspěvky k dějinám KSČ*, 2 (1958).

Kozák, J. *Strana v boji za upevnění lidové demokracie. Únorové vítězství nad buržoazií (1945–1948)*, Prague, 1954.

Kozák, J. 'Význam vnitrostranické diskuse před 8. sjezdem KSČ: aktivní účast členů strany na vypracování sjezdových usnesení', *Příspěvky k dějinám KSČ*, 12 (1960).

Kozelka, B. *Vzpomínky*, Prague, 1968.

Kráčmanová, H. 'České vysokoškolské studentstvo v revolučních událostech na jaře 1945', *Československý časopis historický*, XXIII, 4 (1975).

Krajina, V. 'La résistance tchécoslovaque', *Cahiers d'histoire de la guerre*, No. 1, February 1950.

Král, V. *Osvobození Československa*, Prague, 1975.

Král, V. *Otázky hospodářského a sociálního vývoje v českých zemích v letech 1938–1945*, 3 vols., Prague, 1957–9.

Král, V. *Zářijové dny 1938*, Prague, 1971.

Kramer, J. *Slovenské autonomistické hnutie v rokoch 1918–1929*, Bratislava, 1962.

Krblich, J. *Stará a nová zemědělská politika*, Prague, 1946.

Kreibich, K. *Těsný domov – širý svět*, Liberec, 1968.

Krejčí, J. *Důchodové rozvrstvení*, Prague, 1947.

Kroupa, V. 'Úloha národních výborů při budování SNB a zajišťování vnitřní bezpečnosti (1945–1948)', *Historie a vojenství*, XXIV, 2 (1975).

Kroupa, V. 'Únor 1948 a Sbor národní bezpečnosti' in *Únor a československé*.

Kružík, F. 'Odjezdy čs. dobrovolníků do Španělska 1936–1938', *Příspěvky k dějinám KSČ*, 1966, 4.

Křen, J. 'Beneš – problém politického vůdcovství (1939–1940)', *Revue dějin socialismu*, 1968, 2.

Křen, J. *Do emigrace: západní zahraniční odboj 1938–1939*, 2nd edn. Prague, 1969.

Křen, J. *V emigraci: západní zahraniční odboj 1939–1940*, Prague, 1969.

Křen, J. 'Vojenský odboj na počátku okupace Československa (1938–1940)', *Historie a vojenství*, X, 2 (1961).

Křen, J., Kural, V. 'Ke stykům mezi československým odbojem a SSSR v letech 1939–1941', *Historie a vojenství*, XVI, 3 (1967).

Křížek, J. 'Protisovětské vystoupení čs. legií a změna vztahu Dohody k čs. zahraničnímu odboji v roce 1918', *Historie a vojenství*, XV, 1 (1966).

Křížek, J. *Říjnová revoluce a česká společnost*, Prague, 1967.

Kublík, J. 'Petiční výbor věrni zůstaneme v odbobí Mnichova a za druhé republiky', *Československý časopis historický*, XVII, 5 (1969).

Kural, V. 'Cesta k programu nacionálního odboje', *Revue dějin socialismu*, 1968, 1.

Kvasnička, J. *Československé légie v Rusku 1917–1920*, Bratislava, 1963.

Kvetko, M. 'Na prelome dvoch epoch; V ilegalitě a v povstání' in *Zborník úvah*.

Lacina, V. 'K agrárním koncepcím sociální demokracie a národních socialistů v letech 1945–1948', *Československý časopis historický*, XVII, 1 (1969).

Laluha, I. *Február 1948 a stredné Slovensko*, Banská Bystrica, 1967.

Laštovička, B. *V Londýně za války*, Prague, 1960.

Laštovka, V. *Stále v boji: KSČ na Plzeňsku v boji proti hladu, fašismu a válce*, Plzeň, 1966.

Laušman, B. *Kdo byl vinen?*, Vienna, 1953.

Laušman, B. *Pravda a lož o slovenskom národnom povstaní*, Petrovec, 1951.

Lehár, L. *Pražští kováci v boji za svobodu (1939–1941)*, Prague, 1965.

Lehár, L. *Sjezd velkého rozhodování*, Prague, 1968.

Lenin, V. I. *Selected Works*, Moscow and London, 1968.

Lettrich, J. *History of Modern Slovakia*, London, 1956.

Lettrich, J. 'Odboj a povstanie' in *Zborník úvah*.

Lichnovský, M. 'Otázky upevňování lidově demokratické moci v západní pohraničí v letech 1945–1948 a úloha čs. armády', *Historie a vojenství*, IX, 5 (1960).

Ličko, M. J. 'K otázke spojeneckej pomoci v Slovenskom národnom povstaní' in *Zborník úvah*.

Lipták, J., Špičák, M. 'Únor 1948 a československá armáda' in *Únor a československé*.

Lipták, L'. 'Maďarsko v slovenskej politike za druhej svetovej vojny' in *Príspevky k dejinám fašizmu*.

Lipták, L'. *Slovensko v 20. storočí*, Bratislava, 1968.

Lipták, L'. 'Slovenský štát a protifašistické hnutie v rokoch 1939–1943', *Historický časopis*, XIV, 2 (1966).

Lipták, L'. 'The role of the German minority in Slovakia in the years of the Second World War', *Studia historica slovaca*, 1 (1964).

Lockhart, R. H. B. *Comes the Reckoning*, London, 1947.

Lockhart, R. H. B. 'The Czechoslovak Revolution', *Foreign Affairs*, XXVI, 4 (July 1948).

Luža, R. 'The Communist Party of Czechoslovakia and the Czech resistance, 1939–1945', *Slavic Review*, XXVIII, 4 (December 1969).

Luža, R. *The Transfer of Sudeten Germans*, London, 1964.

Machotka, O. 'Česká národní rada za revoluce' in *Pražské povstání 1945*.

Machotka, O. 'Vznik České národní rady a její předrevoluční činnost' in *Pražské povstání 1945*.

Mackenzie, C. *Dr. Beneš*, London, 1946.

Mainuš, F. *Totální nasazení*, Brno, 1970.

Majer, V. 'Czechoslovakia' in *The Curtain Falls*.

Majer, V. 'Moskevská cesta' in *Československá sociální demokracie v exilu*.

Majer, V. *UNRRA a Československo*, Prague, 1946.

Majer, V. *Zásady reorganisace distribučního systému*, Prague, 1947.

Mamatey, V. S., Luža, R. *A History of the Czechoslovak Republic 1918–1948*, Princeton, 1973.

Maňák, J. 'K problematice struktury a postavení československé inteligence v letech 1945–1953', *Revue dějin socialismu*, 1968, zvláštní číslo.

Maňák, J. 'Početnost a struktura české inteligence v letech 1945–1948', *Sociologický časopis*, 1967, 4.

Maňák, J. 'Problematika odměňování české inteligence v letech 1945–1948', *Sociologický časopis*, 1967, 5.

Maňák, J. 'Sociální aspekty politiky KSČ vůči inteligenci v letech 1947–1953', *Revue dějin socialismu*, 1969, 5.

Masaryk, T. G. *The Making of a State. Memoirs and Observations 1914–1918*, London, 1927.

Mastny, V. *The Czechs under Nazi Rule: The Failure of National Resistance, 1939–42*, New York, 1971.

Medvedev, R. *On Socialist Democracy*, London, 1977.

Mencl, V., Menclová, J. 'Náčrt podstaty a vývoje vrcholné sféry předmnichovské československé mocensko-politické struktury', *Československý časopis historický*, XVI, 3 (1968).

Mencl, V., Sládek, O. *Dny odvahy*, Prague, 1966.

Métadier, J. (ed.) *Solidarity*, London, 1943.

Michels, R. *Political Parties, a Sociological Study of the Oligarchic Tendencies of Modern Democracy*, London, 1915.

Mikuš, J. *Slovakia in the Drama of Europe*, Milwaukee, 1963.

'Místo VII. kongresu Kominterny v dějinách mezinárodního a československého dělnického hnutí', *Příspěvky k dějinám KSČ*, 1966, 1.

Mlýnský, J. *Únor 1948 a akční výbory Národní fronty*, Prague, 1978.

Možná, J. 'Vývoj centrismu v českém dělnickém hnutí na počátku 20. let', *Příspěvky k dějinám KSČ*, 1967, 5.

Mrázek, O. 'Course and results of the nationalisation of industry' in *The Czechoslovak Economy*.

Mrázek, O. *Jak zvýšit životní úroveň pracujících*, Prague, 1947.

Mrázek, O. *Lidovláda v hospodářství*, Prague, 1945.

Národní fronta a komunisté, Prague, 1968. Contributions to a conference of historians in 1966 from Czechoslovakia, Poland and Yugoslavia on the 1938–45 period. Czech edition edited by F. Janáček and J. Hříbek.

Národní správci v zemědělství se osvědčili, Prague, 1946.

Navrátil, J., Domanský, J. *Boj KSČ o lidovou armádu*, Prague, 1962.

Navrátil, J., Hochsteiger, T. 'K otázkám demokratizace velitelského sboru čs. armády v letech 1945–1948', *Historie a vojenství*, XI, 3 (1962).

Nedvěd, J. *Cesta ke sloučení sociální demokracie s komunistickou stranou v roce 1948*, Prague, 1968.

Nejedlý, Z. *O vyšší životní úroveň*, Prague, 1947.

Nejedlý, Z. *T. G. Masaryk*, Prague, 1946.

Němec, F., Moudrý, V. *The Soviet Seizure of Subcarpathian Ruthenia*, Toronto, 1955.

Nosek, V. *Republika lidové demokracie*, Prague, 1945.

Novák, J. 'Promeškaná příležitost', *Příspěvky k dějinám KSČ*, 1966, 5.

Novotný, J. 'KSČ v ilegalitě (1939–1938)', in *Z počátků*.

Očenášek, R. *První hospodářský plán v Československu*, Brno, 1947.

Odboj a revoluce 1938–1945, Prague, 1965. Written by a collective of thirteen authors under O. Janeček.

Oliva, F. *Ekonomické studie*, Prague, 1967.

Opat, J. 'K metodě studia a výkladu některých problémů v období 1945–1948', *Příspěvky k dějinám KSČ*, 1965, 1.

Opat, J. *O novou demokracii*, Prague, 1966.

Otáhal, M. *Zápas o pozemkovou reformu*, Prague, 1963.

Otázky národní a demokratické revoluce v ČSR, Prague, 1955. Contributions to a conference of historians in 1955 edited by M. Klimeš, V. Král and M. Zachoval.

Outline History of the Communist International, Moscow, 1971. Written by a collective of eight authors under A. I. Sobolev.

Palecek, A. 'Antonin Svehla: Czech peasant statesman', *Slavic Review*, XXI, 4 (December 1962).

Pasák, T. 'K problematice české kolaborace a fašismu za druhé světové války', in *Príspevky k dejinám fašizmu*.

Pavel, J. 'Hlavní štáb Lidových milicí v Únoru', *Pražské milice*.

Pavlíček, V. *Politické strany po Únoru. Příspěvek k problematice Národní fronty*, Prague, 1966.

Pěnička, A. *Kladensko v revolučnich letech 1917–1921*, Prague, 1954.

Perman, D. *The Shaping of the Czechoslovak State: Diplomatic History of the Boundaries of Czechoslovakia, 1914–1920*, Leiden, 1962.

Peroutka, F. *Budování státu*, 4 vols., Prague, 1933–6.

Peroutka, F. *Byl dr. Beneš vinen?* Paris, 1950.

Peřina, J. *První sjezd Svazu národní revoluce v Praze 26–28. října 1946*, Prague, 1946.

Plánovský, P. 'Odbojová činnost' na Východnom Slovensku za II. svetovej vojny', in *Zborník úvah*.

Pleva, J. 'Bratislava na prelome rokov', *Príspevky k dejinám v rokoch 1945–1948*, Bratislava, 1966.

Plevza, J. *Československá štátnost' a slovenská otázka v politike KSČ*, Bratislava, 1971.

Plojhar, J. *Vítězný únor 1948 a Čs. strana lidová*, Prague, 1958.

Pokorná, J. 'K taktice "třida proti třídě" v hospodářských bojích československého proletariátu (1929–1932)', *Příspěvky k dějinám KSČ*, 1964,1.

Požárský, Z. *Založení komunistické strany v Severních Čechách*, Ústí nad Labem, 1971.

Pražské milice v únoru, Prague, 1964. Accounts of the activities of the militia in February 1948, edited by J. Sýkora.

Pražské povstání 1945, Washington DC, 1965. A collection of articles by participants in the Prague uprising edited by O. Machotka.

Prečan, V. *Slovenský katolicizmus pred Februárom 1948*, Bratislava, 1961.

Prehl'ad dejín KSČ na Slovensku, Bratislava, 1971, Written by a collective of five authors.

Preiss, J. 'Boj KSČ za revoluční přeměny na Mikulovsku' in *Cesta k vítězství*.

Príspevky k dejinám fašizmu v Československu a v Mad'arsku, Bratislava, 1969. Studies on fascism by eight authors, edited by L'. Holotík.

Príspevky k dejinám v rokoch 1944–1948, Bratislava, 1966.

Program Komunistické internacionály a usnesení VI. sjezdu KSČ, Prague, 1931.

Protokol 1. pracovního sjezdu živnostnictva čs. sociální demokracie 6–7/4/46, Prague, 1946.

Protokol prvního řádného sjezdu Komunistické strany Československa 2, 3, 4a 5/2/23, Prague, 1923.

288 Bibliography

Protokol II. řádného sjezdu Komunistické strany Československa 31/10/24–4/11/24, Prague, 1925.

Protokol III. řádného sjezdu Komunistické strany Československa 26–28, září 1925, Prague, 1967, Second Edition.

Protokol V. řádného sjezdu Komunistické strany Československa 18–23. února 1929, Prague, 1971, Second Edition.

Protokol VII. sjezdu Komunistické strany Československa, Prague, 1936.

Protokol XII. řádného sjezdu čs. sociálně demokratické strany dělnické, Prague, 1919.

Protokol XIII. řádného sjezdu československé sociálně demokratické strany dělnické 27, 28 a 29/11/20, Prague, 1921.

Protokol XIV. řádného sjezdu československé sociálně demokratické strany dělnické 19–22/2/24, Prague, 1924.

Protokol XV. sjezdu československé sociálně demokratické strany dělnické v Praze 1927, Prague, 1927.

Protokol XVI. sjezdu československé sociálně demokratické strany dělnické v Praze 27–29/9/30, Prague, 1930.

Protokol sedmnáctého řádného a jubilejního sjezdu čs. sociálně demokratické strany dělnické 26. až 29. října 1933 ve Smetanově síni Obecního domu hlavního města Prahy, Prague, 1933.

Protokol osmnáctého řádného sjezdu československé sociálně demokratické strany děnické 15–17. května 1937, Prague, 1937.

Protokol XX. manifestačního sjezdu československé sociální demokracie, Prague, 1946.

Protokoly sjezdů KSČ; I. svazek; Ustavující a slučovací sjezdy KSČ roku 1921, Prague, 1958.

Provazník, J., Vlasák, F. *Socialistické soutěžení v ČSR*, Prague, 1960.

Průběh národní revoluce na Kladně, Kladno, 1945.

Průběh plnění hospodářského plánu roku 1947, Prague, 1948.

První sjezd Svazu osvobozených politických vězňů a pozůstalých po politických obětech nacismu a fašismu, Prague, 1945.

Purgat, J. 'Čo predchádzalo Dohode o výmene obyvateľstva medzi Československom a Maďarskom?' *Revue dějin socialismu*, 1969, 4.

Purgat, J. 'Niektoré otázky maďarskej menšiny v Československu' in *Východné Slovensko*.

Rašla, A. *Ľudové súdy v Československu po II. svetovej vojne ako forma mimoriadného súdnictva*, Bratislava, 1969.

Reicin, B. 'Situace a odboj v Protektorátě v letech 1939–1940' in *Z počátků*.

Reiman, M. 'Únor a československá cesta k socialismu' in *K politickým*.

Reiman, P. 'K úvahám o odsunu německé menšiny' in *Československá revoluce*.

Ripka, H. *Czechoslovakia Enslaved*, London, 1950.

Ripka, H. *Eastern Europe in the Post-War World*, London, 1961.

Roušar, P. *Dějiny národního podniku SVIT – národní podnik Baťa* (*1945–1948*), Prague, 1967.

Rudé právo 1939–1945, Prague, 1971. Reprints of issues during the occupation.

Růžička, K. *ROH v boji o rozšíření moci dělnické třídy* (*1945–1948*), Prague, 1963.

Seton-Watson, H. *The East European Revolution*, London, 1950.

Sjezd národních správců z Čech, Moravy a Slezska ve dnech 17. a 18. srpna 1945 v Praze, Prague, 1945.

Skilling, H. G. 'The break-up of the Czechoslovak coalition 1947–1948', *Canadian Journal of Economic and Political Science*, xxvi, 3 (August 1960).

Skilling, H. G. 'The Comintern and Czechoslovak Communism: 1921–1929', *American Slavic and East European Review*, xix, 2, (April 1960).

Skilling, H. G. 'Communism and Czechoslovak traditions', *Journal of International Affairs*, xx, 1 (1966).

Skilling, H. G. *Czechoslovakia's Interrupted Revolution*, Princeton, 1976.

Skilling, H. G. 'The Czechoslovak struggle for national liberation in World War II', *Slavonic and East European Review*, xxxix, 92 (December 1960).

Skilling, H. G. 'The Formation of a Communist Party in Czechoslovakia', *American Slavic and East European Review*, xiv, 3 (October 1955).

Skilling, H. G. 'Gottwald and the Bolshevization of the Communist Party of Czechoslovakia 1929–1939', *Slavic Review*, xx, 4 (December 1961).

Skilling, H. G. 'The Prague overturn in 1948', *Canadian Slavic Papers*, iv, 1960.

Slábek, H. 'O politice komunistických stran v oblasti agrárních reforem (1945–1948)'. *Příspěvky k dějinám KSČ*, 1966, No. 2.

Sládek, O. *Krycí heslo svoboda – Hnutí odporu v jižních Čechách*, Česke Budějovice, 1967.

Sládek, Z. 'Československá politika a Rusko 1918–1920', *Československý časopis historický*, xvi, 6 (1968).

Slánský, R. *Nedopustíme přípravu nového Mnichova*, Prague, 1945.

Slánský, R. *Za vítězství socialismu: stati a projevy 1925–1951*, 2 vols. Prague, 1951.

Slezák, L. 'Zemědělské osidlování pohraničí Moravy a Slezska v letech 1945–1947'. *Československý časopis historický*, xxii, 1 (1974).

Slovenské národné povstanie: dokumenty, Bratislava, 1965 (abbreviated to *SNP*). Documents on the Slovak uprising selected and annotated by V. Prečan.

Slovenské národné povstanie roku 1944, Bratislava, 1965.

Směrnice pro práci národohospodářských komisí, Prague, 1947.

Sněm budovatelů: Protokol VIII. řádného sjezdu KSČ 28.–31. března 1946, Prague, 1946.

Snítil, Z. 'O dvouletce a jejím místě v politice KSČ v roce 1946', *Příspěvky k dějinám KSČ*, 1967, No. 5.

Sobolev, A. I. *People's Democracy, a new form of political organisation of society*, Moscow, 1954.

Souček, V. *Znárodnění průmyslu v ČSR*, Prague, 1947.

Soukup, F. *28. října 1918*, 2 vols., Prague, 1928.

Sova, F. 'Lidové milice – věrná stráž revolučních vymožeností pracujícího lidu' in *Únor a československé*.

Spiknutí proti republice, Prague, 1947.

SSSR dnes, Prague, 1946.

Stalin, J. V. *Problems of Leninism*, Moscow, 1953.

Statistická příručka ČSR, Prague, 1948.

Stránský, Jan *East Wind over Prague*, London, 1950.

Stručný hospodářský vývoj Československa do roku 1955, Prague, 1969. Written by a collective of eight authors under R. Olšovský and V. Průcha.

Sychrava, L. *Svědectví a úvahy o pražském převratu v únoru 1948*, London, 1952.

Široký, V. *Za šť'astné Slovensko v socialistickom Československu*, Bratislava, 1952.

Škurlo, I. 'Celoslovenská konferencia KSS v Žiline roku 1945 a čo jej predchádzalo', *Historický časopis*, XIX, 2 (1971).

Šmeral, B. *Historické práce 1908–1940*, Prague, 1961.

Šmeral, B. *Pravda o sovětovém Rusku*, 2nd edn, Prague, 1966.

Šmídmajer, J. *Závodní rady a odborové hnutí*, Prague, 1947.

Špičák, M. 'Ke vzniku stranickopolitického aparátu ČsLA', *Historie a vojenství*, XXIV, 2 (1975).

Šprysl, J. 'K problematice postavení českého rolnictva v letech 1939–1941', *Historie a vojenství*, XVI, 4 (1967).

Švec, J. 'Únor 1948', unpublished manuscript, 1975.

Šverma, J. *Za socialistickou vlast. Vybrané spisy*, Prague, 1949.

Táborský, E. 'Beneš and Stalin; Moscow 1943 and 1945', *Journal of Central European Affairs*, XIII, 2 (July 1953).

Táborský, E. 'Benešovy Moskevské cesty', *Svědectví*, I, 3–4 (1957).

Táborský, E. *Czechoslovak Democracy at Work*, London, 1945.

Táborský, E. 'The Political Institutions of Czechoslovakia', in J. Métadier *Solidarity*.

Tichý, M. *Z bojov komunistov banskobystrickej oblasti*, 2 vols., Bratislava, 1966.

Ullmann, W. *The United States in Prague 1945–1948*, New York, 1978.

Únor a československé ozbrojené síly, Prague, 1973. Articles on the armed forces in February 1948 edited by V. Kroupa.

Václavů, A. 'Zemědělství v první pětiletce' in *K politickým*.

Vartíková, M. *Roky rozhodnutia – k dejinám politického boja pred Februárom 1948*, Bratislava, 1962.

Vávra, V. 'K historiografické interpretaci poměru T. G. Masaryka vůči sovětskému Rusku v roce 1918', *Československý časopis historický*, XXI, 1 (1973).

Veselý, J. *O vzniku a založení KSČ*, Prague, 1952.

Veselý-Štainer, K. *Cestou národního odboje*, Prague, 1947.

Veselý-Štainer, K. 'Odbojová organisace Obrana národa' in *Z počátků*.

Vetiška, R. *Skok do tmy*, Prague, 1966.

Větší moc národním výborům, Prague, 1947.

'Vojensko-politická linie KSČ a domácí odbojová fronta v okupovaných českých zemích (červen 1941-duben 1944)', *Historie a vojenství*, XXIII, 4 (1974).

Volavka, A. *Zásady nové cenové politiky v zemědělství*, Prague, 1946.

Volf, M. *Sociální a politické dějiny Československa*, Prague, 1948.

Všeodborový sjezd ROH duben 1946, Prague, 1946.

Východné Slovensko pred Februárom, Košice, 1968. Contributions by five authors on Eastern Slovakia 1945–8 edited by M. Firdová.

Vznik a vývoj lidově demokratického Československa, Prague, 1961. Contributions to a conference of historians in 1960 edited by V. Král, M. Klimeš and V. Prečan.

Bibliography 291

What is Your Opinion? Prague, 1947. Results of opinion polls prepared by
C. Adamec, B. Pospíšil and M. Tesař.

Z dějín odborového hnutia na Slovensku (1944–1946), Bratislava, 1970. Documents on Slovak trade unions edited by I. Škurlo.

Z počátků odboje 1938–1941, Prague, 1969. A collection of articles on the 1938–41 period edited by O. Janeček.

Za nové Československo, Moscow, 1944. Articles from *Československé listy* 1943–5.

Za svobodu českého a slovenského národa, Prague, 1956. Documents on KSČ history 1938–45 prepared by the Institute of the History of the KSČ.

Za svobodu. Do nové československé republiky, Prague, 1945.

Základy československé dvouletky, Prague, 1946.

Základy prnví československé pětiletky, Prague, 1948.

Zápotocký, A. *Jednota odborů oporou bojů za socialisaci*, Prague, 1951.

Zápotocký, A. *Naše národní revoluce v roce 1918 a 1945*, Prague, 1946.

Zápotocký, A. *Nová odborová politika*, Prague, 1948.

Zápotocký, A. *O socialistickém soutěžení a mzdové politice*, Prague, 1954.

Zápotocký, A. *Po staru se žít nedá*, Prague, 1947.

'Záznam o rozhovoru s maršálem Stalinem v divadle v Moskvě dne 12.12. 43', *Svědectví*, XII, 47 (1974).

'Záznam z konference (aktivu) funkcionářů KSS 8/4/45 v Košicích', *Československý časopis historický*, XIV, 2 (1966).

Zborník úvah a osobných spomienok o Slovenskom národnom povstaní, Toronto, 1976. A collection of articles on the Slovak uprising edited by M. Kvetko and M. J. Ličko.

Zemědělské brigády – příručka pro zemědělské brigadníky a zemědělce, Prague, 1947.

Zinner, P. E. *Communist Strategy and Tactics in Czechoslovakia, 1918–1948*, London, 1963.

Zvara, J. *Maďarská menšina na Slovensku po roku 1945*, Bratislava, 1969.

Žižka, J. 'Únorová politická krise a státní aparát lidové demokracie', *Československý časopis historický*, XXI, 5 (1973).

Index

Action Committees, 203, 206, 214, 216,
219, 220, 222, 226
Adámek, V., 257, 262
Agrarian (Republican) Party, 7, 10, 20,
23, 79, 92, 95, 126, 129
banning of, 36, 47
and National Socialists, 118, 151,
153-4, 185
agricultural price policy, 79
anti-Communist bloc, 139, 184, 192-3,
198
April Agreement, 104, 130, 155, 171-3,
179, 185
assassination attempt on three ministers,
169, 197
Austro-Hungarian empire, 6, 26
Austro-Marxists, 140

Bajcura, I., 226
Banderovci, 172-3, 177, 205
Banská Bystrica, 41
Bareš, G., 113, 138, 233, 241, 258, 261,
265, 274
Bartošek, K., 247, 250
Bašťovanský, Š., 173, 256
Bednár, Š., 255
Beer, F., 248-9
Belda, J., 4, 5, 243, 248-9, 254, 261-2,
264-6, 268-71, 273
Benčík, A., 248
Benedikt, J., 252
Beneš, E., 2, 15, 20-2, 58-9, 64, 93, 103,
127, 141, 192, 200-1, 203, 207,
243, 246-8, 250
and February events, 196, 206, 208,
210-14, 216
after February, 217, 225, 231
and Germans, 31, 64
and Germany, 162

and Košice government, 46-50
and Munich, 25
and National Socialists, 113-14, 120,
165
and nationalisations, 31, 71
and Prague uprising, 51-2
as President, 54, 58, 158
and Protectorate, 30
and Slovak uprising, 41-3
and Soviet union, 25, 30-2, 46, 128,
211-12
after World War I, 6, 7
World War II plan, 27, 29-34, 36-40
Berger, O., 245, 259
Bernard, V., 259, 267
Bertelmann, K., 251, 255, 272
Bevin, E., 182, 267
Black, R. E., 269
black market, 84, 146, 174, 186, 230
Bloomfield, J., 252, 269
Board of Commissioners, 43, 155-6,
173, 177-9, 216
Bolen, V., 260
Bolgár, E., 274
Bolshevisation, 16-17
Bolshevism, 6, 7, 10, 30
Bouček, M., 248-9, 250, 254, 262, 265,
268-72
Brabec, V., 273-4
Bradáč, Z., 252, 271
Brest-Litovsk, 8
Brezno, 129
Britain, 1, 75, 166
and Beneš, 29, 30, 32
and Prague uprising, 52
and Slovak uprising, 43
Brus, W., 87, 226-7, 242, 255, 273
Bubník, J., 260
Bugár, M., 171, 176-7, 185

293